D1326057

Memoirs
of
Bartholomew
Fair

by
Henry Morley

with a foreword
by David Braithwaite
author of *Fairground Architecture*

HUGH EVELYN LONDON

Published in 1973 by
Hugh Evelyn Limited
9 Fitzroy Square, London W1P 5AH

Foreword © 1973, Hugh Evelyn Ltd
SBN 238 78996 9

Printed in Great Britain by
The Scolar Press Ltd., Menson, Yorkshire

FOREWORD

by David Braithwaite

That little has been written on the subject of fairs, possibly the only true form of public entertainment, is a curious phenomenon. Many have been moved by the sheer impact of the event but their writings are perfunctory, contributing little to a chronological record. For example a bemused Wordsworth, obviously startled by the strange happenings at London's Bartholomew Fair, wrote:

'All movables of wonder, from all parts
Are here—Albinos, painted Indians, Dwarfs,
The Horse of knowledge, and the learned Pig,
. . . All out o' the way, far fetched, perverted things . . .'

Yet prior to Henry Morley's classic work, first published in 1859, no serious attempt had apparently been made to research the origins of fairs and markets, and to formulate an authoritative history of the popular amusements that became their main ingredient. For, once the element of trading had declined, itinerant showmen, with characteristic swagger and panache presented theatrical booths, menageries, freak shows and primitive roundabouts.

This essentialy classless entertainment that attracted nobleman, wealthy merchant and bucolic alike is deserving of more study, and archives remain in profusion. In a modest preface Morley acknowledges: 'Though I have raised and garnered all the knowledge I could get . . . there certainly was more attainable.' Documentation on the travellers is, however, sketchy, incomplete and often contradictory. Because for centuries they have been regarded as vagabonds, there is understandably a reluctance on the part of showmen to recount their family histories. Offering a different viewpoint on this omission Cornelius Walford, in his book *Fairs, Past and Present*, observed 'The fact may perhaps be accounted for in the circumstance that fairs, as now regarded, are associated with notions of frivolity?'

The predominant characteristic of the fair, perhaps even its best quality, lies in its evanescent nature, a happening of the moment soon forgotten. Yet it is intangibly part of a continuing theme, a medium reflecting social change, gently poking fun at idiosyncrasies, capturing the imagination with new and faster-than-last-year joy rides, tempting the exhibitionist to try his skill at a dozen ludicrous games. In terms of landscape, both urban and rural, the fair is a catalyst. From unpromising beginnings with the arrival of an assortment of sheeted packing wagons, the measuring and staking out of plots is scarcely indicative of the transformation about to take place. This transience is beautifully expressed by Morley: 'The little o of the Fair is vapour now, and it was vapour from the first.'

As a writer and historian of distinction, perhaps better known for his *First Sketch of English Literature*, this 'first serious history of any fair' is a unique departure. Diligent research and lively commentary make it a work of immense stature. The reader shares with Morley a degree of astonishment as the social history at once hideous and hilarious, volatile yet peaceable, is unravelled. Perhaps for the first time the rough and tumble world of jugglers, horse dealers, drolls and cheapjacks comes alive in his accomplished prose. Spanning seven centuries, the strident progress from humble beginnings in the priory churchyard to England's chief cloth fair, is meticulously recorded. The wood engravings by the brothers Dalziel are a fine embellishment but they are scarcely equal to Morley's glorious word pictures.

'Just opened! May it please you to look in!' These words, evocative and timeless for they are the very essence of showmanship, drew people from far and near to Bartholomew Fair. In sweltering August, for St Bartholomew's Day is celebrated on the 24th, they converged upon the *smooth field* 'shouldering each other . . . dancing and rejoicing'. Yet the origin of this clamorous affair was far removed from mere jostling nonconformity.

In 1120 Henry I granted the right to hold a fair to a courtier named Rahere, believed at one time to have been his jester. Interestingly Rudyard Kipling, in his story *The Tree of Justice*, delineates him as 'more of a priest than a fool and more of a wizard than either'. On a journey to Rome to seek audience with the Pope, Rahere fell desperately ill. In a vision he was directed to return to the Priory of St Bartholomew and there found a hospital to care for the poor. As an obedient servant his reward was instantaneous healing. The hospital, supported by tolls from the fair, was established in 1123 and in 1973 special celebrations mark its 850th anniversary. Miraculous healings were witnessed among the sick and maimed praying for health at the Priory. Although there were those who asserted the miracles were faked by one Cornelius Agrippa, a juggler, they drew large congregations. Rahere was succeeded by a manipulator of words so adept, it was said, that he delivered rhyming sermons, and thus were brought together substantial sources for the early drama.

Isaiah's prophesy concerning Eden, a text much cherished by Rahere, that 'he will comfort all her waste places; and . . . make her desert like the garden of the Lord' may not have been realised at West Smithfield, but certainly the fair transformed the marshy tract into 'a place of jesting and edification, where (as Morley vividly describes) women and men caroused in the midst of the throng; where the minstrel and the story-teller and the tumbler gathered knots about them . . . while the clerks and friars peeped at the young maids.' The picture is at once confusing and lively, the priory grave-yard full of traders and all around the urgent pleas of spieler and pedlar competing with the distressed cries of animals unwittingly changing owners, while below the flags and bunting musicians and 'guitar beaters' kept up a deafening tempo. Not unmerited was Bishop Richard Poore of Salisbury's terse injunction three centuries later that 'dances or vile and indecorous games which tempt to unseemliness' should be banished from the churchyard.

Anciently the fair was a peaceable coming together of merchants, Magna Carta providing that all merchants should have safety and security while travelling, and be able to sell and buy without any 'unjust exactions'. The Court of Pie Powder, from *pieds poudrés* or dusty feet, was established to settle differences arising among the shifting population of merchants. Adam Overdo will be remembered as the judge in Ben Jonson's comedy *Bartholomew Fair*.

Following the dissolution of the monasteries when the fair was severed from the church, trading continued to increase until Bart's became the chief cloth fair of Eng-land. The hospital was taken over by the City of London while tolls from the priory fair fell to one Richard, Lord Rich. The 'slough of pleasure' was paved over in 1614 and the *field*, once open towards the Essex marshes, enclosed by buildings. The earliest dramas were presented around 1500, while in the 17th century the first 'Wild Beast' shows appeared. A century later the theatrical booths of Richardson, Saunders, Penkethman and Timothy Fielding (not Henry as popularly believed) were well known. Cornelius Walford makes mention of the obvious commercial benefit to the showmen, noting that according to cash returns for 1827 Richardson's theatre took £1,200 and Wombwell's Menagerie £1,700. But a sensitivity which had appeared as early as 1700, when puppet shows were prohibited because it was felt that satire was harmful, began to influence the city authorities. In 1839 measures were taken to suppress the fair and eleven years later the last proclamation was made by a Lord Mayor. The London City Mission pointed out the dangers of moral pollution whereupon the markets committee increased tolls, bringing this once flourishing fair to an abrupt end in 1855. Sadly, the revolution that followed when steam-powered roundabouts supplanted the primitive cartwheel-like devices of the 18th and early 19th century came too late for Bartholomew Fair.

In the late 19th century the travellers formed the United Kingdom Van Dweller's Protection Association. As an organised body they were able successfully to counter restrictive proposals by the Victorian reformer George Smith and today, re-organised as the Showmen's Guild, the work to ensure survival goes on, though hampered by cumbersome legislation and seemingly doomed to prejudice against so-called vagabonds. Directives from above are vague enough for local government to expel the showmen from traditional sites, curtail and infringe ancient rights and denigrate the honest nobility that seems to have motivated the original charters.

The rebuilding of towns and cities and the consequent problems of reorganising traffic are, of course, inevitably taking their toll of the established fairgrounds. Sometimes the reasons for curtailment of a fair are frivolous in the extreme; for example, alleged loss of trade and atmospheric interference caused by the dodg'ems ought to be no more than laughable but unfortunately are not so. The opportunity to plan for open air exhibitions is rarely seized upon and the inhospitable places that are offered for winter quarters are further evidence of an unreasonable hostility.

Built up in the Tuesday Market Place, King's Lynn Mart, opening on St Valentine's Day, marks the beginning of the travelling season. To the more successful showman it continues through to chill November when Loughborough Charter Fair fills the centre of this grey industrial town. The whirling frames ablaze with lights work out their seasonal miracle re-enacting the ancient charters. Oily overalled figures, with watery faces glazed in melancholy, murmur: 'Smaller than last year, fair's dying out.' Yet soon the skidding divertissements will entice even the most gloomy with a gaiety as infectious as ever.

In a world of specialisation, of complex and unintelligible vocations, the compelling simplicity of amusement caterer is strangely misunderstood. Hopefully, this re-issue of the first edition of *Memoirs of Bartholomew Fair* may correct a false view point, introducing a culture rich in history, innately strong and interwoven with the lives of splendid impresario figures. As Quince, the carpenter, haltingly expressed it:

'Our true intent is. All for your delight,
We are not here. That you should here repent you,
The actors are at hand; and, by their show,
You shall know all that you are like to know.'

MEMOIRS

OF

BARTHOLOMEW FAIR.

MEMOIRS

OF

BARTHOLOMEW FAIR

BY

HENRY MORLEY.

WITH FACSIMILE DRAWINGS, ENGRAVED UPON WOOD,
BY THE BROTHERS DALZIEL.

Omnia Mors pofcit: Lex eft, non Pœna, perire.—SENECA.

LONDON:

CHAPMAN AND HALL, 193, PICCADILLY.

1859.

LONDON :
BRADBURY AND EVANS, PRINTERS, WHITEFRIARS.

Inscribed

WITH FRIENDSHIP

TO

JOHN FORSTER,

BY WHOSE LIFE OF GOLDSMITH

THE HOME FEELINGS ARE REFINED:

AND BY WHOSE STUDIES OF THE COMMONWEALTH

THE WISDOM OF GOOD CITIZENSHIP

IS ENLARGED AND STRENGTHENED.

PREFACE.

———◦✦◦———

SINCE I am here occupying virgin foil in a part of the wild diftrict beyond the bounds of cultivated hiftory, I may be pardoned perhaps if my ground is not at once ftaked out in the beft manner, and my fields are not fo trim as thofe combed by the ploughs and harrows of fucceffive generations. This is not only the firft hiftory of Bartholomew Fair, *but the firft ferious hiftory of any Fair ; even the general fubject of Fairs, as far as I can learn, has never been thought worthy of a book. Yet what a diftinct chapter in focial hiftory fhould be contained in the ftory, rightly told, of any Great National Fair !*

When I firft refolved upon the writing of thefe Memoirs, I knew fimply that Bartholomew Fair *was an unwritten portion of the ftory of the people. Bound once to the life of the nation by the three ties of Religion, Trade, and Pleafure, firft came a time when the tie of Religion was unloofened from it ; then it was a place of Trade and Pleafure. A few more generations having lived and worked, Trade was no longer bound to it. The nation ftill grew, and at laft broke from it even as a Pleafure Fair. It lived for feven centuries or more, and of its death we are the witneffes. Surely, methought, there is a ftory here ; the Memoirs of a Fair do not mean only a bundle of hand-bills or a catalogue of monfters. And thus the volume was planned which is now offered to the reader, with a lively fenfe of its fhortcomings. Confcious of what fuch a book might have been, and ought to be, I feel how much of crudity there is in this, and only know too well how dimly the foul of it glimmers through its fubftance.*

There has been no lack of matter to make fubftance. In the Library of the Corporation of London at Guildhall *is a valuable collection of cuttings, handbills, and references to authorities, made by a gentleman who had defigned the publication of a book upon* Bartholomew Fair. *There is in the* Britifh Mufeum *another collection, made with a like purpofe, lefs valuable, but containing much that is not found in the collection at* Guildhall. *In the* Guildhall Library *there are alfo handbills bought by the City, rare tracts, and various MS. notes, from which illuftration of the ftory of the Fair was to be drawn.*

To the Committee of St. Bartholomew's Hofpital *I am indebted for permiffion to examine the old records in their keeping. Let me add that the fault is mine if I have not made ufe enough of the great courtefy with which this formal permiffion was carried out in practice, and of the ready kindnefs with which help was offered me by* Mr. White, *the Treafurer,* Mr. Wix, *the Secretary, and the* Rev. Mr. Mitchell, *Chaplain of the Hofpital.*

Here alfo let me acknowledge the good humour with

which the Rev. Mr. Abbifs, *rector of* St. Bartholomew's the Great, *permitted the irruption of a ftranger into his veftry, and fent him away not empty of the information that he fought.*

Private friends do not need public thanks, but even here I muft not pafs without acknowledgment the help I have had from my friend Mr. James Gairdner, *of the* Record Office, *who has, not only faved me all trouble of fearch among the Public Records, but who, by his exact knowledge of old fources of hiftory, has now and then given the book valuable help.*

Moreover, it would be a capital omiffion if I did not fpecially thank Mr. Henry Hicks, *of Highbury Crefcent, for accefs to fome of the papers of the late* Mr. Richard Hicks, *Deputy of Caftle Baynard Ward.* Mr. Richard Hicks *bound his name in the memory of fellow citizens with the later hiftory of* Smithfield, *and was the member of the Corporation engaged moft prominently in the final fuppreffion of* Bartholomew Fair. *He took notes at the time, and many of them are preferved. There is enough extant evidence of his refearch to have impreffed me greatly with a fenfe of the confcientious work that may be done even by a member of the City Parliament, when he devotes his public energies in all fincerity to any queftion. The jottings upon* Mr. Hicks's *papers bring together, from all forts of books and Corporation records, a great number of details about* Smithfield, *about the hiftory of tolls, and about the relation of the City to the Fair. As to the fuppreffion of the Fair, they contain extracts from the books of the* City Lands' Committee, *now and then alfo notes written by himfelf at the time in the committee-room. It needs not many words to tell of how much ufe thofe papers have been to me.*

Thus, while I may expect allowance to be made for the rough way in which I have ftaked out my little claim upon virgin foil, yet is the foil fo rich that I fear I muft go unpardoned if it fhall prove to have yielded to my tillage but a fcanty harveft. Though I have raifed and garnered all the knowledge I could get about the Fair, there certainly was more attainable: there are pamphlets and collections, doubtlefs, that I have not feen; collectors whom I have not fought. I feel convinced alfo that I muft have overlooked, through ignorance, facts known to many of my readers. Therefore I fhall be moft thankful for all further information that may come to me from any fource.

For as much as this volume can tell of Bartholomew Fair *I have efpecially wifhed to entitle it to credit as, at any rate, an honeft record. For aid in this refpect it is my duty to thank* Mr. H. Sydney Barton, *the excellent draughtfman employed by* Meffrs. Dalziel *the wood-engravers, in taking fketches and facfimiles for the pictures, varying between copies of the rudeft of old woodcuts and the imitation of fine etching upon metal, with which it is illuftrated.* Mr. Barton *has exactly met my wifh for minute faithfulnefs in the copying of everything reprefented. Even when, as in the cafe of the defign for a Bartholomew Fan, or Rowlandfon's fcenes of the Fair, comprehenfive pictures have been broken up into the feveral groups which they contain, no artist's liberty whatever has been taken with any one of the fragments so detached. Accurate work is very hard to find. Most of the illustrations in this book are now for the first time drawn (usually on a reduced scale) from the illuminations, loose engravings, or handbills, in which they first appeared; about half a dozen of them, however, have been reproduced before in other works, and not even in one instance has the copy truly represented the original. In this book, with the exception mentioned in a note upon page 7, nothing of which the original is extant has been represented from a copy. A second exception, mentioned by anticipation in that note, was set aside after the sheet had gone to press, by the discovery of an original map older and more fitted to the text than that of which a copy was to have been used.*

Outside oration is the Fashion of the Fair; therefore I hope, that I have not said too much from the platform of my little show. Secretly I fear that, like all other shows, it will be found more tempting in promise than sufficient in performance. But it is not the part of a wise showman to say that. He has his own appointed peroration. Let him, therefore, discreetly remember that he must ask Gentlemen, Ladies, *and* Children, *to walk in. To maids and boys I sing. The place about our standing is well swept, and there is no dirt of the Fair here to offend them.—* Never Before Exhibited. BARTHOLOMEW the Royal Smithfield Giant. Seven hundred years of age. His Mother's at Rome and his Father's at Bradford. To be seen A-live. *Vivat Regina!—" Shall there be good Vapour?"*

demands an acquaintance of Ben Jonſon's, Captain Knockem Jordan. The little o *of the Fair is vapour now, and it was vapour from the firſt—*

> Sith all that in the world is great and gay,
> Doth as a Vapour vaniſh and decay—

As much alive as ever, then. The ſhow is open.— BARTHOLOMEW THE ANCIENT KING OF SMITH-FIELD, IN HIS ROYAL ROBES, SURROUNDED BY HIS COURT OF CELEBRATED MONSTERS, ALL ALIVE! *Juſt opened! May it pleaſe you to look in!*

H. M.

4, UPPER PARK ROAD,
HAVERSTOCK HILL,
December, 1858.

CONTENTS.

—◆—

CHAPTER IX.

CHAPTER X.

CHAPTER XI.

CHAPTER XII.

CHAPTER XIII.

CHAPTER XIV.

CHAPTER XV.

CHAPTER XVI.

CHAPTER XVII.

CHAPTER XVIII.

CHAPTER XIX.

CHAPTER XX.

CHAPTER XXI.

CHAPTER XXII.

CHAPTER XXIII.

CHAPTER XXIV.

ERRATA.

Page 7, line 2 in note, *for* Profeſſor *read* brother of the Profeſſor.

419, ,, 9 from bottom, *omit* was.

,, ,, 5 from bottom, *for* with the old name *read* in her old part.

420, laſt line but one, *for* memoirs *read* memories.

LIST OF ENGRAVINGS.

Memoirs

OF

BARTHOLOMEW FAIR.

CHAPTER I.

ffyrst shal be shewyd who was ffunder of owere ffaire.

HE beginning of Bartholomew Fair was a grant from Henry the Firſt to a Monk who had been formerly his Jeſter. It was that Jeſter, Rayer, who founded the Priory of St. Bartholomew, in later times transformed into a Hoſpital for the Sick Poor.

By a friar who lived in the Priory not long after the death of Rayer (or as he was called in Latin, Raherus, Engliſhed back into Ra-here,) the life of the Founder was written ; all its laſt incidents being ſupplied from the memory of perſons

on the fpot. By two other friars who lived afterwards in
the Priory, this life—in Latin and in later Englifh—was
engroffed on parchment, carefully adorned with orna-
mental fcrolls and gay illuminated letters. Among the
gilt ornaments and the illuminations we find the beginning of the ftory of the Fair.*

Rayer of good remembrance, as the manufcript
informs us, founded the Priory in honour of the moft
bleffed Bartholomew Apoftle, after the rule of the moft
holy Father Auftin, and lived in it twenty-two years,
ufing the office and dignity of a Prior; not having
cunning of liberal fcience, but having that which is more
eminent than all cunning, for he was richeft in purity
of confcience. Among all the virtues fet down to his
credit we find bright manners and prudent bufinefs in
temporal miniftration. Bufy he was; and it concerns
us that his bufy mind begot the fair for the advantage
of his order : he had alfo a cunning fuited to the prefent
meaning of the word, for in his friar's robes he made
much money as a juggler. But, fays the biographer,
" in what order he fet the fundament of this temple,
in few words let us fhew as they teftified to us that faw
him, heard him, and were prefent in his works and
deeds; of the which fome have taken their fleep in
Chrift, and fome of them be yet alive and witneffeth
of that that we fhall after fay.

" This man, born of low lineage, when he attained

---

* In the Britifh Mufeum, Cotton MSS. *Vefpafian* B ix., Liber
Fundacionis ecclie fancti Bartholomei Londinarum ptinent. prioratui
eiufdem in Wefte Smythfelde (Latin and Englifh). The initial letter
to this Chapter is that of the Manufcript. The heading also, with change
of a word, is that of its firft Englifh chapter.

the flower of youth, he began to haunt the houſeholds
of noblemen and the palaces of princes, where, under
every elbow of them, he ſpread their cuſhions with
japes and flatterings, delectably anointing their ears, by
this manner to draw to him their friendſhips. And yet
he was not content with this, but oft haunted the
King's palace, and among the noiſeful preſs of that
tumultuous court inforced himſelf with jollity and
carnal ſuavity, by the which he might draw to him
the hearts of many one there. In ſpectacles, in meats,
in plays, and other courtly motleys and trifles intending,
he led forth the buſineſs of all the day. And now to
King's attendance, now following the intent of great
men,—preſſed in proffering ſervice that might pleaſe
them,—buſily ſo occupied his time that he might obtain
the rather the petitions that he ſhould deſire of them.
Thiswiſe to king and great men gentle and courteous,
known, familiar, and fellowly he was. This manner
of living he choſe in his beginning, and in this
exerciſed his youth." So runs the record. So—in
ſpectacles, meats, plays, and other courtly motleys—
were laid the foundations of the Royal favour that
beſtowed on Bartholomew in Weſt Smithfield the ſite
of his Priory and of his Fair.

Henry the Firſt was the king upon whom Rayer
waited as jeſter, or minſtrel. He was a king eaſily
moved through ſuperſtition. In one year, we are told
by Fabian's Chronicle, he had divers monitions and
viſions; for, among other fearful dreams, he ſaw
a great company of clerks, with divers weapons,
which menaced him for debt that he ſhould owe unto

them; and, when they were paffed, he was menaced to death of his own knights; and laftly appeared to him a great company of bifhops, which threatened him, and would have fmitten him with their croffes. By this monition, he took remorfe in his confcience, and did great deeds of charity in Normandy and England. One of them was the building of Reading Abbey, which was founded at about the fame time as Rayer's Priory of St. Bartholomew. When Henry died he left two characters behind him. "The fame of him faid that he paffed other men in three things, in wit, in eloquence, and in fortune of battle; and other faid he was over-comen with three vices, with covetife, with cruelty, and with luft of lechery." *

Of our next king, Stephen, Malmefbury records the "readinefs to joke." Even Henry the Second, by whofe charter, foon after Rayer's death, the fair was confirmed, relifhed buffoonery. A robuft man, who kept down a tendency to corpulence by inceffant activity of body, he was a mighty hunter, and, when not reading or at council, had always in his hand a fword, a hunting-fpear, or a bow. In difcuffing bufinefs, he ftood or walked. Yet his wit was lively, and with his intimate friends he was exceedingly familiar. In the day of Becket's power, he and Becket, after they had made an end of ferious affairs, would play together like two boys of the fame age. Fitzftephen, who fays this in his Life of Becket, gives an inftance, which will fhew clearly enough that there was yet vocation for a jefter at the court of the wifeft and moft vigorous of the Plantagenets. One

* Fabian's Chronicle, cap. 229.

day the king was riding by the fide of his chancellor through the ftreets of London, in cold, ftormy weather, when his Majefty faw coming towards them a poor old man, in a thin coat, worn to tatters.

" Would it not be a great charity," (faid he to the chancellor) " to give this naked wretch, who is fo needy and infirm, a good warm cloak ? "

" Certainly," Becket replied, " and you do the duty of a king in turning your eyes and thoughts to fuch objects."

While they fpoke the man came near. The king afked him whether he wifhed to have a new cloak, and, turning to the chancellor, faid, " You fhall have the merit of this deed of charity ;" then, fuddenly laying hold on a fine new fcarlet cloak lined with fur, which Becket wore, he tried to pull it from him, and, after fome ftruggle, in the courfe of which they both nearly rolled from their horfes, Majefty prevailed. The poor man had the cloak, and the applauding courtiers were loud in mirth. In any fuch fcenes, Rayer could perform a part, until he was converted.

His converfion was made manifeft in his defire to go to the court of Rome, " coveting in fo great a labour to do the worthy fruits of penance. He took his way, and whole and found whither he purpofed came. Where at the martyrdom of the bleffed Apoftles, Peter and Paul, he, weeping his deeds, and reducing to mind the fcapes of his youth and ignorances, prayed for remiffion of them, behefting furthermore thefe utterly to forfake. There the clear lights of heaven, the men of mercy, Peter and Paul, he ordained mediators between him and the Lord of all earth. And while he tarried there, in that meanwhile he began to be vexed with grievous ficknefs, and his dolours little and little taking their increafe, he drew to the extremity of life ; the which dreading within himfelf, and deeming the laft hour of his death drew him nigh, he fhed out as water his heart in the fight of God, and all brake out in tears. Then he avowed that if health God him would grant, that he might lawfully return to his country, he would make an Hofpital for recreation of poor men, and, to them fo therein gathered, neceffaries minifter after his power. And not long after, the benign and merciful God beheld the weeping man, and gave him his health. So of his ficknefs recovered he was, and in fhort time whole made began homeward to come, his vow to fulfil.

" Now, when he would purfue his way that he had begun, in a certain night he faw a vifion full of dread and of fweetnefs, when, after the labours and fweating that he had by days, his body with reft he would refrefh. It feemed him to be bore up on high of a certain beaft having four feet and two wings, which fet him in an high place, and when he from fo great an highnefs would inflect and bow down his eye to the lower parts downward, he beheld an horrible pit, whofe horrible beholding impreffed in him the beholder great dread and horror, for the deepnefs of the fame pit was deeper than any man might attain to fee. He fremifhed and for dread trembled, and great cries out of his mouth proceeded. To whom dreading, appeared a certain man pretending in cheer the majefty of a king,

of great beauty and imperial authority, and, his eye
on him faftened, he faid good words : ' O man,' he
faid, ' what and how much fervice fhouldft thou give
to him that in fo great a peril hath brought help to
thee ?'

   " Anon he anfwered to this, faying, ' Whatfoever
might be of beft and of mightieft diligently fhould I
give to my deliverer.'

   " Then faid he, ' I am Bartholomew the Apoftle,*

come to fuccour thee in thine anguifh.   Know me truly
by the common favour and commandment of the Celeftial
court and council, to have chofen a place in the fuburbs
of London at Smithfield, where in my name thou fhalt
found a church.   The afker in it fhall receive, the feeker
fhall find, and the ringer or knocker fhall enter.   Of
the cofts of this building doubt thou nothing, only give

---

   * This feal and the feal of Rahere (next woodcut) were copied by
Mr. Delamotte, Profeffor of Drawing at King's College, London, from
the originals among the archives of St. Bartholomew's Hofpital, and firft
publifhed in a little book of his, " The Royal Hofpital of St. Bartholomew
and Priory, illuftrated by W. A. Delamotte."   Only in thefe two inftances,
and, on a later page, in a fragment taken from a modern engraving of an
old pictorial map of London, are any of the illuftrations to this volume
copies of a copy.

thy diligence, and my part fhall be to provide neceffaries.
Of this work know me the mafter and thyfelf only
the minifter. Ufe diligently thy fervice and I fhall fhew
my lordfhip.' In thefe words the vifion difparyfchydde.

"Therefore Rayer came back to London and of his
knowledge and friends with great joy was received.
With which, alfo with the barons of London, he fpake
familiarly of thefe things. And what fhould be done of
this he counfelled, of them took he this anfwer, that
none of thefe might be perfected but the king were firft
counfelled. Namely, fith the place godly to him fhewed
was contained within the King's Market, of the which it
was not lawful to princes or other lords of their own
authority anything to manumit, neither yet to fo folemn
an obfequy depute. Therefore, ufing thefe men's
counfel, in opportune time he dreffed him to the king,
and before him, and the Bifhop Richard being prefent
(the which he had made to him favourable beforehand),
effectually expreffed his bufinefs, and that he might
lawfully bring his purpofe to effect meekly befought.
And ineffectual thefe prayers might not be whofe author
was the Apoftle, his word therefore was pleafant and
acceptable in the king's eye. And he, having the title
of defired poffeffion of the King's Majefty, was right
glad. And after the Apoftle's word all neceffaries
flowed unto the hand."

The church was founded in the month of March,
1123. The only fruit that had been expofed in this
part of the King's market before the building of the
Priory was that which hangs upon the gallows tree.
"Truly this place," fays our informant, "aforn his

cleanſing pretended none hope of goodneſs. Right unclean it was, and as a marſh dungy and fenny with water almoſt every time abounding. And that that was eminent above the water, dry, was deputed and ordained to the gibbet or gallows of thieves and to the torment of other that were condemned by judicial authority."

Upon another portion of the ground now known as Smithfield (that is, ſmooth field), bordering upon the marſh, great elm trees grew, and it was known as The Elms. The king's market perhaps was held among the trees ; but on the marſh the Priory was founded, around which was held the fair.

When Rayer had applied his ſtudy to the purgation of this place, he was not ignorant of Satan's wiles, for he made and feigned himſelf unwiſe, and outwardly pretended the cheer of an idiot, and choſe for a little while to hide the ſecret of his ſoul ; and the more ſecretly he wrought the more wiſely he did his work. In ſportive wiſe, as an idler, he drew to him the fellowſhip of children and ſervants, aſſembling himſelf as one of them, and, with their uſe and help, ſtones and other things profitable to the building playfully he gathered together ; he played with them, and from day to day made himſelf more vile in his own eyes, until that that was hid and ſecret openly began to be ſhewed to all men. Then in marvellous wiſe he inſtructed with cunning of truth in divers churches. And the multitude both of clerks and of the laity conſtantly was exhorted to follow and fulfil thoſe things that were of charity and almſdeed. Thus in brief time, clerks in the ſame place were

brought together to live under regular inftitution, Rayer
obtaining care and office of the poorhede, and miniftering
to them neceffaries, not of certain rents but plenteoufly
of oblations of faithful people.

" Some faid he was a deceiver.   Before the hour of
his laft diffeverance his houfehold people were made his
enemies.   With pricking of envy many privately, many
alfo openly, againft the fervant of God ceafed not to
grudge and in derogation to the place and prelate of the
fame brought in many flanders."   We will here wickedly
prefs againft the holy prior no heavier flanders than
one or two of the many anecdotes of his juggling—or
of the wonders worked by St. Bartholomew for the
eftablifhment and enrichment of his houfe, which form
the chief part of this hiftory of its foundation.   As our
hiftorian fays, " let us draw near to the narration of
miracles."

When the oratory was being built, " many and
innumerable were fhewed tokens and miracles, but what
for the great plenty of them and negligence of writing of
the fame, they be almoft unremembered."   When the
church was being built, a light was feen at evenfong to
play upon it for about an hour, then fuddenly flafh up
into the fky and difappear.

A man who had for many years appeared in the ftreets
of London dragging his body after him, and who begged
alms in St. Paul's Church, inviting pity for the languor
that deprived him of the ufe of all his limbs, was carried
in a bafket to the new altar of Rayer's Priory, where,
having prayed, he loft all crookednefs and ftraightway
recovered the ufe of his limbs.   And from that time the

noble matrons of the city kept their night watches before St. Bartholomew's altar, and the church became greatly frequented.

Again, fays the hiftorian, "a certain man took away a book.from this place, that we call an Antiphoner, the which was neceffary to them that fhould fing in the church, in that fpecially there was not at that time great plenty of books in the place; when it was fought bufily, and not y-found it was told to Rayer the Prior what was done of the book. And he took the harm with a foft heart patiently." The reft of the ftory is that Rayer was admonifhed, by a vifion in the night, to ride next morning to the houfe in the Jews' quarter where the book was, and where he had of courfe taken good care that it fhould be.

A woman's tongue could not be contained in her mouth. Rayer touched it with relics, and painted a crofs on it with holy water. In the fame hour it went back between her teeth.

A rich man, upland dwelling, came to the church, having heard of the deeds done in it, and faw miracles. Then he faid to the Prior, " Sir, I fhall commit me and all mine to Saint Bartholomew, advocate of this place, and to his fervice I fhall me fubdue, and with my fubftance, as he will infpire me, his clerks honour." Then faid Rayer, " Well haft thou purpofed, and doubtlefs a wife keeper of thy goods thou haft chofen." Some time afterwards that man's kitchen took fire, and he faid " Have not I late me and mine committed to bleffed Bartholomew the Apoftle. And him I have made keeper of my head and of all thing that pertaineth

to me.   If therefore it pleafeth him his to keep to himfelf, he fhall not need our help." So no man troubled
to put out the fire, and it did not fpread farther than
the kitchen.

Sailors in peril faid to each other, "What dread we,
men of little faith, the which have bleffed Barthilmewe
the doer of fo great miracles at London." They appealed
therefore to him for refcue and were refcued, in return
for which help they offered to the church of tapers a
great quantity.

There was a young man, Ofberne by name, whofe
right hand ftuck to his left fhoulder, and whofe head
ftuck to his left hand.   He was unglued at St. Bartholomew's eftablifhment.

At the high feftival of Saint Bartholomew, a boy faid
to have been born blind was led into the church, one
leading him, father and mother following.   And as he
entered the church he fell down to the earth, and there
awhile turned himfelf, now this way, now that way.
Then he rofe up with blood running down his cheeks,
declared that he for the firft time faw his parents, and
called fundry things diftinctly by their proper names.

Rayer joined to himfelf a certain old man, Alfuin
by name, to whom was fad age with experience of long
time.   This fame old man not long before had built the
church of St. Giles at Cripplegate.   And that good work
happily he had ended.   Deeming this man profitable
to him, Rayer deputed him as his companion.   Alfuin,
who had fhown fkill as a collector, carried about the
veffel in which to collect offerings.   A furly butcher,
who was named Godrich, called him a truant, and would

give nothing. Alfuin was importunate, Godrich was obftinate. Alfuin then broke out in thefe words, "O thou unhappy, O thou ungentle and unkind man ! to the Giver of all goods wilt not come ? Take in experience the virtue of the glorious Apoftle, in whom if thou truft, I promife thee that every piece of thy meat that thou giveft me a portion of fhall fooner be fold than other, and nothing to the minifhing or leffening of the price." The butcher caft a bit of meat into his veffel, and fo bade the friars leave him ; to whom Alfuin anfwered, " I fhall not go till my word and promife be fulfilled." He waited, therefore, in the fhop until a man came, who bought from the heap of meat that had fupplied the Priory, and paid without queftioning the price afked by the butcher. But Godrich had charged this cuftomer for the meat taken by St. Bartholomew, as well as for his own. " And from that time they began to be more prompt to give their alms, and alfo fervent in devotion, and ftrained how they might prevent one another in giving"—that is to fay, they competed for the fanctifying of extortion.

Here are miracles enough to affure us who contrived the tale of a confpiracy againft the life of Rayer, which a penitent confpirator revealed. Such a tale gave the cunning Prior opportunity to go before the king " with a lamentable querele expreffing how with untrue defpites he was deformed, and what faftidious outbreaking had tempted him, befeeching his royal munificence that his perfon and the place he had granted him he would defend. The king anfwered that he would apply him to his juft and neceffary petitions, and that furthermore he behefted himfelf to be a defender of him, and of his ; therefore he made his Church with all his pertinence with the fame freedoms that his crown is libertied with, or any other church in England that is moft y-freed; and releafed it all cuftoms, and declared it for to be free from all earthly fervice, power, and fubjeĉtion, and gave fharp fentence againft contrary malignants. Such liberties he confirmed with his charter and feal, and commended to the upholding and defence of all his fucceffors. Rayer, when with fuch privileges he was ftrengthened and com-fortably defended, glad he went out from the face of the king. And when he was come home to his, what he had obtained of the Royal majefty expreffed to fome that they fhould joy with him, and unto fome that they fhould be afraid.

" Also this worfhipful man

propofed for to depofe the complaint of his calamities afore the See of Rome, and of the fame fee writings to bring to him and to his aftercomers profitable, but divers under-growing impediments, and at the laft letting the article of death, that he would have fulfilled he might not."

Thus it was that Rayer profpered greatly by his wife investment of the wit of a Court Jefter in the fpeculation of a Priory; and there can be no doubt that if as a court wit he was lean, as a monk, according to the record we are following, "the fkin of his tabernacle dilated."

It was in the twelfth year of his prelacy, ten years before his death, that Rayer obtained from King Henry the Firft, upon the plea of danger from his enemies, that ampler charter to which reference has juft been made. The Fair had been from the very firft connected with the Church, and in this charter, bearing date in the year 1133, the king declares, after providing for inde-pendent election of a new Prior by the monks in the event of Rayer's death, and confirming privileges and poffeffions of the Priory: — " I grant alfo my firm peace to all perfons coming to and returning from THE FAIR which is wont to be celebrated in that place at the Feaft of St. Bartholomew; and I forbid any of the Royal fervants to implead any of their perfons, or without the confent of the canons, on thofe three days, to wit, the eve of the feaft, the feaft itfelf, and the day following, to levy dues upon thofe going thither. And let all the people in my whole kingdom know that I will maintain and defend this Church, even as my crown; and if any one fhall prefume to contravene this our Royal privilege, or fhall offend the Prior, the canons, clergy, or laity of that place, he, and all who are his, and everything that belongs to him, fhall come into the king's power."

CHAPTER II.

The First Fairs.

THE firft fairs were formed by the gathering of worfhippers and pilgrims about facred places, and efpecially within or about the walls of abbeys and cathedrals on the feaft days of the faints enfhrined in them. The facred building often was in open country, or near fome village too fmall to provide accommodation for the throng affembled at its yearly feaft of dedication. Then tents were pitched, and as the refources of the diftrict would no more fuffice to victual than to lodge its flying vifitors, ftalls were fet up by provifion dealers and by all travelling merchants who look to a concourfe for opportunity of trade. Thus in the time of Conftantine, Jews, Gentiles, and Chriftians affembled in great numbers to perform their feveral rites about a tree reputed to be the oak Mambre under which Abraham received the angels; at the fame place, adds Zofimus, there alfo came together many traders, both for fale and purchafe of their wares. St. Bafil,* towards the clofe of the fixth century, complained that his own church was profaned by the public fairs held at the martyr's fhrines.

* De Afceticis.

Under the Fatimite Caliphs, in the eleventh century, there was an annual fair held even on Mount Calvary.

We may not be juftified in deriving the word Fair, from the Church feftivals under their name of *Feriæ;* it may be derived through the French *Foire,* from another claffical root, and mean only a place to which merchandife is brought. Germans, however, keep the origin of a fair in mind by calling it *Meffe,* or Mafs ; in fome regions it is called, as in Brittany, a *Kirmefs,* or Church Mafs. There is a fecond opinion upon almoft every point in etymology, and there are fome who fay that *Meffe* is the German for a fair, becaufe men feized upon a word which fignified the end of Church and the beginning of chaffer : *ecclefia miffa eft,* the Church is difmiffed.

Bifhops and abbots, of courfe, never overlooked the reafonable fource of profit to their fhrines and the maintainers of them, which would be derived from tolls upon the trade occafioned by themfelves, and carried on within the bounds of their own lawful jurifdiction. Becaufe traders obtained from the Bifhops and patrons of the churches and monafteries, whofe dedication feafts they vifited, licences called *Indultus,* there ftill are to be found in South Germany fome fairs called Dulte ; there is, for example, the Jacobi-Dult at Munich, on St. James's Day. Every fuch fair was called after the faint whofe feaft day brought it into life. There were the fairs of St. James, St. Denis, St. Bartholomew, and at firft their duration ufed to be for the natural period of three days : the day of affembling on the eve of the feaft ; the feaft day ; and the day following ; when there were

c

farewells to be faid to friends, matters of bufinefs to further among ftrangers, and fairings (relics perhaps, or images of faints, the anceftry of our fmall figures in gilt gingerbread) to be procured for relatives at home, before the general difperfion of the holiday affembly.

Until a date later than that of the foundation of the fair in Smithfield, fairs were held very commonly in the churchyard of the facred building about which they were affembled, or even within the church itfelf. In the fourteenth year of Henry the Third the archdeacons within the diocefe of Lincoln were inftructed to inquire into this practice, and it was in that diocefe foon afterwards prohibited. In the fame reign a royal mandate forbade the keeping of Northampton fair within the church or churchyard of All Saints. In the thirteenth year of the reign of Edward the Second, the holding of a fair in any churchyard was prohibited by ftatute. The Abbot of Ely, in King John's reign, preached againft the holding of fairs on a Sunday. In earlier times, fpecial precautions had been taken to enforce order upon facred ground; and it was not unufual, when a fair was held within cathedral precincts, to oblige every man to bind himfelf by an oath at the gate not to lie, fteal, or cheat, till he went out again.

The right of levying toll, fometimes even a right of coinage, like that once granted during Magdeburg fair to the church of St. Moritz, was derived by the clergy from the crown; and to this day, throughout Europe, no fair can be lawfully held, except by grant from the crown, or by prefcription fuppofed to arife from a grant, in cafes where no record of it can be found.

Since the ſmall ſize of the towns and villages of
Europe during the infancy of modern nations, and the
infrequent reſort of ſtrangers to any place except upon
occaſions of religious feſtival, allowed few towns to
become centres of trade, the fairs of the moſt popular
ſaints, to which men flocked from afar in greateſt
numbers, became the chief marts in every country.
They proſpered eſpecially, becauſe the privileges granted
by the crown to the clergy for the holding of fairs were
equivalent to a conceſſion of ſome channels for free
trade, through the midſt of a wildernefs of taxes. Thus,
in France, before a way was opened for trade by the
fair of St. Denis, of which the origin is found in the
reign of Dagobert, rights of *ſalutaticum*, *pontaticum*,
repaticum, and *portulaticum*, abſorbed one-half of a
foreign merchant's goods upon their firſt arrival and
debarkation. But to the fair chartered by Dagobert,
" in honour of the Lord and to the glory of St. Denys
at his feſtival," traders came, exempt, not only from
imperial taxation, but from many of the ordinary riſks
of travel ; and it became, therefore, under the name
of *forum indiſtum* (whence *l'indiſt* and its corruption
to *landit*) an emporium for the iron and lead of the
Saxons, for ſlaves, for the jewellery and perfumes of the
Jews, for the oil, wine and fat of Provence and Spain,
for the honey and madder of Neuſtria and Brittany, for
merchandiſe from Egypt and the Eaſt. The fair which
laſted for ten days following the tenth of October, was
opened by a proceſſion of monks from the Abbey of
St. Denis ; and, in later times, it was uſual for the
Parliament of Paris to allow itſelf a holiday called

Landi, in order that its members might take part in the great marriage-feaſt of commerce and religion.

The granting of the King's " firm peace," or " firmeſt peace," to all perſons coming to, ſtaying in, or returning from a fair, was not a mere technical form. Otto the Great uſed the ſame phraſe on behalf of German fairs in the tenth century; breakers of ſuch peace were ſet under ban; and, where the right of private feud was recogniſed, it was ſuſpended during fair time. Traders, on their way to or from a fair, and in the fair, were free from arreſt, except for debts ariſing out of commerce in the fair itſelf. This immunity was defined in the caſe of the then ancient Frankfort fair, by Charles the Fourth, in the fourteenth century, as freedom to fair-goers for eighteen days before and after the fair, during which they were to fear nothing from Imperial mandate, interdiĉt, ban, or arreſt. As further ſecurity, Frederic the Firſt had ordained that ſuch traders ſhould carry ſwords tied to their ſaddles, or faſtened to the vehicles in which they rode, " not for the hurt of the innocent, but for defence againſt the robber." Again, becauſe there was no ſettled proviſion for the feeding and lodging of a large number of travellers, who paſſed but once a year over roads uſually unfrequented, and through towns but thinly peopled, ſpecial licence was given to the inhabitants of any diſtrict ſo traverſed to convert their houſes during fair time into inns.

The Free Fairs of the continent were thoſe which invited foreign trade, for to them all merchants might enter from abroad exempt from every public impoſt, and ſecure againſt all detention of their goods; they had fimply to pay the tolls of the fair to the church, city, or perfon on whom they had been conferred by royal grant. But this privilege was forfeited if goods were fold out of the fair, or if the trader did not remain during the whole fair time, feeking or awaiting pur-chafers. There were alfo in France and Germany fmall fairs that received only local privileges, and to which foreign trade was not brought by a free opening of ports ; but the great national fairs were always centres of free trade, and the refort to them of merchants from abroad was not only expected, but fometimes even folicited. Thus in the year 1314, Philip the Second, of France, complained to our King Edward the Second, that Britifh merchants had ceafed to frequent the French fairs with wood and other goods, and defired that they might be perfuaded or compelled to do fo.

To add to the attractions of a fair, and more efpecially to induce the rich and powerful to refort to it with full purfes in their purfuit of pleafure, amufements were introduced. The beft entertainment offered to the curious in the firft days of modern hiftory was to be found, not in fixed cities, but among the tents of thofe great fhifting capitals of trade. Thus the nobles of Languedoc betook themfelves in pleafure parties to the fair of Beaucaire, the nobles of Normandy to that of Guibray, German princes and lords amufed themfelves once a year at Frankfort and Leipfic, and in Bartho-lomew Fair there was entertainment good enough for royal vifitors.

Grant of the tolls of a fair was then a conceffion from the crown of no mean value. It would help largely to the eftablifhment and enrichment of a religious houfe, and was prudently fecured by Rayer when he laid the foundation of his priory of St. Bartholomew.   Stourbridge Fair, at one time perhaps the largeft in the world, is traced back to Caraufius; but it was fpecially granted by King John for the maintenance of a hofpital for lepers, which had a chapel in the neighbourhood. Sometimes a fair was granted for the reftoration of a town or village that had been confumed by fire; this was, in the reign of Edward the Third, the origin of a fair held at Burley, in Rutlandfhire.

Owners and governors of fairs were bound to take care that everything was fold according to juft weight and meafure; all goods fold were fold abfolutely, however bad the title to them of the feller, faving only the rights of the King. In every fair there was its own court of prompt juftice, or Pie Poudre Court. Proprietors of fairs were authorifed alfo to appoint a clerk to mark and allow weights, and to take reafonable fees. By extortion they might lofe their franchife, or the franchife might fall by voluntary abandonment or difufe for ten years, and might be forfeited by revolt or excommunication, or if the market was kept open beyond the period fpecified in the grant, a time that was to be declared at each opening by proclamation. Any perfon felling goods in the fair after its time was expired, forfeited double their value, one fourth of the forfeit being due to the profecutor, the reft to the King. Such ftrictnefs was the more neceffary, becaufe thefe inftitutions, however free to thofe ufing them, were commonly oppreffive to adjacent traders. Not only was it unlawful for any two fairs to be fet up within feven miles of each other, but it was ufual to compel all fhopkeepers to ceafe from independent bufinefs in the neighbourhood of any fuch privileged market.   Thus in the year 1248, when Henry the Third ordered a fair at Weftminfter, he compelled the city tradefmen to fhut up their fhops while it was open, and even fuppreffed the fair at Ely for the further leffening of competition.   "Which was done," fays Holinfhed, "not without great trouble and pains to the citizens, which had not room there, but, in booths and tents, to their great difquieting and difeafe, for want of neceffary provifion, were turmoiled too pitifully in mire and dirt, through occafion of rain that fell in that unfeafonable time of year."

The fair on St. Giles's Hill, given to the Bifhop of Winchefter by William the Conqueror for three days, and by Henry the Third for fixteen days, clofed the fhops not only in Winchefter but alfo in Southampton, which was a capital trading town.   Wares fold out of the fair within feven miles of it were forfeit to the Bifhop. Officers were placed on roads and bridges to take toll upon all merchandife travelling towards Winchefter. The Bifhop received toll on every parcel of goods entering the city gates.   In the fair itfelf was a tent of juftice called the Pavilion, in which the Bifhop's officers had power to try caufes for feven miles around.   No lord of a manor could during fair time hold a court baron within that circuit, except by licence had from the Pavilion.   On St. Giles's-eve the mayor, bailiffs, and citizens of Winchefter gave up to the Bifhop's officers the keys of the four city gates, and while the fair lafted the Church appointed its own mayor, bailiff, and coroner. Foreign merchants came to this fair and paid its tolls. Monafteries had alfo fhops or houfes in its drapery, pottery, or fpicery ftreets, ufed only at fair time, and held often by leafe from the Bifhop.

Such was the place occupied in focial hiftory by the firft fairs of modern Europe. For many years after the death of Rayer they continued to be the chief reforts of trade, and even in the fixteenth century there was fo little of commercial life in Englifh towns, that ftewards of country houfes made annual purchafes of houfehold ftores at fairs that might be a hundred miles diftant from the eftablifhments for which they were providing.

Robbery from booths was a capital offence, for which two perfons were executed in the reign of Henry the Eighth.

Many a purchafer, however, fuffered robbery at booths, if the complaints of old writers againft cheating in trade be credible. Thus the monk who wrote in the fourteenth century the Vifion of Piers Ploughman, makes Covetoufnefs tell us:—Firft I learned to lie: wickedly to weigh was my firft leffon. To Wye and to Winchefter I went to the Fair, with many manner merchandife, as my mafter me hight, and it had been unfold this feven year, fo God me help, had not there gone the Grace of Guile among my chaffer.

CHAPTER III.

Bartholomew Jugglers.

"N the name of the holy and undi-
vided Trinity, I, Henry King of
England, William of Canterbury,
and George Bifhop of London, to
all Bifhops and Abbots, Counts,
Barons, Juftices, Gentlemen, and
all men and faithful citizens greeting,
grant to Rayer the Prior and the
regular Canons, their Hofpital free
of all authority beyond epifcopal
ufage, defend all the rights of
Rayer and the Canons, and forbid
that any one moleft Rayer.   I
grant alfo my firm peace and the
fulleft privileges to all perfons
coming to and returning from the Fair of St.
Bartholomew." The charter of 1133, whereof this is
a fummary, and from which the paffage that efpecially
concerns us has already been quoted, was written in a
book with other records, and efpecially the Rental of the
Priory, by Brother John Cok, in the middle of the
fifteenth century.   His maffive volume (worded, of

courſe, in Latin) is ſuperſcribed " The Rental of the
Hoſpital of Saint Bartholomew in Weſt Smithfield,
London ; of all the returns pertaining to the ſame
Hoſpital, whether within or without the city of London.
Compiled and written by Brother John Cok, Treaſurer
of the Hoſpital, at Eaſter A.D. 1456 ; and in the
thirty-ſixth year of King Henry the Sixth, in the
time of Maſter John Wakeryngs, the thirty-fifth
year of his Maſterſhip, the thirty-ſeventh of the
profeſſion of the aforeſaid J. Cok, and ſixty-fourth of
his age." At the end we read : " Written by Brother
John Cok in the evening of his life, A.D. 1468.
To whom may God be merciful. Amen." Brother
Cok, therefore, ſpent twelve years in copying into one
volume the charters, bulls, and other vital documents,
relating to the Priory, and in the compilation of its
then very extenſive rent-roll.   His age was almoſt four-
ſcore when he had finiſhed, and ſtill he had left the
initial letters, chief ornaments of a manuſcript, to be
inſerted by another hand.   In Queen Elizabeth's time
there was extant a manuſcript Bible, written by John
Cok, aged ſixty-eight, of which Stow ſays it is " the
faireſt Bible that I have ſeen."   After John Cok's death,
there aroſe within the Church a ſpirit of reſiſtance againſt
Church corruption ; and there ſeems to have been a friar
in the Priory of St. Bartholomew, perhaps even a
treaſurer, who had licence to complete the decorations of
the Rental, and ſupplied the vacant ſpaces in a paler ink,
with groteſque letters, among which are two that prove
him to have been of doubtful faith.   Of his initial letter
to the firſt charter eſtabliſhing the power of the Prior

and the Canons, a tracing is prefixed to the fummary at
the beginning of this chapter.   Having illuftrated this
document with a pike fwallowing a gudgeon, he, on a
later page, adorns a bull of Pope Honorius for the
raifing of alms from the faithful on behalf of the poor
fuftained in St. Bartholomew's, with an initial letter H,
prefenting this fketch of a paftoral kifs from the fox
faithfully accepted by the goofe :

The Grace of Guile undoubtedly affifted in the founding of the Priory.   Even in its firft days it contained
friars who before his deceafe faid that Rayer was a deceiver.
Cornelius Agrippa, whom the world has denounced as a
juggler, was an honeft fpiritual man ; Rayer, whofe fame
as a faint nobody has queftioned, was a juggler.   Yet the
honeft man lived a wafte life, and the cheat laid the foundations of what is now one of the nobleft charities in
Europe. I can compare only the men themfelves.   In old
times the Church faved or the Church deftroyed a reputation, but the Church was very fallible indeed, and not
difinterefted.   It was by the production of falfe miracles at
the feaft and fair of St. Bartholomew, that Rayer made
his inftitution famous and drew crowds to Smithfield.

In his church, on St. Bartholomew's day, there lay among
the glitter of the votive tapers wretched men, women,
and children: fome truly wretched, hoping in vain for
miraculous relief; fome noifily wretched, who were in the
prefence of God mocking his difpenfations, and intending,
with connivance of the Prior, to perform a lie before the
altar. After the death of Rayer miracles became more
fcarce; "Forafmuch," fays the monk who in the next
generation wrote their hiftory, "forafmuch as the
beginning of great things needeth greater help, when
the remembered prior was yet alive there was then plenty
of miniftered grace." He diftinctly eftablifhed miracles
as a means of attraction to his feaft and fair. It was a
folemnity, we read, "for obventions and gifts, in money,
in houfehold, in corn, and in moveable goods, great
number; and then after a jocund feaft, bufy in this
place was had of recovering men into health;—of them
that languifhed, of dry men, of contract men, of blind
men, dumb men, and deaf men; for this caufe when the
day of his" [the faint's] "nativity into heaven was
known," [in ancient times there had been two opinions
about it] "it was folemnifed and honoured with great
mirth and dancing on earth." The twenty-fourth of
Auguft is this day of St. Bartholomew, on which in
the firft years of the Smithfield Priory and Fair, "men
preffed hither thickly for various caufes, and fhouldered
together," and their prefs was compared to that of the
fick men round the well, at which they waited till the
angel ftirred the waters.

Though Rayer was an impoftor, and denounced as
fuch in his laft days by his own people, it does not

follow that every miracle worked at the Feaſt of
St. Bartholomew in his time and in the days of his
immediate ſucceſſors was invented at the Priory.   The
cuſtoms of the feſtival offered to diſhoneſt perſons
who deſired profit or notoriety direct temptation to ſtand
forward as people on whoſe behalf there was a divine
interpoſition.   Thus, in the time of Rayer, there was a
carpenter of Dunwich-by-the-Sea, profeſſing himſelf to
have been contracted and twiſted in all his limbs, to
have prayed to St. Bartholomew and received promiſe of
help.   Brought to London by a ſhipper, and received
among the poor men of the Hoſpital, he gradually
recovered ; firſt uſing his hands in woman's work,
ſuch as the making of diſtaffs, then when other limbs
ſtrengthened, hewing timber with an axe, then ſquaring
it with the chopping axe, until finally, bleſſing God, he
exerciſed his trade of carpentry within the church in
preſence of the congregation, and eſtabliſhed for himſelf
a buſineſs in London.   In caſes like this, it is natural to
ſuppoſe that the Prior was leſs a deceiver than a man
content to be deceived.

But there was a ſpecial claſs of miracles relating to
the larder of the Priory, in the publication of which
nobody could have been more intereſted than the Prior
and the Canons.   Rayer's colleague and collector, Alfuin,
was apparently a man of kindred genius.   We have
read the Miracle of the Butcher's Meat ; now let us
add to it the Miracle of Malt.   Alfuin, when collecting
the materials for a brew of ale by the monks, went to
a pious woman in the pariſh of St. Giles, Eden, the
wife of Edred.   This woman had but ſeven ſieves of

malt, from which, if fhe fpared any, her own brewing
would be fpoilt; neverthelefs, rather than fend the
holy man empty away, fhe meafured him a fieve full.
Then fhe meafured what remained, and there were
ftill feven fieves full. Surprifed at this, fhe tried again,
and lo, there were eight fieves full. She meafured
again, and there were nine fieves full. She took her
increafe to the church, and publicly bore witnefs to
the marvel.

A ftiff-jointed child, who always "lacked bowable-
nefs," was healed in the church, "and," it is added,
"ferved the Canons there in the kitchen; and, for the
gift of his health, he gave the fervice of his body."

In Rayer's time alfo the wonder-working relics vifited
the provinces. A certain man of Norwich, who had
not taken enough care of himfelf after bloodletting,
loft the power of fleep for almoft feven years, became
lean, fhrivelled, and difcoloured about the mouth.
Unable to work, he fell from a condition of wealth
into poverty. In the feventh year of his misfortune,
when the relics of St. Bartholomew were brought and
put into the Oratory of St. Nicholas at Yarmouth,
"this man drew to the fame relics devoutly, and he
found that he fought; he rang at the door, and our
porter opened to him, and fhowed him magnificently
the bowels of his mercy." He grovelled on the ground,
flept, rofe, and was well.

Let it fuffice to cite, from the other miracles performed at the Feaft of Bartholomew in Rayer's time,
one piece of very clumfy jugglery. A dropfical man
rolled on the pavement, and, it is faid, "at the laft, in

the fight of all men, he caſt out wonder venom, and his inwards were purged from this deadly filth, and all whole returned to his own houſe."

It is to be recorded, alſo, that the Priory, when altogether new, was furniſhed with traditions. Edward the Confeſſor had a viſion of this place, " when he was in the Church of God, replete with manifold beauty of virtue, as the book of his gefts declareth," and ſhone as a holy man, full of the ſpirit of prophecy. Alſo, three men of Greece, pilgrims, entering England of old time, deſired to viſit the bodies of ſaints; and, coming to Weſt Smithfield, proftrated themſelves in the marſh on the ſite of the Priory, and preached to the mocking byftanders of a temple that was to ſtand there, whoſe fame ſhould " attain from the ſpring of the ſun to the going down."

In the year 1143 Rayer died, " after the years of his prelacy twenty-two and ſix months, the twentieth of September, the ſeventh month, the clay houſe of this world he forſook," and there was left by him, ſays the record, " a little flock of thirteen Canons, as a few ſheep, with little land and right few rents; neverthelefs, with copious obventions of the altar, and helping of the nigh parts of the populous city, they were holpen." The author of the record, written about thirty years afterwards, adds : " Soothly they flouriſh now, with lefs fruit than that time when the aforeſaid ſolemniſations of miracles were increaſed." Upon the monument raiſed over the tomb of the departed ſhepherd is an effigy that repreſents him in death, with an angel at his feet, and two of his ſheep with Bibles open at this text in the 51st chapter of Isaiah: 'The Lord shall comfort Zion: he will comfort all her waste places; and he will make her wilderness like Eden and her desert like the garden of the Lord.'

About a year after the Founder's death, in the year 1144, and in the reign of King Stephen, who made Theobald Archbishop of Canterbury, Robert, Bishop of London, admitted as Prior, Thomas Hagno, one of the Canons of St. Osyth (Essex). This Prior's rule lasted for thirty years, and it was very soon after his death, and in the reign of Henry the Second, that the Manuscript History of the Foundation of St. Bartholomew's was written.

In the charter of King Henry the First it had been provided, that after the death of Prior Rayer out of the same congregation should be chosen he who was worthy; but that no one should be chosen from elsewhere, whether by the demand of Pope or Prince, unless, on account of manifest crimes (which Heaven forbid), none of the house were found worthy of the office; in that event, they were to have power of choosing a Prior from some other reputable place. We will infer no evil, however, from the fact that after Rayer's death the office of Prior remained for a whole year in abeyance, and that it was a canon of St. Ofyth whom the Bifhop of London then confirmed in the office. In thofe days there was civil war in the nation, and there might well be diffenfion in a priory. If the houfehold was divided againft Rayer when he died—and there are faid even to have been plots againft his life—the Bifhop might have refufed to accept a Prior from among its inmates; or they may have themfelves agreed to cancel in a friendly fpirit rival claims, by choofing from the church without their walls a fecond Prior who was able to maintain the fame of their eftablifhment. The firft prior was a lay jefter transformed into a clerical juggler, and the fecond prior was an improvvifatore. Prior Thomas, unlike Rayer, was a fcholar, and he had the power of delivering himfelf copioufly in impromptu rhyme; therefore, whenever he wifhed to attract the people to his miniftration, it was his cuftom to preach in doggrel. "This Thomas," fays the hiftorian among the friars, "as we have found in common, was a man of jocund company and fellowly jocundity; of great eloquence and of great cunning, inftruct in philofophy and in divine books exercifed; and he had it in prompt whatfoever he would utter to fpeak meterly. And he had in ufe every folemn day when the cafe required to difpenfe the word of God, and flowing to him the prefs of people from without on this account, He added to him glory who had given him this grace within. He was prelate to us meekly almoft thirty years, and in age an hundred winter almoft, with whole wits, with all Chriftian folemnity he deceafed and was put to our fathers the year of our Lord 1174, of the Papacy of the Bleffed Alexander the Third the 16th year, of the coronation of the moſt unſkunfited" (invictiſſimi—undifcomfited) " king of England, Henry the Second, the 20th year, on the 17th day of the month of January." The flock of canons in the Priory had then increaſed to thirty-five, " increaſing with them temporal goods evenly."

The ſteady increaſe in the wealth of the eſtabliſhment had been due not merely to the learning and the rhyming of the Prior Thomas. As a rhymer and a jocund man it is juſt to believe that the Prior of St. Bartholomew's furniſhed ſomething more than pulpit oratory for the celebration of the yearly feſtival. Poſſibly he wrote miracle plays. Certainly alſo the church ſtill boaſted of its miracles, which, though leſs numerous than in the days of Rayer,—" as a plant, when it is well rooted, the oft watering of him ceaſeth," yet were in particular years eſpecially abundant.

In the year 1148, the twelfth after the death of Henry the Firſt King of England, when the golden path of the ſun brought round the defired joys of feſtival celebration, at a new ſolemnity of the Bleſſed Apoſtle there were beheld new miracles. Feeble men loaded with various diſeaſes lay proſtrate among the lights in the church, imploring divine mercy and the preſence of St. Bartholomew. Preſently ſome were heard rejoicing at releaſe from headache, ſome from lameneſs, or from ſinging in the ears, ſome from bleared eyes ; many joyed at relief from fevers, giving thanks to the honour of the Apoſtle, " certain while everywhere for ſuch thing was given applauſe and gladneſs of all the people." In the left corner of the church—I abridge but retain the ſubſtance and the manner of the narrative—fome were heard weeping amid the gladnefs, where lay a certain damfel deaf and dumb, whofe parents, waiting, lay grovelling on the pavement, and ceafed not from prayer till all things was finifhed of the clergy that was expedient to fo great a feaft. When the canons fang the fecond evenfong, the maid became more grievoufly tormented, frothing at the mouth, beating her breaft, knocking her head againft the ground. When they came to the hymn of our Bleffed Lady, where the altars fhould be lighted, the forefaid maid began with a fharp voice to cry and her members fhe ftretched out. Anon joyfully fkipping forth, her eyes, now new and now clear, with the linen cloth that fhe was clothed in fhe wiped and dried. And thus with ftedfaft ftanding, when fhe was repaired of hearing and of the acceptable light of feeing, fhe ran to the table of the holy altar, fpreading out both hands to heaven.

One Spilman, ploughman at Berwick, an epileptic, was brought to the church at the feaft of the Apoftle, then, receiving his health, kiffed the altar, " and not a little he amended into devotion all that were then prefent." Others received eyefight and bore witnefs; women were cured of the palfy; a crippled girl received the faint's word of healing in a dream.

In the year 1159 at the feaft of St. Bartholomew, many tokens were fhowed in his holy church. A certain woman, grievoufly fick, borne to the church on a horfe litter in the vigil of the Apoftle, about the hour of complin began to recover, rofe out of her litter and came to kifs the high altar, the convent of the church

and many people being prefent.   After the octaves of
the fame feaft, a child was brought by its parents which
had been mad fince the feaft of St. Lawrence, and his
mother faid that he had been borne to many places of
faints but had obtained no remedy.   The child was
cured by St. Bartholomew and fhown to all the people
on the Sunday following.

In addition alfo to the king's firm peace and the ufual
privileges, there was fuggefted by a miracle the fpecial
care of the apoftle over thofe braving the perils of a
journey to the Feftival and Fair.

Thus it was taught that a Kentifh prieft, " coming
near the gladnefs of the glorious feaft," rode a good
horfe that was dear to him, and was, with other men,
bound to the fame church.   At night, they needed their
inn, and found no hoftelry, for which reafon they
camped and turned their horfes out to pafture under
watch.   All fell afleep, and the prieft's horfe broke
loofe.   Then there appeared to the fleeping prieft a
certain man with fhining cheer, and fhook his veftment
foftly.   The prieft, fo awakened, miffed his horfe,
found him two furlongs off, and fkipped upon him.
At London, he bore witnefs that the image he faw in the
Priory was moft like to him that waked him, and " his
horfe that fo delicioufly he loved, and fo negligently had
loft, mightily reftored."

The author of the record fays that many marvellous
things for the prolixity of this treatife and the fimilitude
of miracles he has omitted to write, but he candidly
defines the object of all thefe miraculous interpofitions.
The moral of them all is, Give, give! " that freely

they bring, kindly and joyfully, not only men but women."

A poor woman at Windſor loſt, in a murrain, all her cows but one, and that was ſick. She meaſured the animal's length for the ſize of a taper to St. Bartholomew, and immediately it recovered. — There was a peſtilence among cattle at Enfield. A pious clerk loſt nine oxen, and there remained but a ſick heifer. He vowed it to St. Bartholomew if it recovered, or the price of its ſkin if it died. Suddenly it was well and began to eat hay. It was duly ſent to Smithfield.—A woman living by the caſtle of Montfichet (that caſtle built by Gilbert de Montfichet, a follower of the Conqueror, was afterwards pulled down to make room for the great houſe of the Blackfriars), who, though ſhe ſtood in the bonds of marriage, lived as a nun, ſaw her cow in peril of life over calving. She ſaid to her ſervants that if the cow calved without hurt, ſhe would mark the calf in the ear, and when it was weaned give it to the church of St. Bartholomew. The cow ceaſed to ſuffer, and the calf was immediately born, notched already by the Saint himſelf in *both* ears.

Never did a bleſſed Saint look after the perquiſites of his office more ſtrictly, let it even be ſaid more greedily, than the Saint Bartholomew, who was magnified by the Prior and Canons in Weſt Smithfield. He would even, when it was made worth his while, conſent with thieves. Once, when the king of England beſieged Wales, a merchant had made money by extortion in his traffic with the king's army at Colcheſter, and vowed to St. Bartholomew a part of his unhallowed gains. But

the Saint's fhare he kept by him. This man took fhip
to London, and then travelled further, till upon the way
one of his fellow-travellers robbed him of his money,
which he had placed under his pillow. The Saint then
appeared and lectured the afflicted merchant moft
devoutly on the fin of extortion. But to the prayers of
the plundered thief he accorded the information, that he
had miraculoufly caufed the man who took his wealth to
keep it undiminifhed, and the Saint agreed to contrive
its quiet reftoration, on condition that he received for
his fhare all that had been vowed to him—and more.

A poor man, accuftomed to come annually with his
wife to the Feaft of St. Bartholomew, and bring
oblations, was feized as a known offender againft the
laws (wrongfully, fays the record) by a beadle, carried
off, and chained in a houfe near the Priory. There, in
the night, at the found of the bells and hymns of the
monks, his chain miraculoufly parted from its faftening,
and he was able to efcape, dragging it after him. The
beadle hearing the clank of the chain of his efcaping
prifoner, leapt out of bed, reached his door in time
to fee him running through the moonlight to the
church, and was miraculoufly deprived of the power
either of fhouting or purfuing. The efcaped man
fled to the church, and then gave praife to the pro-
tecting Saint. Again, we are told that a man, bound by
his enemies, was carried by them in a cart. When
paffing the church his bonds were loofened, he fkipped
out of the cart, entered the church, and was fafe. The
church of St. Bartholomew became only a pleafanter
and fafer fanctuary for the prifon-breaker when, before

the congregation, he afcribed his efcape to a miracle worked in his favour by its patron Saint.

London being a port, it was advifable that the brotherhood in Smithfield fhould lay ftrefs on the power of their Saint to affift fea-faring men who brought gifts to the Priory. Eleven fhips from a port in Flanders being feparated in a ftorm, one of them ran aground, and was buried half its depth in fand. On board this veffel, among the weepers, wailers, and miftrufters, was one, riper and fadder of age, who, preaching to them, faid : " I have heard fpecially of one faint and heavenly citizen, I have heard of St. Barthil-mewe, that, among the knights of the heavenly king, is worthy to be called upon, who pleafantly condefcendeth to the prayers of devout afkers. Let us, therefore, lift up our hands to Heaven, and avow, with clear devotion, that, when we come whither we purpofe, to London, we fhall bear thither, in the honour of St. Barthilmewe, a Ship of Silver, after the form of our fhip, made on our cofts, offering it to that church in mind of our deliverance." The vow was made, and immediately the Saint, " with his holy hand, drew forth the fhip by the fore-end." The ftory ends with the delivery of the filver to the Priory.

St. Bartholomew himfelf is elfewhere reprefented, in the midft of the ftorm, touting for cuftom. A merchant was brought to the chapter-houfe, who had a ftory for the canons. At fea, in a ftorm, when he and all his fhip-mates prayed to many faints, he " heard a voice faying, What cry ye upon fo many names of faints, and your patron, by fpecial privilege granted of God to you, ye

laches to call. To whom I faid, Who is that, my
Lord? And he faid, Moft bleffed Bartholomew call
ye in to you, and him ye fhall feel moft prompt helper
in this prefent peril." They called, therefore, upon
St. Bartholomew; and thereupon the elements gave
way to them, and ferved their will. The merchant,
having told this ftory, prefented his oblation.—A merchant of Flanders was taken by the faint from a wreck
in the midft of the fea, and landed dryfoot on the
Englifh fhore.—A failor, clinging to a maft after a
fhipwreck, appealed to St. Bartholomew, who came to
ftill the ftorm, told him that there would pafs a fhip
from Dover for his refcue, and, before departing, gave
him a piece of bread. This morfel of bread the failor
produced at the church, where it was kept as a token
and a relic; fo that we muft number this among the exhibitions popular in the firft days of Bartholomew Fair.

It was not Saint Bartholomew alone who had a
bufinefs to look after in Smithfield. In the eaftern part
of its church the Priory maintained an oratory and
altar to the Virgin. To Hubert, a mild and pious
prieft, worfhipper there, once appeared " the Mother of
Mercy faying, with a honey and fweet mouth: Canons,
fhe faid, of this church, thy brethren, my darlings, in
this place confecrate to my name, fometime paid to me
folemn office of mafs, and devout fervice of faithful
reverence gave to me. And now hath undercrept them
negligence, charity chilleth, that neither have the holy
myfteries of my Son been haunted, neither to me has
wonted praife been given. Therefore, from the high
defcenfe of heavens, by the confent of my fon, hither

I defcend, for your given obfequy of honour to give thanks," &c.   The comment upon this fiction was, How holy muft the fhrine be to which Mary herfelf came down ; and thus, no doubt, there was fecured for the Priory a fenfible addition to its income.

I am not founding an opinion about thefe miracles on the citation of a few, but, at the rifk of being tedious, have told nearly all of them; the reader can judge, therefore, of the drift of the whole mafs.   Only the monotonous details of a few healings in the church on Feftival day will have been paffed over when four more ftories have been detailed.   Thefe relate to the power of the Saint over the devil.

A young courtier, Robert, on the way from North-ampton to London, flept in a wood.   In dreams the enemy came to him, fat at his head in the fhape of a fair woman, and, before departing, put a little bird into his mouth.   He awoke mad, and ran about the country until he was caught and brought to London.   Him the Saint cured.—A certain knight, Radulf, of the houfehold of William de Montfichet, became mad on his way from Effex to London, flid down from his horfe, rent his clothes, fcattered abroad his money, and threw ftones at thofe he met.   He wandered in woods and about hills, was dangerous in crowds, and, after he had been captured, withftood violently thofe who con-veyed him to the church of St. Bartholomew, in which, after he had dwelt two nights, he was reftored to his whole mind again.—Wymund, who ruled St. Martin's church, fituate in the corner of the way that leads to Weftminfter, and dean of neighbouring churches, was

beyond equity given to voluptuous life ; but he trained
virtuously his illegitimate daughter, who trod all things
carnal under-foot.   Then the Serpent transformed himfelf into the likenefs of a fair young man, adorned
with precious ornaments, as one who was a gentleman
of the king's blood, and fuddenly flid into her chamber.
He talked with her in vain.   When the nurfe came
fhe heard the talking, but faw only the maid.   The
Serpent reappeared again and again, with increafed
beauty, and offering increafed temptation ; at laft, being
ftill difcomfited, he fmote that maiden, and deprived
her of her wit.   A great crowd gathered where fhe fell ;
when fhe could fpeak, fhe explained what had happened,
and was borne on a carpet to the church of St. Bartholomew.   The Serpent was by her fide, and faid: "Whither
art thou borne?   Troweft thou that the Apoftle fhall
deliver thee from my hands ? "   At the church door he
redoubled his temptations ; but, as fhe refifted him ftill,
fhe was tormented more than ever.   By the Saint fhe
was delivered from the fiend, and this feat also " was
publifhed everywhere to his praife."

Of the laft miracle recorded we are told, " there be
almoft as many witneffes as men dwelling in the port of
Haftings."   The town of Haftings was on fire.   There
was a venerable matron there, named Cealia, whofe
hufband, named Helyas, having come from abroad into
London, not knowing of the hurt at home, went with
his offering to the church of St. Bartholomew.   In the
meantime, his wife Cealia at Haftings, feeing the flames,
called on the fame Saint, and, having vowed lights to his
church, fhe began anon with a long thread to compafs

the houfe, and left it there fixed. The fire flowed on
to the next houfes, and did not prefume to touch the
thread or the houfe it meafured. The houfe, added the
fpinner of this yarn, is yet to be feen, with its pinnacles
half-burnt, while new houfes clofe by are utterly
deftroyed.

What wonder if, to fee the miracles worked at the
celebration of the Feaft of St. Bartholomew in the firft
years after the foundation of his Priory in Smithfield,
the people came from far and near, and were to be
found " fhouldering each other," as well as " dancing
and rejoicing," in a concourfe at the Fair !

CHAPTER IV.

𝕿𝖍𝖊 𝕱𝖆𝖎𝖗 𝖎𝖓 𝖙𝖍𝖊 𝕻𝖗𝖎𝖔𝖗𝖞 𝕮𝖍𝖚𝖗𝖈𝖍𝖞𝖆𝖗𝖉.

IN the network of London there are few meſhes cloſer
and more intricate than thoſe in which the broken
fragments of the Norman Priory of St. Bartholomew
now lie entangled. Tall houſes, ſome adorned with
grotefque figures, bury between them narrow lanes;
pent-up alleys lie in the ſhade of factory walls that were
once Priory walls, or that contain ſtones from the ruin
of the Priory mortared among their bricks. Within the
bounds of the old Priory encloſure, approached by
gateways which have loft the fence in which they were
built and even the paſſages to which they led, this
diftrict fituated in the heart of the denfe central quarter
of the town correſponds in every ſenſe to its name of
Bartholomew Cloſe. One open piece there is in it, a ſmall
paved ſquare from which the houſes ſeem to have been
not removed, but ſwept afide and crowded into a confuſed
heap with the ſurrounding buildings. Out of the ſquare
of the Cloſe, one may paſs into another part of the maze
through a fragment of Priory, now a dim public
thoroughfare called Middleſex Paſſage.

This looks like the cloifter of a dungeon, but is no
cloifter at all. It is a fragment of the great crypt of

the Priory, overhung by the wreck of a great hall. The hall is broken up, divided into floors and adapted for ufe as a tobacco factory. Into feparated portions of the crypt there is accefs by the doors on each fide of the Paffage.

In one fection there is tobacco ftored, and in another pickles. The way among the pickle barrels is between pointed Norman arches under a high vaulted ceiling, on ground much above the level of the ancient floor. The entrance to the crypt was by a defcent of five-and-twenty feet until earth and rubbifh were poured in,

and the floor thus was raifed for the convenience
of traffic. Tradition holds that at the end of the
long vaulted fubterranean hall there was a door opening into the church. But when he has come from
under thefe vaults, the ftranger may fearch for a little
time in vain before he finds the remaining fragment of
the church into which that clofed gateway was fuppofed.
to lead. Probably he will firft reach, through an alley, a
door and bit of church wall hemmed in between factories.
That is an entrance by which it is moft unlikely that
he will obtain admiffion ; fhould he propofe then to walk
round to the other fide, he muft needs turn his back on
the church altogether, and plunge through the chaos of
brick that hems it in. With trouble, if unaffifted, and
by mere accident at laft, he finds another gateway deep
fet among buildings, and after further fearch he may find,
or may fail to find, an iron railing fixed before the main
entrance of what is now the church of a fmall parifh.
It was the centre of the Priory ; the choir from which its
tower rofe. The nave is entirely gone. The laft line
of a complete fquare of cloifters, ufed in its later days as
a ftable, tumbled down about a fcore of years ago. The
apfe is broken off, and its place filled up with a beggarly
brick wall. But there remain ftill perfect the maffive
fide walls, the arches and their ftrong pillars like the
pillars of a fortrefs. Half way between capital and bafe
of the pillars of that oratory of the Virgin which a
miracle commended once to reverence, now ftands the
floor of the veftry of the parifh church.

Except a window opened for himfelf by a much later
Prior through which he could fee the monks at their

prayers without croffing the threfhold of his houfe, the
walls and aifles on either fide of the church of St. Bartholomew the Great are as they were when Rayer caufed
them to be built. The "ampler buildings" with which
in the fecond Prior's time "the fkin of the tabernacle
was enlarged" could not have included that part of the
church from which everything elfe radiated. One of the
firft miracles alfo was affociated with the building of the
oratory. Upon this point ftones can fpeak. High

columns and arches
maffive as rock itfelf,
enriched only with
the rude ornament
and zigzag work
ufed by the oldeft
of our Norman
builders; unbut-
treffed walls, firm in
their own folid
breadth ; windows
raifed far above the
ground that they
might afford no eafy
way of entrance to
the enemy, and
arcades before them
on which fighting
monks or knights

might ftand if danger preffed to beat back the befiegers;
thefe, in their fturdieft and fimpleft form, are the main
feature of the building.

The tomb of Rayer, under its ſtone canopy, is againſt one of the old walls, and is of younger date. Common opinion, however, holds the painted ſtone figure upon it to be older than the tomb; to be, in faćt, a portrait ſtatue, executed when the features of the firſt Prior were known, by an artiſt competent to reproduce them. Undoubtedly the ſtatue has a real and individual, not a conventional face, and anſwers very well to our impreſſion of the perſon whom it repreſents. If the effigy be truſtworthy we have but to copy its head faithfully, as in the annexed ſketch, ſet it upright, and receive it as the only extant portrait of the founder of the Fair.

S. Barkla del   DALZIEL Sc.

Saint Bartholomew chofe his fite fhrewdly when he afked for ground in Smithfield. It was fimply the beft fituation for a London Priory that wit could find. Rayer was not afraid to make the Saint afk for a piece of the king's market,—the great market held every Friday for the neceffary commerce in horfes, cattle, fheep, pigs, and farm implements, between the country and the town. To this great weekly gathering the brotherhood could look for many of thofe offerings to the altar, upon which they depended for a main part of their income. But that is not all. Smithfield was not only a market, but alfo the daily gathering place of Londoners in fearch of active recreation. It was there that Rayer began his enterprize by playing with the boys and the apprentices, and inducing them, as the legend runs, to accept as a jeft the work of filling up with ftones the piece of marfhy ground on which he had refolved to build. There was a daily throng to Smithfield of perfons who, when there, had leifure to think about the wonder-working fhrine, or to feek entertainment in the miniftrations of the fecond Prior, Thomas, when he exhorted them to godlinefs and liberality in jocund rhyme.

We need look but little farther than to the account of London, written in the year 1174, by the Norman Londoner and clerk, William Fitzftephen, inmate in the houfe of Thomas à Becket, remembrancer in his chancery, fubdeacon in his chapel, and eye-witnefs of his death, for fufficient fulnefs and accuracy in defcribing the pofition of the Priory when it firft opened its gates befide the king's market in Smithfield. At the fame time we fhall be able to make

E

some direct addition to the story of the first days of
the Fair.

London was then assured in her rank as the capital of
England. Winchester, her rival, had lost ground for
ever since the ruin suffered by it in the civil wars, when
Maude besieged the bishop in his castle in the town, and
was herself besieged by Stephen's army. The fires
launched forth by the defenders of the castle destroyed
much of the city, forty churches, and two abbeys.
Another abbey, in which citizens sought refuge, was
stormed and sacked. We may observe, in passing, that
such incidents show what is meant by the thick walls of
Norman keeps and churches. The hand of Manza,
Norman bishop, was almost as familiar with the sword as
with the crozier. After the breaking of the Anglo-
Saxon church, bishoprics of which the seat was in
defenceless places, were transferred to walled towns, as
Sherborne to Sarum, or Selsey to Chichester. In other
places that retained their bishops, as Durham, Rochester,
and Exeter,—though Exeter had been upon similar
grounds, under half Norman influences, a transfer from
Crediton,—strong castles were set. In harmony with
such a temper of the times, the Norman churches,
priories, and abbeys, were always, to some extent, built
with a regard to soldiers as well as saints.

London included, when St. Bartholomew's Priory
was newly founded, thirteen large conventual and twenty-
six parish churches. Its great length was from east to
west, along the course of the Thames; from the Tower
on the east to the two western castles, both well fortified
by Baynard and Montfichet. It was a city contained on

three fides within high and thick walls, through which there was egrefs by feven double gates. To the north wall, beyond which lay the Priory of St. Bartholomew, there were many towers and turrets. London had once been walled alfo on the fouth or river fide, but the tides had undermined and deftroyed that defence, and it had never been repaired. Truft was put in the Tower and the Bridge. It was but a wooden bridge until a few years after the date to which we now refer. Two miles out of town, on the weft, the royal palace, faid Fitzftephen, exalts its head and ftretches wide, an incomparable ftructure, furnifhed with baftions and a breaftwork. The palace of Weftminfter was then, however, confidered to be united to the city by a kind of fuburb, as there was the village of Charing, and there were fome river-fide houfes of great men on the inter-vening ground. Outfide the city walls there were fuburban gardens, rich in trees. The citizen who looked from the north wall with his face towards Weft Smithfield and the Priory, would fee open country : moorland, runlets, brooks, and pools ; a larger fheet of water ; the fmooth field, partly fhadowed by its elms, lying between the marfhy ground and a rich landfcape of "cornfields, paftures, and delightful meadows, inter-mixed with pleafant ftreams, on which ftands many a mill whofe clack is grateful to the ear." The whole was then bounded in the diftance by the outline of the great foreft of Middlefex (not difafforefted until the reign of Henry the Third), "beautified with woods and groves, and full of the lairs and coverts of beafts and game, ftags, bucks, boars, and wild bulls." The way to

Weft Smithfield was through Alders' Gate, or through
the Cripplegate befide which cripples affembled to beg
alms of the pleafure-feeker, for it was the gate of
pleafure haunted by remembrances of pain.   Immediately outfide Cripplegate was a fuburb of a few thatched
houfes, and the church of St. Giles, lately built by
Alfuin, whofe genius as a devifer of miracles had alfo
aided Rayer in eftablifhing his Priory.   The church was
built befide a pool.   London was then a city of which
the inhabitants depended folely for frefh water on their
fprings.   Within the city itfelf fprings bubbled up and
ran as ftreamlets to the Thames.   Old Bourne rofe
from the earth upon the fite now occupied by Holborn
Bars, and ran down a fteep hill into the River of Wells
at Old Bourne Bridge.   Langbourne broke out in
Fenchurch Street.   The River of Wells was formed
partly by brooks from the three great rural Wells,
Holywell (afterwards made filthy by the heightening of
ground for garden plots), Clement's Well, and Clerkenwell, thefe being the beft frequented both by fcholars
from the fchools and by the youth of the city on a
fummer's evening : partly it was fed by runlets from
fome leffer wells near the Clerks' well, known as Skinner's Well, Fag's Well, Tode Well, Loder's Well, and
Radwell.   The River of Wells flowed by a bit of the
path outfide Cripplegate, and entered lower down to pafs
through London as a ftream up which, as far as Fleet
Bridge, ten or twelve of the fmall fhips then built could
come abreaft.   Attached to the moor fields on one fide,
and to the partly fenny, partly firm ground of the green
plain and playground of Weft Smithfield on the other,

was a confiderable fheet of water, called the Horfe Pool. There the beafts were watered at the Friday cattle market. Thither in winter went the citizens for fport upon the ice. Fitzftephen fpeaks of the pool as "that vaft lake which waters the walls of the city towards the north;" and defcribes the fliding on it by the youth of London when it was hard frozen, the riding on blocks of ice dragged over it as fledges, the pulling of one another in long chains of players holding hand to hand, the fkating upon primitive fkates made of the leg bones of fome animal, an iron-fhod ftaff being ufed by the fkater for pufhing himfelf along "with the velocity of a bird." Sometimes the fkaters met in playful battle, when whoever fell had his head fplit to the fkull or his leg broken. Citizens alfo went out through the Cripplegate on fowling expeditions with the hawk and merlin, and they had the right of hunting in Middlefex, Hertfordfhire, the Chilterns, and in Kent as far as the river Cray. Our Smithfield was diftinguifhed as Weft Smithfield from Eaft Smithfield, near the Tower. In Eaft Smithfield, again, there was an old monaftery, dis-tinguifhed as Eaft Minfter from the Weft Minfter at the oppofite end of the town.

Of Smithfield Market, Fitzftephen, writing in the twelfth century, tells us that there was without one of the city gates, and even in the very fuburbs, a certain Smooth Field, fuch both in reality and name. Here every Friday, unlefs it fhould be a folemn feftival, there was a market for fine horfes, whither came, to look or to buy, earls, barons, knights, and a fwarm of citizens. There were prancers, draught horfes, hacks, and charging fteeds, the laft named being thofe ufed as racehorfes. There could be found a trotting horfe for an efquire, or an ambling horfe worthy to be a knight's gift to a lady.

In the Friday market was another quarter for the fale of peafants' wares, implements of hufbandry of all kinds, pigs and cows, oxen, plough mares and cart mares, fome with foal.

In Fitzftephen's account of the entertainments of the town, Smithfield again occupies a confpicuous pofition. Our citation can, on fome points, be illuftrated by the pencil of an almoft cotemporary artift, one of the monks of the Priory, who, in its early days, illuminated a book of Decretals, from which we have extracted the above fketch of a lady's horfe, and of which we fhall fay more hereafter.

Inftead of the ancient fhows of the theatre, to which Fitzftephen as a fcholar can refer, London, he fays, " has entertainments of a more devout kind, either reprefenta- tions of thofe miracles which were wrought by holy confeffors, or thofe paffions and fufferings in which the martyrs fo rigidly difplayed their fortitude." Shrove Tuefday was a fchoolboy's holiday. The Church had in its hands all the education of the rich, and every cathedral was bound legally to provide free inftruction for poor fcholars. London had flourifhing fchools connected with three churches which are not named by Fitzftephen, but which he fays were privileged by grant and ancient ufage. They were St. Paul's, St. Peter's, Weftminfter, and St. Peter's, Cornhill. The laft-named fchool was attached to the moft ancient church in London, of which the foundation was afcribed to Lucius the firft Chriftian king, who lived in the year 160. There was once a well-furnifhed library attached to that church for the ufe of fcholars, which in the beginning of the feventeenth century no longer exifted. But there was then " yet belonging to the church a fchool wherein are taught fuch arts and learnings as are taught at St. Peter's, Weftminfter, mufic excepted." * On Shrove Tuefday Stow records that every boy took to the fchool his fighting cock, " and they were indulged all the morning in feeing their cocks fight in the fchoolroom." After dinner all the youth went into the field of the fuburbs and played football, while the elders and rich men of the city went to the field on horfeback to look on. On the Sundays in Lent troops of young men, fons of the citizens, rufhed out at the gates with lances and fhields to engage in fham fights, and if the king happened to be in the neighbourhood, young men of rank who fought advancement hovered about him and combated together in his prefence. At Eafter there were games at ftriking the target on the water, when many were drenched, and there was the Bridge crowded with laughing fpectators.

---

* The Third Univerfitie of England, &c. &c. A pamphlet by G. B. Knt. (Sir George Buck), 1615.

On summer
evenings the
youth would
run, leap,
wreſtle, caſt
the ſtone, or
contend with
b u c k l e r s,
ſwords, and
arrows. Mai-
dens danced
to the tabor
by moonlight,
boys whipped
large tops, or
joined in a
game with
bat and ball.
Bowls and
n i n e p i n s,
(here allow for
the friar's bad
perſpective
☞), were
among the
ſports, even
dice - caſting,
when homes
were ſcarcely
h a b i t a b l e,
ſeems to have

been accepted as an out-door game.
Since thefe fports natural to Smithfield
muft have been among the recreations
fought on the great Smithfield holiday
provided by the Fair, we turn to the old
friar of St. Bartholomew for pictures of
the games as they were played fix centuries ago.

Appeal was
made to the
fenfe of won-
der on fuch
holiday occa-
fions not by
the monks
only. Among
the firft curi-
ous feats of
fkill   per-
formed for

money at the Fair may have been that of
a woman, who is difplayed among the illuminations in our gay volume of Bartholomew Decretals, balancing herfelf to the
mufic of tabor and pipes, head downwards
and feet in the air, by the palms of the
hands, upon two fword points.

Again, though walking upon ftilts with
boffes on the legs to prevent them from
finking hopeleffly into the quagmire,
was not a rare accomplifhment among

the dwellers by the great fens with which England then abounded, probably the woman fhown in another of the monk's pictures walking on long ftilts with an infant in her arms and a water jug balanced on her head, claimed applaufe and reward for her achievement. To us it certainly will feem more difficult than that of the ancient acrobat, who pipes in triumph, while he fhows a child at work upon the alphabet of tumbling.

The volume from which thefe fketches are taken is a manufcript of the thirteenth century, containing the text of Gregory's Decretals, with a commentary. It is now in the Britifh Mufeum, * but belonged originally to the Priory of St. Bartholomew. It is lavifhly adorned with pictures, which are valuable illuftrations of the manners, arts, and literature of the time. At the foot of every page there is fome incident depicted. Firft, fcripture ftories, as of Jofeph and his brethren, or of Samfon, are told each in a feries of little paintings ; then profane ftories, jefts, fatires, legends of the faints. There is a feries illuftrating the old fatire of Reineke Fuchs, with many noticeable variations, which does not flinch from reprefenting Bifhop Fox as paftor to the geefe. Another feries reprefents a dog hunted, caught, tried, dragged to execution, and hung by the hares, one of whom bites his thumb in defiance of the criminal. Here again there are hares bringing a man before their court, and on another page we fee a ftag chafed by a fnail. There are pictures, illuftrating ftories

* King's MSS. 10 E. IV.

known and unknown; men ply their trades or play, or fight by land and fea; knights jouft, fair ladies ride, hawk, hunt, are courted, are attacked in caftles,— one of them fnips at the head of an invading knight with fwords croffed sciffar-wife,—the mind of the pious illuftrator dwelt with an obvious pertinacity upon the other fex. Giants, dragons, hoftile kings are flain. Wild men and women abound in thefe picture ftories. Gene-rally, after we have been fhown how wicked a monk can be, the pictures go on to tell that he ran wild in the defert until he became a faint, and had his rewards often in the flefh as well as in the fpirit. Even the large picture appended to the firft book of thefe folid and grave Decretals is a caricature, having on one fide a monaftery, on the other fide a fair lady's pavilion. The lady in her doorway, while her hufband peeps out of window, beckons to the monk, upon whom, as he paffes through the monaftery gates, there is a jar of water emptied from above. There is no denial of the ftrength of appetite after the flefh. On one page a prieſt kiſſes the cookmaid while he ſteals her capon from the pot.

A monk, furpriſed with the miller's wife by the miller himſelf, who carries a large mallet, gets poſſeſſion of the mallet and therewith murders the miller. He runs wild, becomes firſt hairy, then holy, and is finally repreſented as a favourite of Heaven, whoſe feet wild beaſts come from afar to lick. A monk and a woman are ſhown in the ſtocks together. They both fold their hands towards the Virgin, who releaſes them, and in their places faſtens the two devils by whom they had been tempted. So it is throughout. A monk tears from a mother her child, then murders the woman, and conceals her under the high altar. He runs wild, becomes hairy, and, when he is holy, receives from the Virgin the mother and child alive again, miraculouſly revived or preſerved. To another claſs of ſtories belongs that of the knight who ſerved too weakly the lady of his love. She becomes exacting, and with every admitted exaction more imperious. He takes to the

wafh for her garments, over which fhe holds her nofe,
wafhes them, fpins for her, makes bread for her, unloofes
the latchet of her fhoe. Her afpect is angrier in every
picture until, in the laft, fhe kills him.

So it was that the friar of St. Bartholomew's drew in
his cell pictures of the world to which he clung, the
world to which his gates efpecially were opened upon the
three days that centered in the feaft day of his Saint.
Of fuch matter was, in the firft days of Bartholomew
Fair, the fpeech or fong of the ftory-tellers, who
abounded at all holiday gatherings. We have but to
give voice and life to all thofe pictures, and we have the
fpirit of the concourfe at the Fair. Cripples about the
altar, miracles of faints, mummings of finners, monks
with their fingers in the flefh-pot, ladies aftride on the
high faddles of their palfreys, knights, nobles, citizens,
and peafants, the toils of idlenefs and induftry, the ftories
that were moft in requeft, the lax morality, the grotefque images which gave delight to an uncultivated
people, the very details of the dreffes that were worn, are
told to our eyes with a wonderful fidelity.

In the next chapter of thefe memoirs, reafon will
appear for inferring that, from very early times, if not
from the beginning, there were practically two Fairs held
in Smithfield, one within and one without Priory bounds.
The outer Fair was poffibly compofed of the mere
pleafure givers and pleafure feekers, who attended on
the company of worfhippers and traders then attracted
to the Priory, and whofe tents were pitched in the open
market of Smithfield, outfide the gates, not free from
toll to the church. Within the gates, and in the Priory

churchyard, the fubftantial fair was held.   Three centuries later we learn from Stow, that there was obferved in
the Priory churchyard the fame practice which Fitzftephen thus defcribes as having been eftablifhed from
the firft :—" On feftivals at thofe churches where the
feaft of the patron faint is folemnized, the mafters con-
vene their fcholars.   The youth on that occafion difpute,
fome in the demonftrative way, and fome logically.
Thefe produce their enthymemes, and thofe more
perfect fyllogifms.   Some, the better to fhow their
parts, are exercifed in difputation, contending with one
another, whilft others are put upon eftablifhing fome
truth by way of illuftration.   Some fophifts endeavour
to apply, on feigned topics, a vaft heap and flow of
words, others to impofe on you with falfe conclufions.
As to the orators, fome with their rhetorical harangues
employ all the powers of perfuafion, taking care to
obferve the precepts of art, and to omit nothing
appofite to the fubject.   The boys of different fchools
wrangle with one another in verfe ; contending about
the principles of grammar, as the rules of the perfect
tenfes and fupines.   Others there are who in epigrams or
other compofitions in numbers, ufe all that low ribaldry
we read of in the ancients ; attacking their fchoolmafters,
but without mentioning names, with the old fefcennine
licentioufnefs, and difcharging their fcoffs and farcafms
againft them ; touching the foibles of their fchoolfellows,
or perhaps of greater perfonages, with true Socratic wit,
or biting them more keenly with a Theonine tooth."
The fchoolbooks upon which thefe wits had been trained
were chiefly Prifcian's grammar with the commentary of

Remigius, Ariftotle's Logic, and the Rhetoric of Cicero and Quintilian.

Though by the cuftom of the Normans every great houfe, noble or religious, was, to the utmoft degree, bountiful in almfgiving, yet it was not in the power of the Priory to feed or lodge all pilgrims, merchants, and idlers who came to the feaft of St. Bartholomew. There was wine fold in fhips, but otherwife only one houfe in London at which food could be bought ready for immediate ufe; that houfe was on the Thames bank, and there might be had fuch dainties as fturgeon or guinea-fowl, as well as coarfer meat. "It is a public eating-houfe," we are told with fome pride, "and is both highly convenient and ufeful to the city, and is a clear proof of its civilization." Neverthelefs, it was but one, and it was diftant from the Priory. Law, alfo, however relaxed in Fair-time, was ftrict againft the entertainment of ftrange guefts in any houfe. There is a painful reminder of the civil ftruggles and the diftruft fet by them between man and man, in an edict very recent at the time of which we are now fpeaking. It was ordained by King Henry the Second that no ftranger fhould be lodged for more than one night, by any man who would not be made anfwerable on his behalf, unlefs upon reafonable excufe, which was to be fhown by the hoft to his neighbours; and when fuch a gueft departs, let him depart, faid the ordinance, in prefence of the neighbours, and in daytime. On the firft night a ftranger lodged in a houfe was accounted unknown, on the fecond a gueft, and on the third a member of the houfehold.

Alfo it is to be remembered that on St. Bartholomew's Day there is, or ought to be, warm autumn weather. Reafon enough, therefore, appears for the belief that during the three days of the fair there were many who not only played or worked by day, but flept by night in the encampment outfide the gates of St. Bartholomew, and that in the fale, century after century, of certain forms of cooked meat, we have, partly, the continuance of a cuftom that arofe out of the neceffities preffing upon the fair when it was firft eftablifhed.

In the churchyard of the Priory, the fair chiefly confifted of the booths and ftandings of the clothiers of all England and drapers of London, who were there clofed within walls of which the gates were locked every night and watched, for fafety of men's goods and wares.

CHAPTER V.

Old Chronicles.

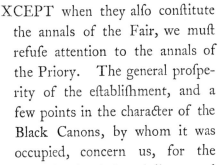

XCEPT when they alfo conftitute the annals of the Fair, we muft refufe attention to the annals of the Priory. The general profperity of the eftablifhment, and a few points in the character of the Black Canons, by whom it was occupied, concern us, for the ftrength of the Fair at firft lay in their privileges and their power. In the days of Stephen, and of his fucceffor, not lefs than the king, even in England, as a fource of power, was the Pope of Rome. Rayer, as we have feen, defigned to obtain for his foundation a fubftantial bleffing out of Rome, but died before his purpofe was accomplifhed. "After his deceafe," writes the recorder of his life, "three men of the fame congregation, whofe memory be bleffed in blifs, fonderly went to fonderly Bifhops of the See of Rome, and three privileges of three Bifhops obtained—that is to fay, of Saints Anaftafe, Adrian, and Alexander—this church with three dowries as it were with an impenetrable

F

fcutcheon warded and defended againft impetuous
hoftility." The three fucceffive Popes whofe Decretals
provide, together with the firft royal charters, the
foundation of the power of the Priory, were Anaftafius the Fourth, Adrian the Fourth (Nicholas Break-
fpear, the one Englifh Pope), and Alexander the Third.
Anaftafius was Bifhop of Rome in the laft year of
Stephen's reign, and the other two Popes were contem-
poraries of King Henry the Second.

A pleafant note of royal patronage beftowed upon the
poor men maintained by the friars of Bartholomew in
the hofpital, which was a part of their foundation, I find
in the clofe rolls. By fucceffive warrants to Henry de
Cigeny in 1223 and other years, Henry the Third
granted an old oak from the foreft of Windfor as fuel
for the infirm in the Hofpital of St. Bartholomew.

In the reign of the fame king there ruled over Rome
and its fpiritual dependencies Pope Gregory the Ninth,
of whom we read in Capgrave's Chronicle that " with
him dwelt a friar preacher cleped Raymond. He was
Penitencer under the Pope; and by his commandment
the friar gathered out of many books that book which
they clepe ' Decretals.' And the Pope wrote to the
Doctors of Law that they fhould in fchool ufe this com-
piling." Of the text book thus impofed upon all
ftudents of ecclefiaftical law, a copy was made for the
Priory of St. Bartholomew. It is that copy of manufcript Decretals to which I have before referred as the
fource of the illuftrations which, in this part of our
narrative, reprefent views of life as fketched in Smithfield by a draughtfman of the thirteenth century.

What fort of men they were by whom, in its firft days, the Fair was managed, this record may alfo tell. Boniface, a wrathful and turbulent man, elected to the See of Canterbury in 1244, came, during a vifitation, to the Priory of St. Bartholomew in Weft Smithfield. He was received with folemn proceffion, but, he faid to the friars, he paffed not for honour; he was there to vifit them. The canons anfwered that they, having a learned Bifhop, ought not, in contempt of him, to be vifited by any other. This anfwer fo much offended the arch-bifhop, that he fmote the fub-prior on the face, faying, " Indeed! indeed! doth it become you Englifh traitors fo to anfwer me?" Then raging with oaths, he rent in pieces the rich cope of the fub-prior, trod it under foot, and thruft him againft a pillar of the chancel with fuch violence, that he had almoft killed him. The canons, feeing their fub-prior thus almoft flain, came and pulled away the archbifhop fo vigoroufly that they overthrew him backward, whereby they faw that he was armed and prepared to fight. The archbifhop's attendants, who were all his countrymen, born in Provence, obferving their mafter down, fell upon the canons, beat them, tore them, and trod them under foot. At length, the canons getting away as well as they could, ran, bloody, miry and torn, to the Bifhop of London to complain, who bade them go to the king at Weftminfter, and tell him hereof: whereupon four of them went thither, the reft were not able from being fo fore hurt. When they arrived, the king would neither hear nor fee them.

In the meantime the proceffion of the bleeding canons had raifed the city in an uproar, where the citizens were ready to have rung the common bell, and to have hewed the Archbifhop in pieces had he not efcaped to Lambeth. Thither they purfued him, and not knowing him by fight, cried aloud, "Where is that ruffian, that cruel fmiter? He is no winner of fouls, but an exacter of money, whom neither God nor any lawful or free election brought to this promotion, but the king did unlawfully intrude him. He is unlearned, he is a ftranger, and he has a wife." But the Archbifhop conveyed himfelf over the river, and went to the king with great complaint againft the canons.

The control even of the Bifhop of London was by the firft charters left open to a doubt that was not urged.

The general character of ancient fairs we find illuftrated, when, four years later, on the 13th of October, 1248, King Henry the Third with many prelates and magnates met at London to celebrate the memory of the Tranfla-tion of St. Edward. The king then caufed a new Fair to be proclaimed at Weftminfter, which fhould continue fifteen days, and prohibited all other fairs that ufed to be kept at that time of the year throughout England, and alfo all trading in the City of London, within doors and without, during that time; that this Fair at Weftminfter might be the more plentifully ftored and frequented with all forts of goods and people.

Upon a fpecial point of privilege relating to the Fair of St. Bartholomew, appeal was made by Ralph Sand-wich, cuftos of the city, to King Edward the Firft at the time when he was engaged in Scotland upon thofe difcuffions which refulted in the eftablifhment of Baliol as a vaffal king. The king's taxes had by royal charters been remitted to the traders at the Fair. The Priory took all the tolls, but there was no ſpecial exemption of it from any claim that could be put in by the city. Though the valuable wares of the clothiers and others were diſplayed within the ſhelter of the Priory walls, not only much of the concourſe at the Fair, but at leaſt alſo its traffic in live ſtock muſt have been without the ſacred bounds. As the Fair throve, its chief articles of traffic were, in the firſt inſtance, cloth, ſtuffs, leather, pewter, and live cattle. It ſpread beyond the Prior's bounds, and a claim was made therefore by the Cuſtos for a half ſhare of the tolls, the claim being urged before King Edward the Firſt at a time when the receipt of all tolls of the city had been transferred from the city to the ſovereign. The king being at Durham, and the matter being laid before him a few weeks before the uſual time of the Fair, he ſigned this order : " Dominus Rex, &c. The Lord the King hath commanded the Cuſtos and Sheriffs in theſe words : Edward, by the grace of God, to the Cuſtos and Sheriffs of London, greeting. Whereas the Prior of St. Bartholomew, of Smithfield, in the ſuburbs of London, by the charters of our Progenitors, Kings of England, claimeth to have a certain Fair there every year, during three days, viz., on the Eve, on the Day, and on the Morrow of St. Bartholomew the Apoſtle, with all Liberties and Free Cuſtoms belonging to the Fair ; a contention hath ariſen between the ſaid Prior and you, the ſaid Cuſtos, who ſue for us, concerning the uſe of the Liberties of the ſaid Fair, and the Free Cuſtoms belonging to it. And Hindrance being made to the ſaid Prior, by you the ſaid Cuſtos, as

the faid Prior afferteth, to wit, concerning a Moiety of
the Eve and of the whole Morrow before faid, concerning
this, We Will, as well for Us as for the forefaid Prior,
that juftice be done as it is fit, before our Treafurer and
Barons of the Exchequer, after Michaelmas Day next,
within a month. We Command you that fufficient
fecurity be taken of the faid Prior for reftoring to us on
the faid day the proceeds of the forefaid fair, coming
from the Moiety of the forefaid Eve and from the whole
Morrow, if the faid Prior cannot then fhow fomething
for himfelf, why the faid proceeds ought not to belong
to us. We Command you, that ye permit the fame
Prior, in the mean time, to receive the forefaid proceeds,
in form aforefaid ; and thereto you may have this Brief.
Witnefs myfelf at Durham, the 9th day of Auguft, in
the 20th year of our Reign." The reply to the inquiry
was unfavourable to the claim of the city, and the
charter of the friars was again confirmed. The queftion
of tolls poffibly remained in fome degree a vexed one
between City and Priory, until, after the lapfe of more
than another century ; it will be convenient, therefore,
to referve for a future chapter what more has to be faid
of the place occupied by London in the early ftory of
the Fair.

A very flight fuggeftion of the filthy ftate of the
Black Canons' quarters will fhow what they muft have
fuffered who were crammed within the churchyard of the
Priory at Fair time. Among documents in the Patent
Rolls is a licence from King Edward the Firft, to the
mafter and brethren of the hofpital of St. Bartholomew
in Smithfield, to cover with ftone and wood the ftream

of water running through the midſt of the hoſpital to
Holborn Bridge, "on account of the too great ſtench
proceeding from it." The licence is ſignificantly dated
(in the midſt of the hot weather) on the twenty-ninth of
June.

On the Eve of St. Bartholomew, the firſt day of the
Fair, in the year 1305, the traders and pleaſure ſeekers,
the friars and the jeſters, clothiers, tumblers, walkers
upon ſtilts, hurried acroſs the graſs of Smithfield from
the ſide on which the Fair was being held to the gallows
under the Elms, where officers of ſtate and a great
concourſe of men awaited a moſt welcome ſpectacle.
The Priory was indeed built on the ſite of a gallows; but
in that ſuburban gathering-place of the people,—place of
executions, place of tournaments, place of markets, place
of daily ſport, place of the great annual fair,—one
gallows tree was not enough to ſatisfy a juſtice that
loved vengeance and had ſlight regard for life. Under
the Elms of which already mention has been made—
Cow Lane now repreſents their ſite—under the Elms, we
read in a cloſe roll, ſo early as in the fourth year of
Henry the Third gallows were built "where they had
ſtood before." An execution during Fair time on that
ancient exhibition ground, was entertainment rarely
furniſhed to the public; for the Church forbade, among
other work, fulfilment of a ſentence of the law on any
holy day of feſtival, and a Fair was a Saint's holiday.
But on this occaſion, law was eager to aſſure the execution of its vengeance. The redoubtable Wallace, hero
of the Scottiſh people, had been taken. The rugged
patriot, ſtrong of heart and ſtrong of hand, had been

brought to London in his chains the day before the Fair was opened, and on the day of the opening of the Fair was arraigned and condemned at Weſtminſter as a traitor, and without even a day's refpite, at once fent on to his death. Under the Elms, therefore, in Smithfield, ſtood all the concourſe of Bartholomew Fair, when William Wallace was dragged thither in chains at the tails of horſes, bruiſed, bleeding, and polluted with the filth of London. The days had not yet come when that firſt part of the barbarous fentence on high treaſon was foftened by the placing of a hurdle between the condemned man and the mud and flint over which he was dragged. Trade in the Fair was forgotten while the patriot was hanged, but not to death ; cut down, yet breathing, and difembowelled. Mummers and merchants faw the bowels burnt before the dying hero's face, then faw the executioner ſtrike off his head, quarter his body, and defpatch from the ground five baſket-loads of quivering fleſh, deſtined for London, Berwick, Newcaſtle, Aberdeen, and Perth. Then all being over, the ſtilt walkers ſtrode back acroſs the field, the woman again balanced herſelf head downwards on the points of fwords, there was mirth again round the guitar and tambourine, the clothiers went back into the churchyard, and the prieſt perhaps went through a laſt rehearſal with the man who was to be miraculouſly healed in church on the fucceeding day.

To this we muſt add the ſtatement of Bartholomæus de Glanvilla, an Engliſhman writing at the end of the fourteenth century, that in his time men and women were publicly fold as beaſts in the fairs of England. We may

add alſo a chronicle of the peſtilence which broke out in
London at the time of Bartholomew Fair in the year
1348, and ended about Fair time in the year following.
During the interval between fair and fair, ſo great had
been the mortality, that, in addition to the burials in
churches and other churchyards, the population of a
city—fifty thouſand bodies—had been interred in a
ſingle burial-ground.   It was that of the Carthuſians,
whoſe houſe was not built until twenty years later.
The graveyard was there firſt, and as it adjoined the
Fair, it muſt in that year have been the great object of
intereſt and terror to the ſlender throng of men who
hardly dared aſſemble, and who, miſſing from the annual
crowd ſo many familiar faces, ſpoke to each other with
a feeble hope of the apparent lifting of the plague.
What mirth was there in that handful of the living,
camped ſo near the ſilent congregation of the dead !

In the fourteenth year of the reign of Edward the
Second, there was a writ iſſued inquiring by what warrant
the Priory held its rights over Bartholomew Fair.   The
writ was part of the machinery of a general inquiſition
into the rights claimed by ſubjects, which had in many
caſes been alienated without licence from the crown, and
gave riſe often to private oppreſſion of the people.   The
Prior of St. Bartholomew pleaded the royal charters of
his houſe, and teſtified upon oath that his predeceſſors
had held ſuch a three-day fair ſince times beyond the
reach of memory.   The juſtification ſatisfied the king's
exchequer, and in the ſeventh year of Edward the Third,
the old rights were confirmed in a new charter, which
reaſſured the king's firm peace to all perſons travelling

towards, ftaying in, or returning from Bartholomew
Fair, and forbidding any fervants of a royal or epifcopal
court to implead any of their perfons, " or without the
confent of the prior and canons on thofe three days, that
is to fay, the Eve of the Feaft, the Day of the Feaft,
and its Morrow, to exact tolls either without the city or
within it, whether in the paffage of roads or bridges, but
let all proceeds that arife according to the ufage of fairs
belong to the canons of the aforefaid church." The
charter again definitely excludes the claim of a moiety
of the proceeds which had fince the reign of Edward
the Firft been fet up on behalf of the city.

In the days of Edward the Third there were a few
fuburban houfes with gardens bordering Smithfield, and
there were others on the road to the Clerks' well.
From brother Cok's manufcript Rental of the Hofpital,
I learn that there was a houfe then on the fouth fide of a
bit of ground owned by the friars, called the Bell on the
Hoop, and that on the eaftern border of the fame plot
was the garden of the Rofe on the Hoop. The whole
community was party to all bufinefs contracts. Thus, in
the fame reign we find William le Fons Mafter of the
Hofpital, by confent of its brothers, letting a piece of
ground in the Spital Croft to John Dobelyn and Joan
his wife. Peter at the Gate and Fulton de Paddington
were among the witneffes to the contract, which was
figned in Clerkenwell Street. The pious brethren were
unwilling to turn money from their doors, and though
they could read, in their own copy of Gregory's Decretals,
admonitions againft the fettlement of money matters on
a day of holy feftival, they have left upon record a

receipt " in full fettlement of all dues from the beginning
of the world to the feaft of Eafter in the year of the
reign of Edward the Third, the three hundred and
fourth after the Conqueft " (1370). The receipt was
figned on Eafter Sunday. Another entry fhows how the
Priory was releafed from law of mortmain by a fpecial
decree of the fame King Edward when, in the eighth
year of his reign, Ealfrid de Catenham, painter of
London, left to St. Bartholomew his houfe in Bifhopfgate,
and how the teftament and the royal releafe were duly
read in full huftings before the citizens of London.
The Hofpital had at this time houfes and lands in many
parts of London—Alderfgate, Cripplegate, Ludgate,
St. Sepulchre's, St. Dunftan's Weft, St. Bridget in Shoe
Lane, and fo forth—and it had alfo poffeffions in the
country. The documents copied into its rental—compiled in the middle of the fifteenth century—illuftrate
many points relating to old London. They do not
relate to the Fair, and we muft pafs them over, but the
reader will pardon me for citing one that almoft reftores
a fragment of the road by the ftrand of the river between
London and Weftminfter as it was in the year 1337.
In that year, the tenth of Edward the Third, there was a
grant by the Priory to Ealfrid de Eyftan and his wife of
a houfe in the Strand, fituated in the parifh of St. Mary
le Strand, held by Laurence the Tailor,—fituated between
the meffuage of Robert de Aldenham on the eaft, and
that of Thomas the Linendraper on the weft, and
extending fouthward over the high road from London to
Weftminfter. Brother Cok's volume is a collection of
charters, decretals, grants, leafes, receipts; in fhort, of

binding documents received or iffued by the friars.
Therefore, while it includes the royal charters upon
which the Fair is bafed, it contains no note whatever of
the annual receipt of toll.   That was a tranfaction which
brought money to the Priory exchequer, but led to the
production of no document requiring prefervation in the
archives.   It is to be obferved alfo that, although we
rightly fpeak of Priory and Hofpital as one foundation,
they maintained two feparate eftablifhments, and it was
to the Hofpital that brother Cok was treafurer.

We turn back from the Strand to Smithfield, acrofs
the city of low wooden houfes, and through Alder's
Gate, whence the eye looks upon field and moorland, rills
and ftanding pools, with churches and a few clufters of
fuburban houfe and garden.   Before us is Leyreftowe,
the burial-ground of the Jews (the fite of Jewin Street),
until late in the reign of Henry the Second the only fpot
of ground in England wherein there was reft allowed to
a dead Jew.   Not far outfide the turreted north wall of
London, is the Smooth-field, bounded on one fide by
the rich Priory, and noticeable for its fheet of befouled
water and its Elms.   We have feen that Bartholomew
Fair was of old affociated by pofition with the city playground and the city gallows, with the Friday market,
and the burial-ground of the plague-fmitten.   There
alfo great tournaments and joufts were held.   Combats
in fport for love of chivalry, combats for life in the
ordeal by battle were to be feen in the lifts at Smithfield
when the Fair was young.   It was a tournament when
parties of knights joined together in the conflict.   In
joufts two only fought together, man againft man.   In

the year 1357 the Kings of England, France, and
Scotland, were among the fpectators of the joufts in
Smithfield. In the forty-eighth year of King Edward the
Third, Dame Alice Perrers, the king's miftrefs, as Lady
of the Sun, rode through Cheap to the lifts in Weft
Smithfield, accompanied by many lords and ladies.
Know that, at the day appointed, there rode forth, at a
proceffion pace, from the Tower of London, under the
bright morning fun, firft a great number of muficians
and trumpeters, then fixty courfers, apparelled for
the joufts, mounted by efquires. Then fixty ladies
of honour, richly apparelled, mounted upon palfreys,
every lady leading forth a knight by a gold chain.
So they proceeded to Smithfield, whither the King and
Queen had come from their lodging with the Bifhop of
London, and where they were feated in chambers, amid
a great company, to fee the joufts. The ladies that led
the knights were taken from their palfreys, and went up
to chambers prepared for them. The efquires yielded
up to the knights their horfes, and the knights, in good
order, mounted. Then, after the helmets were fet on
their heads, and they being ready at all points, proclamation was made by the heralds, and the joufts began.

For a long time after this date the lifts of Weft Smith-field were in ufe. The judicial combat between Horner the armourer and his man Peter, who had accufed him of treafon, introduced by Shakefpeare into the Second Part of King Henry the Sixth, actually took place in the year 1524, between William Cator an armourer of St. Dunftan's parifh in Fleet Street, and John David, his falfe fervant, who afterwards was hanged for felony. The armourer, too freely plied with wine by his good friends, was flain, and in the Exchequer Record, printed by John Nichols, we read the order for the preparation of the ground for the duel to be held upon the thirty-firft of January, with details of the coft of men's labour for fetching the barriers from Weftminfter, expenfes for bars, timber, boards and nails, for cafting away fnow, for rufhes and rakes, for 168 loads of fand and gravel to make level fighting-ground. Alfo there was " paid to officers for watching of the dead man in Smithfield the fame day and the night after that the battle was done, and for horfe hire for the officers at the execution doing, and for the hangman's labour, 11s. 6d. Alfo paid for the cloth that lay upon the dead man in Smithfield, 8d. Alfo paid for 1 pole and nails, and for fetting up of the faid man's head on London Bridge, 8d."

At various times alfo after the acceffion of Henry the Fourth, and notably during the famous days of fpecial perfecution, women and men were burnt alive as heretics in Smithfield, and a part of the Fair was held over the afhes of the martyrs. One of the firft of thefe martyrs was John Bedby, a tailor, burnt in Smithfield in the year 1410. The martyr fires were ufually kindled on that

fpot of ground outfide the Priory gates, over which the
lighter portion of Bartholomew Fair fpread, the ground
occupied by the holiday makers and the tumblers, jefters,
and dancers by whom they were entertained.   Among
the old woodcuts in the firft edition of Fox's Martyrs,
there is one that includes a rude fketch of the Priory of
St. Bartholomew in a plan of the difpofal of the ground
outfide at the burning of three perfons.

The martyrdom here pictured happens to be that of
Anne Afcue and others.   She was burnt in Autumn,
and the ground muft have been ftill black with the afhes
of that Chriftian heroine, over which the dogs danced,
and the devil in the miracle play jefted not very many
days later at Bartholomew Fair.

CHAPTER VI.

Literature and Commerce.

URING the middle ages, when the infant nations of Europe waited for inftruction at the knee of the Church, their mother, fhe was almoft the fole depofitory of thofe germs of knowledge which expanded and bore much fruit in her children after they had come of age. Thoufands of monks, working, pen in hand, reprefented our exifting cohorts of compofitors, and what the printing office is, the monaftery was. There are no great national fairs of which the origin was not ecclefiaftical, and the beginning of them all is to be connected with two great fervices done by the Church to fociety. In fairs, the manlieft form of modern imaginative literature, the dramatic, had its origin. Our playhoufe is an offfhoot from the Church. In fairs alfo, as we have already feen, commerce was, by the influence of the Church, loofed from many of her trammels. There was an approach made to free trade ; there was prompt fettlement of all difputes, and a complete fecurity as to

the validity of contract in all matters of bargain and fale.
Rights of fair were indeed granted to laymen, but no
layman had influence enough over the maffes to eftablifh
permanently as a great popular feftival the fair of which
he took the tolls. To maintain her influence was the
great object of the Church. In an age when men
generally, whatever their vocation, feldom had a refined
fenfe of morality, frauds began, of which fome have to
this day been perpetuated by tradition in the lefs-
enlightened parts of Europe. We have feen how, on
behalf of St. Bartholomew, miracles were forged, and by
the fame of them crowds were attracted to the church
and Fair. What other ways there were of ftrengthening
its influence over the people, the Church energetically
practifed. The fair in the churchyard reprefented vifibly
the people in the fold, and there is a large truth of
Hiftory to be illuftrated by movements of the priefts
among the traders and the feekers after pleafure.

The firft power of the mind revealed in every child
is that of mimicry. The majority of men go to the
grave mimics ; in religion, manners, language they
have learnt their parts, and acquitted themfelves in them
more or lefs refpectably. Nearly all child's play is
effentially dramatic. Wherever there have been men,
therefore, there have been mimics, and fome rude kind
of dramatic fport over affairs of life has been a favourite
amufement. The Church, feizing upon this element of
human character as means of laying a firm hold upon
the people, made of Divine worfhip a fhow, eftablifhed a
repertory of tales for the enlivement of fermons, and
taught fcripture hiftory and fcripture myfteries—after-

wards even preached fermons on abftract morality—in plays. From thofe plays, performed on days of feftival, the modern drama has its origin. Many years after our drama was mature, reminders of its old ways lingered in the places of its birth; and to Bartholomew Fair they clung fo long that there, perhaps, took place the laft performance of a miracle play in this country. The parifh clerk of old, deacon in holy orders, Chaucer has painted as a jolly Abfolon, in a white furplice, with curly hair, red ftockings and fafhionable fhoes. He could bleed, clip and fhave, write title-deeds and receipts, dance, fing, play the guitar, drink, go with a cenfer on a holiday, and when he cenfed the parifh wives look at them lovingly. The parifh clerks of London formed themfelves into a harmonic guild, (chartered in 1233,) and their mufic was fought at the funerals and entertainments of the great. In the year 1390 they played interludes in the fields at Skinner's Well, for three days, Richard the Second, with his Queen and court, being among the fpectators. Again, in the year 1409, in the reign of Henry the Fourth, the clerks played at Skinner's Well for eight days "Matter from the Creation of the World," a great affembly of the noblemen of England being prefent. Joufts in Smithfield then immediately followed. At this well (near Weft Smithfield,) wreftlings were afterwards fubftituted, and in part continued at Bartholomew tide. The wreftlings were continued, as we fhall hereafter find, in clofe affociation with the Fair.

The Matter from the Creation of the World meant, doubtlefs, fuch a cycle of fcripture hiftories, from the creation downwards, as we find in the extant fets

of Miracle Plays performed at York, Chester, and
Coventry. In very early times monks acted fcripture
ftories in their church. Three plays, written in Latin
for fuch reprefentation by a difciple of Abelard are
extant. They are coeval with the founding of the Priory
of St. Bartholomew. Such plays were the drama of the
twelfth and thirteenth centuries; they entertained both
prince and peafant. They came into England with the
Normans, and had paffed from Latin into French, for the
amufement of the court, before they were performed in
Englifh for the more complete entertainment and
inftruction of the people. Latin ftage directions to the
laft bore witnefs to the clerkly character of thofe by
whom they were to be performed. Legends of faints
were at firft the chief fubjects treated, and thefe formed
the true Miracle Plays. Truths of Revelation, told by
dramatic ftories taken out of fcripture were the Myfteries; and in a later day came the Moralities, which
difcuffed moral truths upon a ftage by the perfonification
of the virtue, and by examples out of hiftory wherewith
the human intereft in plays began, and out of which our
modern drama was then rapidly developed. This rapid
development took place in the age of the revival of
letters, when the comedies of Plautus and the tragedies
of Seneca had become known to the clerical playwrights.
Thus, and thus only, did the ancient drama come to
exercife an influence over that of the moderns, an
influence which was in England but a paffing breath.
For among us there arofe a ftate of fociety that helped
to perfect and to force into a ripe dramatic form the
expreffion of that rare genius in which the England of

Elizabeth was rich. So it happened that, before King Herod, Pilate, and the mediæval devil had been fairly banifhed from Weft Smithfield, Shakfpeare had written, and Ben Jonfon was among the booths, turning Bartholomew Fair itfelf into a comedy.

It happens that at Coventry the myfteries were acted by trade guilds at the feaft of Corpus Chrifti, each guild furnifhing its own ftage and acting its own play. It happens alfo that the old accounts of expenditure kept by thefe guilds are extant, and, from the refearch made into thefe fome years ago by Mr. Sharpe, a local antiquary, much has been learnt of the general character of thefe old entertainments. The extant Englifh plays of this defcription do not, however, belong to the moft ancient clafs; and, from what we have learnt of thefe, we muft guard ourfelves againft forming too abfolute a rule for all. Of fuch plays, as has been faid, the firft ftage was the church pavement, upon which they were performed as a religious fervice to awaken zeal. Setting afide fpecial performances for the delight of courts, the next ftep was to act them upon ftages in fome field, or to prefent them on feftival days in open fair, and upon raifed ftages, for the delight and inftruction of the people. The ftages ufed by the Coventry guilds were moveable vans, drawn from ftreet corner to ftreet corner, fo that, during the feaft, the plays, which reprefented a complete cycle of Scripture hiftory, followed each other in every quarter of the town. Chaucer fays of his dainty parifh clerk, the jolly Abfolon, that, " Sometimes, to fhow his lightnefs and maiftrie, He playeth Herod on a fcaffold high." Herod fuited the fine lady's man, as being the character that was moft pompous in fpeech, and moft magnificently dreffed. A high fcaffold, doubtlefs, was the ftage ufed by the parifh clerks of London at their well, about which fpectators ftood and fat upon the rifing ground; and the friars alfo on St. Bartholomew's Day muft have thus edified the people at their Fair. Again, the laft lines of the proclamation of performance prefixed to the feries of plays ufed at Coventry, have been thought to fuggeft that Myftery players moved from place to place :—

> On Sunday next, if that we may,
> At fix of the bell we 'gin our play,
> In N. town, wherefore we pray
>   That God now be your fpeed.

But it is moft probable that this cycle of dramas, written by an old poet, was known and ufed in feveral parts of the country, and that N. ftands fimply for any town in which it was adopted by the clergy or the people. I think it reafonable to believe that the firft dramatic entertainment at Bartholomew Fair was on the ftage erected by the Priory, and that this ftage was for a long time the only one erected. Legends of faints everywhere preceded fcripture hiftories, and the firft plays at the Fair were, therefore, prefentations of great miracles afcribed to St. Bartholomew. There was much latitude allowed for the fancy, and much room for rude ftage effects, in the embellifhment of ftories of this kind. The monks fimply put life upon a ftage into the pictures with which they adorned their books. I have no doubt that, when they were not reprefenting myfteries of Scripture, they fometimes fat in the ftocks

on their high fcaffold, ran wild till they became faints,
and then retaliated on the devil. St. Dunftan feized
that popular charaȼer by the nofe; and perhaps even,
by a well-contrived ftage artifice, the Virgin in the
piȼture ftretched her hand out to hold up the painter
when the envious demon broke the ladder under him.
A fcene like this, fketched by a friar of St. Bartholomew's, in the manufcript of Gregory's Decretals, might
have been taken from the platform in the Fair. Satan,
iffuing from Hell-mouth, has been battering the gates
of Heaven; but is brought into fubjeȼtion by the Virgin,
at whofe feet he grovels in the duft.

In fome, if not in all thefe reprefentations, feparate
ftages or levels indicated the abodes of the Heavenly
Father, of angels and glorified faints, and of men. In a
corner of man's ftage was Hell-mouth, through which
fiends came up and down. It was a grotefque head,
which might vary in defign, but of which the general
charaȼter is reprefented perfeȼtly in the above fketch, and
in the initial letter to this chapter. In a manufcript note
to a Myftery of the Paffion in the Royal Library of Paris
(cited by Hone), it is recorded that, at the reprefenting
of fuch a lay in 1437 on the plain of Veximiel, when the

chaplain of Metrange played Judas (and was nearly dead while hanging, for his heart failed him, wherefore he was very quickly unhung, and carried off), that the " Mouth of Hell " was very well done; for it opened and fhut when the devils required to enter and come out, and had two large eyes of fteel. The devil of the mediæval ftage was always a comic chara&ter, and his conventional drefs admitted of much variety in the grotefque fhaping of the mafk, but all the forms abided clofely by the one ftandard conception. Thus there is clofe likenefs in the difference between the demon of the drawing laft copied, and that taken from the fame fource, which ferves as initial letter to the fifth chapter of this volume, or between either of thofe and this, in which Satan is yielding a foul to the Virgin in the prefence of its guardian angel.

The chara&ter was reprefented in life, as the pi&ure fhows him, by the ufe of a leather drefs trimmed with feathers or with hair. He was, as the Chefter plays

defcribe him, " the devil in his feathers all ragged and
rent ; " or, as the Coventry account books fhow, a perfon
carrying three pounds of hair upon his hofe.   Having
once found his way into Bartholomew Fair, this perfon-
age never quitted it, and was to the laft, with a few
variations of coftume, a regular performer there.

The floor of that firft ftage was beftrewn with rufhes,
and the body of the fcaffolding was concealed under a
decorated cloth.   At Coventry there was a canopy, with
vanes and ftreamers, and a ftandard of red buckram.
A few notes of the more charaĉteriftic entries from the
Coventry accounts will complete a brief reminder of
the charaĉter of the firft ftage-plays aĉted in the Fair.
Among the properties were a gilt crofs and rope to draw
it up, and a curtain to be hung before it, two pair of
gallows, four fcourges, and a pillar.   A barrel for the
earthquake : That was to produce the rumbling.   Four
gowns and hoods, jackets of black buckram with nails
and dice upon them, for the executioners; four more with
damafk flowers ; alfo two jackets, partly red and black,
all for the tormentors or executioners.   Two mitres for
Annas and Caiaphas.   In making the next entries no
irreverence was felt, but I fhould fhrink from quoting
them if they were not effential to a proper notion of the
manner of thefe plays.   God's coat of white leather (fix
fkins).   A ftaff for the demon.   Two fpears.   Chevreul
(or peruke) for God.   Three others and a beard, two of
them (for our Lord and St. Peter) gilt.   A pole-axe for
Pilate's fon.   Gilt faulchion for Herod.   This charaĉter,
reprefented as a gorgeous boafter, had alfo a painted
head, furmounted by an iron creft painted in gay colours,

and decked out with gold and filver foil ; his gown was of blue fatin.   The contraft to fo magnificent a perfon feems to have been Pilate's wife, called alfo Procula, who was attired in worn old clothes when better were not to be borrowed.   We find fuch entries as, For mending of Dame Procula's garments, vii*d*.   To reward to Mrs. Grimfby for lending of her gear for Pilate's wife, xii*d*. For a quart of wine for hiring Procula's gown, ii*d*.   All the characters wore gloves.   Thofe not in mafks had their faces prepared by a painter.   Among mifcellaneous items of charge are fome for the mending of hell-mouth, for its curtain, or for keeping up the fire at it, which was a part of the ordinary ftage effect.   There is a charge for fouls' coats, one for a link to fet the world on fire, and " paid to Crowe for making of three worlds, ii*s*."   In one play we find, alfo, this graduation of the fcale of payment to performers.   Paid, for playing of Peter, xvi*d*. ; to two damfels, xii*d*., to the demon, vi*d*. ; to Fawfton, for hanging Judas, iv*d*. ; paid to Fawfton, for cock-crowing, iv*d*.   Judas, as well as the demon, was a comic character ; the tormentors were all broad comedians ; fo alfo were the foldiers who maffacred the innocents, as well as the mothers from whofe arms the innocents were taken ; the maffacre being prefented as an occafion for much lively interchange of buffets and broad jefts.

Whether Rayer at the court of Henry the Firft, counted entertainments of this nature among the " fpec-tacles, plays, and other courtly motleys," in which he took part, I am unable to fay ; but in the days of his fucceffor in the Priory, who was a man of wit fo lively

that he preached rhymed fermons to the people, Fitzftephen, writing at the time (in 1174), tells us that
" London for its theatrical fpectacles, for its fcenic plays,
has plays more facred, reprefentations of miracles which
have been worked by the holy confeffors, or reprefentations of paffions in which fhone the conftancy of
martyrs." Therefore we drew only a juft inference,
when fpeaking of Prior Thomas, in fuggefting that he
may not only have invented miracles, but that he may
alfo have written miracle plays. He muft have fpecially
avoided the moft obvious opportunity for the ufe of his
talent, if he did not mount the clerks or brethren of his
church upon a ftage in the Fair, and teach them how,
according to the cuftom of the city, they might add to
the attractions of the feftival. Among fome Latin ftories
written in the thirteenth century, we read of there being
feen in a long meadow by the river-fide, a great multitude
of men affembled, who were now filent, now breaking
into laughter. They were " fuppofed there to be
celebrating the fpectacles which we are accuftomed to
call Miracles." Solemn as were the fubjects treated, it
was neceffary that there fhould be in their treatment jeft
enough to provoke in a rude affembly frequent laughter.

Thus we have in the moft ancient times of the Fair, a
church full of worfhippers among whom were the fick
and maimed, praying for health about its altar ; a grave-
yard full of traders, and a place of jefting and edification,
where women and men caroufed in the midft of the
throng; where the minftrel and the ftory-teller and the
tumbler gathered knots about them ; where the fheriff
caufed new laws to be publifhed by loud proclamation in

the gathering places of the people ; where the young men
bowled at nine pins, while the clerks and friars peeped at
the young maids ; where mounted knights and ladies cur-
vetted and ambled, pedlers loudly magnified their wares,
the fcholars met for public wrangle, oxen lowed, horfes
neighed, and fheep bleated among their buyers; where
great fhouts of laughter anfwered to the Ho ! ho ! of
the devil on the ftage, above which flags were flying,
and below which a band of pipers and guitar beaters
added mufic to the din.   That ftage alfo, if ever there
was prefented on it the ftory of the Creation, was the firft
Wild Beaft Show in the Fair ; for one of the dramatic
effects connected with this play, as we read in an ancient
ftage direction, was to reprefent the creation of beafts by
unloofing and fending among the excited crowd, as great
a variety of ftrange animals as could be brought together,
and to create the birds by fending up a flight of pigeons.
Under foot was mud and filth, but the wall that pent
the city in fhone funlit among the trees, a frefh breeze
came over the furrounding fields and brooks, whifpering
among the elms that overhung the moor glittering with
pools, or from the Fair's neighbour, the gallows. Shaven
heads looked down on the fcene from the adjacent
windows of the buildings bordering the Priory inclofure,
and the poor people whom the friars cherifhed in their
hofpital, made holiday among the reft.   The curfew
bell of St. Martin's le Grand, the religious houfe to which
William the Conqueror had given with its charter the
adjacent moorland, and within whofe walls there was a
fanctuary for loofe people, ftilled the hum of the crowd
at nightfall, and the Fair lay dark under the ftarlight.

A great part of the Priory was rebuilt in the year 1410, and after this date its general plan was that which it maintained until the time of its fuppreffion. It became famous for poffeffing one of the firft mulberry gardens planted in this country. The fituation of this mulberry garden was to the eaft of Middlefex Paffage, and in later years, it was under the mulberry trees that the fcholars, at Fair time, held their difputations. Within the gates, the northern part of the Priory ground was occupied by a large cemetery, with a fpacious court or yard, now the paved fquare of Bartholomew Clofe. The old fite of the Cloth Fair in the cemetery is now marked by a ftreet bearing that name.

In a former chapter it has been fhown, how trade throve under the walls of churches, with its fetters loofened and defended from taxation by the fovereign. Bartholomew Fair was, in the firft centuries of its life, one of the great annual markets of the nation. It was the great gathering, in the metropolis of England, for the fale of that produce upon which England efpecially relied for her profperity. Two centuries after the Conqueft, our wealth depended upon wool, which was manufactured in the time of Henry the Second, in whofe day there arofe guilds of weavers. In King John's reign there was prohibition of the export of wool, and of the import of cloth. A metropolitan Cloth Fair was therefore a commercial inftitution, high in dignity and national importance. There was trade alfo at Bartholomew Fair in live ftock, in leather, pewter, and in other articles of commerce; but cloth ranked firft among the products of our induftry, and it was as an annual trade gathering of

Engliſh clothiers and London drapers, that the Fair obtained a place for itſelf in the hiſtory of commerce. Live ſtock was ſold weekly.   In leather and ſkins Stourbridge Fair dealt more than that of St. Bartholomew ; but Bartholomew Fair as the chief Cloth Fair of England, as long as need remained for ſuch an inſtitution, was without a rival.

In the reign of Edward the Third, by whom moſt of the guilds of London were firſt chartered, when, aſſuming a diſtinct dreſs or livery, they became Livery Companies, and exchanged the name of guilds for that of crafts or myſteries, the King himſelf became a Linen Armourer, or as it afterwards would have been called a Merchant Tailor.   This he did that he might manifeſt his ſtrong deſire to eſtabliſh woollen cloth as a ſtaple manufacture of the country.   King Richard Cœur de Lion was a Tailor alſo.   Thus it was made a faſhion for the rich and powerful to join the Company of Merchant Tailors, or ſome other important craft that was thought worthy of eſpecial maintenance, as that of Mercers or of Skinners, who were men of mark when all the great men in the land wore robes of fur.   Having compelled his people to make cloth for themſelves, of home-grown wool, and by other meaſures perfected the wool manufacture, Edward the Third (in 1361), removed the woolſtaple from Calais to nine Engliſh towns, the chief being at Weſtminſter, between Temple Bar and Tothill Fields. Cogniſance was taken at theſe markets of the five ſtaple commodities of the kingdom, wool, wool fells, leather, lead, and tin.   In 1378 Richard the Second removed the woolſtaple to the ground ſtill known as Staple Inn, by

Holborn; and about twenty years later, there was begun at Blackwell Hall a weekly market for the fale of country cloths in London. Such was the pofition taken by the cloth trade, while this Fair rofe in importance by affociation with it as a great annual mart, to which even the foreigner had unreftricted accefs.

The arms of the Merchant Tailors were engraved upon a filver yard, thirty-fix ounces in weight, with which century after century members of their body were deputed to attend in Weft Smithfield during Bartholomew Fair, and try the meafures of the clothiers and drapers. Thus we find in their books a direction that fit perfons fhall be appointed on the Eve of St. Bartholomew, to fee that a proper yard-meafure be ufed. This right of examining the yard-meafures was maintained as long as the Cloth Fair had vigour in it. In 1566 we find that a dealer named Pullen was committed to prifon by the court, for ufing an unlawful yard, which was found in his fhop at the time of the fearch. Stands had become fhops by that time, fo important was the fituation. And in 1612 there is note of a dinner at Merchant Tailors' Hall, "for the fearch on St. Bartholomew's Eve." All this was done fubject to the control and faving the rights of the city.

The Drapers were incorporated in the year 1364, when there was fpecial exemption made from prohibitions of the fale of cloth by any who are not free drapers, in favour of the king's beloved in God the Prior of St. Bartholomew's in Weft Smithfield, and other lords who have fairs in the faid fuburbs. A draper meant originally one who made the cloth he fold, it was the London name

for clothier, very few of the members of the Drapers'
Company being refident beyond the limits of the city.
Therefore, fay the old writers, that Bartholomew Fair
was frequented by "the clothiers of England, and the
drapers of London." Drapers fold their goods chiefly
by the beam fcales; mercers, by the little balance.
Mercers efpecially frequented fairs and markets, where
their ftandings were gay with haberdafhery, toys, and
even drugs and fpices, the fmall articles of traffic upon
which they throve. Mercers attending the French fairs
towards the clofe of the thirteenth century, paid only
half toll when they were not ftall keepers, but expofed
their wares on the ground. They, and the clafs of
pedlers to which they were allied, may have enjoyed a
like privilege in England. But, while many of the
mercers were thus of the brotherhood of Autolycus,
others dealt largely in filk and velvet, and abandoned to
the haberdafher traffic in fmall articles of drefs. Whittington, thrice lord mayor of London, was a mercer.

The general nature of the court eftablifhed in all fairs
for the judgment of caufes arifing out of tranfactions in
the fair itfelf, has been already defcribed. From the
earlieft times of which there is record, it has been known
in England as the court of Piepowder. The court of
Piepowder for Bartholomew Fair was held, of courfe,
within the Priory gates, the Lord of the Fair being the
Prior who fat in the court by his reprefentative. It
abided always by its original fite, being held in Cloth
Fair to the laft. There is no record to be found of any
ordinance by which the court of Piepowder was firft
eftablifhed in this country. There never had been

known a fair in Europe to which fuch a court was not
by ufage lawfully attached. Such courts were held in
the markets of the Romans, which fome writers regard
as fairs, and in which they find the origin of modern
fairs. But the *nundines* of the Romans were not fairs,
they correfponded in character to our own weekly market
days. It is true that the right of market was a grant
from the ftate to great lords and landowners, as the right
of fair afterwards became a grant from the Crown to
monafteries, towns, or men of rank. In this refpect,
and doubtlefs alfo in the ufe of market courts, the
Roman law founded a cuftom throughout Roman
Europe. A law of William the Conqueror, *de
Emporiis*, fhows that there were fuch tribunals in the
ordinary markets of the Normans. But modern fairs,
as we have faid, had their own natural and independent
origin, and are analogous to nothing in the ancient world
but the affemblies formed during the celebration of the
Public Games. There were the Greek church feftivals,
begetting fairs. Thus, a true fair was affociated with
the Olympic Games ; and we learn from Demofthenes,
that all caufes relating to the feftival of Bacchus were
heard on the fpot. The fame practice arofe out of the
fame neceffity. Nobody can affert that the feftivals of
ancient Greece influenced ufages of the Normans in the
tenth or eleventh century.

The court of Piepowder in Bartholomew Fair, or
the correfponding court in any other fair of England,
had jurifdiction only in commercial queftions, and it
tried them before a jury of traders formed upon the
fpot. It could entertain a cafe of flander, if it was

flander of wares, not flander of perfon. It might
hold pleas for amounts fixed in later times at above
forty fhillings, and judgment could be deferred until
another fair; but it could fit only during fair time,
could take cognizance only of things happening during
fair time and within the fair, and could try a thief who
had committed robbery in the fair only when he had
alfo been captured within its bounds. The king himfelf,
if he fhould fit in a court of Piepowder, could not
extend its powers. Neither is it in the king's power to
refume a franchife that has once been granted; fo that a
fair once granted is, by the common law of England,
good againft the king.

But though it was not in the fovereign's power to
enlarge the jurifdiction of the courts of Piepowder,
private wrong was done in their adminiftration; ftewards
and commiffioners of the Lords of Fairs abufed their
power in the courts, to their own advantage. They
tried caufes which they had no right to try, and by the
connivance of unprincipled accomplices, perfecuted honeft
fairgoers upon whom extortion might be practifed. The
abufe of thefe courts, in the feventeenth year of the reign
of Edward the Third, was diminifhing the refort of men
of bufinefs to our great fairs; when the evil was met by
a ftatute which, for the firft time, placed upon the ftatute-
book a formal recital of the nature of the courts of
Piepowder and of the limitation of their privileges.

By the ftatute 17 Edward the Fourth, it was provided,
"that whereas divers fairs be holden and kept in this
realm, fome by prefcription, allowed before juftices in
Eyre, and fome by the grant of our Lord the King that

H

now is, and fome by the grants of his predeceffors, and to every of the fame fairs is of right pertaining a court of Piepowders, to minifter in the fame due juftice in this behalf, in which court it hath been at all times accuftomed, that every perfon coming to the faid fairs fhould have lawful remedy of all manner of contracts, trefpaffes, covenants, debts, and other deeds, made or done within any of the fame fairs, during the time of the fame fair and within the jurifdiction of the fame, and to be tried by merchants being of the fame fair ; which courts at this day be mifufed by the ftewards, under-ftewards, bailiffs, commiffioners, and other minifters holding and governing the faid courts of the faid fairs, for their private profit ; holding pleas by plaints as well of contracts, debts, trefpaffes, and other feats, done and committed out of the time of the faid fair or jurifdiction of the fame (whereof, in truth, they have no jurif-diction), furmifing the fame debts, trefpaffes, &c., to be done within the time of the faid fair, and within the jurifdiction of the fame, (where of truth they were not fo), and fome time, by the device of evil-difpofed people, feveral fuits be feigned, and trouble them to whom they bear evil will, to the intent that they for lucre may have favourable inquefts of thofe that came to the faid fairs where they take their actions ; and whereas divers perfons coming to the faid fairs be grievoufly vexed and troubled by feigned actions, and alfo by actions of debt, trefpafs, deeds, and contracts made and committed out of the time of the faid fair, or the jurif-diction of the fame, contrary to equity and good confcience ; whereby the Lords of the Fairs do lofe great profit by the not coming of divers merchants to fairs, which by this occafion do abftain, and alfo the commons be unferved of fuch ftuff and merchandife, which otherwife would come to the faid fairs;" therefore it is enacted, that the Plaintiff fhall fwear that the caufe in declaration happened during fair time.

Such was the character of the Tribunal of Commerce, known to fair-goers as the court of Piepowder. Its name is corrupted from the French for "dufty feet." Spelman thought this was becaufe juftice is adminiftered in it more quickly than duft can be fhaken from the feet. In Manley's edition of Cowel it is fuppofed that, becaufe fairs were ufually held in fummer, feet were dufty. Blackftone adopts Daines Barrington's obfervation, that Pied puldreaux was the old French name for a pedler. Dr. Pettingall* was troubled with a theory of his own about a "curia rufticorum," and derived the name from the dirty boots which ruftics got among their clods, propping his theory with Plutarch, who fays that the Epidaurians called country folk κονιποδες, which the French tranflator reprefents by *pieds poudreux*. Yet Dr. Pettingall while he fets up one theory demonftrates another, and fupplies us with a claffical quotation apt to it, when he quotes from Cicero on Invention, "If we fee a man with much duft on his fhoes, it is probable he came off a journey." A trader travelling through any place, or felling his wares in it without poffeffing houfe or land upon the foil, might be, at Bartholomew Fair,

---

* On the Courts of Pypowder; by John Pettingall, D.D. Read before the Society of Antiquaries, March 4, 1762.—*Archæologia*, vol. i. pp. 190—203.

H 2

one of the fmall pedlers, or one of the great cloth
merchants.   He was a traveller, whofe part in the foil
was no more than the duft upon his foot.   He was a
Piepowder, or as Dr. Pettingall fhews us that he was
formerly called in the old Scotch Borough Laws, a Duftifute.   The plural ending to the name of the court was
fubfequently dropped, but in the preamble of the Act juft
recited, it may have been obferved that it was known as
a court of Piepowders in former time.   A court for
men who travelled from many parts to a certain fpot on
which they had no refidences, and there traded during
certain days; for whom therefore it was neceffary to
decide by a tribunal of their own, held on the fpot
during the brief time of their fojourn, fuch queftions of
property as might arife among themfelves.

From feveral paffages relating to "fairand man or to
the Duftifute" in the Scotch Borough Law (publifhed
by Skene with the Regiam Majeftatem), it is enough for
our purpofe to take this clear definition of the name:
"Gif any ftranger marchand travelland throw the realm,
havand no land, nor refidence nor dwelling within the
fherifdome, but vagand from ane place to ane other,—
qwha therefore is called pied poudreux or Duftifute."
A definition like this fets at reft all doubt as to the
meaning of a Court of Piepowders.

CHAPTER VII.

The City Fair.

THE queſtion of the right of the city to the tolls ariſing from uſe of its ground outſide the Priory in Weſt Smithfield, had been decided in or before the year 1445. Weſt Smithfield was juſt within the confines of the city liberties, their limit in that direction being Smithfield Bars. In the year named—the twenty-third of King Henry the Sixth—it is on record that four per-ſons were appointed by the Court of Aldermen as keepers of Bartholomew Fair and of the court of Pie-powder. In that court, therefore, the city was then repreſented as joint lord of the Fair with the Priory; the lordſhip of the city being founded on its right over the ground beyond the juriſdiction of the Canons.

In the firſt charter granted by King Edward the Fourth to the City of London, dated on the ninth day of November, in the ſecond year of his reign (1462), there is this clauſe: "We have alſo granted to the ſaid mayor, commonalty, and citizens, and their ſucceſſors for ever, that they ſhall and may have yearly one Fair in the town aforeſaid, for three days; that is to ſay, the 7th, 8th, 9th days of September, to be holden, together

with a court of Piepowders, and with all the liberties
to fuch fairs appertaining : And that they may have and
hold there at their faid courts, before their faid minifter
or deputy, during the faid three days, from day to day,
hour to hour, and from time to time, all occafions,
plaints, and pleas of a court of Piepowders, together
with all fummons, attachments, arrefts, iffues, fines,
redemptions, and commodities, and other rights whatfoever, to the fame court of Piepowders in any way
pertaining, without any impediment, let, or hindrance
of Us, our heirs or fucceffors, or other our officers and
minifters foever."

Some writers upon the hiftory of London have
referred to this charter as containing a grant of a city
fair in Weft Smithfield—a Bartholomew Fair conceded
to London, which was held a few days after that of
which the Priory received the tolls.   But the " town
aforefaid " is Southwark.   " To take away from henceforth and utterly to abolifh all and all manner of caufes,
occafions, and matters whereupon opinions, ambiguities,
varieties, controversies, and difcuffions may arife," in
its previous claufe the charter had " granted to the
faid mayor and commonalty of the faid city who
now be, and their fucceffors, the mayor and commonalty and citizens of that city, who for the time
being fhall be for ever, the town of Southwark, with
the appurtenances."

Thus was eftablifhed Southwark Fair—our Lady Fair
—of which the glory is that it was once dwelt upon by
the genius of Hogarth, and of which the fhame became
fo great after it had ceafed to be a refort of trade that it

was fuppreffed before the clofe of the laft century. This was the firft great fair granted in whole poffeffion to the city of London. There were other London fairs yielding no profit to the city : St. James's Fair, granted by Edward the Firft to the Hofpital of St. James, an inftitution founded by the citizens of London for the maintenance of fourteen women, pious lepers. That hofpital, with its ground, being furrendered to King Henry the Eighth, was adopted by him as the fite of St. James's Palace and Park. There was a fair upon Tower Hill, granted by Edward the Third to the " mafter, brothers, chaplain, and fifters of St. Katherine's, to be held upon the king's ground in all places thereof, oppofite the Abbey of Graces, next the Tower." The fame king had ordained on behalf not only of the city, that " merchant ftrangers," coming to England to fell merchandife, fhall be obliged to difpofe of it in forty days, and that they fhall not keep houfes, but fojourn with the citizens. Thus, the foreign Duftyfoot, his bufinefs done at the fair, was remitted back to his own land, and was not allowed to enter into fettled competition with the Englifh traders. This had been a city cuftom in the days of Athelftan, but was a point upon which Norman legiflation often varied.

While we fpeak of the other London fairs, it may be as well alfo to name and difmifs May Fair, held by a grant to the Abbot of Weftminfter, with revelry for fourteen days, which began on May Day in Brook Field, on the fite of Curzon Street. It was prefented as a nuifance by the grand jury of Weftminfter in 1708, abolifhed for a time, revived and finally abolifhed in the

reign of George the Second, after a peace officer had
been killed in the attempt to quell a riot.

A city fair is a city market of a certain kind, every
fair being a market, although only a few markets are
fairs. For many years before and after the Conqueſt,
traffic was carried on by a great ſyſtem of marketing.
The Saxon laws directed all bargains to be made in open
market, called in Norman deeds market ouvert, and
in the preſence of the boroughreeve or ſome truſtworthy
perſon. The Normans maintained the ſame rule, and
thus it was eſtabliſhed as a principle in common law
that no tranſfer of goods is binding againſt third parties
unleſs made in market ouvert. Nearly the whole trade
of the city of London was in Saxon times tranſacted in a
great chepe or market that ran through the town from
Tower Street to Newgate, and was known as Eaſt and
Weſt Chepe. The ſites of different branches and
diviſions of this central market, which ran as an ali-
mentary canal through the midſt of the city that was to
be nouriſhed, are to this day remembered in the names
of ſtreets. The hill on which the corn-market was held
uſed to be called, and now is called, Cornhill. Poulterers
kept market in the Poultry. Bakers, from that old
capital of the bread trade Stratford at Bow, came daily
with their loaves in long carts to their market-ground in
Bread Street. At London, ſays Active-Life, in the
Viſion of Piers Ploughman, "there was a careful com-
mune when no carts came to town with bread from
Stratford." The woodmongers were in Wood Street;
milk was ſold daily in Milk Street; there was a fiſh-
market in Old Fiſh Street; and in Old Change were the

moneyers. Of this great market ouvert, Cheapfide was the centre. On the fite of the Manfion Houfe ftood then a pair of ftocks in a market named after them, the Stocks Market, ufed firft for meat, and afterwards for wool, and at a much later date for herbs and vegetables.

At the time of the Conqueft nearly all the cities and towns of England were poffeffed by the king or his nobles, as private property or in demefne. They paid fixed rents in kind and fervice ; and in each the fuperior, whether king or inferior lord, impofed various tolls, duties, and cuftoms to be paid by thofe attending the fairs or markets he eftablifhed, fuch demands being made at the lord's difcretion during the firft years of Norman rule. To evade the oppreffion of an arbitrary tax, cities and boroughs fought to compound with the king by payment of a fixed rent inftead of the tolls, which tolls they then levied upon themfelves that the lord's rent might be fatiffied out of the produce. Toll is a generic term, of Gothic origin, which includes every kind of tribute levied upon the movement from place to place of goods or perfons. The term formerly included a multitude of charges, every charge being confidered due for fervice rendered, as the provifion of a trading place, a ferry or a bridge, a wharf or a fet of public fcales known as a beam or tron. But the infliction of thefe tolls, whether by the king's officers, or by the king's favourite to whom they might have been given, or by the fpeculator who had with a large price bought of the king the right of farming them, was ufually cruel. How cruel we may infer from the fact, that in the reign of Edward the Firft, it had been fought to reftrain the greed of collectors by a statute threatening severe penalties; and in the reign of Edward the Third, parliament was petitioned that those extortioners, the officers of the king's beam, might suffer death for their exactions. The collection of such of the king's tolls as were not farmed, was entrusted by the Norman system to the sheriff, who thus became an officer with fiscal powers of such vast interest to the Crown, that his appointment was no longer entrusted to the people.

When Bartholomew Fair was annexed to the Priory by Henry the First, West Smithfield was the king's market, and though the Fair might trespass beyond church-bounds, it was not for the city then to claim a moiety of toll arising from it. The same king who gave his first charter to the Prior Rayer, granted the first real charter to the city of London, and thereby founded its Corporation. That charter granted Middlesex to farm at 300*l.* a year, and gave to the citizens certain freedoms, which included a free passage exempt from tolls and customs over any part of England. In 1197, Richard the First sold to the city for 1500 marks the conservancy of the Thames. In 1199 King John, for 3000 marks confirmed its ancient rights, and restored the fee farm of Middlesex, which had been revoked by Matilda. But at this time, the rent of the London Exchange was a branch of the royal revenue, farmed to a man who in 1202 was more than a thousand pounds in the king's debt. The city chamberlain was appointed by the king, and paid, besides a heavy entrance fine, 100 marks a year for his office. It was not until 1215 that the citizens even received liberty to choose for themselves

their mayor.   Until that date he had been always
nominated by the Crown.   Thirty years later, the
citizens were paying to King Henry the Third more
than feven hundred pounds in yearly duties, of which
eighty-four were raifed by market tolls.   It was at this
time that the king fet up the fair at Weftminfter, which
clofed the fhops of London for a fortnight.   A repetition of that trouble was bought off by a heavy payment ;
but five years afterwards the fame device was again
adopted, and the Londoners were obliged for a fortnight
to fhut up their fhops, and in the middle of winter
expofe themfelves and their goods in Tothill Fields, to
the inclemency of all weathers, on a ftinking or frozen
marfh.   After enduring various exactions, the citizens
in 1266 obtained from this king, for 20,000 marks,
enjoyment of their rights and liberties, with title to
receive the rents and profits of their lands and tenements.   In 1288 Edward the Firft, upon a quarrel
with the city, feized its liberties and did not reftore them
fully until twelve years afterwards.   It was during this
time that Ralph Sandwich, appointed cuftos by the
king, firft afferted the right of the city to divide with
the Priory of St. Bartholomew the tolls of Bartholomew
Fair.   It was not until the year 1399 that there was
granted to the citizens of London, by King Henry the
Fourth, the office of gathering the tolls in Smithfield.
Forty-fix years later we find the city firmly eftablifhed
in its right to the Fair tolls outfide the Priory inclofure,
and appointing, as it has been ftated at the outfet of
this chapter, four perfons as keepers of Bartholomew
Fair and reprefentatives of city jurifdiction in the court

of Piepowder.   Before the fame tribunal the two eldeſt
clerks in the city Sheriffs' court came as attorneys.

The ſketch here given of the gradual ariſing of the
intereſt of London in the tolls of Smithfield is incomplete, for the firſt title to them reſts upon preſcriptive
right, not upon extant evidence.   Of the city juriſdiction over the Fair in Weſt Smithfield, I do not ſay that
it began only in the year 1445 ; but that certainly it
was eſtabliſhed then, if not before.   There were ſeveral
early recognitions of the city's hold over the ſoil in
Smithfield.   Thus in the eleventh year of Henry the
Third, the king granted to the widow, Katherine
Hardell, a recluſe, twenty ſquare feet of land outſide
the Hoſpital of St. Bartholomew, whereon to build
herſelf a hermitage.   The mayor and ſheriffs of London
were commanded to aſſign the ſaid ground to the lady,
who, as an anchorite among the fair-goers, muſt in her
time have been one of the Bartholomew-tide ſpectacles.

CHAPTER VIII.

A Change of Masters: London and Lord Rich.

CROYLAND Abbey, which contained the scourge of
St. Bartholomew, was founded for the honour of God,
the Virgin, and St. Bartholomew of whom the anchorite
Guthlac, parent of the abbey, was especially a servant.
It was a custom at Croyland on Bartholomew's day, in
memory of the Saint's death by flaying, to give knives—
Bartholomew knives—to all strangers who came. The
abbey was rich. A chief cook in it had given forty
pounds—when forty meant in money, what we should
now call four hundred—to provide milk of almonds for
the brethren upon fish days; but Abbot Wisbech, about
the year 1475 abolished the practice of distributing
Bartholomew knives, "a piece of great and needless
expense. Besides this, he obtained a bull of dispen-
sation from the Pope, which permitted the eating of
flesh at Septuagesima." As a sign of the changed
temper of society, this ready suppression of old custom
in the abbey may not have been altogether insig-
nificant. Less reverence for old form, and more
hunger for solid meat, was becoming every year more
surely a part of the public mind. Thousands of

men were looking for emancipation from a fpiritual
Lent.

The laft prior of St. Bartholomew who was acknowledged by a king of England, died in office, and was
the laft prior but one for the Black Canons in Weft
Smithfield. He was a faftidious man, who feemed to
be the head of a luxurious and profperous community.
He repaired the church and opened into it an elegant
window marked with his rebus, a bird-bolt in a tun for
his name Bolton (there is an inn in London ftill named
after it, the Bolt-in-Tun) ; he built anew the manor at
Iflington belonging to the Canons of St. Bartholomew,
and known as Canonbury. He lived in a handfome
priory houfe behind the monaftery church, was fump-
tuoufly hofpitable in a dining-hall not lefs fit for a
prince than for a prior, and ruled within the precincts
of the religious houfe, not only over the friars in it, but
alfo over a fmall colony of cooks and other lay attendants. The fpace within the priory inclofure ranked in
London as an independent parifh—that of Great St.
Bartholomew—and there was a vicar in it, having fpecial
charge over the lay parifhioners. In the fame way, the
adjoining hofpital, built on the fouth fide of Smithfield,
though a main part of St. Bartholomew's eftablifhment
and clofely bound by charters to the Priory, was in its
own inclofure ; was under rule of its own officers, who
were answerable to the Prior ; had its own church ; and
ranked as the diftinct parifh of Little St. Bartholomew.
We turn to the moft ancient map of London extant, Ralph
Aggas's (?) *Civitas Londinum,* 1533, and in the part which
reprefents Weft Smithfield with the Priory and Hofpital

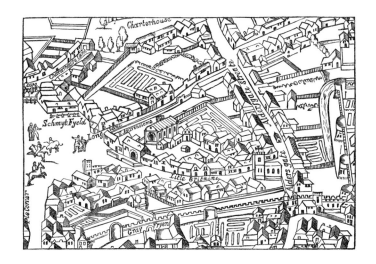

we have a rude picture of the arrangement of the
ground when it was on the point of paffing out of the
hands of the monks.   It is evident that the conftructor
of the map kept very bad proportion in his fketches,
and we may not be abfolutely fure that there were no
houfes where none are fhown.   On the whole, however,
this map is a valuable witnefs.   It tells us that the
Priory wall abutting on Long Lane, was not built
againft in the time of the Black Canons; that they
raifed no permanent houfes along the line of Cloth Fair,
but that they had, north of the church, for the annual
ufe of the trades, an oblong fpace of ground containing
only graves.   The houfes have throughout the map conventional forms; but a ftructure of unufual fize indicates
fufficiently the fite of the great dining-hall above the
crypt, and the fquare enclofed by cloifters is defined,
though we are not fhown the ecclefiaftical character of the
buildings that furround it.   There are the houfes fronting

outwards upon Smithfield and Little Britain, let to lay
tenants and parifhioners. We are fhown the fite of the
feveral detached buildings and outhoufes, behind which
there was a confiderable garden ; this was the Mulberry
Garden, in which, at Fair time, the young fcholars of
London held grammatical difputes under the trees. On
the fouthern fide of the angle of Smithfield occupied by
the Friars, with Duck or Duke Street between it and the
Priory, we fee the old hofpital with its church that is ftill
known as the church of St. Bartholomew the Lefs.

The thirteenth Act of the thirty-firft year of King
Henry the Eighth (May, 1539) confirmed the furrender
of religious houfes diffolved fince the paffing of the
previous Act, and empowered the king to extend its
provifions at pleafure to thofe that remained ftanding.
The Priory and Hofpital of St. Bartholomew then paffed
through the king's hands, and were for ever fundered
from each other. By the fame focial law that deftroyed
one, the other was developed.

Rayer had founded the Hofpital connected with his
Priory for the fick and infirm, for lying-in women, and
for maintenance of infants born within its walls until the
age of feven. King John, in the fifth year of his reign,
had confirmed the bond between the Hofpital and Priory.
There had been many royal grants and charters to
fuftain the place ; tenements had been given by the pious
to fecure prayer for their fouls. Shortly before the
diffolution of the monafteries the Hofpital received
from rents in London, Middlefex, Effex, Berks, North-
ampton, Somerfet, and St. Albans, after deducting
payments to be made, about three hundred pounds,

equivalent to not much lefs than three thoufand in money of the prefent day. The fuppreffion of religious houfes threw upon the roads and ftreets many fick, lame, and impotent people ; for the place occupied by almfgiving in the fyftem of the Roman Church was one means of its happy adaptation to the wants of a more barbarous time, and when the endowed afylums maintained by the Church on behalf of fick and poor ceafed to exift in England, fudden thought had to be taken for the difcharge of a new duty impofed upon men, not as fons of the Church, but as citizens. Anticipating the fuppreffion of religious hofpitals in London, Sir Thomas Grefham, the lord mayor, with the aldermen and citizens, in the year 1537 prayed to the king for the governance of the three hofpitals of St. Mary, St. Thomas, St. Bartholomew, and the new abbey at Tower Hill, " founded of good devotion by ancient fathers, and endowed with great poffeffions and rents, only for the relief, comfort, and aid of the poor and indigent people not being able to help themfelves ; and not to the maintenance of priefts, canons, and monks, carnally living as they of late have done, nothing regarding the miferable people lying in the ftreet, offending every clean perfon paffing by the way with their filthy and nafty favours."

In 1544 the king, in order that there might be comfort to the prifoners, vifitation to the fick, food to the hungry, drink to the thirfty, clothes to the naked, and fepulture to the dead, eftablifhed on the old fite a new hofpital of St. Bartholomew, under a mafter, who was a prieft, and four chaplains, namely, a vice-mafter, a curate, a hofpitaller, and a vifitor of prifoners in New-

I

gate. But the place was neglected and mifmanaged.
The king offering to give the city charge of hofpitals, if
it would provide a portion of the neceffary funds, the
Corporation at once paffed a profpective and conditional
vote of five hundred marks a year. At laft the Bifhop
of Rochefter announced the king's gift and the purpofe
of it in a fermon at St. Paul's Crofs; and on the 27th of
December, 1546, a month before the king's death,
the indenture was figned between Henry the Eighth and
the city of London, which gave to the city, with other
places, Little St. Bartholomew, to be " the Houfe of
the Poor in Weft Smithfield, in the fuburbs of the city
of London, of King Henry the Eighth's foundation."
In the parifh of Little St. Bartholomew there was to be
a vicar and a hofpitaller. London was to give refidence
and income to the vicar; and to lodge and tend in the
Hofpital a hundred poor men and women, maintaining
one matron, with twelve women under her, for neceffary
fervice to the poor, a fteward, a receiver and collector,
porter, butler, cook, as well as eight beadles, who were
to traverfe London and fetch in the poor, fick, lame,
and impotent found in the city and fuburbs, but to expel
valiant and fturdy vagabonds and beggars. A phyfician
and furgeon alfo were to be maintained, with provifion
of apothecary's wares. In confideration of this charge,
the city took the lands of the endowment with a right to
acquire lands to the value of another thoufand marks.
All profit of the eftablifhment was to be fpent on the
poor. There was no profit, but there was a brave outlay
of money and exertions. The Hofpital was in difrepair,
and applied to the ufe only of a few women with their

infants born there under queftionable circumftances. It is no part of this narrative to tell how the mayor and corpo- ration were abufed becaufe the London ftreets were not at once cleared of all objects of mifery. They acquired St. Thomas's for the city; the citizens cheerfully bore a tax that was in fact a poor's rate. The noble work was nobly done. The hofpitals for the fick then formed have grown with the growth of fociety, and—thanks, in no fmall meafure, to the enlightened liberality with which their principle has been fupported by the medical pro- feffion—they now rank among the foundeft inftitutions of the land.

While the Hofpital of St. Bartholomew was being thus difpofed of, courtiers and others eagerly put forward their requefts to purchafe houfes and lands taken from the feveral religious bodies; and among thefe was Sir Richard Rich, Knight, Chancellor of the Court of Augmentations, and in the reign of the next king, Lord Chancellor. He it was who, as Solicitor-General, gave a turn with his own hand to the rack by which Anne Afcue was tortured. Sir Richard Rich was the fon and grandfon of two thriving London mercers. He was born in the city, was in youth light of his tongue and quick of wit, a great dicer and gamefter, and not of any com- mendable fame. He bore no good character for honefty as a law ftudent in the Middle Temple, but was efteemed for the quicknefs of his parts, and throve as a practitioner. In 1532 he was appointed for life Attorney-General of Wales, and in the year following Solicitor-General to the King. He had an eafy confcience in the fervice of the crown—betrayed his friends and ferved his fovereign.

In 1535 he was rewarded with a valuable finecure, and
two years afterwards he was made Speaker of the Houfe
of Commons, in which office he was the king's abject
flatterer, and an important agent in the reconcilement of
the Commons to the fuppreffion of the greater monafteries.   When the king had taken their eftates, they
were put under the management of a royal commiffion,
with Sir Richard Rich, under the ftyle of Chancellor of
the Court of Augmentations, at its head.   He proceeded
to fecure the reward of his fervice in the augmentation
of his fortunes, and the firft bargain he made was the
purchafe (for 1064*l.* 11*s.* 3*d.*) of the Priory in Weft
Smithfield, with all that was upon the ground within its
enclofure, and all rights thereto pertaining.   Among his
other bargains made within the next two years, upon the
lands fubject to his commiffion, were the manor and
rectory of Little Badowe, in Effex ; the manor of
Newarks, in Goodefter (Effex), with its tithes ; and the
tithes of Newland Fee, of the rectory of Goodefter, and
of four prebends late of St. Peter's, Weftminfter.   He
received alfo four manors in Effex that had belonged to
Canterbury Cathedral, one that had belonged to the
monaftery of St. Ofyth, and four Effex marfhes that had
belonged to Holywell.   Thefe and other acquifitions,
with the grant of the diffolved priory of Leeze in Effex,
enabled him to endow fufficiently the two earldoms
acquired by his defcendants.   The love of money grew
upon him. He was made Treafurer of the King's Wars in
France and Scotland.   After the king's death he became
as Lord Rich an Englifh baron, and in October, 1547,
Lord Chancellor of England.

This was the man who profpered in the day of change, when a new world was opened to the minds and hearts of men—when the way of fociety was not the lefs furely forward and upward, becaufe it was marching with foiled feet upon a miry path.   The monks mingle no more with the fairgoers.   The Fair has not departed from the Priory ; the Priory itfelf melted away, and has been loft out of the midft of the affembly of the people.

The Prior's houfe was made into Lord Rich's town manfion in Great St. Bartholomew, and there he lived as Lord Chancellor : for there had been affigned to him, his heirs and affigns for ever, the fite and capital meffuage and manfion houfe of the late monaftery or priory of St. Bartholomew in Weft Smithfield, and alfo the clofe of the faid late monaftery or priory, called Great St. Bartholomew Clofe, and all the limits and precincts of the faid Clofe ; alfo, all thofe clofes, houfes, and edifices, called the fermery, the dorter, the frater, the cloifters, the galleries, the hall, the kitchen, the buttery, the pantry, the old kitchen, the woodhoufe, the garner, and the prior's ftable, of the faid late monaftery within the churchyard; and all thofe houfes (fifty-one tenements), gardens, void grounds, land and foil whatever, within the faid clofe to the faid fite of the faid late monaftery and priory belonging ; and alfo all that water, and the aqueduct and water-courfe coming from the conduit head of St. Bartholomew in the manor of Canonbury. By the fame letters patent, the king farther granted to Sir Richard Rich, knight, his heirs and affigns, " all that Our Fair and Markets, commonly named and called Bartholomew Fair, holden and to be holden every

year within the aforefaid clofe, called Great St. Bartholomew Clofe and in Weft Smithfield aforefaid, to continue yearly for three days, viz. on the Eve of the day
of St. Bartholomew the Apoftle, on the Day . . . and on
the Morrow . . . ; and alfo all the ftallage, piccage, toll
and cuftoms of the fame fair and markets ; and alfo all
our courts of Piepowders within the fair and markets
aforefaid" . . . . (I omit only the legal wafte of words) ;
" and all our rights . . . whatever, of fuch court of Pie
powders . . . : and alfo, all the fcrutiny, emendment,
and correction of weights and meafures . . . and of other
things whatfoever expofed to fale . . . and alfo the
affize and affay of bread, wine, and ale, and other
victuals . . . and all and fingular fines . . . iffues, profits,
and other rights . . . as fully, freely, and entirely, and
in as ample and the like manner and form as William
Bolton, formerly prior . . . or any of his predeceffors
. . . have or hath held or enjoyed, or in anywife ought
to have, hold and enjoy, . . . as fully and entirely and
freely as all and fingular the premifes came to our hands
by reafon or pretext of the diffolution of the faid late
monaftery or priory of St. Bartholomew."

This grant, it will be obferved, faves all the rights of
the city to the Fair outfide St. Bartholomew's enclofure.
It gave, however, to the family of Lord Rich the tolls of
the Cloth Fair, and of all that part which was contained
within the parifh of St. Bartholomew the Great.

CHAPTER IX.

To the Year Sixteen Hundred and Fourteen.

WE need not afk what characters of men, what combinations of events that make up the details of hiftory, produced the change in England that fet Lord Rich in the place of Prior Bolton as joint Lord with London over the tolls of Bartholomew Fair. Here it is out of the midft of the Fair only that we may look at hiftory, and we can fee nothing but the lawful end to which tended the frauds narrated in the early pages of thefe Memoirs. The Fair was nurtured upon fraud, joined to a Church worldly or weak enough to feek profperity through falfehood. The Church was as the men were who fuftained it, good men whom the advance of knowledge and experience through many Chriftian centuries had not raifed to the higheft fenfe of Chriftian honour. Chivalrous knights in thofe old days did not feel infamy in any falfehood that was not a breach of their troth openly plighted. Let us be grateful to our forefathers for all they did, and blame thofe of them only who fank lower than the fpirit of their age. But, at the fame time, there is to be drawn the fharpeft line between our fenfe of error and our judgment of the

erring.   One, when it is certain, ought to be immutable
and ftern ; the other, wavering, and full of tendernefs.
No allowance for a difference of age in man or nation
makes a lie other than a lie ; yet who does not know
that a child's falfehood may be but a fault for an hour's
forrow, while in the man falfe words are a life's infamy.
Lies rot the fubftance to which they belong.   It falls to
pieces, and the truths in it muft join again to form a
purer and lefs perifhable compound.   The people muft
be very wanting in perfiftent energy who, after long and
gradual advance, needed more than the difcovery of
printing, and the confequent activity of intercourfe
among all reafoning men, the fowing of old knowledge
broadcaft by the printers and a brifk fuggeftion of new
knowledge by the thinkers, to get rid of the more
palpable delufions that had been affociated with the
higheft form of truth.   Englifhmen are not lazy, and
they are not fickle ; therefore, the Priory, in good time,
vanifhed from the Fair.   But the Fair loft alfo the form
and the laft veftige of the foul of a religious gathering.
The reformed Church took no tribute from it, and paid
to it no more heed than to other affemblages of men in
purfuit of gain or pleafure.   The Fair was a truth
ftill, and it lived.   It reprefented at the time of the
change, and for a fhort time afterwards, the true need of
fuch a gathering-place of traders as Cloth Fair and the
Clofe were then affording.   It reprefented then, and for
a long time afterwards, the true need of amufement
by the people ; and we fhall fee how, as knowledge
advanced and refinement fpread, better enjoyments than
it could offer drew away from it, beginning from above,

clafs after clafs, till fuch pleafure as it was in its nature to afford became a true thing only to the loweft. When, even to thefe, there were offered and made acceptable purer fources of enjoyment, Bartholomew Fair no longer reprefented any living truth; and as it had long ceafed to be a place of worfhip or a haunt of trade, fo, alfo, it was outgrown by the people as a haunt of pleafure. Therefore, become worthlefs in its laft poffible form, it has, in our own time, vanifhed from the midft of London.

Grotwell, or Cartwell, was the name of the man— himfelf a hangman—who was hanged, with two others, in Henry the Eighth's time, for robbery of a booth at Bartholomew Fair. They were executed in the wreftling-place at Clerkenwell.

Lord Rich, as a profperous political adventurer, having become mafter of the ground within the old Priory enclofure, thought was foon taken for converfion of the foil to its moft profitable ufe as a fource of revenue. In the reign of Edward the Sixth, that part of London not being deferted by the rich and powerful, the owner of the parifh lived in it while Lord Chan-cellor. There alfo lived, foon afterwards, Sir Walter Mildmay, in Queen Elizabeth's day Chancellor of the Exchequer. It was prefently found that the lines of trade marked at Bartholomew Fair by the ftandings of the clothiers and others, would yield more money as ftreets of houfes than as ftreets of booths; and before the clofe of the century we have Stow telling us, that " now, notwithftanding all proclamations of the prince, and alfo the Act of Parliament, in place of booths within

H S BARTON Del.

this churchyard (only let out in the Fair time, and clofed
up all the year after) be many large houfes built, and
the north wall towards Long Lane taken down, a
number of tenements are there erected for fuch as will
give great rents." The line of trading-houfes was
fubftituted for a profitlefs dead wall bordering Long
Lane, in fpite of any one of the many powerlefs Acts

which have been paffed by Parliament againft too much
building in London. Parallel with it, through the
ground vacant of building north of the church, which
that wall had enclofed, parallel alfo with one of the
church walls, a ftreet of confiderable houfes occupied the
fite and kept the name of the Cloth Fair. The cloth
had been expofed in a line of booths, clofe under the
fhadow of the church; and the fketch facing this page
fhows how, on one fide of the ftreet, the backs of the
old houfes built in Cloth Fair by Lord Rich and his
immediate fucceffors, crowd in the fame line againft the
facred building. Of feveral of thefe houfes the frontage
on the roadway of Cloth Fair has been modernifed.
Their backs are unaltered, and fo rotten that the other
day a woman fell into the yard through the over-
hanging floor of one of them. The filling up of the
parifh with houfe after houfe, and that fmothering with
houfes of the piece of Priory retained as church, to
which we have already referred, began with the rule
of the new mafters of the land.

The difputations, held at Fair time, of the fcholars in
the mulberry garden ceafed at the fuppreffion of the
Priory. John Stow witneffed them in his youth. He
fays, " As for the meeting of the fchoolmafters on
Feftival Days at Feftival churches, and the difputing of
their fcholars logically, &c., whereof I have before
fpoken, the fame was long fince difcontinued; but the
arguing of the fchoolboys about the principles of
grammar hath been continued even till our time; for I
myfelf, in my youth, have yearly feen, on the Eve of
St. Bartholomew the Apoftle, the fcholars of divers

grammar fchools repair unto the churchyard of St. Bartholomew, the Priory in Smithfield, where upon a bank
boarded about under a tree, fome one fcholar hath
ftepped up, and there hath oppofed and anfwered till he
were by fome better fcholar overcome and put down;
and then the overcomer taking the place, did like as the
firft. And in the end, the beft oppofers and anfwerers
had rewards, which I obferved not but it made both
good fchoolmafters, and alfo good fcholars, diligently
againft fuch times to prepare themfelves for the obtaining
of this garland. I remember there repaired to thefe exercifes, amongft others, the mafters and fcholars of the
free fchools of St. Paul's in London, of St. Peter's at
Weftminfter, of St. Thomas Acon's hofpital, and of St.
Anthonie's Hofpital; whereof the laft named commonly
prefented the beft fcholars, and had the prize in thofe
days. This Priory of St. Bartholomew being furrendered to Henry the Eighth, thofe difputations of
fcholars in that place furceafed; and was again, only for
a year or twain, revived in the cloifter of Chrift's
Hofpital, where the beft fcholars, then ftill of St. Anthonie's fchool, howfoever the fame be now fallen both in
number and eftimation, were rewarded with bows and
arrows of filver, given to them by Sir Martin Bower,
goldfmith. Neverthelefs, however, the encouragement
failed, the fcholars of Paul's, meeting with them of St.
Anthonie's, would call them Anthonie's Pigs, and they
again would call the other Pigeons of Paul's, becaufe
many pigeons were bred in St. Paul's church, and St.
Anthonie was always figured with a pig following him;
and mindful of the former ufage, did for a long feafon

diforderly provoke one another in the open ftreet with
' *Salve tu quoque, placet mecum difputare ?* '—' *Placet.*'
And fo proceeding from this to queftions in grammar,
they ufually fell from words to blows with their fatchels
full of books, many times in great heaps, that they
troubled the ftreets and paffengers ; fo that finally they
were reftrained with the decay of St. Anthonie's fchool."

The fatchels full of books, with which the boys
belaboured one another, really were the weapons that had
put an end to the old practice of inceffant oral difputation. Schoolmafters and men of learning, years before,
had also taken to the thrafhing of each other with many
books ; and books fcattered abroad " many times in
great heaps," were the remains alfo of their new way of
controverfy. If a man had learning, fociety no longer
made it in any degree neceffary for him to go bodily in
fearch of the general public to a Fair, or in fearch of
the educated public to the great hall of a Univerfity.
Writing was no longer a folemn bufinefs, and writing
materials were no longer too coftly to be delivered over
to the herd of fchoolboys for habitual ufe and deftruction. Written, inftead of fpoken exercifes, occupied
the ' pigs ' and ' pigeons,' who ran riot over the remains
of a dead fyftem.

There is a famous digreffion in Holinfhed to the ftory
of a murder that in his time by its numerous ftrange
details feized upon men's minds, a ftory vigoroufly told
by the old chronicler, and diluted alfo into a play, which
has been improperly enough afcribed by fome critics
to Shakefpeare. Five acts of Shakefpeare would at any
rate not have been feebler than ten columns of Holin-

shed.   The date of the story is the year 1551, not long
after the suppreffion of the monasteries ; and one part of
it illustrates the position held by Bartholomew Fair under
its two separate lordships.   When Arden of Feversham,
that tall and comely personage, matched with a gentlewoman, young, tall, and well-favoured of shape and
countenance, but ill-favoured of heart, after many marvellous and unconscious escapes from the traps laid for
his life, had at laft been murdered at his own hearth by
his wanton wife, her tailor Mofbie, Black Will, and the
reft of her affociates, his body was carried out by the
affaffins into St. Valentine's Fair.   Mafter Arden's
garden at the back of his houfe was feparated only by a
field and by a graveyard from Feversham Abbey, which
King Stephen founded, and in which King Stephen had
been buried.   The fair had been about the abbey, but
the tolls for that part of the fair beyond the abbey
ground had belonged to the town of Feversham.   " The
fair," Holinshed writes, " was wont to be kept partly in
the town, and partly in the abbey ; but Arden for his
own private lucre and covetous gain, had this prefent
year (1551), procured it to be wholly kept within the
abbey ground which he had purchafed ; fo reaping all the
gains to himfelf, and bereaving the town of that portion
which was wont to come to the inhabitants, got many a
bitter curfe."   By the rufhes fticking in the dead man's
flipper, it was feen that Arden had been murdered in a
houfe ; the footfteps in the fnow fhowed that it was out
of the door of his own houfe that he had been brought.
Within the houfe was other evidence againft the guilty.
Having told this, and related the punifhments inflicted

on the murderers, the chronicler returning to the fcene at the fair fays, " This one thing feemeth very ftrange and notable touching Mafter Arden, that in the place where he was laid, being dead, all the proportion of his body might be feen two years after and more, fo plain as could be, for the grafs did not grow where his body had touched; but between his legs, between his arms, and about the hollownefs of his neck, and round about his body and where his legs, arms, head, or any other part of his body had touched, no grafs growed at all of all that time. So that many ftrangers came in that mean time befide the townfmen, to fee the print of his body there on the ground in that field. Which field he had (as fome have reported) moft cruelly taken from a woman . . . for which fhe not only exclaimed againft him, in fhedding many a falt tear, but alfo curfed him moft bitterly even to his face, wifhing many a vengeance to light upon him, and that all the world might wonder on him. Which was thought then to come to pafs, when he was thus murdered, and lay in that field from midnight till the morning; and fo all that day, being the Fair day, till night, all the which day there were many hundreds of people came wondering about him." His body feems to have been left there, as the miraculous print of it was maintained, among the wonders of the Fair, for the well-being of thofe who profited by its attraction.

Arden had been the Lord Rich of that Valentine Fair, of which we are informed that the tolls had of old time been divided between town and abbey. Lord Rich would gladly have procured the whole Bartholomew

Fair to be held on the church ground he had purchafed ; but this being impoffible, he made the moft of
what he had. The old market tolls of Smithfield remained without alteration for three centuries; and it is
probable that the tax levied on the tranfit of goods
through any of the gates of Bartholomew the Great in
Fair time in the days of Strype, was that which had been
taken from the firft: it was a penny for every burthen of
goods brought in or carried out; and to that end,
Strype fays, " there are perfons that ftand at all the entrances into the Fair ; and they are of late years grown
fo nimble, that thefe blades will extort a penny, if one
hath but a little bundle under one's arm, and nothing
relating to the Fair." Then there were the charges
paid infide for houfe-rent, piccage, and ftallage.

Stallage at fairs is the rent paid for ground on which
a ftall is fet for the difplay of wares, or on which any
temporary ftructure is erected ; piccage is payment for
the liberty of picking holes into the ground for a fecure
planting of props in the erection of ftall or booth.
They are, of courfe, a kind of toll, but fimple toll is
the due paid upon things taken into the Fair and fold
there. If there was no fale, there was no toll due.
Thus, there was a charge upon each animal or fcore of
animals fold from the live ftock expofed in the City
Fair, and there might be tolls upon various commodities,
as there is toll in country markets of perhaps a penny or
two upon each bafket of butter and eggs difpofed of in
the market-place. Such toll is legally regarded as payment for value received in the witneffing of fales. Thus,
in the Smithfield Horfe-market, that ufed to be held on

Fridays, and in the Smithfield Hay-market, held on Tuefdays, Thurfdays, and. Saturdays, there was a collector paid by a fixed falary, and fupplied with a houfe free of rent and taxes, who was liable at all times to be called upon to witnefs and regifter fales, efpecially of horfes, and to keep a regifter of all fales of hay and ftraw, open to be read by any one on payment of a penny. The toll on the fale was the fee paid for its regiftration. As to fuch matters there is but one law for fairs and markets. Very jealoufly have the dues taken as toll by fubjects been watched over by Parliament, left they fhould be abufed into a fimple tax levied by fubject upon fubject. No private perfon has a right to levy taxes. All authority to exact market-tolls is, therefore, given in the moft guarded form. If the amount of toll be not fpecified in the grant, it muft be afcertained by reference to the prefcription of long ufage. If there be neither a fpecific grant from the crown nor a fcale of tolls fixed by prefcription, then the fair or market may be held, but no tolls can be taken. Lords of a fair or market may not increafe the eftablifhed rate of tolls. They may diminifh it, as men may abandon that which they poffefs, but they may not feize what is not theirs. So jealoufly is this principle upheld, that when the Corporation, having fpent a hundred thoufand pounds upon improvement of their old market in Smithfield, afked leave of Parliament, by an increafe of toll, to be repaid half that fum in forty years by thofe for whofe advantage the improvement had been, fuch power was denied to them by a majority of four or five to one. When, in September, 1568, the fheep-pens in Smithfield were let by the city to Richard Selby on a leafe for one-and-twenty years, he was bound by a fpecial claufe never to increafe any toll ; and while markets were farmed, fuch a claufe was inferted in all leafes, with a penalty of ten pounds upon every infraction of it. This main point in the law concerning toll taken at markets and at fairs we fhall hereafter have occafion to remember. It is, in fact, a main point in the conftitution of this country. Edward the Firft, who confirmed Magna Charta eleven times during his reign, was the firft king who by a definite ftatute (De Tallagio non Concedendo) decreed that no tax fhould be laid or impoft levied without the joint confent of Lords and Commons. At the Revolution of 1688 this principle was rooted firmly in our foil.

In the grant to Sir Richard, afterwards Lord Rich, of the diffolved priory of St. Bartholomew, there was referve made of the parifh church, of which the living was placed under Sir Richard's patronage. " Whereas, the great clofe of St. Bartholomew hath been before the memory of man ufed as a parifh church within itfelf, and diftinct from other parifhes ; and the inhabitants thereof have had their parifh church within the church of the late monaftery and priory and to the fame church annexed, and have had divine fervice performed by a curate from the appointment of the prior and convent; and whereas, a certain chapel, called the Parifh Chapel, with part of the great parifh church, have been taken away, and the materials fold for our ufe ; neverthelefs, there ftill remains a part fit for erecting a parifh church, and already raifed and built : we do grant to the faid

Richard Rich, Knt., and to the prefent and future inhabitants within the Great Clofe, that part of the faid church of the faid late monaftery or priory which remains raifed and built (namely, the ftill exifting choir, taken according to this grant) to be a parifh church for ever, for the ufe of the faid inhabitants, ... and that all the void ground, eighty-feven feet in length and fixty feet in width, next adjoining the weft fide of the church, fhall be taken for a churchyard." Richard Rich was appointed the firft patron; John Deane the firft rector. King Edward the Sixth confirmed all grants to Rich, who had paid 1064*l.* 11*s.* 3*d.* for his fucceffion to the Black Canons in Smithfield. Queen Mary, however, in the fecond year of her reign, reftored the church of St. Bartholomew to Rome, by granting it to the Black Friars; they ufed it as their conventual church until the reign of Elizabeth who, in the firft year of her reign turned them out; the grants of King Edward were then confirmed by parliament, and the parifh has remained until the prefent day, retaining nothing of its ancient conftitution except the poffeffion of fome fmall privileges which, when it was brought within the city bounds, were not withdrawn. Of the Black Canons, as individual men, there was no memory. They were gone and their place knew them no more. I am told by the rector, that it is a cuftom in the parifh on Good Friday for the churchwardens to proceed to a certain grave and place upon it twenty-one fixpences, which are to be taken up again by twenty-one poor people. A like fum of twenty-one fixpences is then paid to the minifter. Not only was the origin of that cuftom forgotten before modern memory begins, but the very name of the man who is buried in that grave has not been known. There is no document accounting for the usage.

The heirs of Richard, Lord Rich, to whom the lord-ship of the old Priory Fair descended, were the Earls of Warwick and Holland.

So complete was the change, that in Queen Elizabeth's reign, roods and church images were the victims of the martyr fires ; and Bartholomew's Day, in France chosen as the day of triumph for the Catholics, by a great maffacre of Proteftants, was kept in England as a day of triumph for the Proteftants, on which the book-fellers difplayed in their fhop-windows nothing but bibles.

The old days, when it was confidered a great honour for London to contain one eating-houfe, were paffed away, taverns abounded in the town, and were efpecially numerous among the houfes which encroached upon the border of the once void fpace of Smithfield. By the frequenters of the weekly markets, taverns were needed. The moft famous, and one of the oldeft of thofe opened outfide the clofe, was a corner houfe, at the Smithfield end of Knightrider, or Gilt-fpur-ftreet, the main way into Smithfield, along which, of old time, proceffions of knights and ladies, fometimes with kings in their com-pany, had come to the joufts. At the fign of the Pie— the bird, not the baker's-work fo called —there was fuch notable entertainment, that Pie-corner became a familiar name, bearing the name of the inn long after its place was occupied by other houfes. Within the clofe there were inns alfo, of which the chief was one that claimed alliance with the cloth trade and the merchant tailors, by the fign it bore, "the Hand and Shears." It was in one of the chambers of this inn that the court of Pie-powder was held.

But there was other trade to be done in Elizabeth's day with the frequenters of Smithfield. After the gallows had gone weft to Tyburn, the ground from Hofier-lane to Chick-lane was rapidly built upon. The fite was valuable, and when Pennant in his account of London "cannot help indulging himfelf with the mention of William Pennant, an honeft goldfmith, his great, great, great, great, great, great uncle," he fupplies us with a not uninterefting focial fact, in telling how this goldfmith "at his houfe, the Queen's Head in Smithfield, acquired a confiderable fortune in the latter end of the reign of Elizabeth, and the beginning of that of James the Firft." Bartholomew Fair was upon no unfafhionable ground when it was poffible for a Chancellor of the Exchequer to refide in Cloth Fair, and for a goldfmith to make a large fortune by his trade in Smithfield. Yet the worft horrors of Smithfield were fometimes revived to fcare the daylight. Upon the old ground in the year 1575, Elizabeth being queen, two Dutchmen, anabaptifts, were burnt "with roaring and crying."

There was that horror before God, and there was the horror before man of deadly peftilence, that fometimes turned Smithfield, when it fhould have been a place of mirth, into a place of dread. In the year 1593, the keeping of Bartholomew Fair as a refort of fmall dealers and holiday makers, was for the firft time fufpended by the raging of the plague ; and the terms of the proclamation of Elizabeth then made, not only prove that the Fair ſtill maintained its character as a great place of commerce, but alſo furniſh us with a few points of ſpecial information as to the nature of the traffic carried on in it, and the ground allotted to ſome branches of its trade. It is ordered by the queen that, " whereas, there was a general reſort of all kinds of people out of every part of her realm to the ſaid Fair, that in the uſual place of Smithfield there ſhall be no manner of market for any wares kept, nor any ſtalls or booths for any manner of merchandise, or for victuals, ſuffered to be ſet up, but that the open ſpace of the ground called Smithfield, be only occupied with the ſale of horſes and cattle : and of ſtall wares, as butter, cheeſe, and ſuch like, in groſs, and not by retail, the ſame to continue for the ſpace of two days only.

" And for the vent of woollen cloths, kerſeys, and linen cloth, to be all ſold in groſs and not by retail ; the ſame ſhall be all brought within the cloſe yard of St. Bartholomew's, where ſhops are there continued, and have gates to ſhut the ſame place in the nights, and then ſuch cloth to be offered to ſale, and to be bought in groſs, and not by retail, the ſame market to continue but 3 days, that is to ſay, Even, the Day of St. Bartholomew, and the Morrow after.

" And that the ſale and vent of leather be kept in the outſide of the ring of Smithfield, as hath been accuſtomed, without erecting of any ſhops or booths for the ſame, or for any victualler or other occupier of any wares whatſoever.

" And for notice hereof to be given to ſuch of her

Majefty's good fubjects as for lack of knowledge of this her Majefty's princely ordonnance might refort to London to fell or buy fmall wares by retail, and there receive infection, and carry the fame into their countries, her Majefty commandeth that the Lord Mayor of London fhall caufe this her Majefty's proclamation to be prefently publifhed in all the ufual places of the city, in the time of two or three market-days, and to be alfo proclaimed by the fheriffs of Middlefex, Kent, Surrey, and Effex, in fome places of thofe counties near to the faid city, whereby none may refort to the city at this feaft of St. Bartholomew, by pretence of any Fair, but fuch as fhall have caufe to fell or buy the commodities in grofs." Imprifonment without bail, during the queen's pleafure, or further punifhment, was the penalty for infraction of this ordinance, made about three weeks before fair time, on the 6th of Auguft, in the 35th year of the reign of Queen Elizabeth.

The cardinal inference to be drawn from this proclamation is, that Bartholomew Fair, as a place of wholefale commerce, was not to be fuppreffed without more injury to trade than fear of plague would force the queen's advifers to inflict. But this confideration muft be qualified by the fact, that the chief rifk came from the throng of pedlers, hawkers, ftall-keepers, fhowmen, and holiday makers from the country round about; and that the foberer refort of merchants to the Fair, while it was certainly in one refpect a greater good, was in the other refpect alfo a leffer evil. Alfo, there was a wealthy nobleman at court, unwilling to part with a year's tolls from the Cloth Fair and the clofe, and able to urge actively from motives of felf-intereft, confiderations that were, at the fame time, not wanting in juftice.

In the year 1596, a formal agreement was made between Lord Rich and the London corporation, eftablifhing a compofition of the tolls of Bartholomew Fair, and as to jurifdiction in the Fair, placing both parties exactly in the relative pofition occupied by the Corporation and the Priory in Henry the Sixth's time.

Two years later, Bartholomew Fair was vifited by the firft man who has taken the trouble to defcribe what he there faw. Paul Hentzner was a German tutor, travelling in the year 1598 through Germany, France, Italy, and England, who wrote an "Itinerarium" that after his return home was publifhed in fucceffive editions at Breflau and Nuremberg. He wrote for a ftay-at-home public, in the fpirit of a ftay-at-home, to whom all foreign things are ftrange. A tranflation of the part of this Itinerary in which England is defcribed was made by Bentley for Horace Walpole, and printed in 1757 at Strawberry Hill. It was included afterwards in the fecond volume of Dodfley's collections. Hentzner went to Bartholomew Fair. Of courfe he alfo faw and defcribed Queen Elizabeth " in the fifty-fixth year of her age (as we were told), very majeftic: her face oblong, fair, but wrinkled; her eyes fmall, yet black and pleafant; her nofe a little hooked, her lips narrow, and her teeth black (a defect the Englifh feem fubject to from their too great ufe of fugar). . . . . She wore falfe hair, and that red; her bofom was uncovered, as all the Englifh ladies have it till they marry; her hands were fmall, her fingers long, and her ftature neither tall nor low; her air was ſtately; her manner of ſpeaking mild and obliging." Yet under the rule of ſuch a queen, Paul Hentzner counted more than thirty traitors' heads rotting upon the tower of London Bridge. He went to the play, and may have ſeen Shakeſpeare acting, as he did that year, in Ben Jonſon's ' Every Man in his Humour.' He ſpeaks of the excellent muſic, variety of dances, and exceſſive applauſes in an Engliſh theatre—of the coming round of oranges, nuts, apples, ale, and beer; and we ſhall preſently have Ben Jonſon's authority for applying to the ſhows and booths of Bartholomew Fair what Hentzner ſays about one habit of the audiences at the plays, with a proviſion, indeed, that it is their habit every where elſe: "At theſe ſpectacles, and everywhere elſe, the Engliſh are con-ſtantly ſmoking tobacco in this manner."—Truly it is a whimſical thing to look back to the time when, of all countrymen in the world, a German looked upon tobacco with aſtoniſhment, and told his neighbour how the Engliſh were accuſtomed to make uſe of that new thing.—" In this manner: they have pipes on purpoſe made of clay, into the farther end of which they put the herb, ſo dry that it may be rubbed into powder; and putting fire to it, they draw the ſmoke into their mouths, which they puff out again through their noſtrils, like funnels, along with plenty of phlegm and defluxion from the head." The Engliſh of thoſe days, we are told, were ſerious like the Germans, lovers of ſhow, liking to go followed by troops of ſervants; good dancers and muſicians; politer in eating than the French, taking leſs bread, more meat, and much ſugar

in their drink ; quick of body and wit, good failors and
better pirates. Three hundred of them were faid to be
hanged yearly in London. They were much troubled
with fcurvy—one of the diftinguifhed things, by-the-
bye, which was faid to have come in with the Norman
conqueft. " They are powerful in the field—fuccefsful
againft their enemies,—impatient of anything like
flavery ; and" [as Bartholomew Fair could witnefs]
" vaftly fond of great noifes that fill the ear, fuch as the
firing of cannon, drums, and the ringing of bells; fo
that it is common for a number of them, that have
got a glafs in their heads, to go up into fome belfry,
and ring the bells for hours together, for the fake of
exercife."

It is through the eyes of this German obferver that
we have the following glimpfe of Bartholomew Fair in
the year 1598.

" It is worthy of obfervation, that every year, upon
St. Bartholomew's Day, when the Fair is held, it is ufual
for the mayor, attended by the twelve principal aldermen, to walk in a neighbouring field, dreffed in his
fcarlet gown, and about his neck a golden chain, to
which is hung a golden Fleece, and, befides, that
particular ornament which diftinguifhes the moft noble
order of the Garter. When the mayor goes out of the
precincts of the city, a sceptre and fword and a cap are
borne before him, and he is followed by the principal
aldermen in fcarlet gowns with gold chains, himfelf and
they on horfeback. Upon their arrival at a place
appointed for that purpofe, where a tent is pitched,
the mob begin to wreftle before them, two at a time ;

the conquerors receive rewards from the magiftrates. After this is over, a parcel of live rabbits are turned loofe among the crowd, which are purfued by a number of boys, who endeavour to catch them, with all the noife they can make. While we were at this fhow, one of our company, Tobias Salander, Doctor of Phyfic, had his pocket picked of his purfe, with nine crowns, which, without doubt, was fo cleverly taken from him by an Englifhman, who always kept very clofe to him, that the Doctor did not perceive it." Thus, the firft fketch of Bartholomew Fair, made by a mere obferver, meagre as it is, does not omit the pickpocket.

Five years before Hentzner's vifit, general refort to the Fair was forbidden by reafon of the plague. Five years after, the plague clofed the Fair again. James I. then was king, and he firft iffued a proclamation, dated at Windfor, July 11, 1603: "For the fair which hath been ufed to be kept on the fields near our houfe of St. James and city of Weftminfter, commonly called St. James's Fair, about the day of our coronation and for fome days after; to be forborne for eight or ten days after the firft day of the ufual holding thereof, the fame to be held then as ufed to do." St. James's Fair, therefore, after the Palace had been fubftituted for the Leper Houfe, was kept in courtly fafhion, not on the anniverfary of a faint's coronation as a martyr, but on the coronation day of his moft facred Majefty. This order for the poftponement of the courtly Fair was followed by another proclamation, dated July 29, 1603, to the effect that "The folemnities of our coronation being now performed," the nobility of Scotland and all

Englifh noblemen and gentry, not the king's fervants in ordinary, are commanded to repair homewards into the country, to prevent the fpreading of the contagion of the plague. The knight-marfhal is to prevent perfons from infefting the court, and petitions of fuitors are to be received at Kingfton. This was followed on the 8th of Auguft by a proclamation dated from Hampton Court, ordaining for the " defire of preventing an univerfal contagion among our people," that Bartholomew Fair and Sturbridge Fair fhall not be holden, " nor anything appertaining unto them, at the times accuftomed, nor any time till they fhall be licenfed by us."

The next record we find concerns the Fair for the year following, and officially defcribes fome of the ceremonies which helped to imprefs Paul Hentzner with his admiration of the dignity and fplendour of the lord mayor and the aldermen of London. It is a part of the " order of my lord mayor, the aldermen, and the fheriffs, for their meetings and wearing of their apparel throughout the year 1604.

" ON SAINT BARTHOLOMEW'S EVEN FOR THE FAIR IN SMITHFIELD.

" The aldermen meet my lord and the fheriffs at the Guildhall Chapel, at two of the clock after dinner, in their violet gowns lined, and their horfes, without cloaks, and there hear Evening Prayer; which being done, they take their horfes and ride to Newgate, and fo forth to the gate entering in at the Cloth Fair, and there make a proclamation "———

Here I break the text of the order, that the pro-clamation itfelf may be heard.

THE TENOUR OF THE PROCLAMATION MADE ON BAR-THOLOMEW EVE, IN THE AFTERNOON, AT THE GREAT GATE GOING INTO THE CLOTH FAIR, SMITHFIELD.

" The Right Honourable Lord Mayor of the city of London, and his right worfhipful brethren the alder-men of the faid city, ftreightly charge and command, on the behalf of our fovereign lady the Queen, that all manner of perfons, of whatfoever eftate, degree, or condition they be, having recourfe to this Fair, keep the peace of our faid fovereign lady the Queen.

" That no manner of perfons make any congregation, conventicles, or affrays, by the which the fame peace may be broken or difturbed, upon pain of imprifonment and fine, to be made after the difcretion of the lord mayor and aldermen.

" Alfo, that all manner of fellers of wine, ale, or beer, fell by meafures enfealed, as by gallon, pottle, quart, and pint, upon pain that will fall thereof.

" And that no perfon fell any bread, but if it keep the affize, and that it be good and wholefome for man's body, upon pain that will fall thereof.

" And that no manner of perfon buy nor fell, but with true weights and meafures, fealed according to the ftatute in that behalf made, upon pain that will fall thereof.

" And that no manner of perfon, or perfons, take upon him, or them, within this Fair, to make any manner of arreft, attachment, fummons, or execution, but if it be done by the officer of this City thereunto affigned, upon pain that will fall thereof.

" And that no perfon or perfons whatfoever, within the limits and bounds of this Fair, prefume to break the Lord's Day in felling, fhowing, or offering to fale, or in buying or offering to buy, any commodities whatfoever, or in fitting, tippling, or drinking in any tavern, inn, ale-houfe, or cook's-houfe, or in doing any other thing that may lead to the breach thereof, upon the pain and penalties contained in feveral acts of Parliament, which will be feverely inflicted upon the breakers thereof.

" And finally, that whatever perfon foever find themfelves aggrieved, injured or wronged by any manner of perfon in this Fair, that they come with their plaints before the ftewards in this Fair, affigned to hear and determine pleas, and they will minifter to all parties juftice, according to the laws of this land, and the cuftoms of this City.   God fave the Queen ! "

The mayor, fheriffs, and aldermen fitting on horfeback, robed in their violet gowns, having made this proclamation at a point between the city Fair and that owned by the Warwick or Holland family, as the reft of the official rule details, "the proclamation being made, they ride through the Cloth Fair, and fo return back again, through the Churchyard of Great St. Bartholomew's to Alderfgate, and fo ride home again to the Lord Mayor's houfe."

" ON BARTHOLOMEW DAY FOR WRESTLING.

" So many aldermen as dine with my lord mayor and the fheriffs, be apparelled in their fcarlet gowns lined, and after dinner their horfes be brought to them where they dine, and thofe aldermen which dine with the fheriffs, ride with them to my lord's houfe, to accompany him to the wreftling. Then when the wreftling is done, they take their horfes, and ride back again through the Fair, and fo in at Alderfgate and fo home again to the faid lord mayor's houfe.

" The next day, if it be not Sunday for the fhooting, as upon Bartholomew's day, but if it be Sunday, the Monday following."

Tradition declares that the mayor, when he had read the proclamation, drank ale from a filver flagon, and that thereupon the buftle and the bufinefs of the Fair began. The proclamation above cited was abbreviated at a later time, and may have been originally fhorter than it there appears. It muft have been fhorter in the days of Queen Elizabeth, unlefs (as was quite poffible) the city of London exercifed a ftricter than the general rule in the fuppreffion of all traffic upon Sundays. For againft one claufe in the proclamation we muft fet an advertifement, made in the feventh year of Elizabeth's reign for due order in the public adminiftration of Common Prayers, enjoining that " in all Fairs and Common Markets, falling upon the Sunday, there be no fhowing of any wares before the fervice be done."

Up to this time the old Priory Enclofure, reconftituted as a parifh, had not been reckoned among city parifhes. It was beyond the precincts. It was not until the 20th of September, 1608, that in a charter granted by King James the Firft to the city of London, the circuit, bounds, liberties, franchifes, and jurifdictions of the city were fo extended as to include the ground of the late diffolved Priories of St. Bartholomew near Smithfield, (and of its Hofpital) Trinity near Aldgate, of the Blackfriars within and at Ludgate, of the Order of the Bleffed Virgin Mary of Mount Carmel, called White-friars, and the Inn or Liberty of Cold Harbour Lane.

In the year following, a new queftion of jurifdiction was raifed in connection with the Smithfield Fair. Im-mediately after Bartholomew Fair, on the 28th of Auguft, in the year 1609, the Drapers queftioned the right of fearch exercifed by the Merchant Taylors. The Company's books fhow that its clerk was " ordered thereon to attend Drapers' Hall, on the next court day, with a meffage to the following purport, viz., That the Merchant Taylors' Company had right to fearch, and that they had quietly enjoyed the fame fince the 27th of Henry the Sixth, being above 150 years paft, and ftill earlier, as by the Merchant Taylors records appeared, wherein is mentioned a lengthened lawfuit between them and the Drapers, about the same queftion of right of fearch, when a fentence was paffed for the Merchant Taylors."

In 1611 the afhes of the laft martyr-fire in Smithfield fmouldered out. The victim was Bartholomew Leggatt, a pious Unitarian, burnt for diftruft of the Athanafian and Nicene creeds by James the Firft, at the fentence of John King, newly made bifhop of London. Then in the year 1614, between Fairtime and Fairtime, Smithfield was firft paved.

CHAPTER X.

In Ben Jonson's Time.

SMITHFIELD, three years after the laft martyrdom, ceafed to be a broken plain of mud, and of the filth of men and beafts. Rain, and the cattle brought thither for fale, had made the place often almoft impaffable ; and fo foul had been its general ftate, that there were many who would even doubt the power of art to transform it into hard and level ground. Bartholomew Fair, in a wet Auguft before the year 1614, muft have been a flough of pleafure, difficult indeed to ftruggle through. But a king's letter having ordered the Lord Mayor to pave the place, and thereby to remove the fcandal brought upon the city by its ruinous and dangerous condition, in the year 1614 Smithfield was no longer, in that refpect, a public nuifance. At an expenfe of fixteen hundred pounds the paving was accomplifhed. The ground was greatly raifed in the middle, whereby it became a clean and fpacious walk ; channels were made to drain away the water ; and a ftrong railing was fet round about the market-place for the fecurity of foot paffengers from the danger of coaches, carts, horfes, and other cattle, of which Smithfield was then feldom empty.

L

The horfe-pool was decayed, and the fprings being
ftopped up, only the land water fell into a fmall bottom,
enclofed with brick, and called the Smithfield Pond.
Cow-lane, in which was the old houfe of the Prior of
Semperingham, was a lane of houfes, not all of them
new, built over the fite of the ancient gallows. The
laft elm had been cut down. Hofier-lane, and Chick-
lane, were newly become permanent reforts of trade.
Long-lane was being lined with tenements for brokers,
tipplers, and the like. There were brewhoufes, inns,
"fair and comely buildings" on the weftern fide of Smithfield, as far as the Bars ; all thefe erections conftituting
an encroachment upon, and a reduction to about three
acres of, the ancient fpace, whereby, faid Stow, writing
in thofe times, "remaineth but a fmall portion for the
old ufes."

Returning to Smithfield ftones, we fhould add, it
was about this time that the citizens, who were alfo firft
enjoying a more ample water fupply than was furnifhed
by the fprings on their own foil, began to pave the
margins of the ftreets before their doors with broad flag-
ftones for the convenience of foot paffengers. Thefe
Memoirs at the fame time efcape from the flippery
ill-lighted region over which they have been at pains to
keep a fteady footing. In the year of the paving of
Smithfield, Ben Jonfon reprefented in a Comedy, what
Bartholomew Fair, then a moft ancient London feftival,
was in his time. Therefore, we alfo have at laft got
even ground to go upon.

From its birthplace by the church, and in the fair,
the Englifh drama had departed, growing into inde-

pendent life in the wide world, but leaving in the old home many recollections of its childhood. From Myſteries and Miracle plays the drama, ſtill in its childhood, had grown to Moralities, with perſonated virtues to teach morals, and a comic Vice to help the devil's work in raiſing laughter. The Moralities, as they grew older, learnt to enliven their more abſtract dialogues or doctrine with examples illuſtrative of their theme, and ſo included monitory ſcenes from human hiſtory, ſuch as the fortunes of Antony and Cleopatra, Damon and Pythias, or the Siege of Troy. The Vice put on the dreſs of the Elizabethan clown. All this was in the childhood of the drama, whereof memories clung to its birth-place long after it had gone out mature into the world, and had begotten ſons equal in dignity with the beſt poets that have ever laid their ſpell upon mankind. The Fair, like an old Nurſe who once carried the infant child of a great houſe upon her arms, and was not then too ignorant to be its oracle and guide, looks from a lowly hut upon the palace of her nurſling, and croons over to herſelf the old ditties, tells over to herſelf the old ſtories that once ſatisfied the lord of the great houſe, who is ſo tall and ſtately, and ſo choice in mirth, and ſo far-reaching in knowledge.

Once only that bright foſter-ſon croſſed the old woman's threſhold in the days of his great wealth and honour, and ſat chattering and laughing at her feet. She could afford then to be laughed at, for her houſe after all, though dirty and ruinous, was a good houſe. She was a moſt reſpectable ſhopkeeper, ſhe had a whole-ſale trade, and no lack of cuſtom as a retailer of toys and hardware. He was a wayward wilful lad in his fwaddling-clothes, and in his handfome manhood he might laugh at his old nurfe, and welcome. In the name, therefore, of Ben Jonfon, Englifh drama paid a vifit to the Fair in Smithfield. Ben Jonfon's comedy of Bartholomew Fair, though by no means his greateft work, has among his writings one particular diftinction. It is the moft per-fect example of his moft peculiar character among the poets of his time, and it may even be faid of any time. He had a mufe that dwelt in London. His tragic mufe frequented London libraries ; his comic mufe paffed from the court to the city, dropping in at London houfes by the London ftreets. In his comedy of Bartholomew Fair, he is in a denfe centre of London life. So much about one bit of town life as we find in it, is not contained in any other extant play. The burly, kindly man, with " his mountain belly and his rocky face," a polifhed fcholar and a polifhed wit ; fo noble in the outfpoken honefty that has outweighed—at laft—huge maffes of detraction ; the one man who in that day felt to the quick Shake-fpeare's commanding genius, and in the word of a friend's love expreffed a perfect fenfe of it, was not a London poet in the vulgar fenfe. He did not, as a thoufand men have done, talk of all things out of a mind bound down to the perception of but one ; but, with the full foul of a poet and a wide prerogative, he chofe to make a focial being of his mufe, and live with her as the en-livener of his own dwelling-place. Moreover, he was a bold fatirift, whofe fatire being to the town, was of the town. Satire againft the abfent or the diftant was for feebler men. There are other of Ben Jonfon's plays, which in one fcene mention a greater variety of London places than are named in the whole comedy of Bartholomew Fair, where the Fair is all in all, and where we are fo hemmed in with town follies and vices, that the only hint we get of the exiftence of fuch a thing as tree in nature, is the mention of an arbour of green boughs, ufed as a booth for eating pig in. Thofe arbours of green boughs, which difappeared from the Fair, as in courfe of time London expanded, remind us that in the beginning of the feventeenth century, they who croffed Smithfield with their faces to the country very foon were in the open fields. From one fide of it country people entered the Fair through lanes but little built upon, from paths by the brookfide, and over moor and meadow.

Another very noticeable thing in this comedy is the vivid painting of the charaEters through whom the fatirift amufes himfelf with the follies of the Fair. They are many and various, yet every one of them is defined fharply, and they all go through a maze of mifadventure without caufing the leaft confufion to the witnefs of their huge bewilderment. In this particular refpeEt Bartholomew Fair is not excelled by any of Ben Jonfon's works.

Through the centre of the aEtion there moves Adam Overdo, judge of the court of Piepowders. (We obferve in paffing that the final s had in thofe days not yet fallen from the court of Wayfaring traders.) That man of power upon whofe fole jurifdiEtion not King James himfelf may intrude, is poffeffed with the freak of a Haroun Alrafchid. He will walk the Fair in difguife and, habited as a fool, become for himfelf ear-witnefs and eye-witnefs of the enormities that need correction. The watchmen look for him in vain: "How now neighbour Haggise," says one to another who has been on a vain errand, "what says Justice Overdo's worship to the other offen-ders?"—Why," answers Haggise, "he says just nothing; what should he say, or when should he say? He is not to be found, man; he has not been seen in the Fair here all this livelong day, never since seven o'clock in the morning. His clerks know not what to think on't. There is no court of pie-poudres yet."

No court yet, on this four-and-twentieth of August; and it is late in the day, for there has been Puppy the wrestler fast asleep before the booth of fat Ursula the pigwoman,—"a strong man, a mighty man, my lord mayor's man and a wrestler." "He has wrestled so long with the bottle there, that the man with the beard"—that is the bearded face once common on stoneware mugs—"has almost struck up his heels," and some time ago "there has been the clerk of the market to cry him all the Fair over for my lord's service." Now the wrest-ling before the lord mayor is upon Bartholomew Day in the afternoon. The north country clothier has finished his day's work, and cried out too late "I'll ne mare, I'll ne mare; the eale's too meaghty," when he already was "e'en as vull as a paiper's bag."—"My northern cloth," as Puppy, the west country wrestler said for him before he was floored, "do zhrink i' the wetting, ha!"

This sodden north countryman, defined as one "who do's change cloth for ale at the Fair here," is the only ancestor of the merchants of Leeds, Manchester, and Bradford who in Ben Jonson's play indicates the exiftence of the ftill confiderable Cloth Fair in Smithfield. The Pleafure Fair is the fcene of the ftory, and it contains only this one foolifh ftraggler from the body of fubftantial clothiers who were doing bufinefs among themfelves upon Lord Rich's ground. To the Cloth Fair, therefore, fome credit is given in the Play, for it yields to the vice and folly of the day only a ftray fimpleton; but the ftagekeeper in the Prologue difcuffing what might have been written, does not credit the north countryman with want of keennefs: "Ho! an Mafter Tarleton had lived to have played in Bartholomew Fair, you fhould have feen him have come in, and have been cozened in the Cloth Quarter fo finely!"

The Horfe Fair has a reprefentative in Mafter Daniel Knockem Jordan the horfe courfer. A horfe courfer was the man who bought and fold horfes already in ufe, a horfe dealer was he who traded in horfes of his own rearing and training. The horfe courfers, with ribbons fet about the manes and tails of their beafts, for ornament and fign of their being on fale, had their own ground in Bartholomew Fair, and made its dregs the fouler for their prefence. Knockem or Captain Jordan, captain of the roarers, bully in fword, boot and feather, is a man whofe breath reeks of the ftable. He is a knight of the knife, a child of the horn thumb; (a horn on the thumb was ufed to receive the edge of the knife with which purfes were cut;) he is a vapourer who can cut halfpenny purfes or fteal little penny dogs out of the fair; brutal companion, alfo, to the weak among his infamous affociates of the other fex.

To take tolls and manage for its proprietors the

general bufinefs of the Fair there was the Clerk of the
Market. To maintain, on the part of the law, order and
juftice among the keen traders, cutpurfes, and their
confederate balladfingers, pigwomen, coftard (apple)
mongers, bullies and whatever worfe people the Fair
contained,—alfo among the crowd of precocious, eager
boys that duly appear in the play, rioting in the wake of
fome odd perfon who is fo unhappy as to fix their attention,—there was not only the Piepowder Court, with its
juftice and clerks, and the marfhals its ignorant and
ftarveling fatellites, eyes of the criminal law, but there
were the ftocks in the Fair, and there alfo was a whipping
poft. The pond too was large enough for Urfula the
pigwoman to be ducked in, whale as fhe was.

"Many," faid Adam Overdo, "are the yearly enormities of this Fair, in whofe courts of Piepoudres I
have had the honour, during the three days, fometimes
to fit as judge. But this is the fpecial day for the de-
tection of thofe enormities. I am refolved to fpare fpy
money hereafter, and make mine own difcoveries."
Difguifed, therefore, as a fool and paffing with the Fair
goers for "mad Arthur of Bradley, that makes the orations"—to Arthur of Bradley there were in thofe days
many popular allufions, and he was the fubject alfo of a
merry ballad—Adam Overdo mixed with the people of
the Fair.

But it fo happened that the juftice's wife, Miftrefs
Overdo, was eafily perfuaded to tafte what innocent
pleafure fhe could as the companion of her fimple
brother Bartholomew Cokes (Cokes was a name once
anfwering to the character of this its bearer), who called

the Fair his Fair, becaufe of Bartholomew. Cokes meant
to be married to Miftrefs Grace Wellborn, the juftice's
ward, and he had fent his man Wafpe to Proctor Littlewit's to get the marriage licenfe on his day, Bartholomew
Day. He muft fhow his Fair to Miftrefs Grace, who is
a difcreet maiden as fober as fhe is handfome and cafts a
reftrained fcorn upon all his behaviour and fpeeches. But
fhe has been fold to Juftice Overdo as a king's ward and
cannot help herfelf. Before the abolition of the Court of
Wards in the twelfth year of Charles the Second, the heir
of the king's tenant, holding lands in capite, was during
nonage ward of the king, who might fell or prefent the
right of guardianfhip and beftowal in marriage. King's
favourites had made fortunes by traffic in the marrying
of wealthy wards. Juftice Overdo has bought the ward-
fhip of Grace Wellborn, and fhe is doomed by what fhe
calls "a common calamity" to marry his wife's brother, or
fhe can efcape only by paying forfeit of her land. There
was legal remedy in cafe of difparagement, which was a
matching below the bride's rank, or againft decency;
and this is referred to by the gamefter in the Fair, to
whom the poor girl is led to explain her pofition, when
he fays, "Is there no device of difparagement, or fo?
Talk with fome crafty fellow, fome picklock of the law:
would I had ftudied a year longer in the Inns of Court,
an't had been but in your cafe." Cokes, then, attended
by his man Wafpe, takes Grace and his fifter Overdo
into Bartholomew Fair, though Grace truly has "no
fuch fancy to the Fair nor ambition to fee it; there's
none," fhe adds, "goes thither of any quality or fafhion."

But is not Proctor John Littlewit, of the court of

Arches (kept in Bow Church, Cheapside, which as the first church in the city raised upon stone arches, was called St. Mary de Arcubus, or le Bow), is not John Littlewit, one of the Arches, that dwells about the hospital, and one of the pretty wits of Paul's, a person of some quality?   Now Proctor Littlewit goes to the Fair with all his family, namely, Win—not christened Winifred, but Win-the-Fight—his newly married wife, and his wife's saintly mother, Dame Purecraft, with the dame's friend, the reverend elder set over against the meat of Littlewit, the Rabbi Zeal-of-the-Land Busy.   They lived just after the days of sword and buckler men, who clashed their bucklers, and affected to seek quarrel in the Fair.   Kindheart, the tooth-drawer, was a celebrity of the day just gone by : and Bartholomew Fair had been welcoming the Reformation and defying Spain, with a well-educated ape who would leap over a chain in the name of a king of England, and leap back again for an English prince ; but who sat on his tail scornfully, and would not budge, for the Pope or the king of Spain.

Their visit to the Fair happened in this way.   Mr. Littlewit, who has a luck to spin out fine conceits, and, like a silk-worm, out of himself, was pleased by the perception of a pleasant quibble in the drawing out of a licence on Bartholomew Day, the twenty-fourth of August, for a Bartholomew Cokes, of Harrow o' the Hill, in the county of Middlesex, esquire ; and being in good humour with himself and all things, was well pleased to see his wife, Win, come into his room in her velvet cap and her fine high shoes, like the Spanish lady.   He could challenge all Cheapside to show such another : Moorfields, Pimlico-path, or the Exchange in a fummer evening. He was in love with his bright wife and his bright wit. He was none of your Three Cranes, Mitre, and Mermaid men. Other men have wives as fine as the players, and as well dreft. Other men have their works too. Mafter Littlewit was author of a puppet play—a Motion—which was to be performed on that day for the firft time at the Fair. A bachelor friend, Mafter Winwife, happening to call at this time—for he was a fuitor to Mrs. Littlewit's mother, the Dame Purely, —found the happy pair in love with one another, and with all the world, except perhaps Dame Purely and the Rabbi, who kept rule over their houfehold. Mafter Winwife was warned by them, that the widow had been to the cunning man in Cow-lane, who had foretold that fhe fhould never have a happy hour if fhe did not within that very week marry a madman ; t'other man of Moorfields, faid it muft be a gentleman madman. Winwife was advifed to be a little madder than his friend the gamefter, Mafter Quarlous, who had alfo an affection for the dame's fix thoufand pounds. The widow herfelf, he was told, inquired at Bedlam twice a day, and was ftudying the old Elder, come from Banbury, a fuitor that put in at meal-tide, to praife the painful brethren, or pray that the fweet fingers might be reftored. Prefently, Mafter Quarlous alfo looked in upon Littlewit, and was reminded by the dangeroufly brifkwitted proctor, of a promife made over their cups laft night, to join them in a vifit to the Fair. " Before truth, if you have that fearful quality, John, to remember when you are fober, John, what you promife drunk, John ; I fhall

take heed of you, John." The next comer was Mafter
Bartholomew Cokes's man, wanting the licenfe, a terrible
tefty old fellow, and his name was Wafpe, too. He
muft not be kept waiting; he hath both eggs on the fpit,
and irons in the fire; more bufinefs than the buying of
gingerbread there in the Cloifter, or a gilt pouch in the
Fair. He has charge of his mafter: " You are an afs.
I have a young mafter, he is now upon his making and
marring; the whole care of his well-doing is now mine.
His foolifh fchoolmafters have done nothing but run up
and down the country with him to beg puddings and
cake-bread of his tenants, and almoft fpoiled him; he
has learn'd nothing but to fing catches, and repeat
'Rattle Bladder, rattle!' and 'O, Madge!' I dare
not let him walk alone for fear of vile tunes, which he
will fing at fupper and in the fermon times. If he meet
but a carman in the ftreet, and I find him not talk to
keep him off on him, he will whiftle him and all his
tunes over at night in his fleep! He has a head full
of bees! Gentlemen, you do not know him; he is
another manner of piece than you think for: but nineteen years old, and yet he is taller than either of you by
the head, God blefs him! We have been but a day and
a half in town, gentlemen, and yefterday in the morning,
we walked London to fhow the city to the gentlewoman
he fhall marry, Miftrefs Grace; but afore I will endure
fuch another half-day with him, I'll be drawn with a
good gib-cat through the great pond at home, as his
uncle Hodge was. Why we could not meet that heathen
thing all the day but ftaid him; he would name you all
the figns over, as he went, aloud; and where he fpied a

parrot or a monkey, there he was pitched, with all the
little longcoats about him, male and female; no getting
him away! I thought he would have run mad o'the
black boy in Bucklerſbury, that takes the ſcurvy, rogue's
tobacco there." But what inſult to the truſty Hum-
phrey Waſpe, the faithful Numps,—to ſeek him! He
muſt come after him to Proctor Littlewit's; Cokes himſelf, with Grace, and his ſiſter, Miſtreſs Overdo. What
the miſchief! do they think he changed their fourteen
ſhillings worth of ſmall ware—the licenſe—for hobby-
horſes in the Fair! But to the Fair, Maſter Cokes was
bound. "The Fair, Numps, the Fair."—"Would
the Fair, and all the drums and rattles in it, were in
your belly for me! they are already in your brain. He
that had the means to travel your head now, ſhould
meet finer ſights than any are in the Fair, and make a
finer voyage on't; to ſee it all hung with cockle-ſhells,
pebbles, fine wheat-ſtraws, and here and there a chicken's
feather and a cobweb. Gentlemen, if he go to the Fair,
he will buy of everything to a baby there" (the dolls
there were called Bartholomew babies); "and houſehold
ſtuff for that too. If a leg or an arm on him did not
grow on, he would loſe it in the preſs. And then he is
ſuch a ravener after fruit! you will not believe what a
coil I had t'other day to compound a buſineſs between a
Cather'ne pearwoman and him, about ſnatching: 'tis
intolerable, gentlemen."—"O, but you muſt not leave
him now to theſe hazards, Numps".—"Nay, he knows
too well I will not leave him, and that makes him preſume: Well, ſir, will you go now? If you have ſuch
an itch in your feet to foot it to the Fair, why do you

ſtop, am I o' your tarriers? Go! *Will* you go, ſir? Why do you not go ?"

Of courſe he goes. And Proctor Littlewit muſt needs go; for, as he tells his wife, "I have an affair in the Fair, Win, a puppet play of mine own making,—ſay nothing,—that I writ for the Motion man, which you muſt ſee, Win."—"I would I might, John, but my mother will never conſent to ſuch a profane motion, ſhe will call it." But John is a huſband with a wit. He has ideas, "Win, long to eat of a pig, ſweet Win, in the Fair, do you ſee; in the heart of the Fair, not at Pye corner." Roaſt pig was from time immemorial the dainty of the Fair, and to long for Bartholomew Pig was a device common even among married women of a later generation than that to which Mrs. Littlewit belonged. Davenant cites this as part of his impreſſion of the Fair when he has told how

> London's Mayor, in saddle new,
> Rides to the Fair of Bartlemew;
> He twirls his chain and looketh big,
> As if to fright the head of pig
> That gaping lies on every ſtall—

waiting the call of any one in Mrs. Littlewit's poſition. Dame Purecraft fought in vain againſt her child's deſire for the unclean beaſt, pig, and ſhe would do anything to ſatisfy the longing. But faithful juſtification of our zealous brother Buſy might prevail. Buſy was ſought and found faſt by the teeth in the cold turkeypie in the cupboard, with a great white loaf on his left hand and a glaſs of malmſey on his right. Preſently, when he had cleaned his beard, he came. This was the Banbury man

—Banbury being in thoſe days a ſtronghold of the Puritans.

Here let me ſay at once, what there are few now who doubt, that throughout the ſeventeenth century in England the ſincere Puritans were the trueſt gentlemen and beſt maintainers of the country's honour.   But there is nothing ſo eaſy, nothing ſo profitable for a raſcal as the feigning of religious zeal.   Let, therefore, nobody now read the character of Zeal-of-the-Land Buſy as deriſion againſt the whole body of Puritans, who had already declared war againſt the Playhouſe and the Fair. It is a fierce ſatire againſt Religious Hypocriſy.   It is an Engliſh Tartuffe, expoſed to a more paſſionate ſcorn than any Frenchman ever has invoked againſt fraud in religion. Memoirs of Bartholomew Fair now reach a period in which the Puritans muſt occupy a chief poſition in the narrative ; and it is in Ben Jonſon's comedy that upon records of the Fair they firſt make their appearance.

The Rabbi Buſy is the perſon in the play who belongs moſt eſſentially to this part of our hiſtory.   " He is more than an elder, he is a prophet.   He was a baker, ſir, but he does dream now and ſee viſions.   He has given over his trade, out of a ſcruple he took that in ſpiced conſcience, thoſe cakes he made, were ſerved to bridals, maypoles, morrices, and ſuch profane feaſts and meetings.   His chriſtian name is Zeal-of-the-Land, a notable hypocritical vermin.   One that ſtands upon his face more than his faith at all times : ever in ſeditious motion, and reproving for vain glory ; of a moſt lunatic conſcience of ſpleen, and affects the violence of ſingularity in all he does.   A fellow of a moſt arrogant and

invincible dulnefs, by his profeffion he will ever be in
the ftate of innocence and childhood, for he derides all
antiquity, defies any other learning than infpiration, and
what difcretion foever years fhould afford him, it is all
prevented in his original ignorance." That defcription
doubtlefs was meant for a more general cenfure on the
Puritan ; but when the particular Bufy, having purified
his beard, enters to give his counfel to the widow and
widow's daughter, he fnuffles out the language of the
Hypocrite alone : " Verily, for the difeafe of longing it
is a difeafe, a carnal difeafe or appetite, incident to
women ; and as it is carnal and incident, it is natural,
very natural : now pig, it is a meat, and a meat that
is nourifhing and may be longed for, and fo confequently
eaten ; it may be eaten ; very exceeding well eaten ; but
in the Fair, and as a Bartholomew Pig, it cannot be
eaten ; for the very calling it a Bartholomew Pig, and to
eat it fo, is a fpice of idolatry, and you make the Fair
no better than one of the high places.   This, I take it,
is the ftate of the queftion : a high place."—" Good
Brother Zeal-of-the-Land, think to make it as lawful as
you can."—" Yes, fir, and as foon as you can, for it
muft be, fir."—" Surely, it may be otherwife, but it is
fubject to conftruction, fubject, and hath a face of
offence with the weak, a great face, a foul face ; but
that face may have a veil put over it, and be fhadowed
as it were ; it may be eaten, and in the Fair, I take it,
in a booth, the tents of the wicked ; the place is not
much, not very much, we may be religious in the midft
of the profane, fo it be eaten with a reformed mouth,
with fobriety and humblenefs ; not gorged in with glut-

tony or greedinefs, there's the fear : for, fhould fhe go there, as taking pride in the place, or delight in the unclean dreffing, to feed the vanity of the eye, or luft of the palate, it were not well, it were not fit, it were abominable, and not good."

"Nay," fays Littlewit, "we'll be humble enough, we'll feek out the homelieft booth in the Fair, that's certain ; rather than fail, we'll eat it on the ground." "Ay," adds Dame Purecraft, "and I'll go with you myfelf. Win-the-fight, and my brother, Zeal-of-the-Land, fhall go with us too, for our better confolation." Then fays the Rabbi, " In the way of comfort to the weak, I will go and eat. I will eat exceedingly, and prophefy ; there may be a good ufe made of it too, now I think on't : by the public eating of fwine's flefh, to profefs our hate and loathing of Judaifm, whereof the brethren ftand tax'd. I will therefore eat, yea, I will eat exceedingly." So thefe alfo fet off to the Fair.

In the Fair, as I have faid, is Juftice Overdo, folemnly eftablifhing himfelf as a fool for the benefit of public morals. There are the booths and ftalls. There is profperous Lanthorn Leatherhead, the hobby-horfe man, who cries " What do you lack ? what is't you buy ? what do you lack ? rattles, drums, halberts, horfes, babies o' the beft, fiddles of the fineft ! " He is a too proud pedler, owner alfo of a famous puppet-fhow, the manager indeed for whom Proctor Littlewit has facrificed to the Bartholomew Mufes. Joan Trafh, the gingerbread woman, keeps her ftall near him, and the rival traders have their differences. " Do you hear, fifter Trafh, lady of the bafket ? fit farther with your gingerbread progeny

M

there, and hinder not the profpect of my fhop, or I'll have it proclaimed in the Fair, what ftuff they are made on."—"Why, what ftuff are they made on, brother Leatherhead? nothing but what's wholefome, I affure you."—"Yes, ftale bread, rotten eggs, mufty ginger, and dead honey, you know."—"I defy thee, and thy ftable of hobby-horfes. I pay for my ground as well as thou doft. Buy any gingerbread, gilt gingerbread! Will your worfhip buy any gingerbread, very good bread, comfortable bread?"

The cries of the Fair multiply, "Buy any ballads! new ballads! Hey?

> " ' Now the Fair's a filling!
>   O, for a tune to startle
>   The birds o' the booths here billing,
>   Yearly with old Saint Bartle!'

"Buy any pears, pears, fine, very fine pears!"—"What do you lack, gentlemen? Maid, fee a fine hobby-horfe for your young mafter; coft you but a token a week his provender." (Tokens were farthings coined by tradef-men for convenience of change, before farthings were publifhed as King's money by Charles the Second, in 1672.)

"Have you any corns on your feet and toes?"

"Buy a moufetrap, a moufetrap, or a tormentor for a flea?"

"Buy fome gingerbread?"

"What do you lack, gentlemen? fine purfes, pouches, pin-cafes, pipes? what is't you lack? a pair o' fmiths to wake you in the morning? or a fine whiftling bird?"

"Ballads, ballads! Fine new ballads:

" ' Hear for your love, and buy for your money.
   A delicate ballad o' the ferret and the coney.
   A Dozen of Divine Points, and the Godly Garters :
   The Fairing of Good Counfel, of an ell and three-quarters.'

" What do you lack, what do you buy, miftrefs? a fine hobby-horfe, to make your fon a tilter ? a drum to make him a foldier ? a fiddle to make him a reveller ? What is't you lack? little dogs for your daughters ? or babies, male or female ? "

" Gentlewomen, the weather's hot; whither walk you Have a care of your fine velvet caps, the Fair is dufty. Take a fweet, delicate booth, with boughs, here in the way, and cool yourfelves in the fhade; you and your friends. The beft pig and bottle-ale in the Fair, fir. Old Urfula is cook, there you may read :

      " HERE BE THE BEST PIGS AND SHE DOES
      ROAST THEM AS WELL AS EVER SHE DID."

(There is a picture of a Pig's head over the infcription, and) " the Pig's head fpeaks it."

" A delicate fhow-pig, little miftrefs, with fhweet fauce, and crackling, like de bay-leaf i' de fire, la! Tou fhalt ha' the clean fide o' the table-clot, and di glafs vafh'd with phaterfh of Dame Annesh Cleare." (A favourite well near Hoxton, that of Agnes le Clare.)

With Dame Urfula, the pigwoman, more grofs than her own pigs, even Ben Jonfon's rich colouring fhall not tempt us to make any intimate acquaintance. Juftice Overdo has her mifdeeds on record in the Piepoudres. Her booth, gay in front with its fign-board, and arbour, and, on the other fide, fmoky with the fire at which the

M 2

pigs roaft, is a den of infamy, and ufed as the head
quarters of a gang of thieves, headed by Ezechiel
Edgworth, the civil cut-purfe, a polite young gentleman,
in whom the difguifed Juftice Overdo, believing him to
be an honeft, fimple, and mifguided youth, takes a
benign intereft. Knockem the horfe-courfer is of the
fame company, and fo is Nightingale the ballad-finger,
whofe vocation it is to collect crowds, in which Edgworth
and his friends can operate, and, as a man not open to
fufpicion, to receive, when they can be paffed to him,
the purfes cut. Edgworth and he are great friends,
never afunder. He choofes good places near the fulleft
paffages to fing in, and fays his friend to him, " in your
finging you muft ufe your hawk's eye nimbly, and fly
the purfe to a mark ftill, where 'tis worn, and on which
fide ; that you may give me the fign with your beak, or
hang your head that way in the tune." What countryman can fufpect the man who fings him a Fairing of
Good Counfel, of an ell and three-quarters; or is warning
him with all his lungs to mind his pockets, in a Caveat
againft Cut-purfes. Cokes cannot doubt his honour.

Cokes and his friends have had adventures. Cokes has
had his pocket picked by Edgworth of his fmall change,
but he has his purfe of gold, and jingles it, and openly
defies all rogues in the fair to take it. He goes through
the fair with his hand in his pocket, firmly grafped about
his gold, a delicate fine trap, he thinks, to catch the
cut-purfe nibbling. He has been purchafing largely,
and has already loaded the back of his man Wafpe with
toys. " Would I had been fet in the ground," fays
Wafpe, " all but the head on me, and had my brains

bowled at, or threſhed out, when I firſt underwent this
charge." Winwife and Quarlous meet him with his load,
" Are you removing the Fair, Numps ? "—The voice of
Cokes, in barter, here breaks in with, " Thoſe ſix horſes,
friend, I'll have,—and the three Jews' trumps ; and
half a dozen o' birds, and that drum, (I have one drum
already,) and your ſmiths ; I like that device of your
ſmiths very pretty well ; and four halberts—and, let me
ſee, that fine painted great lady, and her three women
for ſtate, I'll have." The frantic Waſpe cries, " No, the
ſhop ; buy the whole ſhop, it will be beſt, the ſhop ! the
ſhop ! " and Cokes is conſidering of that, when the
gingerbread woman calls off his attention. " Is this well,
goody Joan," the toyman aſks, "to interrupt my market
in the midſt, and call away my cuſtomers ? Can you
anſwer this at the Piepoudres ? " But Cokes is ready to
buy ſhop and baſket. The toyman thus appraiſes his
eſtabliſhment : " Sir, it ſtands me in ſix and twenty
ſhillings and ſeven-pence halfpenny, beſides three ſhillings for my ground." Gingerbread woman thus appraiſes hers : " Four ſhillings and eleven-pence, ſir,
ground and all, an't like your worſhip." Whereunto
Cokes anſwers, " It does like my worſhip very well, poor
woman ; that's five ſhillings more : what a maſque ſhall
I furniſh out, for forty ſhillings, twenty pound Scotch,
and a banquet of gingerbread ! there's a ſtately thing !
Numps ? ſiſter ?—and my wedding gloves too ! that I
never thought on afore ! All my wedding gloves gingerbread ? O me ! what a device will there be, to make
'em eat their fingers' ends ! and delicate brooches for the
bridemen and all ! and then I'll have this poeſie put to

them, *For the beſt grace*, meaning Miſtreſs Grace, my wedding poeſie."

Miſtreſs Grace anſwers, "I am beholden to you, ſir, and to your Bartholomew wit." Then whiſpers the civil cut-purſe to the ballad-ſinger, "Yonder he is, buying of gingerbread; ſet in quickly, before he part with too much of his money." Nightingale the ballad-ſinger therefore comes near, and to the tune of Pagginton's Pound, begins:

> " My maſters, and friends, and good people draw near."

"Ballads! hark! hark! pray thee, fellow, ſtay a little; good Numps, look to the goods. What ballads haſt thou?—a Caveat againſt Cut-purſes! a good jeſt i' faith, I would fain ſee that demon, your cut-purſe, you talk of, that delicate-handed devil; they ſay he walks hereabouts, I would ſee him walk now."

Nightingale ſings:

> " My maſters and friends and good people draw near,
> And look to your purſes, for that I do ſay;
> And though little money in them you do bear,
> It coſts more to get than to loſe in a day.
>   You oft have been told,
>   Both the young and the old,
> And bidden beware of the cut-purſe ſo bold;
> Then if you take heed not, free me from the curſe,
> Who both give you warning, for, and the cut-purſe.
> Youth, youth, thou hadſt better been ſtarved by thy nurſe,
> Than live to be hanged for cutting a purſe!"

There are three other verſes, and while they are being ſung, the civil cut-purſe, tickling Cokes in the right ear with a ſtraw, has cauſed him, when off his guard, to take his right hand from his pocket. While he rubs his ear the purſe is gone. Winwife and Quarlous at the edge of the crowd ſee the theft committed. In Whalley's

edition of Ben Jonson's works, that is the scene illustra-
ted by the annexed engraving.   There is one etching on

Barthelemen Fair. Lud Du Guernier inv. et Sculp
1739.

copper before each play, the etchings all uniform and
done by the same Louis du Guernier, were first published

with the work that contained them in the year 1756. I
know not what fmall printfeller afterwards turned the
plate to account by re-iffuing prints from it infcribed
afrefh by himfelf, as a fketch of "Barthelemew Fair.
1739." The woodcut here given is a facfimile of the
re-iffued picture.

Soon afterwards Cokes is a victim to the trick, then
common, of pear-throwing. The coftermonger over-
fets his pears, Cokes joins in the cry, "A mufs! a
mufs!" and is eafed of his hat and cloak during the
fcramble. So far ftripped, he becomes an object for the
attention of the fmall boys of the Fair, who diligently
follow in his wake.

The ftolen goods find their way, for divifion at night
among the confederates, to the booth of Urfula. What
entertainment there is for the public in the "pig-box,"
we may learn from Urfula's directions to her tapfter,
who muft help alfo to wipe the pigs and mend the fire
that they drop not, and bafte and roaft them until they
are paffionate, and have wept out their eyes. "How can
I hope that e'er he'll difcharge his place of truft,
tapfter, a man of reckoning under me, that remembers
nothing I fay to him? but look to't firrah, you were
beft. Threepence a pipe-full, I will have made, of all
my whole half-pound of tobacco, and a quarter of pound
of coltsfoot mixt with it too, to eke it out. I that have
dealt fo long in the fire, will not be to feek in fmoke, now.
Then fix an' twenty fhillings a barrel I will advance on
my beer, and fifty fhillings a hundred on my bottle-
ale; I have told you the ways how to raife it. Froth
your cans well in the filling, at length, rogue, and jog

your bottles, firrah, then fkink out the firft glafs ever,
and drink with all companies, though you be fure to be
drunk ; you'll mifreckon the better, and be lefs afhamed
on't. But your true trick, rafcal, muft be, to be ever bufy,
and miftake away the bottles and cans in hafte, before
they be half drunk off, and never hear anybody call, (if
they fhould chance to mark you,) till you have brought
frefh, and be able to forfwear them.   Give me a drink
of ale .   .   .   .   .   Look who's there, firrah : five
fhillings a pig is my price, at leaft ; if it be a fow pig,
fixpence more ; if fhe be a wife, and long for 't, fixpence
more for that."   Here was enormity for Juftice Overdo
to overhear in his character of mad Arthur of Bradley, to
whom —becaufe a fool's handfel is lucky—Urfula gave a
fixpenny bottle of ale.   "Mad Arthur of Bradley that
makes the orations.   Brave mafter old Arthur of
Bradley, how do you do ? welcome to the Fair !   When
fhall we hear you again to handle your matters with
your back againft a booth, ha ?   I have been one of your
little difciples in my day."   The Juftice prefently beholds
what tempts him to hold forth upon bottle-ale and
tobacco.   Tobacco, "it caufeth fwearing, it caufeth
fwaggering, it caufeth fnaffling and fnarling, and now
and then a hurt."   In the Streights and the Bermudas,
intricate haunts of London pirates, "where the quarrelling leffons is read, how do they entertain the time but
with bottle-ale and tobacco ?   Then for a fuit to drink
in, fo much—and, that being flavered, fo much for
another fuit, and then a third fuit, and a fourth fuit !
and ftill the bottle-ale flavereth, and the tobacco
ftinketh."   The irritated Wafpe falls upon Overdo, who

cries to him, " Hold thy hand, child of wrath, and heir of anger, make it not Childermas day in thy fury, or the feaſt of the French Bartholomew, parent of the maſſacre ! "

In the mean time the watchmen of the Fair are fetched from place to place, but ſo buſy about beggars that they have no leiſure for gentlemen thieves. Beſides there was one of them, Toby Haggiſe, falling under juſt reproach of his comrade Davy Briſtle, "You ſaid let's go to Urſula's indeed ; but then you met the man with the monſters, and I could not get you from him. An old fool, not leave ſeeing yet!" A monſter, according to the derivation of the word, means in the firſt ſenſe a ſhow, a thing to be pointed at, and in that firſt ſenſe it was then uſed in Bartholomew Fair with a tie of the word to living won-ders, ſuch as the dog Toby, the dogs that dance the morrice, the eagle, the black wolf, the bull with five legs,— he was a calf at Uxbridge fair two years agone,—the Hare of the Tabor,* and the great hog, all of which we find named in the play.

The mention of the hog recals to us the Brother Buſy who, leading his flock into the Fair, exhorted them to " walk on in the middle way, fore-right, turn neither to

---

* The Hare that played the Tabor was an ancient monſter, for this ſketch of him is from an illuminated MS. of Hours of the Virgin, painted three centuries before Ben Jonſon's time. Strutt firſt copied it, and his rough copy has been ſeveral times recopied. I need hardly add, that for the above ſketch the draughtſman has gone to the MS. itſelf.

the right hand, nor to the left, let not your eyes be
drawn aſide with vanity, nor your ear with noiſes." The
traders cry, what do you lack? but the Rabbi exclaims,
" Look not toward them, hearken not; the place is
Smithfield, or the field of ſmiths, the grove of hobby-
horſes and trinkets, the wares are the wares of devils, and
the whole Fair is the ſhop of Satan : they are hooks and
baits, very baits, that are hung out on every ſide to
catch you, and to hold you, as it were, by the gills, and
by the noſtrils, as the fiſher doth ; therefore you muſt
not look nor turn toward them." Was he driving his
flock into the pens, that he would let them look on
nothing? Littlewit, reproved by Dame Purecraft for
reading the board over Urſula's booth, aſks how they
ſhall find pig if they do not look about for it. Will it
run off the ſpit into our mouths, think you, as in Lub-
berland, and, and cry " Wee, wee ! " " No," anſwers
the Rabbi Zeal-of-the-Land. " No, but your mother,
religiouſly wiſe, conceiveth it may offer itſelf by other
means to the ſenſe, as by way of ſteam, which I think
it doth here in this place—huh—huh, yes it doth. [*He
ſcents after it like a hound.*] And it were a ſin of
obſtinacy, great obſtinacy, high and horrible obſtinacy, to
decline or reſiſt the good titillation of the famelic ſenſe,
which is the ſmell. Therefore be bold—huh, huh, huh,
follow the ſcent : enter the tents of the unclean, for
once, and ſatisfy your wife's frailty. Let your frail wife
be ſatisfied ; your zealous mother, and my ſuffering
ſelf, will alſo be ſatisfied."

" Mooncalf ! " the horſe-courſer ſhouts, " entertain
within there ; the beſt pig in the booth, a pork-like pig.

Thefe are Banbury bloods, o' the fincere ftud, come a pig-hunting."

"Sippers!" grumbles Urfe, "fippers o' the city; they look as they would not drink off two pen'orth of bottle-ale amongft 'em."

And Mooncalf opines that a body may read that in their fmall printed ruffs.

But Knockem has a wider knowledge of the world than the old hermit of the pig-box, "Away," he fays, "thou art a fool, Urfe, and thy Mooncalf too: in your ignorant vapours now! hence! good guefts, I fay, right hypocrites, good gluttons. In, and fet a couple o' pigs on the board, and half a dozen of the biggeft bottles afore 'em. I do not love to hear innocents abufed; fine ambling hypocrites! and a ftone puritan with a forrel head and beard! good mouthed gluttons; two to a pig, away." "Are you fure they are fuch?" "O' the right breed, thou fhalt try 'em by the teeth, Urfe."

The horfe-courfer, retired within the booth, waits upon Bufy for converfion. As they come out together, Knockem is a profeffed convert, who will take good counfel, cut his hair and leave vapours. He fees that tobacco, and bottle-ale, and pig, and very Urfula herfelf are all vanities. "Only pig," fays the Rabbi, "was not comprehended in my admonition, the reft were: for long hair, it is an enfign of pride, a banner; and the world is full of thofe banners; very full of banners. And bottle-ale is a drink of Satan's, a diet-drink of Satan's, devifed to puff us up, and make us fwell in this latter age of vanity; as the fmoke of tobacco, to keep us in mift and error." "Win," fays Dame Purecraft, "is again longing."

"For more pig," cries the Rabbi hungrily. "There is no more, is there?" Not for more pig, but to fee fome fights of the Fair.

"Sifter, let her fly the impurity of the place fwiftly, left fhe partake of the pitch thereof. Thou art the feat of the beaft, O Smithfield, and I will leave thee! Idolatry peepeth out on every fide of thee!"—Says the man of the ftables, "now his belly is full, he falls a railing and kicking, the jade. I'll in, and joy Urfula, with telling how her pig works; two and a half he ate to his fhare; and he has drunk a pailful. He eats with his eyes, as well as his teeth." The toyman cries: "What do you lack, gentlemen? what is't you buy? rattles, drums, babies——"

"Peace," roars Bufy, "peace with thy apocryphal wares, thou profane publican; thy bells, thy dragons, and thy Tobie's dogs. Thy hobby-horfe is an idol, a very idol; a fierce and rank idol; and thou, the Nebuchadnezzar, the proud Nebuchadnezzar of the Fair, that fett'ft it up, for children to fall down to, and worfhip.

"What is a drum? It is the broken belly of the beaft, and thy bellows there are his lungs, and thefe pipes are his throat, thofe feathers are of his tail, and thy rattles the gnafhing of his teeth."

"And what's my gingerbread, I pray you?" afks Dame Trafh.

"The provender that pricks him up. Hence with thy bafket of popery, thy neft of images, and whole legend of ginger-work.

"The fin of the Fair provokes me," cries the Rabbi, "I cannot be filent.

" Hinder me not, woman.   I was moved in fpirit, to be here this day, in this Fair, this wicked and foul Fair; and fitter may it be called a Foul than a Fair; to proteft againft the abufes of it, the foul abufes of it, in regard of the afflicted faints, that are troubled, very much troubled, exceedingly troubled, with the opening of the merchandife of Babylon again, and the peeping of popery upon the ftalls here, here, in the high places. See you not Goldylocks, the purple woman there, in her yellow gown and green fleeves? the profane pipes, the tinkling timbrels? a fhop of relicks ! "

The jeft is typical.   This Rabbi Bufy was, in Ben Jonfon's age, the character moft dwelt upon and enjoyed by the fpectators of the play.   The other characters were of all generations; he was a man of the day itfelf, and yet more of the day next coming, as the play-writer well knew.   More than an idle jeft was meant when the Rabbi fell on the toys, overthrew the ginger-bread bafket in his zeal and glory to be thus exercifed, and to thofe, who fending him to the ftocks, cried, " Stop his noife," fhouted, " Thou canft not; 'tis a fanctified noife : I will make a loud and moft ftrong noife, till I have daunted the profane enemy."   At the ftocks,—" the pigeon-holes,"—he cried, " No, minifter of darknefs, no; thou canft not rule my tongue; my tongue it is mine own, and with it I will both knock and mock down your Bartholomew abominations, till you be made a hiffing to the neighbouring parifhes round about."   And in the ftocks he declares himfelf, " One that rejoiceth in his affliction, and fitteth here to prophefy the deftruction of Fairs and May games,

Wakes, and Whitſon-ales, and doth ſigh and groan for
the reformation of theſe abuſes."

Set free, and engaged in a new battle againſt the puppets, the Rabbi ſpeaks indeed prophetic words : " I look
for a bickering ere long, and then a battle." He is a
hypocrite trailing through mud upon the ſkirts of a great
Truth. The Rabbi's real character, as well as her own,
Dame Purecraft reveals to one whom ſhe has found in
the Fair, and takes for her appointed madman :

" Good ſir, hear me. I am worth ſix thouſand pound,
my love to you is become my rack ; I'll tell you all and
the truth, ſince you hate the hypocriſy of the party-
coloured brotherhood. Theſe ſeven years I have been
a wilful holy widow, only to draw feaſts and gifts from
my entangled ſuitors : I am alſo by office an aſſiſting
ſiſter of the deacons, and a devourer, inſtead of
diſtributor of the alms. I am a ſpecial maker of
marriages for our decayed brethren with our rich widows,
for a third part of their wealth, when they are married,
for the relief of the poor elect : as alſo our poor handſome young virgins, with our wealthy bachelors or
widowers ; to make them ſteal from their huſbands,
when I have confirmed them in the faith, and got all put
into their cuſtodies. And if I have not my bargain,
they may ſooner turn a ſcolding drab into a ſilent
miniſter, than make me leave pronouncing reprobation
and damnation unto them. Our elder, Zeal-of-the-Land,
would have had me, but I know him to be the capital
knave of the land, making himſelf rich by being made a
feoffee in truſt to deceaſed brethren, and cozening their
heirs by ſwearing the abſolute gift of their inheritance."

The uncared-for madman, then a neceſſary figure in
every true picture of a public feſtival, is a diſcharged
ſervant of the piepowder court, " mad child of the Piepoudres," who flits through the Fair with no thought
but of Juſtice Overdo, and the tremendous efficacy of
his warrant.   Ingenious uſe is made of him in the elabo-
ration of the ſtory of the Comedy.   Of the ſtory,
however, in this place, only that part concerns us, which
belongs eſſentially to the portrayal of the Fair.   We
need not even look at Juſtice Overdo comforting himſelf
with philoſophy as he ſits alſo in the ſtocks.   The ſole
buſineſs of this chapter is to contain all that the play tells
us of the Fair in Smithfield, in Ben Jonſon's time ; and
we have now only to walk into the puppet ſhow, before
we part from our rare guide.

Lanthorn Leatherhead has left his hobby-horſes, and
is dreſſed as a puppet ſhowman : he is the proſperous
mechanic, who makes all the puppets in the Fair.
(Inigo Jones, ſay acute commentators.—Let no one
be " ſo ſolemnly ridiculous as to ſearch out, who was
meant by the gingerbread woman, who by the hobby-
horſe man, who by the coſtard-monger, nay who by
their wares," ſays Ben Jonſon.)   Leatherhead appears
before his booth with his two men ; one plants a flag,
and rolls out the ſign of his invention, while the other
beats the drum.   " All the dirt in Smithfield will be
thrown at our banner to day, if the matter does not
pleaſe the people.   O the motions that I Lanthorn
Leatherhead have given light to, in my time, ſince my
maſter Pod died ! Jeruſalem was a ſtately thing, and ſo
was Nineveh, and the city of Norwich, and Sodom and

Gomorrah, with the rifing of the prentices upon Shrove-Tuefday ; but the Gun-powder plot, there was a get-penny ! I have prefented that to an eighteen or twenty pence audience, nine times in an afternoon. Your homeborn projects prove ever the beft, they are fo eafy and familiar ; they put too much learning in their things now o' days : and that I fear will be the fpoil of this. Littlewit ! I fay, Micklewit ! if not too mickle ! look to your gathering there, goodman Filcher."—" I warrant you, fir."—" An there come any gentlefolks, take two-pence apiece, Sharkwell."—" I warrant you, fir, three-pence an we can."

Sharkwell and Filcher then deliver handbills of " The Ancient Modern Hiftory " (a jeft at the old fchool of Lamentable Tragedy . . . . mixt full of pleafant mirth,) *The Ancient Modern Hiftory of Hero and Leander, other-wife called the Touchftone of true Love, with as true a Trial of Friendfhip between Damon and Pythias, two faithful friends o' the Bankfide.*" " Pleafe you come near, we'll take your money within." " Two-pence apiece, gentlemen, an excellent motion."—" Shall we have fine fireworks ? " afks one as he enters.—" Two-pence apiece, fir, the beft motion in the Fair." Cokes hurries in of courfe, leaving his train of Bartholomew boys at the door. He looks over the bafket full of puppets, and then afks, referring to Marlowe's tranfla-tion of the Hero and Leander from Mufæus, " But do you play it according to the printed book ? I have read that."—" By no means, fir."—" No ! how then ? "—" A better way, fir ; that is too learned and poetical for our audience : what do they know what *Hellefpont* is, *guilty*

N

of true love's blood? or what *Abydos* is? or *the other Seſtos hight?* "—" Thou art in the right; I do not know myſelf."—" No, I have entreated maſter Littlewit to take a little pains to reduce it to a more familiar ſtrain for our people."—" How I pray thee, good maſter Littlewit?" The author then explains: " It pleaſes him to make a matter of it, ſir; but there is no ſuch matter, I aſſure you: I have only made it a little eaſy, and modern for the times, ſir, that's all. As for the Helleſpont, I imagine our Thames here; and then Leander I make a dyer's ſon about Puddle-wharf: and Hero a wench o' the Bankſide, who going over one morning to Old Fiſh-ſtreet, Leander ſpies her land at Trig-ſtairs, and falls in love with her. Now do I introduce Cupid, having metamorphoſed himſelf into a drawer, and he ſtrikes Hero in love with a pint of ſherry; and other pretty paſſages there are of the friendſhip, that will delight you, ſir, and pleaſe you of judgment."

This burleſque puppet play, which had been written by Ben Jonſon ſome time before, is then pleaſantly interwoven with the general ſtory. Its jeſts lie in the abſurd reduction of the higheſt old thoughts, to the loweſt new ones, in the confuſion of plot, the multitude of perſonal encounters,—even Damon and Pythias muſt needs belabour one another,—and in the liberal uſe of language moſt in accordance with the taſtes of the fouleſt people in the Fair. Upon the puppet play Zeal-of-the land Buſy, eſcaped from the ſtocks, ſuddenly falls in with a ſhout, " Down with Dagon! down with Dagon! 'tis I, I will no longer endure your profanations."

" What mean you, fir?" afks the fhowman.—" I
will remove Dagon there, I fay, that idol, that heathenifh idol, that remains, as I may fay, a beam, a very
beam,—not a beam of the fun, nor a beam of the moon,
nor a beam of a balance, neither a houfe-beam, nor a
weaver's beam, but a beam in the eye, in the eye of the
brethren; a very great beam, an exceeding great beam;
fuch as are your ftage-players, rhymers, and morrice-
dancers, who have walked hand in hand, in contempt of
the brethren, and the caufe; and been borne out by
inftruments of no mean countenance."—"Sir, I prefent
nothing but what is licenfed by authority."—" Thou art
all licence, even licentioufnefs itfelf, Shimei!"—" I have
the Mafter of the Revels' hand for't, fir."—" The
mafter of the rebels' hand thou haft: Satan's! Hold thy
peace, thy fcurrility, fhut up thy mouth, thy profeffion
is damnable, and in pleading for it thou doft plead for
Baal. I have long opened my mouth wide, and gaped;
I have gaped as the oyfter for the tide, after thy
deftruction: but I cannot compafs it by fuit or difpute :
fo that I look for a bickering ere long, and then a
battle."

Bufy then offers controverfy, and Leatherhead undertakes that his puppet Dionyfius fhall argue for him.
The argument confifts wholly of recrimination, and at
the end of it, to the great delight of the audiences of
Ben Jonfon's day, Bufy cries out " I am confuted, the
caufe hath failed me." Then fays the puppet, "Be
converted, be converted." " Be converted, I pray
you," urges alfo the fhowman, "and let the play go
on." " Let it go on," fays Bufy, "for I am changed,

and will become a beholder with you." It was well; but a time came when Lord Buckhurft had to write a comment upon this :—

> Many have been the vain attempts of wit,
> Againſt the ſtill prevailing hypocrite.
> Once, and but once, a poet got the day,
> And vanquiſhed Buſy in a puppet play.
> But Buſy rallying, filled with holy rage,
> Poſſeſſed the pulpit, and pulled down the ſtage.

The ſtrength of the Puritans in Banbury dates from a time yet earlier than the induction into the vicarage of Thomas Braſbridge, who in 1590, for Puritan reaſons, ceaſed to be vicar. In 1602 the Zeal of the town cauſed the deſtruction of its public croſs, and the defacing of the ornaments of the cathedral. Banbury had ſent Anthony Cope, and other Puritan members to Parliament; its member for the Parliament of 1623, Sir Eraſmus Dryden, was the grandfather of John Dryden the poet. The vicar of Banbury when Ben Jonſon's Bartholomew Fair was written,—for the four years before, and ſix-and-twenty after that date,—was the famous William Whately, a Cambridge man, and a ſcholar, eminent for bounty to the poor from little means, who had a moſt able body, and ſuch found lungs, that for his ſtyle of preaching he was called "the Roaring Boy of Banbury." Scudder, his diſciple and biographer, tells that "according as his matter in hand and his auditory needed, he was both a terrible Boanerges, a ſon of thunder, and alſo a Barnabas, a ſon of ſweet conſolation." Fuller probably identified this contemporary vicar of Banbury with Rabbi Buſy, when he ſaid, "Indeed he was a good linguift, philofopher, mathematician, divine; and (though a poetical, fatirical pen is pleafed to pafs a jeer upon him) free from faction." Whately was in the habit of ftirring up the faithful at Stratford on Avon, by a periodical lecture. In one fenfe he was Ben Jonfon's fellow worker, for his publifhed works include two volumes of fermons againft hypocrites. A doughty brother labourer with Whately was his fifter's hufband, Robert Harris of Hanwell. He alfo gave at one time, fortnightly lectures to the people of Stratford on Avon, and befides preaching in his own church, lectured at Deddington and Banbury. We are told that troops of Chriftians came on Sundays many miles from all quarters to hear Harris at Hanwell, and on the morrow were in like manner " entertained at Banbury, by Mr. Whately. What a Fair of Souls," cries Durham, the biographer of Harris, "was then held at Hanwell and Banbury by thefe two brothers! How did religion flourifh! how did profeffors thrive!" Againft any fuch Fair of Souls Bartholomew Fair whiftled its fifes, rolled its drums, and fqueaked its trumpets of defiance.

CHAPTER XI.

Oliver's Day.

On the fourth of Auguſt in the firſt year of the reign
of Charles the Firſt, (A.D.) 1625, "the king's moſt
excellent Majeſty, out of his princely and chriſtian care
of his loving ſubjects, that no good means of Providence
may be neglected to ſtay the farther ſpreading of the
great infection of the Plague, doth find it neceſſary to
prevent all occaſions of public concourſe of his people
for the preſent, till it ſhall pleaſe Almighty God, of His
goodneſs, to ceaſe the violence of the contagion, which
is very far diſperſed into many parts of the kingdom
already ;   And therefore, remembering that there are at
hand two Fairs of ſpecial note, and unto which" (let
this conſideration be obſerved) "there is uſually extraordinary reſort *out of all parts of the kingdom,* the one
kept in Smithfield, near the City of London, called
Bartholomew Fair, and the other near Cambridge,
called Stourbridge Fair, the holding whereof at the uſual
times, would in all likelihood be the occaſion of further
danger and infection to other parts of the Land, which
yet, by God's mercy, ſtand clear and free, hath, with
the advice of his Majeſty's Privy Council, thought

good, by this open declaration of his pleasure and neceffary commandment, not only to admonish and require all his loving subjects to forbear to refort for this time to either of the said two Fairs, or to any other fairs within fifty miles of the said City of London, but also to enjoin the Lords of the said Fairs, and others interested in them, or any of them, that they all forbear to hold the said Fairs, or anything appertaining to them, at all times accustomed or at any time, till by God's goodness and mercy the infection of the Plague shall ceafe, or be so much diminished, that his Majesty shall give order for holding them ; upon pain of such punishment as, for a contempt so much concerning the universal fafety of his people, they shall be adjudged to deserve, which they must expect to be inflicted with all severity, his Majesty's desire being so intentive for preventing the general Infection threatened, as he is refolved to spare no man that shall be the cause of dispersing the same. And to that purpose doth hereby further charge and enjoin, under like penalty, all citizens and inhabitants of the said City of London, that none of them shall repair to any fair held within any part of this kingdom, until it shall pleafe God to ceafe the infection now reigning amongst them : His Majesty's intention being, and so hereby declaring himself, that no Lord of any Fairs, or. others interested in the profits thereof, shall by this neceffary and temporary restraint, receive any prejudice in the right of his or their fairs, or liberties thereunto belonging, anything before mentioned notwithstanding." This proclamation, given at the court at Woodstock, best tells its own story.

Again, on the firſt of Auguſt in the year 1630, the Plague being in Cambridge and then threatening London and Southwark, the King remembered that there were " at hand three great Fairs of Special note, unto which there is extraordinary reſort from all parts of the kingdom," and forbade the holding of Bartholomew, Stourbridge, and Our Lady (or Southwark) Fair.

A zeal in the land that was not hypocriſy had been buſy to ſome purpoſe between the year 1614, in which Ben Jonſon's Comedy of Bartholomew Fair was firſt preſented before James the Firſt, and the year 1641, the date which next concerns us in the preſent narrative. The king's " princely and Chriſtian care of his loving ſubjects" was in queſtion.   There was a diſeaſe in the land, for the abatement of which not the king, but the People, had ſent forth a proclamation.

In the year 1641 Charles the Firſt aſſented to the bill for the attainder of Strafford, and Strafford died on the ſcaffold in the preſence of a hundred thouſand perſons.

At Bartholomew Fair time in that year the King was in Scotland, and the Commons were nominating commiſſioners, who, in the name of honourable attendance, were to watch the monarch who had forfeited all truſt.   The ſtate of Bartholomew Fair is repreſented by the oldeſt of the extant tracts profeſſing to deſcribe it, a ſmall quarto of four leaves, containing five pages of print appended to this title-page :

BARTHOLOMEVV FAIRE

OR

Variety of fancies, vvhere you may find a faire of vvares, and all to pleafe your mind

With

The feverall Enormityes and mifdemeanours, which are there feene and acted

LONDON

Printed for *Richard Harper* at the *Bible* and *Harpe* in Smithfield, 1641.

" Bartholomew Fair," we are here told, " begins on the twenty-fourth day of Auguft, and is then of fo vaft an extent, that it is contained in no lefs than four feveral parifhes, namely, Chrift Church, Great and Little Saint Bartholomews, and Saint Sepulchres. Hither refort people of all forts, high and low, rich and poor, from cities, towns, and countries ; of all sects, Papists, Atheists, Anabaptists, and Brownists ; and of all condi-tions. . . . And now that we may the better take an exact survey of the whole fair, First let us enter into Christ Church Cloisters, which are now hung so full of pictures, that you would take that place, or rather mistake it, for Saint Peters in Rome ; only this is the difference, those there are set up for worship, these here for sale." (It will be remembered that the disputations of the scholars were held in these cloisters, still therefore within the Fair, when they were held at all after the dissolution of the Priory.) "But by the way," goes on the tract, "I'll tell you a tale of a precise Puritan, who came in all haste from Lincoln to London, purposely to see the fair, where he had never been before, and coming out of Newgate Market, through Christ Church into the Cloisters, and elevating the snowballs of his eyes, he presently espies the picture of Christ and his twelve Apostles, with the Virgin Mary and many other Saints departed ; at which sight the very thought and strong conceit of superstition set such a sharp edge upon the pure metal of his inflamed zeal, that very manfully, like a man of valour and son of Mars, he steps to a stall well stored with twopenny halberds and wooden backswords, where, having armed himself *cap-à-pie* (as he thought) he begins in a violent passion to exclaim against the Idolatry of the times, that it was grown abominable ; protesting that the woman of Babylon was crept into Christ Church, and that the good motions of the spirit had brought him to town, to make a sacrifice of those idle Idols to his just anger and holy indignation, which begot no fmall laughter to the multitude which thronged about him, that put him into fuch a chafe, infomuch that at the laft, like Roficleare, the Knight of the Sun, or Don Quixote, moft furioufly he makes an affault and battery upon the poor innocent pictures, till the fhop-keepers apprehending him, had him before a conftable, who forthwith committed my little hot fury to the ftocks, where we will leave him to cool his heels, whilft we take a further view of the fair. And now being arrived through the Long Walk, to Saint Bartholomew's Hofpital ; that place (methinks) appears to me a fucking Exchange." A devil's mart, truly ; exchange of filth for baubles of the fair. "Let us now make a progrefs into Smithfield, which is the heart of the fair, where in *my* heart, I think there are more motions in a day to be feen, than are in a term in Weftminfter Hall to be heard. But whilft you take notice of the feveral motions there, take this caution along with you, let one eye watch narrowly that no one's hand make a motion into your pocket, which is the next way to move you to impatience. The fair is full of gold and filver drawers : Juft as Lent is to the fifhmonger, fo is Bartholomew Fair to the pickpocket ; it is his high harveft, which is never bad, but when his cart goes" (Tyburnia way) "up Holborn. The City marfhals are as dreadful to thefe youngfters as the Plague is to the London Actors. That reftrains them from playing, and they hinder thefe from working ; you may quickly know thefe nimble youths, and likely find them very bufybodies in a quarrel which nothing concerns them. . . . Some of your cut purfes are in fee with cheating coftermongers, who have a trick now and then to throw down a baſket of refuſe pears, which prove cloake pears to thoſe who ſhall loſe their hats or choaks" (I cannot ſay that the miſprints are not meant to be funny, therefore re-produce them,) " in ſtriving who ſhall gather faſteſt. They have many dainty baits to draw a bit, and (if you be not vigilant) you ſhall hardly eſcape their nets : fine fowlers they are, for every finger of theirs is a lime twig, with which they catch dotterels. They are excellently well read in Phyſiognomy, for they will know how ſtrong you are in the purſe by looking in your face ; and for the more certainty thereof, they will follow you cloſe, and never leave you till you draw your purſe, or they for you, which they'll be ſure to have (if you look not to it) though they kiſs Newgate for it.

" It is remarkable and worth your obſervation, to behold and hear the ſtrange ſights and confuſed noiſes in the fair. Here a Knave in a Fool's Coat, with a trumpet ſounding, or on a drum beating, invites you and would fain perſuade you to ſee his puppets ; there a Rogue like a Wild Woodman, or in an antick ſhape like an Incubus, deſires your company to view his motion ; on the other ſide Hocus Pocus with three yards of tape or ribbon in's hand, ſhowing his art of Legerdemain to the admiration and aſtoniſhment of a company of cocko-loaches. Amongſt theſe you ſhall ſee a gray gooſe-cap (as wiſe as the reſt,) with a What do ye lack? in his mouth, ſtand in his booth ſhaking a rattle, or ſcraping on a fiddle, with which children are ſo taken, that they pre-ſently cry out for theſe fopperies ; And all theſe together make ſuch a diſtracted noiſe, that you would think Babel were not comparable to it. Here there are alfo your gamefters in action; fome turning of a whimfey, others throwing for pewter, who can quickly diffolve a round fhilling into a three half penny faucer.

"Long Lane at this time looks very fair, and puts out her beft clothes with the wrong fide outward, fo turned for their better turning off; And Cloth Fair is now in great requeft : well fare the Ale houfes therein ; yet better may a man fare (but at a dearer rate) in the Pig market, alias Pafty nook or Pie Corner, where pigs are all hours of the day on the ftalls piping hot, and would cry (if they could fpeak) Come eat me ; but they are . . . . dear, and the reckonings for them are . . . faucy. . . . . . Thefe unconfcionable exactions, and exceffive inflammations of reckonings made that angle of the fair too hot for my company ; therefore I refolved with myfelf to fteer my courfe another way, and having once got out, not to come again in hafte.

> " Now farewell to the Fair ; you who are wife,
> Preferve your Purfes, whilft you pleafe your eyes.

FINIS."

Of the commercial importance ftill at this date attached to fairs, I find an indication in the warden's accounts of expenditure preferved among the records of the Skinners' Company.* In 1606 there is an item, " To the Wardens for their allowance in riding to Stourbridge

---

* Thanks are due to Mr. Kenfit, the Clerk of the Skinners' Company, for his courtefy in giving me information, and permitting me to refer to records that might have contained matter effential to this Hiftory.

Fair, £3 6s. 8d., and 13s. 4d. to me the Renter Warden for my pains." But ten years afterwards the beginning of a change may be implied by the fact that the wardens ceafed to go in perfon to the fairs. It is the accountant who receives, "in allowance towards his charges in riding to Stourbridge Fair, £6," and for the journey to Briftol Fair, £6 13s. 6d.

St. Bartholomew's Cloth Fair, well fupplied with ale-houfes, was at this date ftill a place of much refort; and of the family receiving toll from it we muft now trace the line, for in due time we fhall reach a Lady of the houfe, whofe name became, for the reft of the Fair's life, known only too well to the dwellers about Smithfield.

Of Richard Rich, the Lord Chancellor, firft Lord and founder of the family, by whom the tolls of Bartholomew Fair, formerly due to the Priory, were bought for himfelf and his heirs, we have already fpoken. He died in 1568, leaving behind him ill-fame and a mafs of treafure.

His fon Robert, fecond Baron Rich, was one of the friends of Effex, who went with him in his expedition to Ireland in 1573, and fhared fome of his "mifery, by plague, famine, ficknefs, continual toil, and continual wants of men, money, carriages, victuals, and all things meet for great attempts." He died in 1581, to be fucceeded by his fon and heir, another Robert, the third Baron Rich.

The third Baron was alive, and was ftill only Lord Rich on that 31ft of October 1614, when Ben Jonfon's Bartholomew Fair was firft produced at the Hope theatre in Bankfide. He procured the rank of Earl of

Warwick, two or three weeks before the Fair time, four years afterwards. What do you lack? what do you buy? was the cry of the Stuarts, recklefs and bankrupt traders, huckfter-kings. James the Firft invented baronetcies as a way of raifing money, charging £5000 for a baronetcy, and £20,000 for an earldom.

This was the Lord Rich who had married the Lady Penelope Devereux, daughter of Walter, Earl of Effex, the bright Stella who had Sidney for an Aftrophel. The dying hope of Effex was, that if God fo moved their hearts, Sidney might be the hufband of his eldeft daughter, then about fifteen years old. She grew to be a lady of furpaffing beauty, and was by her friends fold into unwelcome marriage with Lord Rich, "a man" fays Heylin, "of an independent fortune, and a known eftate, but otherwife of an uncourtly difpofition, unfociable, auftere, and of no very agreeable converfation to her." Aftrophel then fang of her :—

> " Rich in all beauties that man's eye can fee,
>   Beauties fo far from reach of words that we
>   Abafe her praife faying fhe doth excel :
>   Rich in the treafure of deferved renown,
>   Rich in the riches of a royal heart,
>   Rich in thofe gifts which give the eternal crown ;
>   Who though moft rich in thefe and every part
>   Which makes the patents of true worldly blifs,
>   Hath no misfortune but that RICH fhe is."

Of her fang alfo Spenfer, when as Colin Clout he praifed the beauties of the Englifh Court :

> " Ne lefs praifeworthy Stella do I read,
>   Though nought my praifes of her needed are,
>   Whom verfe of nobleft fhepherd lately dead,
>   Hath praifed and raifed above each other ftar."

As Lady Rich, tolls of Bartholomew Fair helped to adorn her perſon.   But this exalted lady was a falling ſtar, who did not ever remain " rich in the riches of deſerved renown."   Even at the altar ſhe had made proteſt againſt her unhappy marriage.   Afterwards, loved much abroad and little loved at home, the heart that Lord Rich never aſked for, ſhe gave to another.   There was an actual before there was a judicial ſeparation from her huſband. After three months of ſecond marriage, ſhe was left the widow of Montjoy, Earl of Devonſhire, whoſe fair fame periſhed at the Court, when he reſolved to end in ſacred honour what he had begun in ſhame.   King James was even ſlow to forgive Laud for having tied that ſecond knot.   Poor lady,

> " Wit's ornament, earth's love, love's paradiſe,
>   A faint divine, a beauty fairly wife,"—

ſhe was a woman of bright wit and noble temper, ſet with a dry cruſt in the midſt of all temptations of the banquet.   Robert Lord Rich took in ſecond marriage a full-purſed Lancaſhire widow,—two years after the firſt acting of Ben Jonſon's Bartholomew Fair,—and was ſaid, a year afterwards by Chamberlain, " to be in great perplexity, or rather crazed in brain, to ſee himſelf over-reached by his wife, who hath ſo conveyed her eſtate, that he is little or nothing the better by her, and, if ſhe outlive him, like to carry away a great part of his."   There were three ſons and three daughters of Lord Rich and his firſt wife, but no children by the ſecond marriage.   It was for the deſcendants therefore of Stella that he by help of money obtained, in 1618, his

earldom.   He had wifhed to be made Earl of Clare ; but
Clare being a like title with Clarence was, fays Camden,
" a higher honour than could well fuit with a family in a
manner upftart."   The earldom of Warwick, which
had become extinct in 1561, upon the death of Ambrofe
Dudley, was conferred, therefore, on Robert, third Baron
Rich, whom as a wealthy mifer unhappy in marriage,
the world mocked with the name of Cornucopia.   From
him I need hardly fay that the prefent Earls of Warwick
do not trace defcent.   The earldom, after the extinction of
the line of Rich, paffed in the year 1759 to the defcendants of its firft poffeffors.   Robert Rich having obtained
this earldom, and given to the manfion in Cloth Fair the
name of Warwick Houfe, lived but a few months longer.

The eldeft fon of Cornucopia, again a Robert, held the
earldom of Warwick forty years (1618—1658).   This is
the Earl of Warwick who was Lord High Admiral under
the Long Parliament, a man who was liberal-handed, and
full of wit and energy and cheerfulnefs.   He was three
times married : firft to a rich heirefs, daughter of Sir
William Hatton, and from her alone he received children.
It was a grandfon of his who married one of the Protector
Cromwell's daughters.   The fecond fon given to Robert
Rich of the money-bags, by Stella, was Henry Rich,
who became Earl of Holland.   Henry Rich was a
handfome man, of winning prefence, and a gentle converfation.   Therefore, after two or three campaigns in
Holland, he attached himfelf to the Court, and fought,
fays Clarendon, to be efteemed the creature of the Duke
of Buckingham, and the friend of the Earl of Carlifle.
He courted thofe who ruled the King.   He was made

Knight of the Bath in 1611, and in 1618 Captain of the King's Guard. He married the daughter and heirefs of Sir Walter Cope, who brought with her a good fortune, and the manor and feat of Kenfington, of which he was fhortly afterwards, in 1623, made Baron. The Duke of Buckingham then prevailed with his fovereign to place the Baron Kenfington about the perfon of the Prince of Wales, as Gentleman of the bed-chamber to his Royal Highnefs. He was employed alfo at the Spanifh court, upon diplomacy relating to Prince Charles's wedding with a daughter of the King of Spain. In 1625 he was made Earl of Holland, in Lincolnfhire, and foon afterwards inftalled as Knight of the Garter. He was the firft ambaffador fent into France to treat of the marriage between Charles and his Queen, and being left, after the Duke of Buckingham's affaffination, high in favour, he took pains to ingratiate himfelf with the Queen, as well as with the King, and fought againft the Duke of Portland, and all who were oppofed thereto, the increafe of her authority. Thus, knowing her to be the king's mafter, he earned her particular truft, and contrived to become one of the moft profperous men at the court of Charles the Firft. He was made General of the Horfe in the army raifed againft the Scotch covenanters, in 1639; but he retreated when he came to face the Scotch at Dunfe, and afterwards received with evident good will their overtures for the fuppreffion of a civil ftrife. Returned to court, he put afide a challenge from the Earl of Newcaftle, and he was not employed in the next Scotch expedition, becaufe there were engaged in it the counfels of Strafford, who had once angrily fuggefted that the King would do well to take the Earl of Holland's head, and who was met by the Earl thereafter with open hatred. He was prefently appointed one of the King's Commiffioners to treat with the Scots at Ripon, and was among thofe who were induced to regard their defires with favour. He ferved the office of chief juftice in Eyre, and was accufed of oppreffion and ex-action : but taking offence at the King's refufal to create at his requeft a baron, when he could have made ten thou-fand pounds by the tranfaction, he altered his courfe ; and when, as general for the difbanding of the armies after the fecond Scotch expedition, he returned to his houfe at Ken-fington, the Earl of Holland belonged to the popular party. It was he who read to the King in 1642 the defire of both houfes that his Majefty would refide near Parlia-ment. He was therefore removed from his office of Firft Gentleman of the bed-chamber. In January 1643, he was one of the Comiffioners fent by Parliament to the King with propofitions of peace, he himfelf being at all times difpofed to eftablifh peace on eafy terms, for he had much property imperilled by a doubtful ftrife. Soon afterwards he was, with the Earl of Bedford, a deferter from the Parliament, received into the King's garrifon at Wallingford with a cold welcome. But he had already eftablifhed, from the time of her landing, a private underftanding with the Queen, and being reftored to her favour, fancied that he faw his way before him. He joined the King's army at Gloucefter, fought well at the battle of Newbury, and returned to Oxford with King Charles who, ftill diftrufting him, faw through the arts of a courtier in which he was proficient. He was unwife

enough to fpeak highly at court of the power of Parliament; "which," faid the King, "was a ftrange
difcourfe for a man to make, who had fo lately left them
becaufe he thought the King's condition to be the better
of the two." When, difappointed in every way by
King Charles, he returned to the feet of the Parliament,
his declaration was, that he had fought the King as a
peace-maker, and quitted him again becaufe he was
averfe to peace, and in the power of the papifts. The
Earl's eftate had been fequeftered when he went into the
royal camp, and the fequeftration was continued after his
return from it, in the fame year 1643, and was not
removed till fome time afterwards. The Earl alfo was
committed to prifon, and excluded from the council of
the popular leaders. In 1648 he had again changed
fides, and planned a rifing on behalf of the King.
Propofing the relief of Colchefter, he held a public
rendezvous at Kingfton on Thames ; but fome troops of
horfe under Colonel Rich, put him and his levies fuddenly
to rout. The Earl, fugitive for a day or two, was taken
at St. Neot's by the few horfemen who purfued him,
finally tried, condemned, and executed on a fcaffold
before Weftminfter Hall, a month after the execution of
the King, in March of the year 1649.

In that fame year, the civil ftrife was reprefented in
Bartholomew Fair, by a pamphlet in the form of a
booth-play, entitled " A BARTHOLOMEW FAIR-
ING, New, New, New: Sent from the raifed fiege
before Dublin, as a Preparatory Present to the Great
Thankfgiving Day. To be communicated onely to
Independents." It was iffued without any printer's

name, being figned only " London : Printed in the year
1649."

Charles the Firft had in that year fuffered for high
treafon againft the liberties of England.   Ormond had
proclaimed Charles the Second, and the Prince was to
make his ftand at Dublin.   Cromwell then, after fome
delay, accepted from the council of ftate the title of Lord
Lieutenant-General and General Governor of Ireland,
and undertook to quell Irifh rebellion with certain means
that he demanded, and with the help of Ireton, hufband
of his eldeft daughter Bridget, as his fecond in command.
Before Cromwell's arrival, the Duke of Ormond (who,
after a march from Carlow, during which he had taken
caftles and garrifons, was befieging Dublin with nineteen
thoufand men or thereabouts, and awaiting the arrival of
ten thoufand more) had been attacked by Lieutenant-
General Jones iffuing out of Dublin with four thoufand
foot and twelve hundred horfe.   Jones had received, two
days before, Cromwell's advanced guard from England,
with the news that Cromwell himfelf was at hand ; and
upon this encouragement, at once put to the rout the
befieging army of the Duke of Ormond, and forced his
retirement to Kilkenny.   This event happened on the
fecond of Auguft, and the tidings of it that reached
England were, on the twenty-fourth of Auguft, the chief
talk of the citizens at Bartholomew Fair.   Auguft the
twenty-ninth had been appointed as a great Thankfgiving
Day.   It was on the fifteenth of Auguft that Cromwell and Ireton landed at Dublin, and prepared to
fubdue an ifland of which the inhabitants—as a mafs
unbroken and favage—had, for the paft eight years, been

independent of the Englifh, " and," fays Godwin, " as
one man, looked towards the affertion of Englifh afcen-
dancy in the functionaries of the prefent Englifh Parliament, with an unmingled and indefcribable horror."
With this brief reminder of its date we may fum up the
contents of the Royalift pamphlet difperfed as a Bartholomew Fairing, among the people affembled in Smithfield
from all parts of the country on the 24th of Auguft,
1649.   Thus it opens with a

Prologue.

A *Pedler in hafte* with an *Horn.*

" Stand off, make room, give way, for I come Poft,
    My Fairings do run wild from the *Irifh* Coaft;
    Poor *Cram* a *Cree* untrouz'd, *O hone! O hone!*
    Hath loft his cows, his fheep, his Bagh, all 's gone :
    All is tranfported hither, view it, view,
    Patrick is to be fold at *Bartholomew.*
    All saints muft bow in the old *Calender*
    Unto *Saint Ireton,* and Saint *Oliver :*
    Pompey and *Cæsar*'s Wars are now begun.
    Thus for a *Ceremony,* and poor jars,
    The Saints do keep us ftill in civil wars.
    This Bartholomew will be the laft, I fear,
    Fair we fhall fee : the next is Py-powder.
    Take every one, a Fairing now, be fped,
    You *Prefbyter,* a *Bifhop* in *Ginger-bread :*
    You Cavaliers, what will you buy ? or how ?
    How go by Goldfmiths' Hall, the State's milcht cow ?
    You Independents buy no trifling matters,
    Hobby-horfes, babies, difhes, or platters :
    You are for King's revenues, Crowns and Jewels,
    And *Hangings* too, or you'll ne'er have your due elfe.
    Come buy thefe curious Pendents, and thefe knots,
    They are Scotizing Saints, Saintizing Scots.
    You Papifts, which have juggled with the *King,*
    Buy you thefe *Crosses,* now the Saint's-bells ring.

You honeſt Citizens who yet ſtand true,
Gainſt *Pres*, and *Dep*, and *Pap*, and *Div*: and *Jew*:
Take ye this Book, and on the day of joy,
Laugh at old *Nol*, and drink to the *black Boy*.

The pamphlet belongs to the days when ridicule was held to be a good and ſufficient weapon againſt men who were engaged in ſolemn and ſtrong battle, not only againſt the laſt lines of defence left to popery in England, but alſo againſt the civil yoke which principles of Roman doctrine helped to bind on the necks of the people. Paſſive obedience, a blind faith in certain men and certain ceremonies, were not more the eſſence of Romaniſm than of the Church which Charles the Firſt had fought, in the guiſe of a Reformed Church, to impoſe upon his ſubjects. The Scotch people rejected it, and ſwore to their covenant of reſiſtance. The Engliſh people, wherever the re-action was a true one againſt the old forms of impoſture, aſſerted their own independence; and ſome were firm, while ſome were violent, againſt dead forms of civil and religious deſpotiſm. Theſe Memoirs began by ſhowing us in Bartholomew Fair a credulous multitude, eaſily practiſed upon by the groſſeſt frauds. Againſt this we now ſet that which time has brought about, a day of violent re-action. The chaff of popery is being ſwept by a rude ſtorm, out of the people's threſhing-floor. The ſtrong reſolve to baſe their religion on the Bible only, drove men to a paſ-ſionate ſtudy and exaltation of the Holy Scripture, to an unſettled Bible worſhip, to a fervent, half devout and half defiant uſe of Scripture language in the daily intercourſe of life, glorious to contemplate in men of taſte and education, but at firft glance ludicrous among the men of feeble intellect, whofe zeal, moreover, was perhaps only the hotter for their lack of judgment. Behind the triumphant army flocked a fubtler hoft of hypocrites and thieves, men vapouring religion as the jackal of a camp may vapour courage. Religion is the cloak none like to pluck at rudely, therefore the beft cloak for the meaneft vices; and whenever zeal is active, there are the thieves making their den in the temple. Hypocrify is loud in prayer, and a too open utterance of deep religious emotion muft in our own days always beget diftruft. But in the days of the great ftruggle difcuffed by the crowd at Bartholomew Fair in the year 1649, depths of men's hearts were ftirred, and they were bound to active utterance of their moft facred feelings. They were in battle for the very title to poffefs their fouls in peace. An obtrufive fervour, which to-day would be a fure fign of difhonefty or weaknefs, then was a ftrong man's weapon in defence of liberty. We do not now walk in Cheapfide or Piccadilly, fword in hand; but the fteel flafhed in the hands of our forefathers that we might be able to walk weaponlefs. Zeal-in-the-Land Bufy has no more place in a modern market-place, than an old man-at-arms with morion and broadfword. But we fpeak now of days when a man might be as blindly violent as that Elder from Banbury, and yet be an honeft man, and yet be an efficient helper of a nation's holy caufe.

The charge of hypocrify is always the moft obvious weapon of attack againft religious zeal, and I have no doubt that the main body of Cavaliers, until they had been inftructed by fome rough experience, honeftly took their opponents to be hypocrites. They were open alfo to a charge of gluttony. Zeal-in-the-Land Bufy ate his two pigs and a half to a dinner; and in the tract to which we are now coming, the beft part of the jeft againft the faints confifts in fhowing how they feed. God gave us bodily fenfes and their innocent delights, as well as a foul and its pure afpirations. Re-action againft a form of worfhip that put the delight of the fenfes where the fpiritual afpiration fhould have been, led to a vain attempt at the complete reverfal of the error. Men who denied themfelves too many of the finer pleafures of the ear and eye, were eafy prey to the temptations of the table.

The reference to " Goldfmiths' Hall, the State's milcht cow," in the Prologue to the Bartholomew Fairing, is an allufion to the ufe then made of that building. It was, from the year 1640 till the Reftora-tion, the Exchequer of the Parliamentarians, in which was ftored up all the money accumulated by fequeftra-tions of the royalifts' eftates. There are three other fmall points to be remembered in connection with this Bartholomew Fairing. Committee-men's wives figure in it, becaufe Englifhwomen were in thofe days fpecially active on behalf of the popular caufe, and had even carried to Goldfmiths' Hall, jewels and trinkets to affift in raifing funds for fupport of the army of the Parlia-ment; a Thimble and Bodkin Army it was fometimes called on that account. Apprentices of London are caricatured in it, becaufe they alfo fided generally with the Parliament; and the whole caricature is exprefled in the form, odious to Independents, of a play, theatres having at that time been clofed for feven years.

There are five acts. The chief topic of the play is the reftoration to the people of the New Park at Richmond, which King Charles had formed by unwarranted enclofure of the public land.

ACT THE FIRST. Enter three Independent committeemen's wives, Mrs. Avery, Mrs. Tryall, and Mrs. Woolaftone.

Mrs. Avery fays : " Good day to you, fifters ; I may give you the good fpeed, for I know you to be of the Houfehold, for unlefs it be to fuch (it was Mr. Fenne of Coventry's opinion, and a good one) we might not give it truly." Mrs. Tryall fays that her teacher, Mr. Whateley, of Banbury, was of the fame mind ; but thinks that they three may kifs. They do fo. Mrs. Woolaftone obferving, " Verily yes, fifter, it is now holy, when holy perfons ufe it ; we make everything holy we ufe ; for the creature was made for us, and creature-comforts too, be they higher or be they lower." Mrs. Avery, delighted with the pretty word, creature-comforts, fteps afide and writes it down.

Mrs. Tryall fays, " It was very long ere the Parliament thought upon us, in that point ; but I knew they would put home at laft. Mr. Marten promifed upon his Honefty (an Oath truly that I have kept with me), that we fhould in time be remembered for our Bodkins, Silver fpoons, and Caudle cups, and now they have done it to the purpofe ; this gift of the New Park, infooth, fifter, was it not a pat, a very pat and appofite, a very pertinent, and, as Mr. Goodwine faid, a very fuitable

and agreeing prefent for us? We had no place of
air before, but common with infidels, the cabs and
cabbages, the Gray's Inn Rufflers and Hyde Park
Jezebels, who did profane and unhallow thofe good
places and otherwife wholefome recreations." Mrs.
Avery declares that their hufbands muft buy them a
coach, the place being too far for a fedan. Againft
fedans alfo, then fomewhat newly introduced, the lady
muft cry, Fy. One lady having propofed that the
hufbands buy a coach, another is for horfes, and in the
New park they will have old doings. Says Mrs. Tryall,
" I have acquainted Mr. Marten with our intentions,
and he faith he will move the Houfe and will not be
denied now Cromwell's gone ; and we fhall have an
ordinance for a cheefecake houfe, and there fhall be a
fummer-houfe too, and meet withdrawing-places." The
lady ends with a compliment to Mr. Marten's gallantry,
and Mrs. Woolaftone replies that " the noble Lieutenant-
General is as underftanding every whit himfelf. They
call him Ironfides ; alas ! he is flefh and blood as other
men are, and after the conqueft of Ireland and thofe wild
favages, he will return and do wonderfully." The talk of
the faints becomes indelicate, and the ladies prefently
long for the day of Jubilee, when Cromwell fhall have
come back again : " it fhall be St. Oliver's Day, the
Aldermen fhall be in their fcarlets, and the Livery in
velvet, all our hufbands fhall be in velvet from head to
foot." " O dear," cries Mrs. Avery, " in good footh,
fifter, it will be very pomponatious. But are you
refolved upon the meeting there ? I will fend my three
difhes, befides wine and fweetmeats, and a rofebag, and

other knacks.   But my hufband cannot poffibly go, he is fo given to the world, he is a very Martha." Of courfe, none of the hufbands can go, they muft invite to their feaft in the park fome of the young divines.   Then there are two clever apprentices.   Mrs. Woolaftone's man Ralph has made the prettieft things upon the prefent, and fo magnified the Parliament as paffes all underftanding.   Mrs. Tryall's man is a poet too, honeft Roger, a knight's fon;—London apprentices in thofe days really might be knights' fons, now and then;—his father is a Cavalier who, with the refidue of his eftate after his compofition, bound him to her hufband.   So they will feaft, remembering to bring the codling tart, and to put good ftore of ambergris in the warden and quince pies, and meaning fo to feaft the apprentices and the Levites, with marrow pies, that they fhall take New park for Marrow bone.

ACT THE SECOND.   Enter three Independent minifters, Mr. Lerned, Mr. Olduns, Mr. Bew, as in a chamber, talking a moft atrocious imitation of blank verfe, in which they congratulate each other that,

> " our Harveft
> Is not as the lean country-pulpit-thrafhers,
> Who work for the tenth cock and Eafter book.

They have fifty-two days in the year of fweat not reft, and thereto almoft three hundred holidays.   Mr. Olduns explains,

> Monday 's our prime feftival, Luna
> Begins our merriment, and Venus ends;
> For Saturn makes us melancholy; then
> We are for text and expofition, that is
> But half holiday, fome fack, fome notes;

The morn at Sion College, the afternoon
At　　　　　　in Coleman Street : where we agree
What part o' th' news to preach ; what pray'r, what ufe
(Such as the State prefcribes), and the work's done,
This work of double honour.

Prefently Mr. Lerned draws a bottle from beneath the table, faying,

" Come fit, my friends.
　Come forth (my Pofteller) this is Tonfeca
　The learned Spaniard, this, this is the book
　Which gives us learning and a politic look :
　By virtue of this author, Don-Canary,
　We fpeak what truth we pleafe, or elfe it vary.
　　　　　　　　　　　(*Fills into the glafs.*)
　Look how the fpirits dance, fee how they fkirr it ?
　We that drink this, muft needs hold forth the Spirit.
　Olduns, this lufty glafs to all thofe eyes
　Whofe whites we lift, as I do this, to th' fkies.
　　　　　　　　　　　　　(*Drinks*)

And Mr. Olduns drinks refponfively,

To thofe that figh at every *Lard* and *ah*,
And *hum*, we make upon the fabbath day.

Prefently there is a knock at the door, a fwift hiding of the bottle and glafs, and a fetching out of

Reynolds' Sermons, whofe moft learned books
Are the gulled people's baits, and we the hooks.

The knock is only that of Mr. Woolaftone's apprentice, Ralph —" Ralph Shorthand ! what my ftenographical fermon-catcher, my mafs of repetition, and conferver of my fmall wares of Divinity, little pedler of my dominical labours, how doft thou, fweet youth ? What is thy bufinefs ?" He brings a letter from his miftrefs, and brings money alfo with it, " the *argentum vivum* of the laſt edition : no *Carolus* upon their white boys, nor *Dei gratiâ* neither, but *Anno Libertatis*, and what is it ? *Crucis novæ ?* "   The letter is of invitation to the feaſt, and is received with welcome; fo are the pieces of new coinage.

> This ſhows the State is fixt,
> And learned too : O let me kiſs this croſs
> The ſign of vanquiſhed ſuperſtition,
> The ſign of Reformation in the State
> As well as Church ; for this we bleſs and curſe ;
> Thus we will carry croſſes; in our purſe.
>
> MR. BEW.   With what regard of words ! and godly tokens
> Are we invited to this feaſt !   This whiſtle,
> This ſilver whiſtle of the Saints is ſhrill,
> Theſe charmers may e'en charm me where they will.
>
> MR. OLD.   Next Sunday we will hold forth of thankfulneſs,
> And praiſe the open handedneſs o' th' Saints :
> Our thanks to thoſe who miniſtered to our wants.

Ralph then prefers to Mr. Lerned humble ſuit.   It would for ever make him with his miſtreſs, to have an handſome ſmart copy of verſes on the Park and preſent Thankſgiving.   " Pray, ſir, think : you have it, if you but ſcratch i' the fantaſtical ſide.   Sir, I have a piece of ſingular tobacco for your Muſe.   The very prime of the leaf.   Ochechampano Poca-Hunto's father, great cuſtos of the Indies, drinks not ſo good.   Againſt night, I pray thee, let them be compoſed, fair wrote, and ſcratched under where the emphaſis muſt lie."   Mr. Lerned undertakes to do this, and breaks up the ſitting, becauſe he needs time ; he is a hind at proſe, but a dull ox at verſe.   The ground is then clear for the entrance of the other apprentice, Roger Truſty, the Cavalier's ſon, bound, after his excluſion from the univerſity, to a mercer and committeeman.   He works alone upon the ſubjeƈt of the Park, and fays things more familiar than civil of his miftrefs.

ACT THE THIRD. Enter three committeemen, Mr. Woolaftone, Mr. Avery, Mr. Tryall. They have given their wives a holiday in the Park, but intend to fteal upon them. Meanwhile, as men of the day, they talk a little politics. One did not think the gain of godlinefs had been fo quick. No myftery, no traffic half fo fure. No hazards run. For firft, we know we are faints ; and that granted, the world's our own, and we may fafely take all that we fee or covet. All the reft are aliens, only we are heirs of the houfe.—This, fays Tryall, is our fweet title. The Scriptures are a mine of endlefs treafure if applied aright.—Upon that principle Woolaftone tells how he made all the fortune he poffeffes by betrayal of a truft. It was the eftate of an orphan whofe father had died in arms againft this bleffed Parliament.

> I firft
> Difcovered my engagement; then difclofed
> The foul delinquency, and for a flight
> Reward unto the chairman (fome two or
> Three thoufand crowns, a very toy, a toy)
> For fervices (I never yet knew done),
> And for my loffes (truly I was loft
> But for this happy windfall), and becaufe
> I was affected to the ftate (as no man more),
> And for I was a man of known integrity
> (None ferve the ftate but fuch), I was voted
> Lord of the whole eftate, and the Orphan
> Profcribed and difinherifon'd. He's fent
> Into Barbadoes with inftructions
> Unto a mafter, to unlearn his birth,
> Which, if he can forget, he may do well,
> Then he may live, and prove in time a planter.

Mr. Avery thinks that his friend has proved his truft

abundantly into the ſtate, the end of Feoffe-ſhips. The youth, with a little help of *aqua vitæ*, ſtockings and hats, old ling and martlemas, may riſe to a fortune great as Craven's was.—Mr. Woolaſtone replies that he cares only for the act of good, and has precedent in Sir John Danvers, that honoured knight, and now great ſtateſman, who proved the earl, his brother, a delinquent for ſome pounds lent to the King, and overthrew the will, cozening his own ſiſter and all the legatees. The friends then fall upon talk about the accuſation againſt them of ſacrilege in buying Biſhops' lands. As if their land were Heaven. If it were, they wouldn't purchaſe it. The Houſe is far enough from ſuch an act; that were ſacrilege i' the higheſt, and not on any terms to be committed. " No, heaven at no rate! Little England for my money!" " A little Ireland too will now do well," hints Tryall, and the talk turns upon

> That renegade lord
> Apoſtate Inchiquin, who hath committed
> The high offence, revolting *to* the King.
> 'Tis he that plagues us, he hath diſmunſter'd
> He hath diſmunſtered me (Deil Inch him for't)
> Of full three thouſand acres (his very name
> Makes every Inch I have about me quake),
> Which if I could have quietly enjoyed,
> I would not have engaged in Biſhops' lands.

MR. AVERY. Ormond and he ſhall ne'er be pardoned, nor
> Montroſe, Hopton nor Langdale, no nor Dives—

MR. TRYALL. I was afraid of Ireland once, I gave it
> For an unwholeſome air, bogs and quagmires;
> But Colonel Jones hath cleared it all again,
> With the State's Thunder, Powder and Money.

MR. WOOLASTONE. It was a plot of Cromwell's all this while
> (And Monk will juſtify it) to loſe ſo much:
> To make the buſineſs ſeeming deſperate,
> To his eternal honour to reſtore it.

This was the plot, if Ormond had ta'en Dublin ;
He fhould have put in governors, then marched
And joined with Johnny Prefbyter in Scotland,
Then fhould thofe governors have fold it back
(For what's the City money for, but that ?)
Unto the high Lieutenant, that once ours,
Cromwell had powdered after Ormond, whiles
Good Sir Arthur Hafelrigg and Lambert
Rebuilt the wall betwixt the Piƈts and us,
And kept them out of England, pent in Scotland.
This was the plot, which none but fure ones knew :
This is the day to raife more money for't.

MR. TRYALL. It fhall be levied, what we fay 's a law,
This is the word, Do it, or Cromwell comes ;
We'el fetch him with a whiftle, if they boggle,
He lies in Wales on purpofe at a lurch ;
(Upon pretence of waiting on the winds)
But the truth is, it is to awe thofe here
The Leveller and difcontented party.
He'll fquirt you regiments into Dublin,
And fright off Ormond with a whiff of 's tail.

MR. AVERY. The Welch do love him mainly.

MR. WOOLASTONE. They have reafon.
He is their coufin very near allied,
Once Ap-Lord Lieutenant General,—Ap-All ;
Ap-Tudor, Ap-Queen Elizabeth, Ap-Befs,
Ap great Proteƈtor prefently ; the States
Muft have a grave, and who is fitter for 't.

They talk then of the change of lords, delightful as variety of meats. Kings were too ftately, thought it much to feaft a fubjeƈt ; but the State condefcends to take a lodging, and tell fecrets of the Houfe to citizens' wives, who tell their hufbands what they learn, and pump the junto for intelligence. "And on that confidence we buy king's lands, bifhops or anything. They work it all." Therefore the wives are entitled to their holiday feaft in the park. But they fhall not mifs the pleafure of their hufbands' company.

P

Letters from Cromwell, announcing that he had failed from Ireland, reached London on the twenty-firft of Auguft ; but the fact that he had failed was evidently not known to the writer of this pamphlet, when, immediately after the arrival of the news of the Raifed Siege before Dublin, he began and hurriedly completed his appeal to the paffions of the crowd that was a few days afterwards to be affembled at the Fair. Of the point of the other political allufions very brief reminder is fufficient. The Earl of Inchiquin, Lord Prefident of Munfter, had " difmunftered" the commonwealth, firft by manœu-- vres againft Lord Lifle, to whom, when he arrived from England he played the part of an adverfary in the form of an ally, in the voice of a friend crying check to him at every move he made. Inchiquin was a royalift who, having been offended by his own party, had joined the Parliament, but at the end of two years returned to his old mind, and profited as long as he could by the opportunity of acting as a traitor in the camp to which he had deferted, before he returned to his right pofition as an open foe. He had helped Ormond greatly, and before Ormond's defeat at Dublin and the change of fortune following on that, Monk had been driven out of Ireland ; Dublin and Derry only ftill held out againft the forces of the Stuart. That the tone of the preachers ridiculed in this pamphlet was open to the interpretation fet upon it by the Cavaliers, there can be no doubt. The fermon preached by its " daily Orator before the Throne of Grace " to the Houfe of Commons on that twenty-ninth of Auguft, the Thankfgiving Day, for which the Bartholomew Fairing was a preparation, fhows

us how the learned preached ; and if their preaching put
a flaming fword into the hand of him who liftened, what
muft have been the manner of men whofe zeal was
untempered by knowledge and difcretion.   William
Cooper, M.A., Minifter of the Gofpel at St. Olave's,
Southwark, preaching from a text relative to the fiege
of Jerufalem in the 12th chapter of Zachariah, faid,
" Obferve then the parts and parallel together : you
have here, firft, a very formal and formidable laying a
fiege ; fecondly, we have a fignal raifing of that fiege :
thirdly, we have the caufes and confequents of both : In
the firft, two things are confiderable, firft the befieged,
fecondly, the befiegers.   The befieged is no mean city,
but a Mother in Ifrael, Jerufalem, the metropolis of
Judea, the glory of the Earth, the city of God is
invefted and beleagured ; the beloved city is furrounded
and ftraitened by her adverfaries.   2. The befiegers ; a
numerous Hoft, all the people round about ; fundry
nations, bad neighbours, fuch as bear evil will to Sion."
What would be the comment of a Cavalier upon a
paffage like the following ?   " Such a contrariety is
there between Jerufalem and her enemies, that as the
two fcales of a balance, put weight in one, preffeth down
and lifts the other up : the rife of Sion is the fall of
Babylon ; the death of the witneffes makes the inhabitants
of earth merry, *Revelations*, 11, 10.   When Jeremy
and his people lamented in tears, their enemies laughed,
mocking at their Sabbaths.   Again the Saints have their
turn at laft, they fhall laugh laft, *Ifaiah*, 65, 13, 14.
Behold, my fervants fhall rejoice, but ye fhall be
afhamed ; my fervants fhall fing for joy of heart, but ye

fhall cry for forrow of heart, and howl for vexation of
fpirit, *Revelations.*   Now this is a fpecial act of divine
juftice, to give every one his turn : and not only fo, but
by the Law of Retaliation to make his people fhift their
burdens upon their oppreffors fhoulders : The burdens
that oppreffors lay on the back of the righteous, fhall
fall heavy upon themfelves, breaking their bones, and
preffing them down into the pit.   This they get by
laying loads on the Saints of God."   This direct preaching of the Law of Retaliation received the thanks of the
Houfe of Commons, and was printed by its defire.
"What a diftinguifhing love is here in gracious God,"
fays Mr. Cooper, "that puts fo vaft a difference between
men and men, between party and party ; accounting his
own honourable, his enemies bafe ; his own precious, his
enemies vile : the Lord like a lion goes forth, and tears
whatever he meets with, to feed his young, be it men or
beafts."   Again he fays, "It is ever fatal to affault the
Jerufalem of God.   In their engaging againft Jerufalem,
they do but march the neareft cut to their own graves.
It's an evident token the Lord intends to blaft a Perfon,
Family, or Nation, if he permits them to advance and
act hoftilely againft his people."

Such preaching inevitably tended to beget among the
ignorant, opinions, which in the talk of the men introduced into that third act of his tract, all Bartholomew
Fair knew to be hardly an exaggeration of the Cavaliers.
There were oppreffions alfo, and there were infamous
betrayals of truft by private men, who hypocritically
fought only their own advancement, in the concourfe of
the faints : and it would be unfair to Mr. Cooper not to

fhew how he fpeaks like a Chriftian upon this topic.
He fpeaks of petitions left unopened by the Parliament,
during a prefs of public bufinefs.   " I befeech you," he
fays, " let your ears be open to thofe cries which reach up
into Heaven, and beat loud alarms in the ears of divine
juftice.   Oh, take care and heed, that the oppreffions in
the land may not be fuch as may caufe the tears of the
oppreffed to fpeak.   They have no comforter, while on
the oppreffor's fide there is power; fome cry for bread
to feed their bodies, others cry for bread to feed their
fouls: fome cry for juftice, others for mercy ; fome fink
under their burdens, others play the tafk-mafters upon
their brethren, laying on them more load ; fome grow
rich upon others' poverty, and fome proud by others'
riches."   He tells the members of the Houfe that they
muft unload heavy burdens, heal the breaches between
brethren, and let the oppreffed go free, and that then
" the Lord will be tender of you and yours, and will
build you a fure foundation."

The Minifter was labouring over his ftate fermon,
(which is full of erudition) while the Cavalier was
peppering his gibe, and we may underftand either of
them the better for a glance over the other.   After this
talk between the acts we take our feats for the remainder
of the play.

ACT THE FOURTH.   Enter Ralph and Roger as
at New Park Gate.   Ralph pays the carochman who
has brought the ladies, drink-money above his hire.
The two apprentices, about to order the feaft, exchange a word or two about their approaching wit-
combat.

The three minifters, leading the three Committee men's wives, enter the Park.

> MR. LERNED. Thefe were fometimes high places, and the groves
> Where Ahab burnt unhallowed gums to Baal.
> But now a fanctified inheritance,—

and fo forth. " The herbage is of grace, the trees all elder.

MRS. WOOLASTONE. What are thofe creatures that trip it fo, with the high things upon their foreheads? They have goodly foretops.

> MR. LERNED. Thofe are the favoury meats o' th' place, the diet
> Old Ifaac longed for (we call Venifon),
> Which Efau hunts, but only Ifrael eats.
>
> .　.　.　.　.
>
> MRS. AVERY. We fhall foon defpatch
> Thefe deer upon Thankfgiving-days for Cromwell,
> And then we'll keep our dairies here, the country
> Charming 's too grofs for Saints, we'll have glaffes,
> And fervants, lufty fervants of our own,
> And we will fee it come, The buttermilk
> We'll fell unto the Cabs and eat the cream,
> The cream o' th' kine ourfelves in ftately difhes.
>
> .　.　.　.　.
>
> MRS. TRYALL. Deer was the tyrants' game, but bulls is ours.
> Bifhops and plays were in a day put down,
> I well remember; and Bull-baiting allowed.

They will have geefe, goflings, and pigs of their own, on their own grounds.

> and ne'er
> Be jeered with Bow and Bartholomew Fair Meetings;
> Nor James, nor Sturbridge: our hufbands fhall ply them,
> We and our Levites will ply there.

The Levites announce that the repaft is fet in order. Roger is informed as to the character of Eve's dinner-table on the grafs, which had fix molehills round a knot of turf; Mr. Lerned thinks that was much like the feat of her of Babylon. The minifters and the Committee men's wives fit to their dinner, and the hufbands come behind the trees with hautboys, cornets, and fmall mufic. Even behind the trees their talk together is of Colonel Jones and Ormond. Mr. Tryall thinks that "Cromwell with his running army will o'er run Ireland, and take all, the Divell (God blefs him) is in him, he will have all, all's his."

ACT THE FIFTH. Reprefents the feaft.

All the three minifters fay grace in turn, and upon the depiction of the Three Graces the Cavalier artift evidently has beftowed fome pains. One is in verfe, two are in profe. Such parodies are always painful, and I quote only the firft:

MR. LERNED. Blefs uf-um-blefs us (Lard) and thefe thy gifts,
Marcies and Creature comforts: By thefe fhifts
Thou try'ft our thankfulnefs,-um-this great ftore,
(Lard) it doth make us praife thee more, and more.
Thou takeft from the mouths of Cavaliers,
And fill'ft our bellies with good things of theirs.
Thou feedeft Ravens (Lard) who call on thee,
Young Ravens (Lard) thou feedeft fuch as *we*.
They cannot praife thy name, they eat indeed,
But we do eat and praife, and praife and feed.
So that our life is nought but a thankfgiving
For every eaten thing, both dead and living.
From ftirring oyfters, unto Capon ftiff
And cold, we eat through faith, and corned Beef.
This Venifon Pie, a wild untamed beaft
Alive; is dead, provifion for the bleft.
All forts of Pie-meats (Lard) blefs unto us,
And fanctify our ftomachs, by it thus.
Let not our wembs be ftraitened, but enlarge
Our ventricles unto the whole difcharge,

Even unto fuccetts, confects, dry and moift,
Let us go thorough, and be not debaucht;
Be it as thy fervant prays, unto his wifh,
That he may tafte the Lard in *every* difh.
So be it.

From Mr. Bew's grace I quote one paffage, "um—
we are travellers—um—here is our inn, here we have a
good bait, a very plentiful bait. It will not wrong us
to fweep the manger, to make clean work. For we are
not as other hypocrites, reprobates, and enemies of the
ftate, but unto us thou haft given, from them thou haft
taken, (bleffed be thy name A Lard) they are at rack
and manger, but we are at full meal. Thrice bleffed
we, if we now fhow in our receptions, embracings, and
takings in unto us thy overtures, our unwearied gratitude,
more than feeding-on-by-heart thankfulnefs."

Mrs. Woolaftone is complimented on her carving. An
Italian carver handles not fo clean, nor cuts fo large a
limb and full. Roger, the apprentice, utters his
aftonifhment at the platter-loads that difappear. Mr.
Lerned calls to Ralph for a plenteous glafs of claret,
"fuch as I always ufe after the third remove of my
trencher." Mrs. Woolaftone calls for " fome white
wine, of that the merchant fent my hufband for his
brother's quick difpatch at Squeezing " (Goldfmiths')
" Hall." Though the elect may not drink healths,
they may be topers, and the wine being in, it is
ordained by the Cavalier playwright that truth fhall
appear.

" MRS. TRYALL. May we not tope about a little,
fifter; with the Levites' approbation.—MR. BEW. Ay,
and example too.

"Mrs. T. Healths are profane. Maſky Tope, ſiſter Abigail *(drinks)*.

"Mrs. A. Tope, ſiſter Dorcas *(drinks)*.

"Mr. L. A dry tope now, an't pleaſe you, ſiſter. Mrs. W. What's that? Mrs. T. That's a ſalute. Mr. L. Tope about. *(Kiſs the Levites.)* Mrs. W. A Tope to the Lieutenant General. Mrs. A. To Mr. Marten too a tope . . . Mr. B. Now a wet tope upon the occaſion. Let's not forget the valiant Colonel Jones, and Captain Oatway. Fill largely Ralph. *(All drink.)* Mr. O. Now one tope to Mr. Goodwyn the elder *(drinks)*. Mr. B. He is a faint ſure? Mr. O. I mean in oppoſition to younger. Mr. B. I have toped. I do tope to you, brother, to the worthy viſitors of Oxford, a ſwinging tope. Mr. L. They deſerve it highly, they have reformed that place to the purpoſe. There's no duſt left behind the door, they have made clean work, they have ſwept all out. To good Sir Nat. Mr. Bew. The malignants ſay he is an aſs.

"Mr. Lerned. He? An aſs? and ſo am I. Mr. Old. And I. Mr. Bew. And I. So they ſay Cheynell and Wilkinſon are mad.

"Mr. Lerned. They mad? And ſo am I. Mr. Old. And I. Mr. Bew. And I. Nay, they ſtick not to ſpeak unreverently of Dr. Reynolds and Dr. Harris, and call them hypocrites, and diſſembling knaves.

"Mr. Lerned. They knaves? So am I. Mr. Old. And I. Mr. Bew. And I.

"Roger. This was the beſt tope yet; had it been ſung it would have gone to the tune of *Thou Knave* excellently well."

It is worth obfervation that this paffage guides us to an unfufpected origin of the word toper. The word is not in Shakefpeare, and I believe is not to be found in any author of a date anterior to the commonwealth. Our beft dictionaries give fuch doubtful etymologies as that toper is derived from the German topf, for pot; from top becaufe the drinker's wine flows over the top of his glafs, or by tranfpofition of letters from potor. Nobody feems to have remembered that *toper* is a verb of the French dice-players, that means the fetting of an equal ftake againft one laid already on the table. Tope! was the exclamation of the gambler when he accepted the challenge of his partner of the game to fet coin againft coin. Transferred to the drinking-table it meant glafs againft glafs; as you drink, fo do I. The word went out even into general fociety as a mere exclamation of affent. The French courtiers in the train of Henrietta Maria may firft have brought it to England; and when the Puritans abandoned drinking of healths, it would appear by the paffage above cited, that they fell back on the cry of Tope, and gave it currency enough to eftablifh firmly the word toper among the Englifh people. Then, when it had been ufed by Dryden and by other authors who lived after the time of the commonwealth, it became claffical Englifh.

To the topers of Bartholomew Fair in the year 1649, the Cavalier who offered them his Fairing on occafion of the raifing of the Siege of Dublin had but little more to fay. He brought the hufbands in to join the feaft of faints, and they were welcomed by their wives and by the minifters, who bade them fit down, for the meats were bleſt and thoroughly ſanctified. There needs no repetition; the creature cannot fall from grace. The two apprentices are then called to their wit-combat, which ends the play. It ought to contain the ſting of the whole ſatire; we have been prepared for it from the firſt, and when we come to it,—Ralph witleſſly ſings changes upon the witleſs notion of

> Not ſuch a preſent ſince good Noah's Ark
> As this of the new State, their Fine New Park,

and bewilders us with arks and parks, much to the delight of his hearers in the play, who ſeem to underſtand him. At laſt ſays Mr. Lerned, " Now, conclude, Ralph, ſmartly, with the ſting in the tail, as all epigrammatical poems ſhould.

> RALPH. Tis all our own,—it comes; Be wondrous merry,
> The next good news: All *Ireland's London Derry.*"

It was thirty-ſeven years ſince the large grants of land in Derry, then made to the corporation of London, had received the name of Londonderry. London now might aſk all Ireland for its Derry. There was no wit here, indeed, but there was a ſtrong expreſſion of the eager expectation with which men then watched the iſſue of Cromwell's expedition to a land in which there had been left to the Parliament only two places to call its own.

The other apprentice ſings as a Cavalier of gold and goblets changed to parks.

> Each bodkin in this new alembic proves
> A Tree; ear-rings and thimbles ſtart up groves.
> Gilt ſpoons are ſaplings and the orphans' food,
> Pap with a Hatchet, it is nurſed with wood.

The widow's jointure here moſt ſtately ſhews,
She calls for 't in, the Feoffees ſay It grows.

.   .   .   .   .

Engage, engage apace, while the State lives,
She is a liberal governeſs, ſhe gives.
This is a taſte to the city of their loves,
Lend all you have ; and you ſhall all have groves.
Then though the King return with Foreign Force,
And take your Foreſt, what are you the worſe.
When theſe are gone, the State more favour yields,
They give Parks now, and then Elyſian Fields.

" You are a little too bitter, ſirrah," Mr. Lerned
cries, and the painfully witty Roger anſwers, " Satyrs
in woods, ſir, are moſt proper." The ladies falling out
over the merits of the two apprentices, throw pie,
muſtard, and ſugar at each other. Mr. Olduns riſes, with
hat off, to exorciſe the ſpirit of trouble and feaſt-inter-
ruption ; and the huſbands entering with muſic that plays
" ſeveral ſmart tunes," the ladies tope both dry and wet,
in ſign of reconciliation, and are led off by the miniſters
in a pretty dance, while the huſbands, ever intent on
the ſtate of the nation, run over the diurnals. " The
Moderate Intelligencer" was one of the many little
quarto journals crowded with print, that expreſſed the
ſtir among the people in thoſe days ;—" the Moderate
Intelligencer," ſays Mr. Woolaſtone, " is very full this
week ; what a comfortable letter is here from Colonel
Jones ? What ! was it Ormond's Fair, that there were
ſuch rich prizes taken ? Who would have taken it for
a ſiege ? And you will—we will—ſend and buy it all.
'Twill be good chaffer." The end is that

His Lordſhip's ſhipped : we are Princes all.
MR. AVERY. I muſt unto my court at Squeezing Hall,

There wait thofe Oranges, thofe humbled things :
While we fit uncontrolled like petty kings.
MR. WOOLASTONE. We will have the fong, and fo conclude :
Our wives to their caroches, we to our horfes. Levites to their
Books. Boys to their fhops, and Mufic to the fcraps.

THE SONG.

To the Tune of *In the Merry Month of May*.

I.

In the merry, merry month of June
When the rofe fades ; but venifon
Ranges ftately by the woodfide,
With head branched in her pride.
Then the State looked down upon
Citizana and Citizon.

II.

The States that ftyled are the free
More than thofe of Germany :
Free of flefh, as any State,
Gave us Venifon for our Plate.
They will give us anything,
A New Park for an old King.

III.

What Returns are thefe for our loans
No man grudgeth, no maid groans.
She that laid her bodkin down,
In New Park has a green gown.
And if that be not enough
What is far more pleafing ftuff ?

There are two verfes more before the

(*Clofe.*)

Thus Enge-land for a Crown of Gold
Is with a filly Willow Garland fooled
Thus Enge-land by fuccefsfull knaves,
Is become a State of Fools and Slaves.
Thus for a Park, like a fort of owls,
The Charter's loft of the Foreft of Fools.

In an epilogue of indignation Roger feems to compare
the traffic and turmoil going on throughout the country
to a Fair, and ends as ufual with a blunt point thruft
very fiercely.

> The Fair is hell.
> Difference there is twixt that and Bartholomew,
> That brings Brimftone and Fire, this the Cold Dew.

The fimple hiftory of the Park which is the foundation
of the Cavalier's attack upon the Puritans, is that King
Charles the Firft, by enclofure of common lands belonging
to the people, added to the Old Park at Richmond the
two thoufand two hundred and fifty-three acres ftill
known as the New or Great Park.   In the formal lift of
his encroachments upon public liberty drawn up before
his trial, this feizure of public land had been included ;
and foon after the King's death, two months before this
Bartholomew Fair, that is to fay in June 1649, the New
Park, as their own land, had been given back to the ufe
of the people.   In plain words, reftoration was made of
the ftolen property.

The Puritans did not fupprefs Bartholomew Fair.
There were, indeed, no dramas performed in it by living
actors, but the State did not condefcend, like Rabbi
Bufy, to engage in controverfy with the puppets.   It
was for the Corporation of London, if it pleafed, to
exercife control, and there was a Lord Mayor who, as we
fhall fee, did make himfelf eminent for an attack
upon the wooden Dagons of the fhow.   Againft the
fool in his motley none made war ; Cromwell himfelf
had in his private fervice four buffoons, and had he
vifited the Fair, true hero as he was, might have been

well difpofed to mount a hobby-horfe. Therefore the
clown ftill jefted, and the toyman thruft his baubles in
the face of the Roundhead, while the Cavalier's lady with
a conftellation of black ftars about her nofe, a moon of
ink on her chin, and a coach and horfes, a very fafhionable patch, on her forehead, laughed at the fhort hair
under the broad-brimmed hat of the offended gentleman.
Well might fhe laugh at the miferable fcarecrow in plain
cloak and jerkin, and in boots that fitted him, for he had
no love locks and no peaked beard like the gallant at
her fide; he wore only a little pecked band inftead of a
laced collar, and as for his breeches,—not only did they
want ornament and width, but they even fhowed no
elegant bit of fhirt protruding over them! Acrofs the
Smithfield pavement, Cavaliers in boots two inches too
long, and with laced tops wide enough to contain each of
them a goofe, ftraddled about; compelled to ftraddle, in
order that the long and jingling fpur of one boot, hooked
into the ruffle of the other, might not bring down the
whole man into the gutter. Women, I fay, might note
fuch things, but the men were in earneft. The dainty
Cavalier in the hiftorical fhirt, embroidered with the deeds
of profane heroes, might glance from the fpeckled face of
his companion towards the clean cheeks of the Puritan
maid in the religious petticoat, worked over with texts
and fcripture fcenes; all had their vanities, their froth of
weaknefs floating loofe above the ftorm; all had an eye
for the jeft of the Fair, but under it lay in a heaving
mafs the folemn earneft of the time. The Fair brought
together from almoft all parts of England, men who
had urgent thoughts to exchange, harmonies and con-

flicts now of principle, and now of paſſion to expreſs.
The deſtiny of fatherland was hidden for all in a future
black with doubt. Men brave and honeſt had their
ſouls pledged in allegiance to an earthly king, over
whom and againſt whom others, as brave and as honeſt,
ſet up the rights given to them by the King of kings.

A true Bartholomew Fairing, then, for the year 1649,
was this of which we have diſcuſſed the purport. The
talk of the Fair was in it. Zeal might be there crying out
againſt the puppets, Licenſe might be there preaching the
cauſe of the monarchy to Urſula the pig-woman, type of
all that is groſs and ſenſual in the Smithfield feſtival, and
winning from her and hers a ready outcry againſt
interference of the Puritans with honeſt pleaſure. But
it was not only to the tribe of Urſula that Cavaliers, then
abroad in the Fair, looked for applauſe and countenance.
There were ſupporters of the commonwealth battling
with all their hearts for civil liberty, who did not ſeek
religious liberty by ſharing in the proteſts of the Puritans;
and there were Puritans—nay, there were the very
ſaints of Banbury—who felt themſelves bound in conſcience to pay tribute unto Cæſar, and who had on that
ground proteſted formally againſt the execution of King
Charles the Firſt. All were eager, there were few who
were not earneſt, and there were none to whom the news
from Dublin was not, even in the midſt of the Fair, a
matter of more preſſing intereſt than all the Monſters of
the booths. The Fair was become an aſſembly of the
people, for whoſe ſuffrages contending parties ſtrove.
The very Lords of the Fair had in that year borne
witneſs to the heat and urgency of the great ſtruggle

through which the land was paffing. From the cor-
poration of London, holder of the Fair in Smithfield,
there had been a Mayor difmiffed as difaffected to the
Commonwealth, and a fucceffor forced upon the citizens.
Of the family of Rich, holding the Fair in Bartholomew
Clofe, the two chiefs, brothers, attached to one another
in the houfehold, were divided in the ftate. The head
of one of them had been ftruck off at the gate of
Weftminfter Hall; the other was a main prop of the
Commonwealth, and Cromwell's friend.

The Rich family has to be kept in fight during this
portion of our ftory. In a few paragraphs, therefore, let its hiftory be fummed up for the next half
century.

The Earl of Warwick, a ftout but temperate fupporter
of the Puritans, had, in the King's time, been much
honoured and trufted in the Houfe of Lords. It was
he who had been appointed by the Lords and Commons, on behalf of England and againft the King's wifh,
Vice-Admiral under the Earl of Northumberland; who
had, in obedience to the orders of the Parliament,
removed from Hull to London the King's magazine of
arms, cannon, and ammunition; and who, when the
King difcharged the Earl of Northumberland of his
commiffion, which he would not confent to refume on
the authority of Parliament, took by that authority his
place of Lord High Admiral. The firft ufe made of
the new broadfeal of the Parliament was to confirm his
patent. He was a hearty, honeft, charitable man, whofe
influence was great, not only among leaders of the
popular caufe in London, but alfo among his friends

Q

and tenantry in Effex. Clarendon terms the Earls of
Manchefter and Warwick the two pillars of the Prefbyterian party; and tells us that the Earl of Warwick,
piqued by fome flight put upon him as Lord High
Admiral, was privy and confenting to his brother's
defign for the royalift rifing which was difcomfited fo
eafily at Kingfton, and which brought the fchemer of it
to the block. Yet the Earl of Warwick at that very time
was, by appointment of the Parliament, threatening the
fleet of the Prince of Wales at fea; and when, "becaufe it
was well known that the Earl was privy to the engagement of his brother, and had promifed to join him," the
prince tempted him by letters and friendly meffages,
the meffenger "quickly returned with an anfwer from
the Earl which (in terms of duty enough) humbly
befought his highnefs to put himfelf into the hands of
the Parliament ; and that the fleet with him might
fubmit to their obedience ; upon which they fhould be
pardoned for their revolt." This was not the behaviour
of a traitor to his caufe. Probably he had heard of the
Earl of Holland's wild defign, and was by family affection
reftrained from betraying plots that muft inevitably fail.
When they had failed, he ftrained every nerve to fave
his brother's life, pleaded his paft fervices, his age and
infirmity, engaged all the Prefbyterians on his behalf,
and after long and warm debate failed only by three or
four votes to refcue him from death. He ftill remained
true to the Commonwealth, was Cromwell's faft friend,
was the nobleman who in Weftminfter Hall helped in
the robing of him as Protector, and to whofe grandfon
—another Robert, and a fhort-lived hufband—Cromwell

gave his youngeſt daughter Frances for a wife. He gave her, it is ſaid, ſo joyouſly that, at the wedding-feaſt, he threw ſack-poſſet over ladies' clothes, daubed ſtools with ſweetmeats, and pulled off and ſat upon his old friend's wig. A formal courtier, dancing at this feaſt, had his lip made black like a beard by one of the Protector's four buffoons, and, being offended thereat, nearly ſlaughtered him for his impertinence. There was hope for Bartholomew Fair revels when ſuch ſport was reliſhed in the Houſehold of the Lord Pro-tector. The Earl and his newly married grandſon both died a few months after this wedding, in the year 1658.

But the grandſon ſo married to Frances Cromwell was the only male child of an intervening Robert, the Lord Admiral's eldeſt ſon. This young man's premature death having deprived his father of a direct heir, the title paſſed to his uncle Charles, his father's brother, and the ſecond ſon of Earl Warwick the Admiral. But when this Charles died alſo without iſſue (in the year 1673), the earldom of Warwick came with its eſtates, including the lordſhip of Cloth Fair, to the ſon (again a Robert Rich) of the Lord Admiral's brother, the beheaded Earl of Holland, and of the Elizabeth who had been heir to Sir Walter Cope of Kenſington. Sir Walter was the brother of a Sir Anthony Cope, already mentioned in theſe pages, who had ſerved in the Puritan intereſts for the borough of Banbury, during five Parliaments of Elizabeth, and who was King James's firſt High Sheriff of Oxfordſhire. Marriage into this family had in-fluenced the mind of Henry, Earl of Holland; and,

doubtlefs, had caufed fome of his vacillation between the
contending parties of the State. But Elizabeth, his
wife, Sir Walter's heirefs, appears to have been a lady
of high fpirit, and, after her hufband's execution,
bore no good-will to the party by which he had been
condemned. She continued as a widower to occupy
Holland Houfe, her own inheritance. It had been built
by John Thorpe for her father, afterwards improved by
her hufband, and it was again enlarged by herfelf, when
fhe was fole miftrefs of it, in the year 1654, a widow,
and a mother of nine children. In her eldeft fon Robert,
who was three times married, and who was not mafter
of Holland Houfe until after his mother's death, the
two earldoms were firft united; and after the year 1673,
joint Lord of Bartholomew Fair with the corporation
of London was Rich, Earl of Warwick and Holland.
The firft lord who held the titles jointly died after
holding them two years, and was fucceeded then by a
fon Edward, married to Charlotte Middleton, daughter
of a Welfh baronet, the lady who, after her firft lord's
deceafe in 1701, was re-married to Mr. Addifon. The
firft hufband had left her with a fon named Edward
Henry, three years old, upon whofe fmall head the two
Earls' coronets defcended, and who became the little
Lord alfo of the Fair within the bounds of St. Bartholomew the Great.

CHAPTER XII.

𝔇𝔞𝔤𝔬𝔫.

BARTHOLOMEW FAIRINGS, in the form of political pamphlets, had been in ufe before the year of the King's execution. One fuch work, entitled "General Maffey's Bartholomew Fayrings to Colonel Poyntz," was afcribed to John Lilburne, in eight 8vo pages of anfwer to it printed in 1647, under the name of "Reformados Righted, being an Anfwer to a paltry piece of Poetry, entitled" as above. Some paffages from this anfwer are in the Guildhall book of MS. collections; but they are mere abufe, and can illuftrate nothing. The only point in it is, that the refpondent, as Lilburne had expreffed abhorrence of fmokers, talks of making pipe-lights of his verfes:

> If Derrick don't prevent our taper
> And burn it in Smithfield for a libellous paper.
> Oh, how 'twould vex our idle pamphleteer
> To fee his Fairing executed there:
> Yet fuch a punifhment too noble is
> For fenfelefs rhymers. Let thy doom be this,
> May never reader henceforth look for thee
> But in a whipping poft or pillory.

That Bartholomew Fair held its own while the playhoufes were filenced, there is abundant evidence to prove. Evelyn, in his diary, under date Auguft 28, 1648, notices his coming to London from Says' Court, and feeing " the celebrated follies of Bartholomew Fair." In the fame year, a quarto pamphlet, called " An Agitator Anatomifed," notices the puppet-playing. Nearly as old as this, and, although undated, probably to be taken as the firft advertifement of a wild-beaft fhow in the Fair of which there is extant record, is the following :

" JUST ARRIVED FROM ABROAD,

" And are now to be feen or fold, at the firft Houfe on the Pavement from the end of Hofier Lane, during Bartholomew Fair,

" A large and beautiful young Camel, from Grand Cairo, in Egypt. This Creature is twenty-three years old ; his head and neck are like thofe of a deer."

In the year 1651 the Houfehold Book of Sir Edward Dering, Bart, of Surrenden Dering, in Kent, records as expenditure on the 3rd of September : " Item, Baubles at Bartholomew Fair, 4*s*." That entry might have been important to our hiftory, as the firft intimation we have of the Duration of Bartholomew Fair for a longer time than the three days in Auguft firft appointed for it. But it happens, unfortunately, that, about the year 1650, the practice of adopting from abroad the computation of new ftyle, although not yet eftablifhed by the law in England, had been recognifed by the Commonwealth in public documents, which employed fuch dates as the $\frac{21}{31}$ June. Therefore, Sir Edward Dering's 3rd of September may really have been, and probably was, Englifh Bartholomew's Day, the 24th of Auguft.

Some old verfes about the Fair, written in the time of the Commonwealth, and in the year 1655, fhow that it then ftill throve, that the cut-purfes were not fuppreffed, and that Fat Urfula was ftill meafuring her ale at the rate of fix cans to a quart. The rope-dancer performed within four walls to penny audiences, and the memory of the old Miracle Plays and Moralities was being cherifhed among the puppets. Bows and arrows were fold among the pigs at Pye Corner, and the leather market had begotten, near Smithfield Bars, an offspring of its own in Shoe-makers' Row. Thus runs the " Ancient Song of Bartholomew Fair," quoted in the fourth Volume (p. 169,) of D'Urfey's " Pills to Purge Melancholy " :

> In fifty-five may I never thrive,
> If I tell you any more than is true,
> To London che came, hearing of the fame
> Of a Fair they call Bartholomew.

> In houfes of boards, men walk upon cords,
> As eafy as fquirrels crack filberds;
> But the cut-purfes they do bite, and rob away;
> But thofe we fuppofe to be ill-birds.

> For a penny you may zee a fine puppet play,
> And for twopence a rare piece of art;
> And a penny a can, I dare fwear a man
> May put zix of 'em into a quart.

> Their zights are fo rich, is able to bewitch
> The heart of a very fine man-a;
> Here's patient Grifel here, and fair Rofamond there,
> And the Hiftory of Sufanna.

At Pye Corner end, mark well, my good friend,
 Tis a very fine dirty place;
Where there's more arrows and bows, the Lord above knows,
 Than was handl'd at Chivy-Chafe.

Then at Smithfield Bars, betwixt the ground and the ftars,
 There's a place they call Shoemaker Row,
Where that you may buy fhoes every day
 Or go barefoot all the year, I tro!

But the pofition occupied by Bartholomew Fair during the Commonwealth will be beft underftood if connected with a recollection of the ftruggles of the ftage during that period. Whatever Prynne may have fuffered for his Hiftrio-maftix, or Stagers' Scourge, publifhed in 1633, the intereft excited by the book was mainly due to the fact that it expreffed an actual paffion felt by a large body of the people. Only nine years later is the date of an ordinance of the Lords and Commons concerning ftage plays, commanding them to be forborne as out of joint with days when England was " threatened with a cloud of blood by a civil war." Again, in the year 1647, there had been an Act paffed to the effect that all ftage galleries, feats, and boxes fhould be pulled down by warrant of two juftices of peace; that all actors of plays for the time to come, being convicted, fhould be publicly whipped; and that all fpectators of plays for every offence fhould pay five fhillings. Prynne could have afked no more than that. Many players out of occupation fought in the ranks of the Royalifts. Some waifs collected in one fpot during a lull in the great ftorm, were to be feen together on three or four fucceffive nights in the year 1648, performing at the Cock-pit. They were broken in upon and difperfed by foldiers.

In Oliver's day, however, there was much fecret connivance at dramatic entertainment. Private performances
were held now at one place, now at another a few miles
from town, fometimes at noblemen's houfes ; and among
noble patrons there was none fo prominent as the one in
whofe family part of Bartholomew Fair was an inheritance. Of the fecret performances at Holland Houfe
there is efpecial recollection. At fuch meetings the
performers were paid by a collection made among thofe
prefent. At the great feftival times of Chriftmas and
Bartholomew Fair, it was found poffible to bribe the
officer who commanded at Whitehall, and to open the
theatre in St. John Street, the Red Bull, which from
its vicinity to Smithfield, was efpecially the Bartholomew
Fair playhoufe, for a few performances. Even then,
however, they were difturbed fometimes by the foldiery.

Remembrance is here due to Robert Cox, a good
comedian who, during the fuppreffion of the playhoufes,
wrote drolls or farces which were acted under the difguife
of rope-dancing, he himfelf ufually taking the chief
character. He reprefented thus the living drama in the
Fair ; and it is faid that by his performance of the part of
Simpleton the Smith, at a country fair, he fo impreffed a
blackfmith who was prefent with his genius for fmith's
work, that he offered him the poft of journeyman at
twelvepence a-week extra wages.

At the Reftoration the old actors who furvived were
formed into a company that performed at feveral of the
old playhoufes, including the Red Bull, until the new
theatres were built, for the erection of which Killegrew
and Davenant had, in 1660, each received a patent.

Lady Holland's Mob is an inftitution of the Fair, which feems to have been founded in the time of the Commonwealth. It is a Mob without a Literature, which has no account to give of itfelf; neverthelefs the date of its beginning is not hard to guefs. We remember that the fuppreffed players had, under the Commonwealth, a fpecial gathering place for fecret performances in Holland Houfe. The ladies of this family after the coalefcing of the peerages, were Lady Warwicks. The firft Lady Holland, as we have feen, was that heirefs of Sir Walter Cope who brought the Kenfington eftate into the family, wife of the Earl who was beheaded by the Parliament in the fame year with King Charles the Firft. She it is, who, in the days of the Commonwealth, was miftrefs of Holland Houfe; and her fon's wife was the only other Lady Holland. It was this energetic lady who fet builders to work on the houfe, and entertained the condemned players. She, therefore, muft have been the Lady Holland of the Mob.

During the Commonwealth feveral attempts were made, by London Mayors, to put fome check on the freedom of Bartholomew Fair. One of thefe magiftrates, Sir John Dethick, was knighted by Cromwell foon after the Fair-time (on the 5th of September) in 1656. It is not unlikely that this was the Mayor who preffed hard againft thofe puppet fhowmen and others that had begun the bufinefs of the Fair, as he conceived, twelve hours too foon, and were already at work when he arrived at Smithfield to proclaim the opening. An undated broadfide, of which the only copy acceffible to me is torn upon one margin, and has loft therefore fome rhymes from the fecond column of its verfes, bears on this incident, which feems to be affociated with the origin of Lady Holland's Mob. I copy it, indicating by a bracket where I have given, for the miffing words, conjecture of what poffibly they may have been.

The Dagonizing of *Bartholomew Fayre* caufed b[y the Lord Majors Command, for the battering downe the va[nities of the Gentiles, comprehended in Flag and Pole, appertayning to Puppet-play.

The 23 of Auguft being the day before the Apoftolicke Fayre.

> On Auguft's foure and twentieth Eve,
> The Cities Soveraigne and the Shrieve
> To Smithfield came if you'll believe
>   to fee th' ungodly flagges.

> The Livery men were fore put too't
> Though fome wore fhoe and fome wore boot
> They 'ere all conftrained to trans on foot,
>   God fave 'em.

> Entring through Duck Lane at the Crowne
> The foveraigne Cit began to frowne,
> As if 't abated his renowne,
>   the paint did fo o'retop him.

> Downe with thofe Dagons then, quoth he,
> They outbrave my dayes Regality,
> For's pride and partiality
>   Jove crop him.

> Ile have no puppet-playes, quoth he,
> The harmlefse-mirth difpleafeth me,
> Begun on Auguft twenty three,
>   'tis full twelve howres too early.

> A yonker then began to laugh,
> 'Gainft whom the Major advanc't white ftaffe,
> And fent him to the Compter fafe,
>   Sans parly.

Another wight (in wofull wife)
Befought the Major, his pupetries,
That he would not Babell-onize,
    (Urfula-talk omitted.)

Another Mortall had a clout,
Which on a long pole did hang [out
At which the Major turned up h[is fnout
    for he was then ad[vancing

Mounted with him came both [fhrieves
And Catchpoles with their ha[ndy fleeves;
They fhew'd much like a den [of thieves,
    though pra[ncing.

With that my Lord did filenc[e call,
He op'd his mouth and thus [did bawl:
Tis fitteft quoth he that the [ftall
    unto the walls [be tumbled.

There was a Varlet (clofe a[t hand
To execute (gold chaines [command
Pull'd wight away ftraight, [from his ftand-
    ing, fo[r he grumbled.

He that fhew'd wonders n[ext below
Spoke in behalfe of his fin[e fhow;
Quoth he, we fpit no fire [at you,
    nor fuch like pu[re ones.

Befides we fhew his Excel[lence hand.
Quoth Major, that is [not my command;
Gods-nigs tis time t[o clear the land
    [Of this affurance.

On top of Booth fat [Jack Pudding
(Lord would be loath [to let him fwing)—
I'me fure he wifht [that he could bring
    ye[ars to his Highnefs.

But when his Lo[rdfhip looked on high,
John fet up th[en a devil's cry,
And glad he w[as to fee him fly,

    So was Mr. FINIS.

These verses tell us that the Fair, "begun on August twenty-three, is full twelve hours too early." The proclamation was made late in the afternoon, but the showmen and traders opened their booths early in the morning. Lawful objection being made to this, a riotous assembly met, on the night before the day of the Mayor's proclamation, at the public house within Cloth Fair, in which the Court of Piepowder was held, the Hand and Shears,

—now transformed into a tall brick gin-palace,—and at midnight sallied forth, bearing along, in later years, the effigy of a woman to represent Lady Holland (who must have been instigator and, it would seem, first leader of the mob), and the mob—knocking at doors, ringing bells, clamouring and rioting some five thousand strong during three hours of the middle of the night,—proclaimed for itself, in its own way, that

Bartholomew Fair was open.   The firft irregular proclamation was for many years made by a company of
tailors who met the night before the legal proclamation,
at the Hand and Shears, elected a chairman, and as the
clock ftruck twelve, went out into Cloth Fair, each with
a pair of Shears in his Hand.   The chairman then proclaimed the Fair to the expectant mob, and all fped on
their errand of riot, to aroufe with the news of it the
fleepers in the neighbourhood of Smithfield.

In the year 1661 it was ordered by proclamation that
the coinage of the Commonwealth fhould no longer be
current than the laft day of November in that year.
The *Kingdom's Intelligencer*, for Auguft 22, 25, in the
year following contained this notice, referring obvioufly
to the Fair then open : " Whitehall, Auguft 23. There
hath been a difcovery of divers perfons who have coined
both gold and filver, and of other perfons who have
vended the fame, in great quantities, &c. intending to
utter the fame to Clothiers and at Fairs ; which is publifhed to the end that honeft perfons be not deceived by
receiving fuch monies."

It feems to have been very foon after the Reftoration
of King Charles the Second, that a tract, entitled " News
from Bartholomew Fair.   Or, the World's Mad : being
a Defcription of the Varieties and Fooleries of this
prefent Age," was, with allowance, " Printed for the
General ufe of the Buyer, and Perticular Benefit of the
Seller."   It had for motto " Rifum teneatis amici ?"
and this frontifpiece reprefenting a modified Puritan, in
prefence of Jacob Hall the fafhionable rope-dancer,
exhibiting the vanities of drefs.

It begins "Faith, gentlemen, you may juftly fay I have picked out a mad fubjeﬅ to treat on," and dilates in four pages upon the faithleﬀneſs of the two ſexes to one another. "What Chriﬅian," it aſks, "can refrain from bewailing this preſent age, deteﬅing and abhorring the pride and luxury, the execrations, oaths and curſes, profaneneſs and blaſphemy, ebriety, fornication and adultery, that infatuated mankind (O Miſerabile Dictu) is now immerﬅ in, and wholly addiﬅed to : what precipitate haﬅe they make to hell and damnation, or as if there were no Heaven, none to call them to an account for their crying ſins and tranſgreﬅions ; it's probable they conclude with Muggleton, they have the power of damning and ſaving in their own hands ; and that notwithﬅanding their reiterated villanies they are aﬀured of ſalvation : Thus they daily go on to aﬅ all miſchief, that their deprived appetites ﬅretched on the tenters of invention can deviſe, in which moﬅ of their precious time is ſpent, to the negleﬅ of their more precious and immortal ſouls. All theſe things (Candid Reader)

confidered, I hope I may without much rhetorick be excufed for faying, the world's mad, or the devil's in 't." That is the end and point of the fmall differtation on four quarto leaves, which offered feeble proteft in the Fair againft the licence fafhionable in the days of Charles the Second.

Of that licence there is pitiable evidence in another extant tract, bearing date in the firft year after the Reftoration, 1661, which contains fix pages of filth, ' by Peter Aretine,' printed for ' Theodofus Microcofmus,' a fequel to five pamphlets of which the contents are inexpreffibly difgufting.   The title of this pamphlet begins by promifing ' Strange news from Bartholomew Fair;' the reft of it I do not care to quote.   All to be learnt from it is, that in Duck Lane and Pye Corner were many dens of wickednefs, that bawds were alfo thieves, that they were punifhed by whipping, and that there were ftill zealots who came into the Fair.

The licence of the Reftoration, mainly arifing from the low perfonal character of the King, but greatly promoted by the natural tendency to reaction after the excefs of feverity ufed by the Puritans in fuppreffing what was not to be fuppreffed, at once extended Bartholomew Fair from a three days' market, to a fortnight's— if not even at one time a fix weeks'*—riot of amufement.

Mr. Samuel Pepys, whofe love of amufement has borne fruit in thefe days to many a working ftudent, was at the time of which we now fpeak, Clerk of the Acts of the

---

* The Hiftory and Origin of Bartholomew Fair.   Publifhed by Arlifs and Huntfman, 37, Bartholomew Clofe, anno 1808. fm. 8vo, pp. 26.

Navy, and was refident in Seething Lane. His diary contains feveral points of information on the fubject of the Fair. On the 25th of Auguft—the morrow of St. Bartholomew's Day—in 1663, Mr. Pepys going at noon to the Exchange, met a fine fellow with trumpets before him in Leadenhall Street, and upon enquiry found that he was Clerk of the City Market; three or four men attended him, carrying each an arrow of a pound weight in his hand. This was the beginning again by the Lord Mayor, Sir John Frederic, of the old city cuftom. His Lordfhip had been, the day before, with the Aldermen in Moorfields, for the Bartholomew's Day wreftling. That day was appointed for the fhooting, and the officer, as Mr. Pepys thought, was riding through the city to proclaim or challenge any to fhoot. On the day following—third day of the Fair—there was to be a civic hunting, alfo by old cuftom. The reftoration of fo much of the Mayor's prefence was not fought in Smithfield. " It feems the people of the Fair cry out upon it, as a great hindrance to them."

But it was not only the fafhionable trifler upon town who, after the Reftoration, fought matter of amufement or reflection in Bartholomew Fair. Even John Locke, the philofopher, elbowed his way with the reft of the world, in the Smithfield crowd, as we find from one of his letters to John Strachy at Briftol, dated from Cleves in 1664. " Near the high altar," he writes, " in the principal church at Cleves, was a little altar for the fervice of Chriftmas Day. The fcene was a ftable, wherein was an Ox, an Afs, a Cradle, the Virgin, the Babe, Jofeph, fhepherds and angels, dramatis perfonæ.

R

Had they but given them motion it had been a perfect
Puppet Play, and might have deferved pence a piece;
for they were of the fame fize and make that our Englifh
puppets are; and, I am confident, thefe fhepherds and
this Jofeph are kin to that Judith and Holophernes
which I had feen at Bartholomew Fair."

In the *Newes* and *Intelligencer* of the King's cenfor,
Roger L'Eftrange, commenced in the previous year as
the modicum of newfpaper which was to keep the profane
multitude from being pragmatical and cenforious, and
gifted with an itch for meddling with the government,
we read of the end of St. James's Fair in a market that
was probably, in its eftablifhment, more profitable to the
royal purfe. In the *Newes* of July 28, 1664, is this
announcement: "Whitehall, July 27. The Fair at St.
James's is put by, as confidered to tend rather to the
advantage of loofenefs and irregularity, than to the
fubftantial promoting of any good, common and bene-
ficial to the people." And in the *Intelligencer* of
October 10, we learn that there was a "Market proclaimed at St. James' Fields, Tuefday, 27 September,
1664, for all fort of provifions, Mondays, Wednefdays,
and Saturdays, and for all fort of Cattle in the Haymarket, every Monday and Wednefday."

The year 1665, the year of the Great Plague, which
Defoe has made for us the truth itfelf inftead of the
word of it, the year alfo of the comet, "of a faint, dull,
languid colour, and its motion very heavy and flow," was
no year for Bartholomew Fair. It was fupprefled that
year, and again clofed in the year following, by reafon
of the plague. Plague which had made fo many vifits,

and had even been naturalifed in London between the
years 1636 and 1647, after 1648 had all but entirely
ceafed. There was not plague under the Commonwealth ; but after five years of the Reftoration it came
in again, as a moral plague did alfo, with more than its
former virulence. Of the time of Bartholomew Fair,
in the autumn of this year, Thomas Vincent, one of
the nonconforming minifters, who, when the conform-
able minifters had fled, refolved to ftay with the people,
wrote : " Now people fall as thick as the leaves in
autumn when they are fhaken by a mighty wind. Now
there is a difmal folitude in London ftreets ; every day
looks with the face of a Sabbath day, obferved with a
greater folemnity than it ufed to be in the city. Now
fhops are fhut in, people rare and very few that walk
about, infomuch that the grafs begins to fpring up in
fome places, and a deep filence in every place, efpecially
within the walls." No Bartholomew Fair, therefore, in
1665. At the beginning of September, ufual Fair time,
in that year, bale fires burnt night and day, for the
cleanfing of the air, in every ftreet, till they were put
out by heavy rain. In the year following, though
Plague was abated, the holding of Bartholomew Fair
was not accounted fafe ; and fo there was again no
Bartholomew Fair when, on the 2nd of September,
within the time to which the holding of the feftival
had been extended after the Reftoration, the Great Fire
of London began. Flames two miles long and a mile
broad, fmoke fpreading fifty miles, were at that Fair
time in London ; and the Fire would not have fwallowed
up the booths if they had been erected, for it ended at

Pye Corner. The houſes at Pye Corner that eſcaped the Fire, and lay upon its borders, were not taken down until October, 1809. The ſuppreſſion of the Fair during theſe two years is mentioned in Clavell's " Catalogue of Books publiſhed ſince the Plague."

In the year after the Fire, the Fair was held again ; and Mr. Pepys rejoiced in it, and on the 28th of Auguſt, as he ſays, " went twice round Bartholomew Fair, which I was glad to ſee again, after two years miſſing it by the Plague."

Of one of the ſhows of the Fair this year there is a handbill preſerved :

" At Mr. Croome's, at the Sign of the Shoe and Slap, near the Hoſpital Gate in Weſt Smithfield, is to be ſeen,

"THE WONDER OF NATURE,

" A Girl, above Sixteen Years of Age, born in Cheſhire, and not above Eighteen inches long, having ſhed the Teeth ſeven ſeveral Times, and not a perfect Bone in any part of her, only the Head ; yet ſhe hath all her ſenſes to Admiration, and Diſcourſes, Reads very well, Sings, Whiſtles, and all very pleaſant to hear.

" God Save the King.

" *Sept.* 4, 1667."

On the 30th of Auguſt in the ſame year, Pepys tells us that he found at the Fair a crowd about the puppet-ſhow in which was the King's Miſtreſs, Lady Caſtle-maine, introduced by the king ſix years before in the midſt of his court to his newly-married wife. " I to

Bartholomew Fair to walk up and down; and there, among other things, find my Lady Caſtlemaine at a puppet-play (Patient Griſel), and the ſtreet full of people expecting her coming out. I confeſs I did wonder at her courage to come abroad, thinking the people would abuſe her: but they, ſilly people! do not know the work ſhe makes, and therefore ſuffered her with great reſpect to take coach, and ſhe went away without any trouble at all." Of courſe her ladyſhip, having glorified fat Urſula's eyes with her preſence, took coach with great reſpect; ſhe was on her own ground at Pye Corner.

Court people and ladies of all qualities were at home in the Fair in theſe days. On the 29th of Auguſt, 1668, Mr. Pepys, having found poor entertainment at the playhouſe, was dull. "So I out, and met my wife in a coach, and ſtopped her going thither to meet me; and took her and Mercer and Deb. to Bartholomew Fair, and there did ſee a ridiculous obſcene little ſtage-play, called 'Marry Audrey,' a fooliſh thing, but ſeen by everybody; and ſo to Jacob Hall's dancing of the ropes, a thing worth ſeeing and mightily followed."

Jacob Hall, the rope-dancer, was a pretty man, and was ſaid to divide with the king the affections of the Lady Caſtlemaine, from whom he received a ſalary. A few days afterwards, at Southwark Fair, Mr. Pepys having been greatly worked upon, like all people that ſaw it, by the puppet-ſhow of "Whittington," went again "to Jacob Hall's dancing on the ropes, where," he goes on to record, "I ſaw ſuch action as I never ſaw before, and mightily worth ſeeing; and here took acquaintance with a fellow that carried me to a tavern

whither come the mufic of this booth, and by and by
Jacob Hall himfelf, with whom I had a mind to fpeak,
to hear whether he had ever any mifchief by falls in his
time. He told me, Yes, many, but never to the
breaking of a limb. He feems a mighty ftrong man.
So, giving them a bottle or two of wine, I went away."

The favourite of the King's miftrefs affected daintinefs
of drefs, if we may truft this copy of the oldeft engraving
from an unnamed portrait by Van Ooft, firft faid by
Ames in 1748, to reprefent the famous rope-dancer, and
fince admitted as a picture of him into Grammont's
Memoirs.

The throng to the performances of Jacob Hall was
great. Once when he was putting up a booth at
Charing Crofs for his rope dancing, he and his workmen
were fent for by a tipftaff, and becaufe he would not
enter into a recognifance not to build on, he was
committed ; upon which compulfion he abandoned his

defign. Neverthelefs, by the intereft of his patronefs
with all that was frivolous at Court, or by his own
pertinacity, he did eftablifh a rope dancing booth at
Charing Crofs, and when he prefently afterwards began
to erect alfo a ftage in Lincoln's Inn Fields, upon a
petition of the inhabitants, there was an inhibition from
Whitehall, and he was told alfo by the Chief Juftice
that his Charing Crofs booth was a nuifance to the
parifh. Some of the inhabitants there, being in Court,
faid, that it occafioned broils and fighting, and drew fo
many rogues to that place, that they loft things out of
their fhops every afternoon.

> When Jacob Hall on his high rope fhews tricks,
> The Dragon flatters; the Lord Mayor's horfe kicks;
> The Cheapfide crowds, and pageants fcarcely know
> Which moft t'admire, Hall, hobby horfe, or Bow.

Thefe lines from verfes on Bow Church and fteeple in
Dr. Wild's "Rome rhymed to Death" (1683) fhow that
the great rope-dancer performed alfo in Cheapfide when
there were city pageants. Great and fmall poets alike
gave bits of their minds to Jacob Hall. Dryden
alludes to him in the epilogue to Lee's Mithridates
King of Pontus; Dr. John King, of Chelfea, pins
him in a riddle. Dryden connects his name with that of
St. André the dancing mafter, and adds fomething to
our knowledge of what was done in the Fair by flack-
rope dancers.

He afks

> Have not you feen the dancing of the rope?
> When Andre's wit was clean run off the fcore,
> And Jacob's capering tricks could do no more,

A damfel does to the ladder's top advance,
And with two heavy buckets drags a dance;
The yawning crowd perk up to fee the fight,
And flaver at the mouth for vain delight.

Dr. King in his collection of riddles fays:

Ceafe to wonder, I pray, good people, all
At the feats and performances of Jacob Hall,
Or nimble rope-dancer; fince I faw juft now
Ten couple dance over the back of a cow
Upon a fmall pack-thread by the help of a fow.
Tell me this, you fhall be Apollo, I vow.

You who would be Apollo, anfwer to this: Ladies and Gentlemen who dance in fhoes.

William Blaythwaite in a letter to Sir Robert Southwell, dated Whitehall, September 4th, 1679, defcribing a vifit to Bartholomew Fair, made on the preceding day, by Sir Edward Dering, my Lady Mrs. Helena Percival, Mifs Helena, Mifs Betty, and himfelf, fays, " what we faw was the dancing on the ropes performed firft by Jacob Hall and his company, then by a Dutch dancer, who did wonderful feats. From thence we went to the Elephant, who I think was more terrible than pleafant to the young fpectators."

In the Guildhall collection of materials towards a hiftory of Bartholomew Fair, there is a copy made by the collector, of a broadfide printed at about this time, " by and for A. M., and fold by J. Walter, at the Hand and Pen in Holborn," which will add fome colouring to our picture of the Fair in the time of Charles the Second. In quoting this or any other memorial, let it be underftood that I alter nothing, but,

in the name of cleanlinefs, omit whatever is mere
Urfula talk.

" ROGER IN AMAZE ; OR, THE COUNTRYMAN'S RAMBLE THROUGH BARTHOLOMEW FAIR.

(To the Tune of the Dutchman's Jig.)

Adzooks ches went the other day to London Town
  In Smithfield fuch gazing
  Zuch thrufting and fqueezing
   Was never known.
A Zity of wood, fome volk do call Bartholomew Fair,
But ches zure not but king and queens live there.

In gold and zilver, zilk and velvet each was dreft,
  A Lord in his zattin
  Was bus'ly prating
   Among the reft.
But one in blew jacket came in, which fome do Andrew call,
Ad'fheart talked woundy wittily to them all.

At laft adzooks, he made fuch fport I laugh'd aloud ;
  The rogue being fluftered
  He flung me a cuftard
   Amid the crowd.
The Volk fell a laughing at me, then the vixen faid,
' Be fure Ralph, give it to Dolly, the dairymaid.'

I zwallowed the affront, but ftaid no longer there :
  I thruft, I fcrambled
  Till further I rambled
   Into the Fair.
When Trumpets and Bagpipes, Kettledrums and Fidlers all were
  at work
And the Cooks zung, ' Here's your delicate Pig and Pork.'
  . . . . . .

I thruft and fhoved along, as well as ere I could :
  At laft I chanced grovel
  Into a dark hovel
   Where Drink was fold.
They brought me cans, which coft a penny a piece, ad'fheart,
I'm fure twelve ne'er could fill our country quart.

> Che wint to draw her parfe, to pay them for their beer,
>> The devil a penny
>> Of money che'd any
>>> Che'll vow and fwear.
> They doft my hat for a groat, then turned me out of doors.
>
> .   .   .   .   .   .

From the countryman we turn back to the expert townfman at the Fair. On the 1ft of September 1668, Mr. Pepys to the Fair, and there faw feveral fights; among others, the Mare that tells money and many things to admiration. Three days afterwards the fame gentleman went "to the Fair to fee the play of Bartholomew Fair with puppets," meaning not acted by puppets, but with the puppet fhow included in it. Ben Jonfon's play received the doubtful honour of King Charles the Second's fpecial approbation. Firft reftored to the ftage, after forty years fuppreffion, on the 7th of September, 1661, it was performed feveral times before the King, and the Fair itfelf rioted in the difcomfiture of Rabbi Bufy; but, blind to the equally hateful picture drawn of itfelf by the great dramatic fatirift, made its booths merry with the Elder and the Pigwoman. It is well to remember that while Charles the Second, fcoffing at religion, where the fatirift had fcoffed at the vain fhow of it, patronifed Ben Jonfon's Bartholomew Fair, there is faid to have been an interdict put in his reign on the Maid's Tragedy of Beaumont and Fletcher, which clofes with the moral, that:

> On luftful kings
> Unlooked for fudden deaths from heaven are fent.

And, whether that be true or not, Mr. Waller felt it to

be only loyal that a new fifth act fhould be written,
expunging the judgment on the

> Shamelefs villain !
> A thing out of the overcharge of nature ;
> Sent, like a thick cloud, to difpenfe a plague
> Upon weak catching women ! fuch a tyrant,
> That for his luft would fell away his fubjects ;
> Ay, all his heaven hereafter !

And putting in place of it a happy end, with the prayer
that fixed the perfonal interpretation then in every man's
mind :

> Long may he reign that is fo far above
> All vice, all paffion but excefs in love.

Creditable to Mr. Samuel Pepys is his cogitation on
the Fair within the Fair : " And is an excellent play ;
the more I fee it, the more I love the wit of it ; only the
bufinefs of abufing the Puritans begins to grow ftale,
and of no ufe, they being the people that at laft will be
found the wifeft."

On the feventh of September, in the fame year of the
Fair, Mr. Pepys was " with Lord Brouncker (who was
this day in an unufual manner merry, I believe with
drink), J. Minnes and W. Pen to Bartholomew Fair ;
and there faw the Dancing Mare again (which to day I
find to act much worfe than the other day, fhe forgetting
many things, which her mafter beat her for, and was
mightily vexed), and then the dancing of the ropes, and
alfo the little ftage-play, which is very ridiculous."

On the day following Mr. Pepys received fo earneft
an invitation to Stourbridge Fair from Roger Pepys
that he refolved to let his wife go, which fhe was to do

next week. Bartholomew Fair, Southwark Fair, and Stourbridge Fair,—fince the extenfion of Bartholomew Fair,—were all kept in September.

In the year 1671, the corporation of London was diffatisfied with the profits of the Fair accruing from the arrangement then fubfifting, and referred it to the Comptroller to let the ground for the City, and report the profits, &c., to the firft court after the Fair. This was done, and the tolls of the Fair were not farmed but received directly by the City until July 30 in the year 1685, when they were leafed to the fword-bearer for three years at a clear rent of a hundred pounds a year. At the expiration of two years a committee having reported that the net annual profit for thofe years had amounted to not more than fixty-eight pounds, the City Fair, then lafting fourteen days, was, on his application, leafed to the fword-bearer for one-and-twenty years at the fame rent.

In the meantime the civic authorities had already taken formal notice of the " Irregularities and Diforders " of Bartholomew and Lady Fairs, and had in 1678 referred it to a committee " to confider how the fame might be prevented, and what damages would occur to the City by laying down the fame."

This is the firft hint of fuppreffion that arifes in the ftory of the Fair, and its arifing is almoft fimultaneous with the decay of the great annual gathering as a neceffary feat of trade. There is no year in which it can be diftinctly faid that then the Cloth Fair died. Even at this hour, when the Fair itfelf is extinct, there are in the ftreet called Cloth Fair, on the fite of the old mart, one or two confiderable fhops of cloth-merchants, who feem there to have buried themfelves out of fight, and to be feeding on traditions of the place. In Charles the Second's time Leeds had afferted its importance, and the cloth trade in the North of England was already outgrowing the old ways of commerce; Hercules was beginning to neglect his go-cart. The cattle fair was ftill confiderable, but London needed and had weekly cattle-markets, and one of thofe might be a fhow-market, if a great annual cattle-fhow were needed. At a much later date than that at which we have now arrived, (in 1715) we read in Dawk's New's Letter that "on Wednefday Bartholomew Fair began, to which we hear, the greateft number of black cattle was brought, that was ever known." The trade of the fair, therefore, was not extinct when the firft queftion of its fuppreffion arofe in the City of London. There was alfo a grave queftion whether the City had legally a right or power to fupprefs it.

Poor Robin's opinion of the commerce of Bartholomew Fair at this date we find in a catalogue of Jefts upon Fairs in his almanac for 1674. Among fuch quips as, " January 1 at Cogfhall in Effex for 𝕵𝖊𝖊𝖗𝖘, January 25 at St. Martin's for 𝕾𝖍𝖔𝖈𝖐-𝕯𝖔𝖌𝖘, January 28 at Dunftable for 𝕷𝖆𝖉𝖎𝖊𝖘 𝕮𝖍𝖆𝖕𝖑𝖆𝖎𝖓𝖘," &c. &c.—he defcribes Bartholomew Fair, thus: "Auguft 24 𝕬𝖙 𝕾𝖒𝖎𝖙𝖍𝖋𝖎𝖊𝖑𝖉 𝖋𝖔𝖗 𝕵𝖆𝖈𝖐-𝖕𝖚𝖉𝖉𝖎𝖓𝖌𝖘, 𝖕𝖎𝖌𝖘 𝖍𝖊𝖆𝖉𝖘 𝖆𝖓𝖉 𝕭𝖆𝖗𝖙𝖍𝖔𝖑𝖔𝖒𝖊𝖜 𝖇𝖆𝖇𝖎𝖊𝖘."

CHAPTER XIII.

The Hustling of the Pope.

ENOUGH has been read of the ſtory of the Fair to
ſhow that it was as truly as the Houſe of Commons,
part of the Repreſentation of the Engliſh People ;
not, indeed, its Lower, but its Loweſt Houſe. When
Spain threatened us with an Armada, the monkey of
the Fair was taught to ſhow defiance of the King of
Spain. When Gunpowder Plot was the topic of the
day, it was the great ſhow of the Fair, played to
eighteen or twenty penny audiences, nine times in an
afternoon. When England broke looſe from civil and
religious deſpotiſm, the Puritan was in the Fair preaching down vanity ; and the Cavalier was in the Fair with
all the puppets on his ſide, crying down exceſſes of
religious zeal. From among the exceſſes there came
out at laſt a quiet mean.

We arrive now at another period of anti-papal ferment.
Our ſtory does not aſk who ſtood behind Titus Oates, or
what was the firſt purpoſe of thoſe who deſigned the fable
of the Popiſh Plot to kill the king. In October, 1678,
the upheaval of thought among the people, cauſed by
it, began. On the firſt of November, the Houſe of

Commons refolved, " That, upon the evidence that has already appeared to the Houfe, this Houfe is of opinion, that there hath been and ftill is, a damnable and hellifh plot, combined and carried on by Popifh recu-fants, for the affaffinating and murdering the king, and for fubverting the Government, and rooting out and deftroying the Proteftant Religion." Bartholomew Fair was of the fame opinion, and acted on it in its booths. The Fair acted on it in the year 1680, a play, called " the CORONATION of QUEEN ELIZABETH, with the RESTAURATION of the PROTESTANT RELI-GION ; or, the DOWNFALL of the POPE. Being a moft excellent PLAY, As it was ACTED, BOTH AT *Bartholomew* and *Southwark* FAIRS, This prefent year 1680. With great Applaufe, and Approved of, and highly commended by all, the *Proteftant Nobility*, *Gentry*, and *Commonalty* of ENGLAND, who came to be Spectators of the fame. LONDON, Printed for *Ben Harris*, at the *Stationers' Arms*, under the *Piazza*, in *Cornhill*, 1680." The copy of this play (24 pages, Quarto) in the Library of the City of London, here ufed, is fuppofed to be the only perfect copy extant.

In 1680, when it was acted, the ferment raifed among all ranks or degrees, which nobody could conceive who was not a witnefs thereof, was at its height. On the 26th of June, the Duke of York, heir to the crown, had been by perfons of rank and influence, prefented before the Grand Jury at Weftminfter, as a Popifh recufant. The queftion of his exclufion from the throne was being difcuffed throughout the country at Bartho-lomew Fair time, and his rival in the minds of the

people, Monmouth, "the Proteſtant Duke," was at
that time in the Weſt of England, "with chariots,
horſemen, and a numerous train," receiving evidence,
as calm as it was overwhelming, of the Proteſtant
determination of the people. Then it was that the
great play of Bartholomew Fair was the play of which
I have juſt cited the title.

This is the addreſs, "To the Protestant Reader.
Kind Reader. After the great applauſe this Play
has gained upon the ſtage, I have thought fit, for
the better ſatisfaction of the Curious, to publiſh it to
the World, that all may plainly behold my ſincere
Intentions herein, which was only to lay open the
Cruelties and Villanies of *Rome*, more to the Life,
than they have been expoſed ſince the beginning of this
late horrid and moſt barbarous Plot ; for, upon ſecond
thoughts, I conſidered, that many who only ſaw this Play,
were not of ſuch profound Capacities, as to let it take a
firm Impreſſion upon their Memories ;"—we ſhall know
preſently, whether it is a thing to be remembered only
by men of profound capacity ;—" therefore, that all
might the better weigh each particular circumſtance, as
their leaſure ſerved them, I have preſumed to ſend it
abroad into the World, though, no doubt, amongſt a
thouſand Foes, whoſe Malice unqueſtionably will endeavour to aſperſe and fully the candid Reputation it
has already gained amongſt ſeveral Noble Perſonages of
this Nation, whoſe ſound Judgments are undeniable :
the reaſon of it, is, perhaps, becauſe it plainly ſhows
them as in a Mirror, the purity of our Religion, and
the groſs Abſurdities and Cruelties of the *Pope* and

Church of *Rome* in their proper Colours, not gilded over with borrowed Ornaments or Fictions, which never were ; but howfoever, under the friendly patronage of all truly Loyal Proteftants, I have fent it abroad to tell the World the Noble Exploits, Heroick Refolutions and Victories, of that bleft Queen who managed all the Plots and dire Confpiracies of Rome, to the laft moment of her long and profperous reign.

> So I remain a Lover of all that own the Name of Proteftants, and live up to the Dictates of the Sacred Profeffion, to ferve them in all fincerity.
>
> J. D.

The People then, under a king who made England inglorious abroad, were reverting ftrongly to the days of Queen Elizabeth, and dwelling on them in a tone that boded ill to any but a Proteftant fucceffor of the reigning Stuart. The Play of the Coronation of Queen Elizabeth was in three Acts, fhort enough to fecure an end to the whole performance every half-hour. Its theme was, of courfe, a Popifh Plot againft the Sovereign : and thefe were

THE ACTORS.

Queen Elizabeth.
1 Bifhop ⎫ Proteftants.
2 Bifhop ⎭
A Lord, General to the Queen.
Another Lord.
1 Popifh Cardinal.
2 Popifh Cardinal.
Tim, a Tinker.
Brufh, a Cooper.
Honeyfuckle, a Cook.
The Pope.
Devil.

2 Jefuits defigned to kill the Queen.
Dulcemente, a Nun, ravifhed by the Pope,
Cardinal Moricena, her Father,
2 Ghofts.   2 Devils more.
Singers and Mutes, &c,

Act I.

"Scene I.—*The noife of Kettle-Drums and Trumpets are heard, at which the Curtain rifing, difcovers the Queen fitting under a Cloth of State, in her Royal Robes, attended by her Lords and Ladies of Honour; two Bifhops fupporting her Crown, and two Popifh Cardinals ftanding at a diftance: the Scene imagined to be Whitehall.*

" 1 *Bifh*. Long live Elizabeth, of England, France, and Ireland, Queen; fole Protector of our Lives, Fortunes, and Religion, under whofe facred Rule may it fhine brighter than unclouded Stars.

"*A Lord*. May Foreign Nations fly to do you Homage, and kings find Succour under the Shelter of your Wings; Princes and Potentates bow down before you, as the Univerfal Goodnefs of the World: Ne'r was England fo happy in a Monarch, nor we in fuch a Royal Miftrefs.

" 1 *Bifhop*. May the Aethiopians forget the Sun, and fall down and worfhip you, whofe Sacred Influence governs thus Mankind.

"*Queen*. My thanks to all, but I muft refufe that worfhip which the Immortal Powers have only bidden to themfelves, yet muft own you, next to the Powers above, who have given me Effence, and preferved my Life from Dangers great; placing me upon this Throne to Rule a Tottering State, driven by fierce Storms of Malice, o'r the deep Billows of devouring Envy; encompaffed on every fide with Foes, yet fearlefs will I act.   Firft then, To fettle Religion, the deareft part of Government, and fureſt Rock for Princes to build upon, ſhall be my ſpeedy care to begin : I'll reform my own Houſe, and after that the Nation" (this, probably, was, like the next ſentence, a popular reference to the ſucceſſion queſtion, hailed with ſome particular applauſe). "Therefore all you who pay Obedience to the See of Rome, or think ſupremacy due to the Pope, we here diſcharge you and baniſh you our Court. You my Lord Cardinals, as chief, muſt ſhew the way, and in your rooms ſuch faithful Miniſters I'll place, as ſhall be worthy of ſo great a charge.

Bloodſhed and Rapine ſhall to Rome retire,
Murther and Luxury which feed the fire, *Exeunt all but the*
Shall to the Scarlet Beaſt for Succour fly, *2 Cardinals.*
And unimploy'd within his boſom die.

" 1 *Cardinal.* Is it come to this ?

" 2 *Card.* Now Hereſie begins to peep abroad, that in Maryes days was laid as low as Earth.

" 1 *Card.* Oh I could curſe her Heart out, nay, my own, for not preventing it before it had took root.

" 2 *Card.* Horrors and Death, why were our hands ſo tame, when one brave ſtroak had done it at the Altar.

" 1 *Card.* Where was this Devil, *Rome's* great coun- ſellor ; where was he, I ſay, that he foreſaw not this Monſter, to have puſhed it in the Mould of Nature, or have ſtrangled it in its Infancy, e'r it grew to ſuch a gigantick ſtature, now enough to ſhake the very Throne of Rome.

" 2 *Card.* It is not yet too late, the Seeds are newly ſown, and e'r they root too deep, we may pluck them up ; or by lopping off the Cedar, make the Shrubs bend pliant as we pleafe.

" 1 *Card.* Let us about it then, and lofe no time ; methinks I could as freely ftrike the Heretick, as one affured Salvation.

" 2 *Card.* Tis that muft crown our Wifhes; the Queen once Murthered, the reft are eafily reduced unto the See of *Rome ;* let's on then, no opportunity muft be omitted to get her fpeedily difpatched. 'Tis meritorious no doubt: Blood and Murthers are Rome's chiefeft Glories."

Great applaufe in the booth, furely, at this natural remark of the Cardinal's, which the other Cardinal tops with a likely prayer.

" 1 *Card.* O Pius Quartus affift us with thy Prayers, and Hell, if thou hop'ft a glutting Harveft, protect the beft Religion."   [*Exeunt.*

To a Bartholomew Play comic fcenes were effential, and the comedy confifts very much in Urfula-talk which is not worth repeating. It is the Pope who is befouled with it, as the polite reader will be pleafed to take for granted.

" SCENE II.—*Enter* Tim *the Tinker,* Brufh *the Cooper, and* Honeyfuckle *the Cook, with feveral other Rabble.*

" *Tim enter.*] Come, Neighbours, come,—This day is as we may fay, a Holy Day, for this day Queen Elizabeth is crowned King of England, and therefore we ought to keep it Holy.

" *All.* We ought, we ought.

" *Brufh.* How Neighbour, Holy ! Pray Neighbour, have a care what you fay, for methinks talking of keeping a day Holy, ſounds as if we intended to keep a day for his Holineſs.

" *Honey.* Who's that talks of his Holineſs? His Holineſs is . . I ſay no more, I ſay no more.

" *Tim.* Indeed, Neighbour Bruſh, my neighbour Honeyſuckle is in the right on't; for ſince King Elizabeth has baniſhed Popery out of England, I ſay . .

" *Bruſh.* Ay, but Neighbour, this had been Treaſon a year ago.

" *Tim.* But now we have got a King Elizabeth, 'tis no Treaſon, Neighbours; Agad I think myſelf as good a Chriſtian now, as any man of no religion whatſoever.

" *Bruſh.* A year ago, I had like to have been burnt for a Heretick, becauſe the watch took me with a Bible in my pocket, which I had had there at leaſt a quarter of a year, and never thought on't.

" *Tim.* Nay, I had like to have gone to pot too, for ſaying . . . : but thoſe times are gone, they are I thank my Stars, or elſe we ſhould all have ſmoak'd for ſpeaking againſt the Pope. Well, I am but a Tinker, but if I could have turned Papiſt, I never needed to have mended Kettle more.

" *Honey.* How's that, never mended Kettle more, that had been brave.

" *Tim.* No, for you muſt know I am a great Politician, and a great Stateſman ; that is, a man of the State: and a man of the State is a Stateſman, mark ye me Neighbours.

" *Honey.* Why, then we are all Stateſmen.

" *All.* All, all Stateſmen.

" *Tim.* Yes, every Man and Mother's Child that don't

go to Church too often; for if ye go to Church too often, People takes ye to be Religious, and then ye are looked upon as all Plotters, Traitors, Confpirators, and the like ; for under Religion the Pope acts all his Villanies : and everyone knows that he is the greateft Churchman in the World.

" *All.* He is, he is, he is—

" *Brufh.* But come Neighbours, to make right ufe of this Holyday, let us go to the Alehoufe, and there drink till we are drunk, come home and beat our wives, and fo to fleep : come, come, come Neighbours, come.

[*As they are going out, enter two Cardinals.*]

" *Honey.* Ha, what ha' we got here, two young Popes ?

" *Brufh.* No, no, they are Cardinals.

" *Tim.* How, Canibals ! Neighbours, ud's lud, they look as if they were a hungry, I had beft have a care they don't eat me. But now I think on't, Gentlemen, Pray how dare you ftay in London, fince King Elizabeth has Banifhed Popery out of England ?

" 1 *Card.* Why, you know we ought to have preach'd to you but— [*Here they run upon 'um rudely.*]

" *All.* But what, but what ?

" 2 *Card.* Why, ye are a company of Incorrigible, Impertinent, and Exorbitant Wretches—

" *Brufh.* How's that, Neighbours, Exorbitant !

" *Tim.* Ay, that's a hard word Neighbours. . . .

. . . . Therefore I think, Neighbours, thefe He Popes ought to be chaftifed.

" *All.* They ought, they ought—

[*Here they fall upon 'um with Broom-ftaves.*]

" *Card.* Pray Gentlemen, pray Gentlemen be civil.

" *Tim.* Down on your Knees then, down on your Knees, we ſay, and beg our Pardons, and that quickly.

" *Card.* O curſed Fate! But better this than worſe [*Aſide*]. We do, we do, Gentlemen, and are ſorry for what we have ſaid.

" *Tim.* Well, now I know 'um, that's he that burnt my Neighbour Mole the Sexton for a Heretick, who was of no Religion.

" *Bruſh.* And that ſly ſcarlet Rogue. . . *Honey.* And that's the fellow . . ; but 'tis no matter, we'll Plague 'um for it now we have got 'um in our clutches; they had better have been at Rome i' faith.

[*Taking off their Hats and Mantles, they rudely force them out.*

" *All.* Come, come. Away with 'um, away with 'um. [*Force them out.*

" *Tim.*

Thus like two Roman Hero's handy-dandy,
We'll go to the Alehouſe to be Drunk with Brandy.

[*Exeunt in the Cardinals Hats, and other ornaments.*

" SCENE III.—*The Scene draws off, and diſcovers the Romiſh Conclave, the Pope, Cardinals and Biſhops, as in cloſe conſult.*

" *Pope.* Now let the joy of Rome be great, and let every individual Father cry, Long live Religious Soul and Scourge of Hereſie, Mary of England, Eldeſt Daughter to this Holy See, read here.

[*Delivers a Paper to a Cardinal.*

" 1 *Card.* How's this, 300 burnt alive in a Church as they were Preaching Hereſie and cloſe Rebellion againſt this Holy Catholick and Apoſtolick See: Ten more ſuch Sacred Murthers would have made the haughty

Turk and ftubborn Flemming to have owned you the Supreme Head of the Univerfal Church.

" 2 *Card*. 'Tis great and Meritorious, let him be Canoniz'd for a Saint, that firft invented this Religious way of fending Troops of Hereticks to Hell together.

" *Pope*. Let it be done, 'tis my Command it be fo ; for the Propagators of Religion ought to be cherifhed though in Blood ; and let our fpeedy thanks be fent to our beft Daughter, for taking fuch effectual care to blaft the growing Herefie, and keep it underfoot.

" 1 *Card*. She ought to be Sainted whilft on Earth, and when wrapped up into the brighter Manfions, far above this lower world, be Enthroned a Goddefs, and adored, who found herfelf uneafie in her thoughts and reftlefs, till opportunity gave leave to throw her Self and Crown at your Sacred feet, defiring to be received into your bofom.

" *Pope*. And by fo doing has fenced herfelf within a Wall of Addamant, too fecure for Envy, or the prying Fates to reach ; and her Ambaffadors fhall ftill have the preheminency in all our Courts.

" 2 *Card*. Who dares difpute it, if it pleafes you, when all the glories of the Earth depend upon your Will ? Monarch's but a Name you lend to pleafure haughty Man withal, and when you pleafe to call it back, Kings are as foon devefted of their Honours, as are your meaneft Slaves.

[*Enter the* Devil *in the fhape of a Jefuit, as in great Confternation.*

" *Pope*. Ha ! Your Eyes fpeak wonders, and forebode fome difmal Meffage to the See of Rome.

" *Devil*. Difmal indeed, the Flower of Rome is gone,

the Star that lately ſhone ſo bright in your great Firma-
ment, is ſet; the Sacred Empreſs of the Northern Iſles,
the angry Power have ſnatched away, Mary of England's
dead.   [*All riſing come forward.*

"*All.* How!

"*Devil.* Cold as the face of Ice, and in her ſtead the
haughty Magnanimous Siſter's Crown'd—But Crown'd
to make Religion and her Ancient Seat ſtagger and fall
before her.

"*Pope.* Curſ'd diſaſter.

"*Devil.* All of the Church of Rome ſhe has diſ-
graced, and the greateſt Places of Truſt about her
Perſon, are given to Hereticks; no Roman is to be
ſeen in London now, but ſuch as ſculk in corners, or
thoſe of ſuch puny Souls that ſwallow all the Execrable
Oaths they impoſe."

We ſhould remember here that the Teſt Act was
recent when this play was acted. In 1673 the force of
law had been given to the reſolution of the Houſe of
Commons "That all perſons who ſhall refuſe to take
the Oaths of Allegiance and Supremacy, and receive the
Sacrament according to the rite of the Church of
England, ſhall be incapable of all public employment,
military and civil."

"*Pope.* Let them ſwallow all they can Impoſe, we
make it Lawful, we'll grant the Diſpenſations for ſo
doing; no matter if the whole outſide taſte of Heretick,
so within they remain firm to us—

"*Devil.* Something muſt be done to change the Scene,
leaſt other Nations taking Example from her, ſhould fall
from their Obedience, and throw off your yoak.

" *Pope.* There fhall; Nor muft we linger in a Caufe of fuch a vaft Importance; for Herefie, like Weeds, grows faft, and if timely care be not taken to prevent it, the World, e'r we can root them out, will be Infected.

[*Speaks to the* Cardinal.

Father, your advice in this great Affair.

" 1 *Card.* She muft be Murthered, and that without delay.

" *Devil.* Spoke like a Saint that would fain be in Hell before his time.   [*Afide.*

" *Pope.* Murther's too grofs a name, or founds too harfh in People's ears; let her be made away fecretly: Sign a fpeedy Warrant for her Death.

[*The* Cardinal *takes the Warrant, and having Signed it, delivers it to the* Pope, *who gives it to the* Devil.

" *Pope.* Here take this, and with our ample Pardon, though it be for the blackeft Murther's Hell e'r knew, . . .

> For to promote Religion naught 's withftood,
> Empires muft fall, and Kingdoms fet in Blood.
> Blood muft cement the tottering State of Rome,
> And Heaven fhall warrant all the Ills we doom.
> To fix Religion in its bleffed abode,
> Should be the mighty Bufinefs of a God :
> Murther's the end, the Trat'refs fhall not live,
> Who kills for Rome, Rome's Vicar will forgive.

[*Exeunt* Pope, Cardinal, Bifhops, *&c·*

" *Devil.* I can but laugh now, to think how thefe old Fools are cheated: This is the Warrant that Signs the Pope's deftruction. That muft needs be a hopeful Religion that has the Devil to it for a Tutor. 'Tis Murther and Poifon that brings them to the Popedom, where for a while, they enjoy all earthly Pleafures; but

then, by dire Miſchance, or their own Luxury, Death
ſnatches them from hence, and then they are hurried
Headlong down to my great Maſter.

> For he which in Pleaſure gives his Soul to dwell
> A Pope on Earth, muſt be a Devil in Hell.
>
> [*Exit.*"

So ends the firſt Act of this Bartholomew Fair
Drama. The Fair that dated its fame from a pilgrimage
to Rome, to which in its young days the juggling of
monks cauſed thouſands to travel through the marſhes
and the foreſt tracts of England, where men had rejoiced
and traded at the gates of the Priory, and in which
the monk's cowl had been a commoner ſight than the
fool's cap, was a Roman feſtival no more. Nothing
delighted its frequenters better, than that the Pope
ſhould be well huſtled in it. There is weak literature
in this play of Queen Elizabeth; but there is ſtrong
life. Think of it on its platform in the booth, recal
the eager faces and the animated ſhouts of a crowd, in
which Engliſh nobles took part with the rabble of the
Fair. "Therefore, all you who pay obedience to the
See of Rome, or think ſupremacy due to the Pope, we
here diſcharge you, and baniſh you our Court." The
determined power of the people, lay beneath the ſhouts
that anſwered to appeals like theſe. At that hour they
were kindled with the purpoſe of aſſuring to themſelves
their liberties, and when, ere long, the time was ripe for
their juſt effort, it was not made in vain. Very rude
and, in one ſenſe, very ignorant was the delight of the
multitude in the viſible rough handling of a pair of
Cardinals, the beating them with broomſticks, the ſtripping

off of their frippery, and carrying it about the ftage in ignominy, on the perfons of a pair of fots. It was uncivil and unjuft, no doubt, to call the Pope every bad name, to reprefent him as a breaker of all Ten Commandments, and to provide him with the Devil as his right-hand man. But there were three centuries of a nation's healthy growth implied in this. The grotefque figure, with the horns and tail, invented by themfelves, which holy friars in the old miracle plays had prefented to the crowd of the Fair as the Prince of Darknefs whom they were continually vanquifhing, at laft ftood for themfelves upon the fcene of their old triumphs over herefy; and upon the ground once made fruitful by the afhes of the martyrs, entered " the Devil in the fhape of a Jefuit, as in great Confternation."

Now let the curtain rife again, upon

Act II.

" Scene I.—*Enter two Cardinals.*

" 1 *Card.* This is the time the friendly Fates to Rome have fet to cut the root of Herefie, and Crown Religion Monarch in the Throne; E'r to Morrow's dawn the haughty Ufurprefs fhall be no more."

The fecond cardinal afks who are the Murderers, and the firft cardinal informs him that they are two fellows bred up in villany, whom he has agreed with " for fo many maffes to kill the Queen, and " he adds, " if they bring them off fhort of Heaven, there is no Truth in our Religion."

" 2 *Card.* You may as well mifdoubt Eternity, as Holy Unction, Mafs, and Prayer.

" 1 *Card.* Should they fail, I would ftrike the blow myfelf; methinks I could as eafily do it as I can merit my Salvation. [*Enter the* Devil *in the fhape of a Jefuit.*

" *Devil.* Loft, loft and undone for ever. Fly—fly— the Treacherous Secretaries of the Ambaffador, juft as the blow was going to be given, have unravelled all the Secrets of the Plot, and laid them open for each vulgar eye to pry into."

However, the affaffins have only a glimmering of what has paffed, and ftill " lurk about the Court, refolving this night to kill the Queen." The Devil is fent off to give them all encouragement, and goes faying, "I go Imperious Cardinals, but 'tis my Mafter's Intereft I confult, not yours; though you are they that reap our Harveft of dire Sin, 'tis we that have the Profit of the Scarlet grain to fill our Stores. I'll leave ye to your Fates, it will not be long e'r [*Afide*] the law fhall ftrangle you; when all your quibblings will not fave you."

Exit Devil and the Cardinals, after finding fome more villany to fay, go off with this couplet—

> " What's done for Rome muft needs, if great, be good,
> He merits Heav'n whofe Soul is bath'd in Blood."

"Scene II.—*Queen's Garden. Enter two Affaffines in the Habits of Jefuits,*" (alas, poor Jefuits!) " *with Daggers in their hands.*

" 1 *Affaffin.* This is the Night defigned to wafh our hands in Blood of Hereticks, to cut down that high Cedar that has made herfelf Rome's Envy; nor fhall we want Gold for perfecting fo brave a work; the enterprize muft be with Refolution undertook, and as fearlefs we muft on, as did that brave Burgundian, who killed the Prince of Orange.

" 2 *Affafs*. Remember Raviliac, and let us boldly
undertake an act fo meritorious ; nor let our hands
be flack to ftrike our fatal Daggers home into her
breaft ; plunge them to the hilt, and when we've
drawn 'um out, laugh loud, as being pleafed to fee
the ftreaming gore be-crimfon the pale furface of the
Earth.

" 1 *Affafs*. See where the Queen comes, attended only
by one Gentleman. Now's the time to cut the Root of
Herefie, and if fhe 'fcape us may we be accurfed for
ever. Methinks the blow's already ftruck, and Death
has hufhed her filent in his frozen Arms.

" 2 *Affafs*. Let us abfcond awhile, the better to
furprize her.   [*They retire and ftand unfeen.*

[*The* Queen *enters with one* Gentleman.

" *Queen*. Are all things done according to my order.

" *Gent*. They are. In all things I have been obedient
to fulfil your Royal Pleafure.

" *Queen*. What faid the French Ambaffador to his
Accufation ?

" *Gent*. Haughty and bold, like any guiltlefs man
he did behave himfelf before the Council, denying
that he knew ought againft our Sacred Life, or was
not obliged to tell it if he did ; he only alledg'd,
That it was not in the Power of any Council to tax
the King's Reprefentative, much more to demand
fuch Queftions of him as none but his Mafter ought
to know.

" *Queen*. 'Tis clofe and dark as all their other Actions
are, but we'll not meddle with Lemafpin more ; only
tell him our juft refentments, that we banifh him our

Court, and speedy care shall be taken to send him quickly to his own land.

> What Powers Divine Protect, Rome cannot harm,
> Nor can the Scarlet Beast our Senses charm ;
> Pistol nor Poison ne'r can make her start,
> Who has Heav'ns Sacred Armour for her Heart.

> [*Exeunt* Queen *and* Gentleman. *The Assassins come out from their Ambuscade and follow them.*

" 1 *Assass.* Now, now's the time, strike home. Now for cutting the very root of Heresie, that it shall never sprout in England more ; let's on, let's on, I say.

" 2 *Assass.* My heart fails me, I cannot touch her.

" 1 *Assass.* Cowardly slave, art thou not paid for Murther ?

" 2 *Assass.* Not as you are assured Salvation ; therefore strike you, and that quickly, or I'll kill you, and so end the dispute.

" 1 *Assass.* Villain, thou darest not.

" 2 *Assass.* You shall see I dare.

> [*Here they fight with their Daggers, during which,* Tim, Brush, *and* Honeysuckle, *with several others, enter.*

" *Tim.* Why how now, what's to do here ? What ! two Fellows a-Fighting in the Queen's Garden.

" *Honey.* I'll be hang'd if these Fellows have not a hand in the Plot, and come hither to kill the Queen.

" *Tim.* It may be, it may be so, therefore, I think it fit that we seize 'um, and carry 'um before a Justice of Peace to have 'um examin'd.

> [*Here they seize them, upon which they tremble, and endeavour to hide their Daggers, &c.*

" *Tim.* Pray, Gentlemen, of what Trade or what Calling are ye ; for know, Gentlemen, I have Power to apprehend ye, and make ye give a better account of yourfelves, and what bufinefs you had here.   Ha, what are thefe!   Truly, Gentlemen, thefe are fufpicious weapons.   [*Finding the Daggers.*

" *Honey.* Ud's lud, fee ye here, as I take it Neighbours, if I am not miftaken, they fhould be Butchers by their Knives.

" *Tim.* Well, come Gentlemen, I muft carry you and thefe before a Magiftrate, and have you both examined; and I'll promife you, Gentlemen, I'll be fo kind to you, that I won't leave you till I fee you both fairly hang'd; Come away with 'um, away with 'um; bring 'um along, bring 'um along.

" *All.* Along with 'um, along with 'um.
                                    [*They force them out.*"

SCENE III.—*The Scene draws off, and difcovers the* Pope *fitting by a* Nun.

The Pope is indelicate.   The Nun reminds him of her vows.   The Pope gives her free difpenfation, tells her, however, that Religion is a trade, and that " none but Women and Fools do believe that we can Save or Damn for Moneys whom we pleafe; or that Salvation can be bought and fold."   The Nun obtains further information of this fort from the Holy Father, who afks her how fhe can imagine " that the Clergy could confift or live without fuch foft, dear things as are your fex in general."   While he embraces her,
                          [*Enter the* Devil *in the Habit of a Jefuit.*
and fays, " Why this is as it fhou'd be," and offers further counfel for which, the Pope, embracing him, fays, " Thanks my deareft, beft of friends (thou haft

been always kind to me) I'll take thy counſel, and expect thee when to-morrow dawns."

> [*Exeunt* Pope, *leading the* Nun, *and as they are going out the* Devil *with a Dagger offers to ſtrike him.*

But he thinks better of it : He has made a promiſe, and the Pope, ſafe game, will die by the ſnare in proper time. This devil's great maſter ſits as partner in the popedom, "But," ſays to the Britiſh Public the rebellious imp, "it ſhall be my future buſineſs to ſupplant them both, and ſo at once to rid the Chair of a Luſtful Pope and an Imperious Devil."

> Pope thou art ready, and we all agree
> When thou com'ſt to Hell to keep a Jubilee.

Tim, Bruſh, Honeyſuckle, and others enter next, upon their way to ſee the Hanging of the two Aſſaſſins. Bruſh goes out and returns with news that they are hung already. The talk begets a challenge to a fight between Tim and Honeyſuckle, and, of courſe after due vilification of the Pope, the act ends with Tim's monition, "Come, come, Neighbour, for one cherriping Cup, and then to the Fight." [*Exeunt omnes.*

ACT III.

SCENE I.—*The Scene opens and diſcovers the* Pope *and* Nun *ſitting upon a Couch.*

In the midſt of their amorous talk the Nun remembers with dread her Father Cardinal Moricena, but the Pope threatens him with a Sleeping Pill if he prove troubleſome. [*Enter the* Devil *in the ſhape of a Jeſuit.*

"*Devil.* Fly, fly, or all will be diſcovered, Cardinal Moricena's at the gate." The angry Cardinal in fact

T

enters, and ftabs the irreligious Nun his daughter, who dies in his arms, laying the blame of all her guilt upon the Pope. The Pope and Cardinal come to high words. The devil whifpers to the Pope, "Kill the old Coxcomb, Sir, he will be babbling elfe. Kill him, I fay, or elfe you cannot be fafe."

"*Pope.* Moricena, let me embrace thee thus. [*Stabs him.*

"*Morice.* Ah, I'm flain. [*Dies.*

"*Pope.* Take that for railing at the Pope, and that for prying into his fecret love.

"*Afide Devil.* Evil counfel is a fure way to pufh a man upon damnation, and I am fure he wants not much of that.

"*Pope.* Well, what's next to be done?

"*Devil.* Fly Rome, Sir, without lofs of life or honour; this Cardinal reviled much the people's hearts, and when the murther's known, they'll feek revenge. Take all your jewels, and things of greateft value, eafieft portable; and in fome far country fpend the refidue of your days in pleafure.

"*Pope.* It will grieve me much to be depofed, but more to fuffer a fhameful and ignominious death; by the hands of thofe that were my flaves:—I was a fool to kill him—

> For men though great, yet are not always good,
> Who, like to Rome, delight to deal in Blood.   [*Exit* Pope.

"*Devil.* Well, like his fhadow I muft follow him wherefoever he goes, his thread of life is almoft fpun, and then he falls to my great Mafter's fhare—

> I'll hafte, and in deftruction pufh him on,
> And then I'll leave him in confufion.   [*Exit* Devil."

SCENE II.—*Enter* Tim, Honeyſuckle, *and others.*

Tim crying Victoria, Victoria, Victoria. He has beaten Honeyſuckle in the fight, upon which Honey-ſuckle declares, as he was bound to do, for the Pro-teſtants, reviles the Pope, and in token of reconciliation

" *He Dances an Antick Jigg.*

" *Tim.* So, well done, Cook, now I like thee, i' faith.

[*Enters* Bruſh *to them.*

" *Bruſh.* Arm, arm, Neighbours. Arm, or we ſhall be all burnt, burnt for Hereticks.

" *Tim.* How's that, Neighbour, all burnt for Hereticks?

" *Bruſh.* Ay, all for Hereticks; for the Pope with the whole Spaniſh Armado, is come into the Hope, laden with Faggots, Irons, Whips, Racks, and Gibbets, to torture, hang, and burn us all for being Proteſtants.

" *Tim.* How, the Pope come into the Hope! Uds-lud, then let us go hope to catch the Pope; and if we do catch the Old Gentleman, we'll ſo ſinge his Tail, that he ſhall never forſake the countrey. Now will I go muſter up all my Kent Street Regiment" (that was an alluſion meant for popularity in Southwark Fair), " and if I pull him not by the Beard, ſay Tim's a Coward. Come along, come along, along, along.　　　　　[*Exeunt.*

[*Enter the* Pope, *led by the* Devil *in his own Shape.*

" *Pope.* Where haſt thou brought me, through theſe gloomy ſhades of Night?

" *Devil.* Aſk thyſelf—know'ſt thou this Figure, once thy ſervant, and now thy Maſter. I counſelled thee in all, raiſed thee at firſt, and gave thee Popedom; bore thy

Meſſages o'er Sea, and laid and managed all thy Plots
againſt the Hereticks; but thou haſt bought my Service
dear, at the price of thy poor ſoul.   I had thee too in
Bonds, and all to make thee one to Lucifer my Maſter:
The time's expired, thy Glaſs is run, and long thou
can'ſt not ſtay; therefore, I'll leave thee to that fate
thou meriteſt, and the Hereticks ſhall give thee.

> [*The Scene ſuddenly draws off, and diſcovers Hell full of Devils,*
> *Popes and Cardinals, with the Ghoſts of* Moricena *and* Dulce-
> menta *wounded: To them the* Devil *enters.*

"*Pope.* What ghaſtly Viſions? this my eyeballs ſtart,
my Blood runs backward, and chill Horror freezes up
the Spring of Life.

> [*Enter one who ſings, in anſwer to a Noiſe behind the Scenes, &c.*

SONG.

Voice.   Where, where's the Pope?
Anſwer.   Come to die in a Rope:
            Or his breath expire by the flames of hot fire,
            To meet the juſt Plagues that his ſins do require.
Voice.   Pray what is his crime?
[*Anſwer.*] For coming to Popedom before 'twas his time;
            For Murther and Whoredom, for Poiſon and Rape,
            For killing the Father and making eſcape,
            From the Chair of St. Peter to a Heretick City;
            Mid'ſt the Rabble, to ſuffer without any pity.
            A round, a round, a round, incloſe the Pope round;
            Puſh him and toſs him on Prongs; all yet quicker,
            Till he cryes there's no hope, for bloody, bloody Pope,
            And a cheating old fool of a Vicar.

> [*Exit Singer.*"

The Pope cries, "Curſed diſmal fate, muſt all my
Glories and incumbent Honours ſink into the duſt!
O Popedom, thou gilded Pill, whoſe outſide ſeems
enticing fair, but being took, thou hurrieſt Mankind
upon his ſure deſtruction,

Oh, I could curſe thee, but 'tis now too late,
And I with patience muſt endure my fate.

[*As he is going out,* Tim, Bruſh, Honeyfuckle, *and others of the Rabble come running in, and almoſt beat him down.*"

The reader, who has borne with a good deal, here, perhaps, marvels how Tim and the Rabble found their way ſo eaſily to the Infernal Regions. Let him re-member, that at this time Davenant was laying the foundation of the art of ſcene-painting upon a better ſtage, and that in a booth at the Fair, during the reign of Charles the Firſt, the reader was to imagine all the places that he ſaw—as indeed in this drama, the very firſt direction ſays, " the Scene imagined to be White-hall." There was a great convenience attending this old plan, of which Bartholomew Fair dramatiſts could take advantage as they pleaſed. The locality not being obtruſively ſuggeſted to the eye, a ſpeaker was or was not in a given place, or he was now here and now there, according to convenience. Fancy was free, and there was no painter's work calling it to order when it choſe to riot in a few vagaries.

" *Tim.* Ha, what have we got here, a Mamamouche?

" *Honey.* I'll be hang'd if this fellow han't run away from his Colours; Uds-foot look here, he has brought the key of the Cupboard away with him for haſte.

[*Laying hold on the Key that hangs by his ſide.*

" *Tim.* Pray, Sir, if a man may be ſo bold to aſk, what are you, Sir? [*A diſmal Voice from above.*

" *Voice.* He's a Pope."

The Pope denies : the Voice ſays, " He lies." Tim argues that the Voice muſt be believed, " for it can't lie

fo long as it fpeaks againft the Pope." There are to
be bonfires that night for the Victory over the Spanifh
Armada, " and this Pope having been the caufe of the
burning of many a Heretick ; what fay ye, if we
fhould return him like for like, and burn him ?—Hold,
ftop the Pope there !   [*He offers to go out, they pull him in.*

" *All.* Ay, ay, that wou'd be brave, that wou'd be
brave.

" *Tim.* Then take him up, and let's march along
with him from hence.

> To Temple Bar, where being come,
> We'll facrifice this mighty Pope of Rome.

" *Pope.* O Gentlemen, Gentlemen, for Heaven's fake,
Gentlemen, Oh !

" *All.* Ay, ay, up with him, up with him.

> [*They get him aftride upon a Coalftaff, and lift him upon their
> Shoulders, fnatching off his Triple Mitre, Mantle, and other
> Ornaments, they put them upon themfelves; then hollow and
> dance round him.*

" *Tim.*

> For know, if you your felf to us do commit,
> You foon fhall find, we love neither Pope, Prieft, nor Jefuit.

" *Pope.* Gentlemen, Gentlemen, nay Gentlemen.

> [*They go out with him, hollowing and throwing up their hats.*"

Queen Elizabeth then enters with her General, Lords,
and Attendants, has with them a few words of big talk,
and is prefently furrounded by Tim and the rabble,
who " have been a-fighting, an't pleafe your Majefty,
and have beaten the Pope, and taken the Pope ; and
now we are come to get your Majeftie's leave to let us
burn the Pope."

" *General.* And where will you get one.

" *Tim.* O, we have a Pope, a lufty Pope, a ftrapping Pope, a rumping, thumping Pope, a Pope that will fry like Bacon, an't pleafe you.

" *Queen.* Ufe your freedom, you have our leave; but do it with difcretion, without Riot or Tumult; left Grace once given and then abufed, fhould turn the Sword of Juftice againft my Friends.

" *Tim.* Hark you there, fhe calls us all Friends.

" *All.* O law—

" *Tim.* O 'tis brave King Elizabeth; I'll warrant your Worfhip we'll ufe him as we ought. Come, come, to burn the Pope, to burn the Pope; Away, away.

[They go out leaping and fhouting.

" *Queen.*

Thus Heaven fhowers Bleffings on the head of Kings,
And does Protect them with Immortal Wings.
Rome may Confpire, and Hell with her Combine;
Yet cannot harm, though Pope and Devil join.

[They go out.

[Enter fix Dancers, who Dance a Set-Dance, which ended, they go out; then a Woman Enters and Dances a Jig."

That is the end of the Play. Burning the Pope, it fhould be faid, was in thofe days a favourite paftime of the Londoners. When, a few years afterwards, the Stuarts were being finally driven from the three kingdoms, a falfe rumour of King William's death in Ireland came to France, there was great rejoicing in Paris, and fays Voltaire, ofier images of William were burnt by the people, " as they are ufed to burn the Pope in London." On the feventeenth of November following the Bartholomew Fair in which this Play of

Queen Elizabeth was acted, a very pompous pageant in nine parts fet out from Whitechapel Bars and marched to an effigy of Queen Elizabeth at Temple Bar, where the Pope received fentence and was burnt " before Queen Beffes' throne." In the prelude to this pageant, fays an account written for the occafion,—doubtlefs by Elkanah Settle, who, for the time, was manager—after the Captain of the Pope's Guards on horfeback and ten pioneers, " Next walks a Bellman finging, and faying in a loud doleful voice, *Remember Juftice Godfrey.* A dead bloody corpfe reprefenting Sir *Edm. Ber. Godf.* is carried on horfeback, fupported by a Jefuit behind, who hath a bloody dagger in his hand." After this fad prelude, a very large Banner is carried betwixt two, reprefenting on the one fide, the " Cabal of the Jefuits at *Wild Houfe* all hanging on one Gibbit ; and among 'em another Twelve, that would betray their Truft or Confcience. On the other fide is reprefented Gammer *Celliers* with a Bloody Bladder, and all her other Prefbyterian Plot Forgers ; and Proteftants in Mafquerade ; and all this in colours on a Cloth." Hereupon followed the Anti-Papal Pageants planned in the fame temper. The laft difplayed a Martyr before a Bifhop and a conclave of Monks, " and all the theatre round about ftrew'd and hemmed with racks and inftruments of cruelty." The details of the coftly fpectacle were engraved on copper-plates, and poffibly it was this fpecial ceremony of the burning of the Pope, performed in November, to which at the end of Auguft the Bartholomew Play pointed in its laft allufions.

In the fame year, in one of a feries of antipapal tracts,

𝕿𝖍𝖊 𝕻𝖔𝖕𝖊'𝖘 𝕳𝖆𝖗𝖇𝖎𝖓𝖌𝖊𝖗, *by way of Diversion*, (printed by *A Godbid* for *L. C.*, 1680), the following comparison is made between the Church of Rome and Bartholomew Fair. "This as well as that consists wholly of *noise*, and *nonsense*, and *mischief*, a Company of *Knaves*, set up to babble a Rabble of *Fools*. The *Wares* of both are much alike, *Toys and Baubles, gaudy shews and Tricks of Legerdemain*. At *Smithfield* you have *Babies and Hobby Horses*, at *Rome*, consecrated *Roses*, and holy rotten *Bones*, and pretty little *Pocket-gods*, onely you must pay a devilish deal dearer for these than for the other. Here you have *Monsters and Wonders*, there you have prodigious *Saints* and whisking *Miracles*, whilst the *Priest* as *Jack-pudden* makes the *Parade* to the *Show*— *Here, here, here's the onely true Infallible Church, Sirs! Here's Antiquity and Visibility, and Unity, and Universality ; step in then, and take your places, Gentlemen, whilst they may be had ; for, trust me, ere long you will scarce get in for the crowd.* Here too you have the several *Orders* of Rascals, *Mendicant* Ragamuffins without Shirts ; subtil *Jesuits*, that smile in your Face and pick your Pocket ; grave *Capuchins* . . . . whole droves of wandering *Nuns* . . . . And to complete the parallel, here you have the *Devil* and *Pope*, as plenty as Pig and Pork ; and what would you have more if you were at *Rome*, though even in a Year of *Jubilee ?*" Thus we find that not in one booth of the Fair only was the hustling of the Pope in that day the pleasure of the people. His was a figure common in the Fair, and he there rivalled the Merry Andrew in his efforts to secure derision.

CHAPTER XIV.

Rebellers.

RACHEL, Lady Ruſſell, might have ſhared, in theſe days, with Lady Caſtlemaine, the pleaſures of the Fair. As ſhe is finiſhing a letter to her huſband, on the 24th of Auguſt, 1680, ſhe is interrupted, and before cloſing it, writes: "My Siſter and Lady Inchiquin are juſt come from Bartholomew Fair, and ſtored us all with Fairings." The Maſter of the Revels was an officer who had always enjoyed, under the Stuarts, valuable conſideration for his patent. In the time of James the Firſt, we have heard Lanthorn Leatherhead, juſtifying his Motion by aſſerting that he had "the Maſter of the Revel's hand for 't." Charles the Second, though he and all the Stuarts traded in the ſale of patent offices, liberally gave away this place to Thomas Killegrew, whoſe jeſts diverted him. Killegrew and Sir William Davenant, both received at the Reſtoration patents to build New Theatres. Killegrew's was opened as the Theatre Royal, on the ſite of Drury Lane; Davenant's was in Lincoln's-Inn-Fields, his company being ſworn by the Lord Chamberlain as ſervants of the Duke of York. They both began by breaking down the old

practice of caufing women's parts to be performed by
men.   The pains taken by Sir William Davenant to fecure fuitable and rich decoration for his ftage, entitled
him to rank as the founder of the modern practice of
fcene-painting.   Thomas Killegrew died at the age of
feventy-three, in the year 1684.   At leaft feven or eight
years before his death his office as Mafter of the Revels,
had been tranfmitted to his fon.   For he was ftill living
when there appeared in the *London Gazette* of April
13-17, 1682, this advertifement: "Whereas, Mr.
John Clarke, of London, bookfeller, did rent of Charles
Killegrew, Efq., the Licenfing of all Ballad Singers

for five years; which time is expired at Lady-day laſt : theſe are, therefore, to give notice to all Ballad Singers that they take out Licenſes at the Office of the Revels at *Whitehall*, for Singing and Selling of Ballads, and ſmall Books, according to an ancient Cuſtom.   And all perſons concerned, are hereby de-ſired to take notice of, and to ſuppreſs all Mountebanks,

Rope-Dancers, Prize-Players, Ballad-Singers, and ſuch as make ſhew of Motions and ſtrange Sights, that have not a Licence in Red and Black Letters, under the Hand and Seal of the ſaid Charles Killegrew, Eſq., Maſter of the Revels to His Majeſty ; and, in particular, to ſuppreſs one Mr. Iriſh, Mr. Thomas

Varley, and Mr. Thomas Yates, Mountebank, who have no Licence, that they may be proceeded againſt, according to Law."

With the office of Maſter of Revels was allied that of Serjeant Trumpeter of England, which entitled its poſſeſſor to a certain fee from every one who blew a wind inſtrument publicly (except at the Theatres Royal), and, therefore, gave juriſdiction over the Merry-andrews and Jack-puddings in every Fair throughout England.

In the *Loyal Proteſtant* for Thurſday, September 7, 1682, is this advertiſement, fully detailing all the privileges of the office.

" ☞ Whereas ſeveral Perſons do preſume to Stroll about the Countries, to make ſhow of Lotteries, Plays, Rope-Dances, Dumb-Shows, Models, Mountebanks, Ballad Singers, Newſhawkers, Scotch Pedlers, and other Unlicenſed People ; and alſo thoſe that make uſe of Drums, Trumpets, Fifes, and other Wind Muſick, without Licence from Gervaſe Price, Eſq., Serjeant and Comptroller of all His Majeſty's Trumpets, who is Intitled thereto by His Majeſty's Patent, under the Great Seal of England. Theſe are therefore to deſire all Mayors, Bayliffs, Sheriffs, Juſtices of the Peace and Conſtables, to apprehend and Impriſon all ſuch Perſons that ſhall preſume to act herein, without Licenſe in print, under the Hand and Seal of the ſaid Gervaſe Price, Eſq., and to give Notice thereof to the ſaid Serjeant Trumpeter at his Lodgings in Whitehall, ſo that they may be ſent for, to anſwer the Contempt before the Right Honourable the Lord Chamberlain."

Afterwards this demand of the Serjeant Trumpeter was fhown to be illegal.

In the fame Number of the *Loyal Proteftant,* and in the preceding Number for the 26th of Auguft, is an announcement of " the Famous *Indian Water Works,* adorned with feveral new Additions, which have been continuing fince this time Twelvemonths, together with *Mafquerades, Songs,* and *Dances,* to be feen in the *Old Elephant's Ground,* over againft *Ofier Lane,* in *Smithfield,* during the time of the Fair; which will not be publicly expofed any more till the next *Bartholomew Fair.*" Alfo, we learn from the fame " *Loyal Proteftant*" that " At Mr. Saffry's, a Dutch-woman's Booth, over againft the Greyhound Inn, in Weft Smithfield, during the time of the Fair, will be Acted an Incomparable Entertainment, call'd THE IRISH EVI-DENCE; THE HUMOURS OF TIEGE; or, ... ; with variety of Dances. By the firft New-market Company." The title of this play fuggefts a very different treatment of the Irifh Teague to that which expreffed the temper of the nation feven years later. Somebody alfo announced that he had loft " in a Hackney Coach, or otherwife, coming from Bartholomew Fair, a Silver and Gold Fringe, Waift-Belt, and a Sword Inlaid with Gold," fuch announcement being a corroboration of the obvious fact, that people of all conditions frequented Bartholomew Fair after the Reftoration. There is an advertifement alfo, fhowing the rough fide of the fcene. It is " for three horfes ftolen by James Rudderford, a Mountebank, and Jeremiah March, his Clown."

It was by no means all pleafure behind the boards and

canvas of the booths.   There were fees enough to pay,
and griefs enough to fuffer.   One of the fights fhown
alive, was of a child, faid to have been born back to back
with a live bear.   Let any one who loves children, feel
the abomination of the fraud that bound a child and
a bear back to back for the amufement of the public.
In the *Domeftick Intelligence* for September 4-7, 1682,
publifhed during the time of Bartholomew Fair, we
read, how "The GERMAN WOMAN that danc'd where
the Italian Tumbler kept his Booth, being over againft
the Swan Tavern, by Hofier Lane end in Bartholomew
Fair, is run away from her Miftrefs, the Fifth of this
inftant; She is of a Brownifh Complexion, with Brown
Hair, and between 17 and 18 years of Age; if any
perfon whatfoever can bring Tidings to one Mr. Hone's,
at the Duke of Albemarle's Head, at the end of Duck
Lane, fo that her Miftrefs may have her again, they
fhall be rewarded to their own Content."

The Lord Mayor, in faddle new, the Sheriffs, and the
Aldermen, were, at this date, ftill riding, in perfon, to proclaim the Fair on the eve of St. Bartholomew—at about
five o'clock in the afternoon—from the gate entering into
the Cloth Fair ; Lady Holland's Mob having proclaimed
it at twelve o'clock the night before.   The Civic Court
attended alfo at the wreftling upon St. Bartholomew's
Day, and at the Shooting on the 26th of Auguft.

From a contemporary book of "Wit and Drollery,"
I have already quoted the allufion to this march of the
Lord Mayor.   "The Order of my Lord Mayor, the
Aldermen, and the Sheriffs, for their Meetings, and
wearing of their Apparel throughout the whole year,"

printed in 1682, confirms the record of the poet. Of
Bartholomew Fair itſelf we quote from the ſame volume,
("Wit and Drollery; Jovial Poems," 1682; it is not
contained in the firſt edition of that book, publiſhed
in 1656) this little epitome :

> " Here's that will challenge all the Fair
> Come buy my nuts and damſons and Burgamy pears!
> Here's the woman of Babylon, the Devil and the Pope,
> And here's the little girl juſt going on the Rope!
> Here's *Dives and Lazarus* and the *World's Creation*,
> Here's the *Tall Dutch Woman*, the like's not in the Nation.
> Here is the Booths where the High Dutch Maid is,
> Here are the Bears that dance like any Ladies ;
> Tat, tat, tat, tat, ſays little penny Trumpet ;
> Here's Jacob Hall, that does ſo jump it, jump it ;
> Sound Trumpet, ſound, for ſilver Spoon and Fork,
> Come, here's your dainty Pig and Pork."

Sir Robert Southwell's ſon, the Hon. Edward Southwell, being in London with his tutor, Mr. Webſter, at
Bartholomew Fair time in the year 1685, received this
letter from his father written on the 26th of Auguſt,
from Kingſweſton.

> "Dear Neddy,
>
>   "I think it not now ſo proper to quote you
> verſes out of Perſius, or to talk of Cæſar and Euclide,
> as to conſider the great theatre of Bartholomew Fair,
> where, I doubt not, but you often reſort, and 'twere not
> amiſs if you cou'd convert that tumult into a profitable
> book.   You wou'd certainly ſee the garboil there to
> more advantage if Mr. Webſter and you wou'd read, or
> cou'd ſee acted, the play of Ben Jonſon, call'd Bartho-
> lomew Fair : for then afterwards going to the ſpot
> you wou'd note, if things and humours were the ſame

to-day, as they were fifty years ago, and take pattern
of the obfervations which a man of fence may raife
out of matters that feem even ridiculous. Take then
with you the impreffions of that play, and in addition thereunto, I fhould think it not amifs if you then
got up into fome high window, in order to furvey the
whole pit at once. I fancy then you will fay—*Totus
mundus agit hiftrionem,* and you wou'd note into how
many various fhapes humane nature throws itfelf, in
order to buy cheap, and fell dear, for all is but traffick
and commerce, fome to give, fome to take, and all is by
exchange, to make the entertainment compleat.

" The main importance of this fair is not fo much
for merchandize, and the fupplying what people really
want ; but as a fort of Bacchanalia, to gratifie the multitude in their wandring and irregular thoughts." (Note
this.)

" Here you fee the rope-dancers gett their living
meerly by hazarding of their lives, and why men will
pay money and take pleafure to fee fuch dangers, is of
feperate and philofophical confideration.

" You have others who are acting fools, drunkards,
and madmen, but for the fame wages which they might
get by honeft labour, and live with credit befides.

" Others, if born in any monftrous fhape, or have
children that are fuch, here they celebrate their mifery,
and by getting of money forget how odious they are
made. When you fee the toy-fhops, and the ftrange
variety of things, much more impertinent than hobby-
horfes or gloves of gingerbread, you muft know there
are cuftomers for all thefe matters, and it would be a

U

pleafing fight cou'd you fee painted a true figure of all thefe impertinent minds and their fantaftick paffions, who come trudging hither, only for fuch things. 'Tis out of this credulous croud that the ballad fingers attrackt an affembly, who liften and admire, while their confederate pickpockets are diving and fifhing for their prey.

" 'Tis from thofe of this number who are more refin'd, that the mountebank obtains audience and credit, and it were a good bargain if fuch cuftomers had nothing for their money but words, but they are beft content to pay for druggs, and medecines, which commonly doe them hurt.

" There is one corner of this Elizium field devoted to the eating of pig, and the furfeits that attend it. The fruits of the feafon are everywhere fcatter'd about, and thofe who eat imprudently do but haften to the phyfitian or the churchyard.

" There are various corners of lewdnefs and impurity. . . . And how many robberies are beforehand committed on houfes and high-ways to raife a ftock againft this licentious occafion ! Here it commonly ends in quarrels and bloodfhed, fo that either the chirurgeon is fent for to plaifter up the wounds, or the conftable to heal the peace, and truth breaking out among malefactors, Mr. Juftice has fufficient grounds for his mittimus, and Captain Richardfon favours them with houfe-room, and Mr. John Ketch conveys them at length to their long and deferved home.

" So here, by the by, you may alfo obferve, that fome grave men who think they have nothing to doe with the fair, do yet find imployment by it.   There is the judge, the divine, the phyfitian, who all have work by the confequences of this unruly affembly.

"I have formerly told you that I look'd upon human nature as a great volume, wherein every man, woman, and child, feem'd to be a diftinct leaf, or page, or paragraph, that had fomething in it of diverfity from all the reft, not but that many humours, natures, and inclinations, might fall under the fame chapter, or be rang'd under the fame common head. Yet ftill there is fuch diftinction of one from the other, as a difcerning mind will find out. And, indeed, it never was otherwife, even in the whole mafs of things, fince the creation; for two things, if they did not differ, would not be two, but the fame.

"I have told you alfo, how that in fome leaves, and indeed whole chapters of this volume, there is many times fo little fenfe or matter for imitation, that thofe leaves are to be turned over very faft, and yet the variety and very deformity of fhapes they contain, do all help to illuftrate nature, and put you into admiration to fee other leaves and chapters how they are replenifhed, and feem to be the epitome of all that was good and valuable in the reft."

The careful man then adds much prudent counfel before he fubfcribes himfelf to his dear Neddy as "ever

"Your moft affectionate father,

"ROBERT SOUTHWELL."

The Captain Richardfon mentioned towards the clofe of this extract was Keeper of the Old Bailey.

A few days before Bartholomew Fair time, in the year

1687, "His Majefty being informed that divers perfons continue to exercife Lotteries, and new invented Games refembling Lotteries within the Cities of London and Weftminfter, and other parts of this Kingdom, contrary to the exprefs prohibition of His Majefties Letters Patents, Granted to the Indigent Officers, has been pleafed to command, that all Magiftrates and others whom it does concern, do take effectual care to fupprefs all fuch Lotteries as are not duly Licenfed by the Commiffioners and Patentees for the faid Indigent Officers, and particularly at Bartholomew Fair, and publick Meetings."

That appeared in the *London Gazette* for the 15th of Auguft, 1687. In the *Gazette* for Auguft 23rd, 1688. "His Majefty having granted to Randolph Afhenhurft, Efq., Stephen Hales, Michael Cope, and Tho. Afhenhurft, Gentlemen, the fole Exercife of the Royal Oak,"—a gambling game dedicated to the honour of King Charles the Second,—" Raffling and all other Lotteries, and games refembling Lotteries," prohibited the ufe of thefe games by any one who had not obtained a Licence from the Patentees.

In the *Theatre of Compliment* (1688), are fome verfes on the Fair which end with a line illuftrative of the check thus put upon Lotteries.

> Here is the Rarity of the whole Fair,
> Pimper-la-Pimp, and the Wife Dancing Mare;
> Here's valiant *St. George and the Dragon*, a farce;
> Here's *Vienna Befieged*, a moft delicate thing;
> And here's Punchinello, fhown thrice to the King.
> Then fee the mafks to the Cloifters repair,—
> But there will be no raffling all this Fair.

At the fame time a fquabble between Charles Killigrew, Efq., Mafter of the Revels, and Mr. Symms, Comptroller of the fame, as to the right of giving licences, was opportunely fettled, when the Fair was juft at hand, in favour of Mr. Killigrew. So there was to be no more miftake as to the perfon from whom fhow-men were to buy their title to exhibit.

The moft famous of the Merry Andrews of that day was William Phillips, of whom there are feveral en-gravings. It would be pleafant if we could identify this jefter with the unknown William Phillips, by whom a tragedy was written. It was publifhed in 1698, as "the Revengeful Queen." There is another Tragedy afcribed to him, called "Alcamenes and Menelippa." Even in his day, had this man been really the tragedian, he would not have been the firft to live a clown's life with a tragic fenfe of life under his gaiety. The annexed pic-ture reprefents him not as a Tragedian, but as a Merry Andrew:

This reprefents the fame man as a "Bartholomew Fair Mufician."

Among the Harleian MSS. (5961), is the title page only of "A new Fairing for the Merrily Difpofed: or the Comical Hiftory of the Famous Merry Andrew, W. Phill. Giving an Account of his Pleafant Humours, Various Adventures, Cheats, Frolicks, and Cunning Defigns, both in City and Country. London: Printed by J. Willis, and fold by moft Bookfellers, 1688." 12mo.

Among the Advertifements in the *Gazette*, for April 1, 1689, we find a formal announcement bearing witnefs that Charles Killigrew, Efq., remained Mafter of the Revels when the Stuarts had ceafed to be Kings of England. "Thefe are to give Notice, That all Stage-players, Mountebanks, Rope-Dancers, and others who fhow Motions and Strange Sights, do repair to Charles Killegrew, Esq., Mafter of the Revels, at his Office at Somerfet Houfe, to renew their Lycenfes, their former being void, And that none do prefume to make any public fhews in Town or Country, without a new Licence from the faid Mafter of the Revels."

It may here alfo be added that among the advertife-ments which appeared during Fair time in the year 1690, is one of a pamphlet, now not to be found, entitled, "The City Revels, or, the Humours of Bartholo-mew Fair. By J. G. Gent. Sold by Randal Taylor near Stationers-Hall, and by moft Bookfellers. Price, Stitcht. 6*d*."

In juftice to the Mountebank this volume fhould contain a fpecimen of his art as an orator. There is a little undated book, publifhed about the year 1690, entitled, "The Harangues or Speeches of feveral Famous Mountebanks in Town and Country." The leaft extravagant and moft affectedly candid of the fpeakers is Tom Jones, a part of whofe addrefs I quote :

"Gentlemen and Ladies,

"You that have a mind to preferve your own and your Families' Health, may here, at the expenfe of a Twopenny Piece, furnifh yourfelves with a Packet, which contains feveral things of great ufe, and wonderful operation in human bodies, againſt all Diſtempers whatſoever.

" Gentlemen, Becauſe I preſent myſelf among you, I would not have you to think I am an upſtart, gliſter-pipe . . . . Apothecary.   No, Gentlemen, I am no ſuch perſon.   I am a regular Phyſician ; and have travelled moſt kingdoms in the world, purely to do my Country good.   I am not a Perſon that takes delight, as a great many do, to fill your ears with hard words, in telling you the nature of Turpet Mineral, Mercuri Dulcis, Balſamum Capiviet, Aſtringents, Laxations, Hardboundations, Circulations, Vibrations, Salivations, Excoriations, Scaldations.   Theſe Quacks may fitly be called Solimites, becauſe they preſcribe only one ſort of phyſick for all Diſtempers, that is, a Vomit.

" If a Man has bruiſed his Elbow ; Take a Vomit, ſays the Doctor.   If you have any Corns, Take a Vomit. If he has torn his Coat, Take a Vomit.   For the Jaundice, Fevers, Flux, Gripes, Gout, nay even the diſtempers that only my Friend, the famous Doctor Tuff, whom you all know, knows as the Hocognicles, Marthambles, the Moon-Paul, and the Strong-Fives, A Vomit ; Tantum.   Gentlemen, theſe Impoſtors value killing of a Man, no more, than I value drawing an old ſtump of a tooth, which has long troubled any of you ; ſo that I ſay, they are a pack of Tag-Rag, Aſſi-fœtida, Gliſter-pipe Doctors.

" Now, Gentlemen, having given you a ſhort account of this ſpurious race ; I ſhall preſent you with my Cordial Pills, being the Tincture of the Sun, having Dominion from the ſame Light, giving Relief and

Comfort to all Mankind. They caufe all Complexions to Laugh or Smile, in the very taking them, they prefently cure all Dizzinefs, Swimmings, Dulnefs in the Head, and Scurvy.

"In the next place I recommend to you my incomparable Balfam," and fo forth. Prefixed to the volume here cited, is a picture of the Mountebank and his Zany on their Platform. When they have ended their appeal, the Jack-pudding will dance upon the tightrope.

CHAPTER XV.

After the Revolution.

A NEW view of "the Humours of Teague," which had amufed a good-natured public in the Fair not many years before, poffeffed the Englifh People when the laft of our Stuart kings, driven from England, was battling his caufe on Irifh ground, with foreign arms and a wild Irifh help. A Bookfeller who had iffued Popifh Plot Cards to amufe the public, now produced "Orange Cards, reprefenting the late King's Reign, and Expedition of the Prince of Orange," fome of which were to reprefent, "The Prince of Orange Landing, the Jefuits Scampering," &c., "curioufly illuftrated and engraved in lively figures, done by the Performers of the firft Popifh Plot-Cards, and is the only true fort; if there be any others they are counterfeit." Such helps to the diverfion of the patriot, advertifed in *Mercurius Reformatus, or the New Obfervator*, at Bartholomew Fair time, in the year 1689, were enlarged by the appearance of a play publifhed in the year following, to which reference is made by Lord Macaulay in his Hiftory. "This drama," he fays in a note, "which, I believe was performed at

Bartholomew Fair, is one of the moſt curious of a curious claſs of compoſitions, utterly deſtitute of literary merit, but valuable as ſhowing what were then the moſt ſuccefsful claptraps for an audience compoſed of the common people." It is from its character evidently a booth play, not profeſſing to have been performed at either of the licenſed playhouſes, and was acted, probably, both at Bartholomew and Southwark Fairs.

We have been dwelling at ſome length on another play of the ſame claſs which is more diſtinctly illuſtrative of the ſtory of the Fair, for the Wild Iriſhman never took a defined place, as the Pope did, among our Mountebanks and Zanies. It will ſuffice, therefore, now to deſcribe ſhortly, the Tragi-comedy that tells how King William ſailed for Ireland, and was further to tell in a Second Part, what he did after his arrival. Moſt probably it did, in ſome forgotten continuation, really make doggerel of the Battle of the Boyne. The extant Firſt Part is entitled, "the Royal Voyage, or the IRISH EXPEDITION : a TRAGICOMEDY, acted in the years 1689 and 90. Regis ad Exemplum. *Claud.* London ; Printed for *Richard Baldwin,* in the *Old Bailey,* A.D. 1690." The eſſential paſſages in the addreſs " To the Reader," are theſe : " Know ye, firſt and foremoſt, that the Name of this following Play relates to another part yet to come, which will more ſignally fill the Title ; though this has enough of the *Royal Voyage* in it to make that good and proper in this, as well as the other. The *Conqueſt of Granada* is only begun in the firſt part, nay, no more than the Siege on't, yet the propriety of the Title none ever queftioned to that part as well as the other. The next thing I'm to do you, to wit, is, that the end of this Play is chiefly to expofe the Perfidious, Bafe, Cowardly, Bloody Nature of the Irifh, both in this and all paft ages, efpecially to give as lively a fcheme as will confift with what's paft, fo far of the worfe than Heathenifh Barbarities committed by them on their Peaceable Neighbours, in that Bloody and Deteftable Maffacre and Rebellion of Forty-one, which will make the Nation ftink as long as there's one Bog or Bogtrotter left in it." Though his way of writing allows great Liberty, the author fays he has confined himfelf even to the "Chaftnefs of an Hiftorian, examining as the reader will find, all the material Objections thofe wicked people can make to our accufations." He apologifes for having introduced into his play one Irifhman "brave and honeft (as far as his caufe would let him be) to foil the reft;" and adds, "if I have gone a little beyond the pale and left truth behind me, it is a pardonable fault, and the more eafily, becaufe perhaps it mayn't be fo common to err on the fide of good nature." The good-natured poet adds, that he cannot mifreprefent the Irifh when he fpeaks anything ill of them. This is like the opinion of the rabble in "the Coronation of Queen Elizabeth," that the voice muft be truftworthy which abufed the Pope.

The Dramatis Perfonæ of the Royal Voyage are, "Tyrconnel, Primate, Archbifhop of Cafhel, Nugent, Neagle, Irifh Lords, Hamilton, Macarty, Talbot, Butler, Clancarty, Macdonald, Irifh Soldiers, Meffengers, Officers, &c.

" Governor of Inniſkilling, Collonels, Souldiers, &c., Governor of Derry, Collonels, Souldiers, &c., Engliſh Captains with Relief to Derry, Engliſh General, Souldiers, Officers, &c."

This peculiar liſt illuſtrates the author's profeſſed Deſign to be particular in his enmity, but name no names upon the Engliſh ſide, leſt he ſhould be found too partial in his praiſe.

The play deals with high matter; the iſſue of the happieſt of Revolutions, and the moſt determined ſtruggle made by Ireland to throw off the yoke that bound it beſide England. The greateſt ſiege in Britiſh Civil hiſtory, the Siege of Londonderry, is meant to be told in one of its Acts. Its purpoſe was to preſent the news, together with the Engliſh feeling of the day, in fleſh and blood. In the firſt Act it preſents, at Dublin Caſtle, James's Lord Deputy, Tyrconnel, who by his oppreſſion of the Proteſtants in Ireland, had, during the paſt three years, been embittering the feud between the Siſter Iſlands. He is ſurrounded by the Iriſh chiefs, and glorying in his ſucceſs. He has made Ireland a Refuge for the Church—

> But never ſhall we her fair ſpring reſtore,
> As pure and limpid as it was before,
> Unleſs we hollow the polluted Flood,
> And purge out Heretick-Stains with Heretick's Blood.

This thought warms the old veins of the Roman Archbiſhop of Caſhel, who begins to gloat over memories of the maſſacre in 1641, when Sir Phelim O'Neil, producing a commiſſion from King Charles the Firſt, headed an outbreak full of horrible acts of maffacre and cruelty againft the Proteftant Englifh fettlers. Macarthy (Commander in Munfter), who is the one good Irifhman apologifed for by the author in his preface, rebukes the Archbifhop, and is argued with by his Grace in Roman fafhion—that to "keep no Faith with thofe that have none," is a proper doctrine, and one upon which King Louis, eldeft fon of the Church, has thriven famoufly. Macarthy's fenfe of mercy is almoft apoftafy, and he is "*ipfo facto* excommunicate" in the Archbifhop's eye; but in Tyrconnel's mind he is too loyal and brave a fubject of King James to be quarrelled with by thofe who wifh fuccefs to James's caufe. With a hundred thoufand men in arms, and only a handful of men in Ireland to withftand them, "Let's o'er to England" advifes Nugent,

> "That golden Land, where Palms and Laurels wait us,
> Delicious Murthers, and fweet Maffacres:
> Hang, Drown, Stab, Burn, Broil, Eat, Damn our proud Conquerors."

But an approving fellow-counfellor dilates upon the beauty of "fair words, good terms, fweet-honied proffers" to delude the Englifh "kind-believing Fools," till Derry and Innifkillen have been wrefted from them. And a fecond Irifh Lord enlarges upon the defire of a firft Lord to ftay in Ireland and beguile the Englifh, for,

> The Englifh fooner Cheated are, than Beaten;
> We muft expect a formidable Army
> Shortly in our Bowels; though their Hands
> Are raifing long, they generally fall heavy.

At any rate they muft get Derry and Innifkillen, and, if poffible, avoid a famine in the land by keeping the Cattle from the Rapparees.   The hot Primate curſes this lukewarmneſs.   Were not the gentlemen, now ſo moderate, thoſe who in council preſſed to have the Prince proclaimed?   Yes, it is anſwered, but the King had not then quitted England, and given up all that was there to Orange.   Tyrconnel interrupts the diſcuſſion with intelligence of the reception given to King James in France, and of the ſtrong ſuccours thence expected.

> But firſt the Northern Rebels let's ſubdue,
> At Derry and at Inniſkilling too ;
> The Firſt your lot (*to Hamilton*), the Second falls to you (*to Macarthy*).

Hamilton, who had been truſted on a miſſion by King William, and on reaching Ireland had revolted from his truſt, receives this charge with boaſts, alluding lightly to his word, his " few looſe vows, perhaps an oath or two, and airy honour pawned."   Later in the play there is an alluſion to the ſuicide of John Temple, who had commended Hamilton to confidence, and afterwards took fatally to heart the iſſue of his counſel. Macarthy, who is ſent to Inniſkillen, ſays that he cannot promiſe much, for he leads raw and wild troops againſt an enemy both deſperate and firm, but he will do his beſt.   Tyrconnel knows he will, and bids him take the beſt troops while he writes fair offers to the rebels.

After this diſcuſſion, *exeunt omnes*, and " Enter an Iriſh Rabble, Men, Women, and Children; the Men with Swords and Clubs, the Women with Skenes, the Children with wooden Swords and Knives."   Very expreſſive, truly, of a riſing of the entire population. " A Piper before 'em (as was their uſual Cuſtom) with a Prey of Black and Small Cattle, which they had robbed the Englifh of."

The Speakers are Nos. 1, 2, 3, 4, 5, of the Rabble.

" 1ft o' TH' RABBLE. Rare times, by Saint Patrick; the beft that Ireland ever faw, by my Soul joy; why, who would be at the Trouble to raife and breed Cattle of their own, when the Heretick dogs can do 't to our hands without any pain.

" 2.—Right, Neighbour Teague; and, befides, they are all our Tenants, not we theirs; for I heard Father Dominick, our Prieft, make a Swear, that this was all our country, Five Thoufand Years before the New Moon was made, and the Englifh Thieves never came hither to rob us of our own till the next year after the Flood was over." With much more talk of the fame texture; difplaying the thievifhnefs of Irifh Priefts, and incidents of cruelty in the prefent rifing that promptly fuggeft an exchange of frightful recollections from the O'Neil Maffacre of 1641. Then, " that lubberly breed of Black Cattle here," being Englifh property, " we'll find fome way or other to torment, as well as get rid of 'em, and they'll have little caufe to complain, that are ufed as well as their Mafters."

" Let's ferve 'em as we did the Fellow I told you of. Tie 'em to a ftake, and cut off pieces of their flefh alive." So it is done. The play was really acted, and one wonders greatly whether the favage fpirit of the rabble of the Fair was fatisfied with a literal maffacre of an ox at each reprefentation of the " Tragicomedy," according to the ftage direction. " They Sing an Irifh Song, Dancing round a fat Englifh Ox, tied to a Stake;

and as foon as that was over, fall altogether upon it,
cutting out pieces of it alive, and broiling them upon
the coals.   In the meanwhile, a fmall party of Englifh
furprife and fall upon 'em ; on which, all the Rabble fet
up the Irifh yell, and run away without ftriking a ftroke."

The Englifhmen having in bad verfe exchanged re-
flections upon Irifh courage, depart to cut their way
to the relief of the garrifon at Derry.   From this
diverfion, we are taken back to Tyrconnel and his
friends in Dublin Caftle, and hear from them how they
have by Neagle's advice, got rid of their Proteftant ally
Mountjoy, by fending him with Chief Baron Rice, on
a miffion to King James, in Paris, where he is fafely
lodged in the Baftille.   But at this time, James is expected from Breft daily, and on his arrival, in the
Archbifhop's opinion—

> " his fingle Name wou'd do,
> Without an army, and infpire new courage
> If any wanted it—'twas he alone,
> Who through the laft falfe, dangerous Trimming Reign,
> Screen'd off the fury of the Rebels from us ;
> Got that proud Heretick, imperious Ormond,
> Oftener than once removed.   'Twas he who found
> The Treacherous Effex, who buoy'd up the Englifh
> And their decaying Interefts againft us—
> He found him out at laft, fpite of his Policy,
> And did reward him in due time and place.
> But when kind Fate,—or of her own accord,
> Or jogged by fome Officious Catholick Hand—
> Broke Charles his Linfy-Woolfey Line of Life,
> When our bright Star afcended his Meridian
> And fhot his Beams from London to our Ifle,
> What Loyal Face was feen without a fmile ?
> Scarce will our joy or jufter be or more,
> When with his Royal Feet he treads our fhore."

A Courier arrives, who has feen the pompous

entertainment of the Royal Exile, by Great Lewis and his Court, and who left a fquadron at Breft full of money and men, ready for failing. The Roman Primate takes this occafion to fuggeft that the approaching opportunity of following the good counfel 𝕶𝖎𝖑𝖑 𝕬𝖑𝖑— muft not be loft. Another Courier brings word that the King has landed at Kinfale. Tyrconnel gives orders for rejoicings, but the people have already made their bonfires of the houfes of the Englifh. This gratifies the Primate. The Courier delivers a copy of a fpeech made to King James by the Recorder of Kilkenny— a burlefque flourifh of courfe—and the Act ends with prefent expectation of the King in Dublin, and the equally ftrong and immediate expectation of a poft from the North, telling the fate of thofe two ftubborn towns, Derry and Innifkillen.

The firft Act, then, tells clumfily, but with evident regard to the fequence of events, what happened in Ireland to the time of the landing of James at Kinfale. The fecond Act tells in the fame temper the ftory of the defence of Innifkillen, and the third Act is defigned to be a fummary prefentment of the fiege of London-derry. The fourth Act tells of Schomberg's landing in Bangor Bay, of his march through the pafs of Newry, of his encampment in Dundalk, facing a powerful enemy at Drogheda; of the treafon in his camp; the peftilence; the retirement to Newry. The fifth Act, which is very fhort indeed, difplays the defperate ftate of Schomberg's troops by reafon of the ficknefs; the courage of the ftarving Englifh; the cowardice (of courfe) of the Irifh; and the arrival of

King William at Carrickfergus, juſt when he was moſt
wanted. In the laſt ſcene is diſplayed " the Royal Fleet
at the Bay of Bangor. The Mary Yacht with the
Standard. All the ſhore enlightened with Bonfires."
A booth continually acting plays of this deſcription,
would, in fact, be a dramatic news-room, giving the
news always in combination with a ſtarved and angry
ſort of leading article fuddled with verſe.

The literary rank of THE ROYAL VOYAGE is no higher
than that of other booth plays, and it is duller than
moſt others of its claſs, becauſe it amuſes us by fewer
flights into the ſublime of abſurdity. But it is cre-
ditably diſtinguiſhed by the fact that it is from beginning
to end decent. The comic ſcenes, eſſential to a booth
play, uſually depended for their fun upon the gratification of a love of dirt ingrained in the mind of the
rabble ; upon Urſula-talk for the pig-woman and her
large army of adherents. Now the author of the Royal
Voyage was a man who could not deſcend into this
fouler region of claptrap, and who, although he was
an author Littlewit, was at the ſame time an Engliſh
gentleman. In the midſt of the ſtrong current of
bitter feeling upon which he was borne, together with
his countrymen, he not only foils the bad Iriſh with an
Iriſhman who is the nobleſt perſon in his play, but he
alſo, in the midſt of wrath, remembers to make one
of his captains warn the Engliſh ſoldiers, who are
rudely triumphing over a ſucceſsful ſhot :—

> " Never inſult over an enemy
> Conquer'd or ſlain,—if either, that's enough,
> The reſt is baſe. 'Tis true o're you they wou'd,
> But even there o'recome 'em as in battle."

X 2

It is good to feel that this was a fafe claptrap, a fentiment fure in any age to win applaufe even from the fierceft mob in England.

For his fun the author of this Tragi-Comedy mainly depends on a difplay of the bad foldiering and cowardice of the Irifh. He begins his Second—or Innifkillen— Act, by fhowing Macarthy in defpair about his men, putting them through their exercifes. When he cries, " Face to the Right !" they " all fall into confufion, fome facing one way, fome t'other." They are rearranged by an officer, and blunder on till at the words, " To the left about !" they throw down arms and run away. Macarthy orders a frefh party in ; " The officer draws out others. Gives the words. They do all well enough 'till he bids 'em Fire—one half never does it at all, the other, one after another, and moft of them wink, and fhoot juft in one another's faces,—at which, concluding themfelves kill'd, one part drops down and t'other runs away." Macarthy and the officers abufe their men, and can hope nothing for their expedition. Macfhane, O'Donnel, Teague, and other foldiers reappear, difcuffing their performances at drill. " By my fhoul now," fays one, " if poor Teague faw the like in my life. Why my goffip tied a red ribbon about my left hand that I might be fure to know it from my right—and the ugly dog-rogue of an Englifh Serjeant bid me turn to the right, and put me quite out." Prefently they brag, fence in the air, club mufkets to fhow how they would brain the Englifh ; when the fally of a few Englifh from their fort fuddenly puts not only thefe men, but all Macarthy's troops to rout and confternation. Macarthy reviles his pafte-board army ; worfe than an army wove in mufty arras, for that will at leaft ftand to be cut in pieces. He refolves at once to prove his fate by an attack on Ennifkillen, but the garrifon comes out: when there is a grand battle fought upon the ftage, of which the end is that of the Irifh " fome throw themfelves into the bog, and are knockt on the head there; others afk Quarter, and throw down their arms," &c. Macarthy dafhes in gallant defpair among the enemy, difcharges his piftol at a party of Ennifkillen men, who fire at him. He falls ; a foldier clubs his mufket to knock out his brains. Irifh officers exclaim, " Macarthy ! " and with words of refpect he is taken prifoner while fwooning with his wounds. The fally, the rout, and the capture of Macarthy are hiftorical events.

In the Third—or Londonderry—Act, there is but one fcene meant to be comic, and that furely a grim one. The Governor firft appears with his colonels and captains, to unfold in talk the boldnefs that clofed Derry againft the troops of James, the fending for help to England, the ftrength of the army under Hamilton, the peril of the crifis for the town.

> If we fucceed, Hiftory will record
> Our actions louder than Oftend or Troy.

In Hamilton's camp, Maumont (called Mamow), and Pufignan are introduced, impatient of refiftance.

MAMOW. Begar me vill batter 'em down with 1, 2, 3, Potgun.
Vat de Diable do they mean ? Do they not know
My great Maiftre fend his Lieutenant-General Mamow
To pull down all de Walls, and burn, kill, kill,
De Man, Woman and fhucking Shild dat fight vid his
Brother of England ?

The cruelty of the French troops is hiftorical, fo is
the battering of the town next related, the fally partly
fhown upon the ftage, then changed to a " fight behind
the fcenes" to be defcribed fully, together with the
incident of Maumont's death by a Captain who brings
tidings to the Governor in Derry. The victorious
troops enter and receive praife, after which we immediately return to the Irifh camp, lofing fight of all days
between the firft and fecond great encounter incidental
to the fiege, one happening in April, and the other
happening in June. The new attack is planned, which,
with the incident of the fall of Mountgarrat, is prefently defcribed by the Governor, who is fuppofed to
be witneffing it from the town walls. Troops enter
with important prifoners, who are received courteoufly.
It is defigned that they fhall enter into a difcuffion of
political affairs with their captors and reprefent weakly
their fide of the moral to the argument that battle is
determining. The didactic fcene might not be borne at
once by a booth audience; the fpectators, therefore, are
prepared for it, by the relief of this interpolation :—

SCENE VI.

𝔗𝔥𝔢 𝔦𝔯𝔦𝔰𝔥 𝔠𝔞𝔪𝔭.

*Enter an Irifh Funeral, of one of their Commanders kill'd in the laft Action.
Tapers, Crones, Dirges, Two fat Friars finging—and praying for his
Soul.*

SONG BY THE PRIESTS.

I.

Reft thy Soul in Blifs, dear Friend !
Now beginning, n'ere to end :
At Purgatory be not fcar'd,
Its Flame fhall never finge thy Beard.

Mount torights to Heav'n, nor ſtay
To call at the Half-way-houſe by th' way.

2.

On thy Soul, while here below,
If ſome little ſpots did grow :
Murder, Perjury, or Rape,
Or ſome ſuch other ſmall Eſcape :
By thy meritorious Fall
Thou haſt o're atton'd 'em all.

3.

Innocent as Child unborn
On the golden wings of morn
Mount to bliſs, and pray for thoſe
Struggling with their faithleſs Foes :
Aid thy Friends who thee adore
As thou other Saints before.

[*They put him into the Grave, and the* Iriſh *kneel down by him,
tear their Hair, throw up the Dirt, and lament his Death
with inſufferable Howlings, as their manner is, ſinging this
ſong over his grave.*]

IRISH SONG.

Ah Brother Teague !   Why didſt thou go ?
   Whillilla lilla lilla lilla lilla lilla loo !
And leave thy Friends in grief and wo,
   Aboo aboo aboo aboo aboo aboo aboo !

Hadſt thou not ſtore of Houſehold-ſtuff,
   Whillilla, &c.
Potatas and Uſquebagh enough ?
   Aboo, &c.

Three Sheep, one Gaſſoon, and a Cow,
   Whillilla, &c.
A Garden, Cabin, and a Plough ?
   Aboo, &c.

Hadſt thou not Bonny-clabbar ſtore ?
   Whillilla, &c.
If not enough, wee'd giv'n thee more.
   Aboo, &c.

Why wouldſt thou, Teague!   Ah tell me why,
　Whillilla, &c.
Thus play the Fool and maake a dy ?
　Aboo, &c.

Why didſt thou touch the fatal Shore,
　Whillilla, &c.
Where we ſhall never ſee thee more ?
　Aboo aboo aboo aboo aboo aboo aboo !

[*While they are in the midſt of their Harmony comes a Shot from
the Town, and kills the two Fryars and ſeveral others,—all
the reſt ſtart up and run away.*

Immediately we are upon Derry walls, hearing the
ſoldier rejoice that he has ſpoiled their howling, which
was more inſufferable than their cannon; but when
another ſoldier laughs at the ſlaying of the prieſts, he is
admoniſhed by his Captain, in the manner before ſaid,
not to inſult over a fallen enemy.   The priſoners and
captors then come out and hold their argument, in which
the noticeable faċt is, that the beſt view of the caſe treats
Ireland only as a conquered dependent of the Engliſh
crown.   The priſoners tell of the boom acroſs the
Lough, and in the next ſcene the Governor and his
Colonels, from Derry walls, ſee and deſcribe to the
audience the forcing of the boom.   The Aċt ends with
the entry of the relieving Captains, and the news that—

Schombergh ſpeedily is here deſigned
With twenty thouſand men to march for Dublin
And end the war.

This prepares the Speċtator for the Fourth Aċt,
which deſcribes the ſufferings of Schomberg's army, and
contains no comic ſcene.   Its laſt ſcene is, " Dundalk
as before.   *Moſt of the Soldiers ſick, many dead, the*

reſt pining."   It ends with the order to march back to
Newry—

there to quarter till
Recruits and better Seaſons call for Action.

The laſt Act is of four ſhort ſcenes, and but three
pages.   The firſt ſcene is with the Iriſh at Dundalk,
ſimply to explain that they mean to force the Newry
Paſs.   The ſecond ſcene is this.

SCENE II.—*The Newry.*

A Party of Iriſh—Officers, Soldiers, &c.

OFFIC. March quick and cloſe—They take not yet th' Alarm.
The Town's already ours—The Priſoner whom
We lately took, informs there's ſcarce a hundred
Yet left alive, and thoſe half ſick and languiſhing ;
The reſt or careleſs are or deſperate,
Nor dream of that warm viſit we ſhall make 'em.
[*The Centry diſcovers 'em, and fires three times, retiring.*

OFFICER. Diſcovered . . But too late for their prevention ;
In—and we're Conquerors—
[*They enter the Town—Several Officers come out in their ſhirts,
and are knockt o'th' head. A Drummer beats an Alarm, and
a few of the Engliſh gather in the Streets.*

ENG. OFFIC. Ha—are you come ſo far to hinder us
From dying now in quiet—Fellow Souldiers,
You ſee 'em—Rally here behind this Cart,
And give one Charge—if they march not back
At their accuſtomed pace—I'll e'ne run for 'em.
[*The Engliſh charge—The Iriſh run.*

[*Enter ſeveral Engliſh Soldiers crawling upon their Hands and Feet
with their Muſquets in their Hands.*

OFFICER. Poor Wretches—What d'ye mean—You'r fitter for
Your Beds or th' Hoſpital, than War and Action.

1 SOULD. Noble Captain—Let me have but ſhot at 'em
And then I'll dy contented.

2 SOULD. Now we're their Matches, 'twere not fair to fight 'em,
If ſtrong and well as they.
[*They both get up to a Bank, fire their Pieces at the Iriſh and fall
dead themſelves.*

After their officer has praifed them, *exeunt omnes*, and we are at Belfaft : " Heaven fmiles again," and Englifh fupplies come daily—as a General relates in a fpeech of ten lines, forming the whole fcene.   Then appears the Royal Fleet, and the Mary yacht with the Standard, the Bonfires enlighten all the fhore.   A meffenger brings to the General, good tidings from Carrickfergus, at which cries the General—

> " Let all the Bogs in Ireland quake for fear.
>   Their Fate is come—The Pageant King muft run ;
>   And once agen fly from the confcious Sun.
>   And in fome Monaftery hide his Head
>   Midft lonely Tombs, and the polluted Dead.
>   While that bright Hero who fupplies his place,
>   Sways his ftrong Scepter with fo great a Grace :
>   In trembling France fhall give new wonders Birth,
>   And rend the witherd Lilies from the Earth."

The Curtain falls ; not upon this play only, but upon all free dramatic politics in Smithfield.   After the Revolution, there came Governments that would not tolerate the criticifm of the fhowman.   That public entertainer fell back, therefore, upon Sufanna and the Elders, or the Siege of Troy ; or he advanced to a new form of Miracle-play, in which Magicians took the place of Saints, and the Devil held his ground in company with Punchinellos, comic Serving-men, and country Shallows.

CHAPTER XVI.

Monsters.

WE muſt never loſe ſight of the fact, that Bartholomew Fair throve while it was a true element in London
life ; and although, even at the time of which we are
now ſpeaking, the Corporation of London had already
raiſed the queſtion of its ſuppreſſion, it ſtood firm yet for
another century, becauſe it was a true thing ſtill.   In
this chapter I ſpeak only of its Monſters : with a book
before me, once owned by Sir Hans Sloane, into which,
I think, it was Sir Hans himſelf who paſted Handbills
about ſome of the natural Prodigies which intereſted
London from the days of Charles the Second to thoſe of
Queen Anne.   The greater number of them belong to
the reigns of William and Mary and Queen Anne ; the
lateſt is one iſſued directly after the death of " his
late Majeſty," King George the Firſt.   They commonly
profeſs to deſcribe things exhibited by his or her
" Majeſties' Authority "—like the quack medicines of
our own day—becauſe a fee had been paid to Government by every ſhowman for his licence.

But they had other " Majeſties' Authority."   The
Kings and Queens of Europe in the years before and
after 1700, ſhared in the taſte of all claſſes, for

men who could dance without legs, dwarfs, giants, hermaphrodites, or fcaly boys. The tafte ftill lingers among uncultivated people in the higheft and the loweft ranks of life, but in the reigns of William and Mary, or Queen Anne, it was almoft univerfal. Bartholomew Fair, with all the prodigies exhibited therein, was not as it now would be, an annual difplay of things hardly to be feen out of a fair, but was, as far as Monfters went, only a yearly concentration into one fpot of entertainments that at other times were fcattered over town and country. The very mountebanks took lodgings in ftreets, and iffued their addreffes upon paper.

Since the days of Queen Elizabeth, when the wonders of the outlying world began to pour in rapidly upon the Englifh people, a thirft for marvels, and a credulity, in the beginning very natural, had tempted the exhibitor to feek for Monfters from abroad. This Shakefpeare even goes out of his way to fatirife, when he makes Trinculo fay, while firft pondering over Caliban, "Were I in England now (as once I was), and had but this fifh painted, not a holiday fool there but would give a piece of filver: there would this monfter make a man; any ftrange beaft there makes a man; when they will not give a doit to relieve a lame beggar, they will lay out ten to fee a dead Indian." To the nation deftined for a world-wide rule, the myfteries of diftant regions of the world were then firft opening. An eager, all-embracing curiofity, however abfurd in many of its forms, was then as fuitable as all the wonder through which a child comes to its firft acquaintance with the life outfide the nurfery. What

was begun in reaſon was continued in frivolity.   For
the tone of ſociety in England was degraded by the
Court of Charles the Second; ſoon afterwards there
came a ſtrange ſtagnation over nearly the whole mind
of Europe, and for reaſons into which we muſt
not here inquire, the diſpoſition of the rich in England continued to be throughout nearly the whole
eighteenth century indolent and trifling.   The taſte for
Monſters became a diſeaſe; of which the nation has in
our own day recovered with a wonderful rapidity in
preſence of events that force on the development of
all its powers.   Bartholomew Fair is gone, and there
are few Engliſh boys who now would care to ſee the
giant, under whoſe arm it pleaſed Charles the Second to
walk.   Handbills are not uſually dated, but there is
one iſſued in Southwark Fair, containing the year 1684,
when this young giant's age was ſaid to be nineteen.
That will ſettle the date of the following announcement.

" Miracula Naturæ ;

" *Or, A Miracle of Nature.*

" Being that much-admired Gyant-like Young Man,
Aged Twenty Three Years laſt June ; Born in Ireland,
of ſuch a Prodigious Height and Bigneſs, and every
way proportionable, that the like hath not been ſeen
in *England* in the memory of Man.   He was ſhown
to His Late and Preſent Majeſty, and Several of the
Nobility at Court, Five Years ago ; and his Late
Majeſty was pleaſed to walk under his Arm, and he
is grown very much ſince.   And it is generally thought,
that if he lives Three Years more, and Grows as he

has done, he will be much bigger than any of thofe Gyants we read of in Story: For he now reaches with his Hand three Yards and a-half; Spans Fifteen Inches: And is the Admiration of all that fees him.

"*He is to be feen at* Cow-Lane-End *in* Bartholomew Fair, *where his Picture hangs out.*

"Vivat Rex."

But fuch wonders, human or beftial, were not to be feen in the Fair only. The Clever Mare, admired by Mr. Pepys, had her own lodgings in town, out of Fair time, and received company all the year round. Jacob Hall fet up his rope-dancing booth, when there was no Fair, in Lincoln's-Inn-Fields, or at Charing Crofs. In the poem of the Long Vacation, contained in the firft edition (1656) of "Wit and Drollery, Jovial Poems, by Sir F. M., Ja. S., Sir W. D., F. D.," &c., it is not a migration of the Fair people, but of the regular town fhowmen that is thus defcribed.

> Vaulter good, and dancing lafs
> On Rope: and man that cries hey tone;
> And tumbler young that needs but ftoop
> Lay head to heel, and creep thro' hoop;
> And man that doth in cheft include
> Old Sodom and Gomorra lewd.
>
> .   .   .   .
>
> And fhew that while the puppets play,
> Though none expoundeth what they fay:
> And Ape led captive ftill in chain
> Till he renounce the Pope and Spain,
> And white oat Eater that doth dwell
> In ftable fmall, at sign of Bell,
> That lifts up hoof to fhew the pranks
> Taught by Magician ftyled Banks.

Men were agape conftantly for marvels.

In the time of Cromwell's Protectorate, there had been a particular Relation ſent from Sluys, in the Low Countries, touching a monſter there lately born, a Double child, with one of its faces ſo miſhapen, that the eyes ſtood where the mouth ſhould be, both together, opening without eyelids, but above had hairy eyebrows. It had no noſe, and ſeemed to have a mouth under the chin inſtead of over it, with other yet more wonderful peculiarities. In 1674, a pamphlet edified the Londoners with an account of " the Northumberland Monſter," born to Jane Paterſon of Dodington. A creature, having the Head, Mane, and Feet, of a Horſe, with the reſt like a man, which, immediately after birth, was ſcalded to death by advice of the Schoolmaſter of the Town.

There was publiſhed in 1682, as a broad-ſheet, news from an Eminent Merchant in Oſtend, of two girls joined together by the Crowns of their Heads. " The one often ſleeps, while the other is awake, cries, and eats; and they are oftentimes both awake, and both eating : I have ſeen them," ſays the Eminent Merchant, " both aſleep, and both awake, and one aſleep and the other awake. The Heads are ſo united together that when that which is awake turns itſelf, the Neck of the other turns alſo : they will never be able to go, ſit, or ſtand ; for if the one ſhould ſit, or ſtand upright, the other muſt ſtand on her Head with the Heels upward. Their Face, Noſe, and Eyes are not directly oppoſite to one another, but ſomewhat ſideways, ſo as that one looks toward you, and the other from you. Many People come daily to ſee them, and give 3 Stivers

a-piece." Then there was, in the reign of William and
Mary, to be feen every day (during his ftay in Town),
at the Blue Boar's Head, in Fleet Street, Prince Giolo,
fon to the King of Moangis or Gilolo, with a particular
geographical addrefs, including the Longitude of his
own Ifland Kingdom. This unfortunate Prince was
fhipwrecked on the coaft of Mindanao, when on a
voyage with his young fifter and his mother Nacatara.
The fifter was feized in marriage. He and his mother
were fold, and embarked for Europe, but he only lived
to reach England, and became famous as the 𝔓𝔞𝔦𝔫𝔱𝔢𝔡
𝔓𝔯𝔦𝔫𝔠𝔢, the juft wonder of the Age. "In him the whole
Myftery of Painting or Staining upon Human Bodies
feem to be comprifed in one ftately piece. The fore-
part of him fhown in engravings are not half his
charm. The more admirable Back-parts afford us a
lively Reprefentation of one quarter part of the World,
upon and betwixt his Shoulders, where the Arctic and
Tropic Circles centre in the North Pole on his Neck,"
and fo forth; romantic particulars are added in the
hand-bill, and it is ftated that "if any Perfons of
Quality, Gentlemen, or Ladies, do defire to fee this
noble Perfon, at their own Houfes, or any other convenient place, in or about this City of London; they
are defired to fend timely notice, and he will be ready
to wait upon them in a Coach or Chair, any time they
pleafe to appoint, if in the day time."

There was alfo to be feen, at the King's Head near
the Maypole in the Strand, a Man about Twenty-one
years of Age, with one Head and two Bodies, the
Miracle of the whole world. With him went "the

Monſter's Brother, who came out of the Great Emperor of Mogul's Country, from Surat; and are both here ſince baptized in the Chriſtian Faith, and become Chriſtians. They had the honour to be ſhewn before their Majeſties and all the Nobility at Court." In 1699 there was born a child, afterwards exhibited at the Sign of Charing Crofs, at Charing Crofs, with but one Body and two Heads.

Notice was alfo given to " Admirers of Curiofities," that at the Charing Crofs Coffee Houſe, in the Corner of Spring Gardens, there was " arrived from France a Man Six-and-Forty Years old, One Foot Nine Inches high, yet fathoms Six Foot Five Inches with his Arms. He walks naturally upon his Hands, raiſing his Body One Foot Four Inches off the Ground : Jumps upon a Table near Three Foot high with one Hand, and leaps off without making uſe of any thing but his Hands, or letting his Body touch the ground. He ſhews ſome Part of Military Exercife on his Hands, as well as if he ſtood upon his Legs. He will go to any gentleman's houſe if required."

In June 1698, there was ſhewn at Moncreff's Coffee Houſe in Threadneedle Street, " for ſixpence a-piece, a Monſter that lately died there, being Humane upwards, and Bruit downwards, wonderful to behold. And a very fine Civet-Cat, ſpotted like a Leopard, and is now alive, that was lately brought from Africa with it. They are expoſed to View, from Eight in the Morning, to Eight at Night." At about the ſame time there was newly come to the lower end of Brookfield Market, near the Market-Houſe, " a little Scotch Man, which has been admired by all that have yet feen him, he being but two Foot and fix Inches high ; and is near upon 60 Years of Age. He was marry'd feveral years, and had Iffue by his Wife, two fons (one of which is with him now). He Sings, and Dances with his fon ; and has had the Honour to be fhewn before feveral Perfons of Note at their Houfes, as far as they have yet Travelled. He formerly kept a Writing-fchool ; and difcourfes of the Scriptures, and of many Eminent Hiftories, very wifely ; and gives great fatisfaction to all fpectators ; and if need requires, there are feveral Perfons in this Town, that will juftifie, that they were his Schollars, and fee him Marry'd." This Scotchman alfo exhibited at the King's Head in Smithfield.

There was exhibited by David Cornwell, a man who drew ftumps for ten fhillings and teeth for five, at the Ram's Head in Fenchurch Street, the " Bold Grimace Spaniard," who " liv'd 15 years among wild creatures in the Mountains, and is reafonably fuppof'd to have been taken out of his cradle, an Infant, by fome favage Beaft, and wonderfully preferv'd, 'till fome Comedians accidentally paff'd through thofe parts, and perceiving him to be of human Race, purfu'd him to his Cave, where they caught him in a Net. They found fome-thing wonderful in his Nature, and took him with 'em in their Travels through *Spain* and *Italy*. He performs the following furprifing Grimaces, *viz.* : He lolls out his Tongue a foot long, turns his Eyes in and out at the fame time ; contracts his Face as fmall as an Apple ; extends his Mouth fix Inches, and turns it into the fhape of a Bird's Beak, and his eyes like to an Owl's ;

turns his mouth into the Form of a Hat cock'd up three ways; and also frames it in the manner of a four-square Buckle; licks his Nose with his Tongue, like a Cow; rolls one Eyebrow two Inches up, the other two down; changes his face to such an astonishing Degree, as to appear like a Corpse long bury'd. Altho' bred wild so long, yet by travelling with the aforesaid Comedians 18 years, he can sing wonderfully fine, and accompanies his Voice with a thorow Bass on the Lute. His former natural Estrangement from human Conversation oblig'd Mr. *Cornwell* to bring a Jackanapes over with him for his Companion, in whom he takes great Delight and Satisfaction."

In Bridges Street in Covent Garden, over against the Rose Tavern, was to be seen "a Living FAIRY, suppos'd to be a Hundred-and-Fifty years old, his face being no bigger than a child's of a Month : was found Sixty Years ago ; Look'd as old then as he does now. His Head being a great piece of Curiosity, having no Scull, with several Imperfections worthy your Observation."

At the sign of the Golden Lion, near the May-pole in the Strand, was a man-child having in his right eye the words Deus Meus, and the same written in Hebrew in his left eye. At Young Man's Coffee House, Charing Cross, was a Little Man, Fifty Years of Age, Two Feet Nine Inches high, and the Father of Eight Children, who " when he sleeps, puts his Head between his two Feet, to rest on by way of a Pillow, and his great Toes one in each Ear." A shew of the Fairs was a " Mail *Child* born with a *Bear* growing on his Back alive."

There was an Hermaphrodite at the King's Head, over againſt the Mews' Gate, Charing Croſs; there were giants and gianteſſes from all parts of the country; there was the little German woman, " Dwarf of the World," who, in July, 1700, was at the Brandy Shop over againſt the Eagle and Child in Stocks Market, and was " carried in a little box to any Gentleman's Houſe, if deſir'd." There was a High German woman without hands or feet, who could ſew, thread needles, ſpin fine thread, and fire piſtols, to be ſeen " together with the merry Humours of Jenny and Robin, which is very pleaſant and Divertive." There was an Eighth Wonder of the World, born without arms, combing his head and ſhaving his chin with his feet, taking off his hat with his toes to ſalute the viſitors, and with his feet uſing a knife and fork and filling a glaſs from a bottle, threading needles, writing ſix fair hands, and ſo forth. There was a boy covered with hedge-hog briſtles, and another boy covered below the neck with fiſh-ſcales. This laſt named Monſter, before it came to England, was exhibited at Naples in the year 1681.

" A collection of ſtrange and wonderful creatures from moſt parts of the world, all alive," was to be ſeen in Queen Anne's time, over againſt the Mews' Gate at Charing Croſs, " By her Majeſty's Permiſſion."

" The firſt being a little *Black Man*, being but 3 foot high, and 32 years of age, ſtraight and proportionable every way, who is diſtinguiſhed by the Name of the *Black Prince*, and has been ſhewn before moſt Kings and Princes in *Chriſtendom*. The next being his wife, the *Little-Woman*, NOT 3 foot high, and 30

years of Age, ftraight and proportionable as any woman
in the Land, which is commonly called the *Fairy Queen,*
fhe gives a general fatisfaction to all that fees her, by
Diverting them with Dancing, being big with child.
Likewife their little *Turkey-Horfe,* being but 2 foot odd
inches high, and above 12 years of Age, that fhews
feveral diverting and furprifing Actions, at the Word of
Command. The leaft Man, Woman, and Horfe that
ever was feen in the World A-live. *The Horfe being
kept in a Box.* The next being a ftrange Monftrous
Female Creature that was taken in the woods in the
Deferts of ÆTHIOPIA in Prefter *John's* Country, in the
remoteft parts of Africa . . . . The next is the noble
Picary, which is very much admir'd by the Learned.
The next being the noble *Jack call,* the Lion's Provider,
which hunts in the Foreft for the Lion's Prey. Likewife a fmall *Egyptian Panther,* fpotted like a *Leopard.*
The next being a ftrange, monftrous creature, brought
from the *Coaft of Brazil,* having a Head like a Child,
Legs and Arms very wonderful, with a Long Tail like
a Serpent, wherewith he Feeds himfelf, as an *Elephant*
doth with his Trunk. With feveral other Rarities too
tedious to mention in this Bill.—And as no fuch
Collection was ever fhewn in this Place before, we hope
they will give you content and fatisfaction, affuring you,
that they are the greateft Rarities that ever was fhewn
alive in this Kingdom, and are to be feen from 9 a
Clock in the Morning, till 10 at Night, where true
Attendance fhall be given during our ftay in this Place,
which will be very fhort. *Long live the* QUEEN."

Such were not rarities of Bartholomew Fair to tempt

away, once in a twelvemonth, the pence from the pockets
of the crowd; but they were entertainments fcattered
about the town, vifited by gentlemen and ladies, noblemen and Royal Princes, fent for to private manfions for
the curiofity of the luxurious, and not difdained even
by the Saturnine George the Firft.

In the firft years of George the Second, Mathew
Buchinger, twenty-nine inches high, born without
Hands, Feet, or Thighs, played on the Hautboy, and
on the Strange Flute, in concert with the Bag-pipe,
Dulcimer and Trumpet; wrote and drew with a pen;
played cards and dice; performed tricks with cups and
balls; and, fays the handbill that commends him to
attention, "his playing at Skittles is moft admirable.
All thefe being done without Hands, makes all that fee
him, fay, he is the only Artift in the World. His
performing fuch Wonders, has gained him the Honour
of fhewing before Three fucceffive Emperors of Germany; and, moft of the Kings and Princes in Europe,
in particular, feveral times before his late Majefty, King
George. He likewife dances a Hornpipe in a Highland
Drefs, as well as any man,—without Legs."

Even William the Third fhared the prevailing tafte
for marvels. There is a broadfheet in praife of
Mr. William Joyce the Kentifh Man, fhewing how
"on Wednefday laft, being the 15th of this Inftant
November 1699, there was ENGLISH SAMPSON
HIS STRENGTH PROV'D before the **KING**." This
man's "frequent and repeated (tho' unparallel'd) performances in and about the City of *London* and parts
adjacent, gain'd fo much fame and applaufe in moft

parts of *England*, that his Majesty *King William* had a desire to see him perform something Extraordinary, and accordingly on *Wednesday* last, he was introduced before His Majesty at *Kensington.*" He then lifted to a considerable height a solid piece of lead weighing a Ton and fourteen pounds and a half, " to the admiration of His Majesty and His Nobles, who were eyewitnesses thereof." A rope being tied about his middle, he was tugged at by " an extraordinary strong horse," which was whipped to exertion, but did not succeed in moving him. Afterwards, having fastened the rope to two posts, one being of extraordinary magnitude, he twitched the rope to pieces as if it were packthread, then put his arms about the posts and broke them down. " At which strange performance His Majesty was mightily well Pleas'd, (and it is said) has orded him a considerable Gratuity, besides an honnarable entertainment for both he and his acquaintance." On the previous day Mr. Joyce had, at Hampstead, in the presence of some hundreds, pulled up by the roots a tree of a yard and a half in circumference, " modestly computed to Weigh near 2000 weight."

Bodily strength is a respectable monstrosity, fit enough to be set before a king; but the general illustrations here given of the taste of the whole town, abundantly prove that, for some time subsequent to the accession of William and Mary, the Monsters in the Booths of Bartholomew Fair were not, as such things now are in country fairs, there in mere observance of a peculiar traditional usage, but were the true and vigorous expression of a taste then predominating in all classes of society.

From the actual handbills I now copy fome of the announcements of exhibitors at Bartholomew Fair, from the date of the Revolution to the death of George the Firſt :

"In Bartholomew FAIR.

"*At the Corner of* Hoſier Lane, *and near* Mr. Parker's Booth ; *There is to be ſeen* A Prodigious Monſter, lately brought over by Sir *Thomas Grantham,* from the great Mogul's Countrey, being a Man with one Head and two diſtinct Bodies, both Maſculine; there is alſo with him his Brother, who is a Prieſt of the Mahometan Religion.

"*Price Sixpence, and One Shilling the beſt Places.*"

"The tall *Black,* called the *Indian* KING, who was betrayed on Board of an Engliſh Interloper, and Barbarouſly abuſed on Board of that Ship, by one *Waters* and his Men, and put in Irons ; from thence carried to *Jamaica,* and ſold there for a ſlave, and now Redeem'd by a Merchant in *London ;* the like hath not been ſeen in *England.* Now to be ſeen at the *Golden-Lyon,* near the *Hoſpital-Gate,* in *Smithfield,* in his *Indian* Garb, for 2*d.*"

"*A Changling Child.*

"To be ſeen the next door to the *Black Raven* in *Weſt Smithfield,* during the time of the Fair, being a living Skeleton, taken by a *Venetian* Galley, from a Turkiſh Veſſel in the *Archipelago.* This is a Fairy Child, ſuppoſed to be born of *Hungarian* Parents, but

chang'd in the Nurfing, Aged Nine Years and more ;
not exceeding a Foot and a-half high. The Legs,
Thighs, and Arms fo very fmall, that they fcarce
exceed the bignefs of a Man's Thumb, and the face
no bigger than the Palm of one's hand ; and feems fo
grave and folid, as if it were Threefcore Years old.
You may fee the whole Anatomy of its Body by fetting
it againft the Sun. It never fpeaks. It has no Teeth,
but is the moft voracious and hungry Creature in the
World, devouring more Victuals than the ftouteft Man
in *England.*

" *Vivant Rex et Regina.*"

" Next door to the *Golden Hart* in *Weft-Smithfield*,
between the *Hofpital-Gate* and *Pye-Corner*, during the
time of *Bartholomew Fair*, is to be feen the Admirable
Work of Nature, a Woman having Three Breafts ; and
each of them affording Milk at one time, or differently,
according as they are made ufe of. There is likewife
to be feen the Daughter of the fame Woman, which
hath Breafts of the like Nature, according to her Age ;
and there never hath been any extant of fuch fort, which
is Wonderful to all that ever did, or fhall behold them."

" This is to give notice to all Gentlemen and Ladies,
" That there is to bee feen a Child alive about a year
and a half old that has three Leggs ; Two off one fide,
and off one equal length. It hath alfo fixteen too's ;
fix growing on one foot with two. The ftrangeft work
of nature that was ever feen."

That announcement is copied from a contemporary tranſcript. We may take with it a fragmentary account of a monſter born the 28th of March, 1706, with " one Body, Two Heads, four Armes and Hands, four Legs and Feet with Toes and Fingers, having Nails upon them very perfect ; but that which is moſt remarkable and Amazing, is this, that it was Born with Teeth in each Mouth, which are plain and Viſible to all Spectators."

There was alſo ſhewn at the Fair in Queen Anne's time, next door to the *Greyhound,* a child with water on the brain deſcribed as " but Thirty weeks old, with a prodigious big Head, being above a yard about, and hath been ſhewn to ſeveral Perſons of Quality." In the advertiſement next quoted, there is a ſingular illuſ- tration of the taſte of the town for monſters in Queen Anne's day.

" *By Her Majeſties Authority,*

" *At the* Hart's-Horn Inn *in* Pye-Corner, *during the time of* Bartholomew Fair, *will be ſeen thoſe ſtrange rarities following,* viz. :—A Little *Farey Woman,* lately come from *Italy,* being but Two Foot Two Inches high, the ſhorteſt that ever was ſeen in *England,* and no ways Deform'd, as the other two Women are, that are carried about the Streets in Boxes from Houſe to Houſe, for ſome years paſt, this being Thirteen Inches ſhorter than either of them. If any perſon has a deſire to ſee her at their own Houſes, we are ready to wait upon them any Hour of the Day.

" Likewiſe a little *Marmazet* from *Bengal,* that dances

the *Cheshire Rounds*, and exercises at the word of command. Also a strange Cock from Hamborough, having Three proper Legs, Two Fundaments, and makes use of them both at one time.

"Vivat Regina."

A bill issued from Three King Court, Fleet Street, in the reign of George the First, invites the public to the "Wonderfull *Tall* Essex Woman, that had the Honour to shew herself before their Royal Highnesses, the Prince and Princess of Wales, and the Rest of the Royal Family, last *Bartholomew Fair*, with great applause." So that the Fair even then had royal visitors. A Woman with two heads one above the other, also two Mandrakes, and a surprising Thunderbolt had been to the palace, and there " shewn to the King, and all the Royal Family."

———

" *By His Majesty's Permission*,
" *Next Door to the* King-Head, *in* Smithfield, *during the time of* Bartholomew Fair.

"For the Satisfaction of all curious enquirers into the Secrets of Nature, is to be seen a Woman Dwarf, but Three Foot and one Inch high, born in *Sommerfetshire*, and in the Fortieth Year of her Age, who discourses excellently well, and gives great Satisfaction to all that ever saw her.

" ☞ *Note*, there is neither Loss of time, or any other inconveniency in vewing this Mistery of Nature.

"Vivat Rex."

We may as well pair the dwarf woman with a giant man.

" *In* Smithfield, *dureing the time of* Bartholomew-Fair ; *between* Hofear-Lane *and the* Swan-Tavern, *at the* Saddler's-fhop.

" Is to be Seen a Tall *Englifh-man*, Eight Foot High, but Seventeen years of Age. He was never fhewn before.

" He is to be feen any Hour of the Day (at the Place above mentioned), from 8 in the Morning till 8 at Night."

The poor tradefman refident in Smithfield feems to have turned many a penny by the letting of lodgings to a Monfter during Fair-time. There were exhibiting lodgers alfo in the numerous Inns called into exiftence by the weekly market held in Smithfield, and rejoicing annually in the Fair. The refort to the Inns being great, an innkeeper probably would fet a high price on his exhibition-room, although a popular fight on the premifes muft have attracted cuftom to his houfe. Either for the fake of economy, or becaufe all the Inns were occupied by other fhowmen, keepers of giants and other curiofities, not having booths of their own, and of a fort with which the market was becoming over-ftocked, tranfacted bufinefs in rooms behind and over fhops. But that the Inns were regarded as the more eligible fhew-places, is manifeft from the preference given among fhops to thofe that happened to be next door to an Inn. " Next door to the Black Raven ; " " Next door to the Golden Hart ; " " Next door to the Sign of the Greyhound ; " " Next door to the King Head ; " " Over againft the Rofe Tavern ; " were fituations evidently chofen with an eye to bufinefs.

CHAPTER XVII.

At the Beginning of the Eighteenth Century.

DOLLS, now fo dear to all young daughters of England, were not known by that name before the reign of William and Mary. They were called fometimes " poppets " but more ufually " babies." Bartholomew Babies have been often mentioned in thefe pages; and the references to them formerly made by men who were not otherwife alluding to the Fair, fhow that they were in unufual repute. Fewer dolls certainly were nurfed; and of thefe the Bartholomew Babies, elegantly dreffed and carefully packed in boxes, feem to have been regarded as the beft. In Nabbes' Comedy of " Tottenham Court " (1638) this phrafe occurs, " I have packed her up in't, like a Bartholomew Baby in a box. I warrant you for hurting her." Poor Robin's Almanack for 1695, fays, " It alfo tells farmers what manner of wife they fhall choofe; not one trickt up with ribbens and knots like a Bartholomew baby, for fuch an one will prove a holyday wife, all play and no work."

The only lexicographer I find who indicates the modern origin of the word " doll," is Richardfon. In his Dictionary it is obferved, that " Dryden tranflates

Pupæ in Perfius, 'Baby-Toys;'" and, in a note, fays, that "thofe Baby-Toys were little Babies, or Poppets, as we call them." But even Richardfon guefles the derivation of the word to be from the Dutch dol, fenfelefs; others derive it—wonderful are fome of the thoughts contained in dictionaries—from idol. Neverthelefs, Richardfon quotes, as an old word of endearment, " pretty little Doll-pol;" which is, but in brief, Dorothy Mary. Becaufe to the fair fex belong pretty faces and gay dreffes, and doubtlefs alfo for other reafons known to the toy-maker, dolls, with a few ridiculous exceptions, have, at all times, been feminine. Bartholomew babies were illuftrious; but their name, as the licence of the Fair increafed, was of equivocal fuggeftion. Therefore, when fome popular toyman, who might have called his babies pretty Sues, or Molls, or Polls, cried diligently to the ladies who fought fairings for their children, " Buy a pretty Doll " (it was at a time too, when the toy babies were coming more and more into demand), the conqueft of a clumfinefs was recognifed. Mothers applied for Dolls to the men at the ftalls, and, ere long, by all the ftalls and toy-booths the new cry of " Pretty Doll " was taken up. We have good reafon to be tolerably certain that Bartholomew Fair gave its familiar name to a plaything now cherifhed in every Englifh nurfery. A provincial toyman could not have enforced the change; and there was no tradefman in London who could diffufe, as private dealer, a new name for the toy in which Bartholomew Fair dealt moft efpecially, and dealt alfo among throngs.

The Fair ftill reprefented, in its booths and in its crowds, fome part of the political feeling of the nation. In 1693, Admiral Killegrew and Sir Ralph Delaval, chiefs of the Britifh fquadron that was to protect the Smyrna merchant fleet againft the force of the French navy bent on intercepting it, returned to England, leaving Rooke with twenty men-of-war to fpeed on to a mercantile difafter in the bay of Lagos. In the December following, Killegrew and Delaval were ftruck out of the Commiffion of the Admiralty, but in September they had run the gauntlet of the Fair. The fhowmen, in a play made for the occafion, reprefented them as flying to the fhelter of the Tower, from the guns of a few French privateers. The Jack-Pudding played chorus, and commented to large applauding audiences, not only on the affairs of the Admiralty, but alfo on other departments of the State, with fo much freedom, that his profperous career was ftayed at laft by a ftrong body of conftables, who carried the players off to prifon. This incident Lord Macaulay relates on the MS. authority of one of the letters fent by the French refugee, L'Hermitage, to the States-General. There will arife prefently another occafion for obferving how much lefs tolerant of the free fpeech of the Fair upon politics, was the government of William of Orange than, in times more perilous, was that of the high-minded Englifh Statefmen of the Commonwealth.

The Fair ftill was attracting fafhionable company. In the *London Gazette* of Sept. 9, 1695, we read that there was "Taken from a Gentleman's fide on Friday

[Sept. 6], at 7 at night, in Bartholomew Fair, a small French rapier, the hilt steel inlaid with gold ; the handle silver, double gilt, the upper part of the blade next the stile being 'graved. Whoever returns it to the owner, Mr. Champney, at Mr. Secretary Trumbull's Office, Whitehall, shall have 10s. more than what any goldsmith or sword-cutler will give for it."

But, in spite of visitors with silver and gold rapiers, the strong feeling of the Corporation of London was still setting steadily against the evil that was in the Fair. In 1691, and again in 1694, a reduction to the old term of Three Days was ordered, as a check to vice, and in order that the pleasures of the Fair might not choke up the avenues of traffic. In 1697 the Lord Mayor, on Bartholomew's Day, published an ordinance recorded in the *Postman*, " for the suppression of vicious practices in Bartholomew Fair, as obscene, lascivious, and scandalous plays, comedies, and farces, unlawful games and interludes, drunkenness, &c., strictly charging all constables and other officers to use their utmost diligence in prosecuting the same." But there was no suppression of the puppet theatres. *Jephtha's Rash Vow* was performed in that year at Blake's Booth, as in the year following at Blake and Pinkethman's. Again, on the 18th of June, 1700, stage-plays and interludes at the Fair were for that year prohibited. They were again prohibited by the Mayor who ruled in the year 1702.

But the showmen appeared to be too strong for the citizens, as they were, of course, too strong for the Serjeant Trumpeter, and other patented tax-claimers,

who are met with from time to time in plaintive adver-
tisements, urging their claims on a rebellious tribe. In
the *Postman* for the 26th of March, 1698, the Trumpeter mentioned the twelve-pence a day due to him
from every one who blew without a licence, and
reminded those "wishing to be easy and discharged
from paying him," that they might have their licences
(as heretofore), for twenty shillings a year.

In the year 1698, a Frenchman, Monsieur Sorbière,
visiting London, says, "I was at Bartholomew Fair. It
consists of most Toy shops, also Fiance and Pictures,
Ribbon shops, no Books; many shops of Confec-
tioners, where any woman may commodiously be treated.
Knavery is here in perfection, dextrous Cut-purses and
Pickpockets. I went to see the Dancing on the Ropes,
which was admirable. Coming out, I met a man that
would have took off my Hat, but I secur'd it, and
was going to draw my Sword, crying out, ' Begar !
Damn'd Rogue! Morbleu,' &c, when on a sudden I
had a hundred People about me, crying, ' Here, Monsieur, See *Jephthah's Rash Vow ;*' ' Here, Monsieur, see
The Tall Dutchwoman ;' 'See *The Tiger*,' says another ;
' See *The Horse and No Horse* whose Tail stands where
his head should do ;' ' See the *German Artist*, Monsieur ;' ' See *The Siege of Namur*, Monsieur :' so that
betwixt Rudeness and Civility, I was forc'd to get into
a Fiacre, and with an air of haste and a full trot, got
home to my lodgings."

Bartholomew Fair was at this period farmed by the
City, for a hundred a year, to its Sword-bearer ; and the
City profits of the Fair formed part of the endowment

z

of the Mayoralty. In the previous year (1697), there had been printed a propofal to allow the Lord Mayor 4000*l.* a year for the maintenance of his office, inftead of a feries of enumerated perquifites, among which one item is " Bartholomew Fair—100*l.*"

The following announcements reprefent fome of the bufinefs of the Fair, in the laft year of the feventeenth century. The firft is a copy of a bill then pofted in Smithfield and its neighbourhood :

" Advertifement of a Great Raffling, which is to be in the Cloyfters this Bartholomew Fair, 1699.

" There being a quantity of curious fillagreen work, fet with divers ftones, the very beft that ever was feen in England, formerly made in a nunnery and prefented to a Lady of Quality lately deceafed, which coft above 300*l.* the making, befides the filver, is now fet at but 200 guineas, there being Ten pieces in number, which is propofed to be raffled for, and that there be two hundred guineas paid into the receiver's hands, who will give the bearer a billet which will entitle him to as many raffles as he had paid guineas. And if not raffled for, then the guineas to be returned. Billets may be had of Mr. Pinfold, in Lombard Street; Mr. Harrifon and Mr. Ludds, in Cheapfide ; Capt. Jenkins, in Effex Street; Mr. Clark, in the Strand ; Mr. Willcock's, in the Minories (Goldfmith's) ; Mr. White, at the King's Arms in the Hofpital (where the goods may be feen)."

The gambling fpirit was then ftrong in England, bubble companies were arifing, and the advertifement juft cited is remarkable in two refpects. It is a lottery fcheme in the name of a raffle, put forward in the very next year after a ſtatute had declared lotteries to be public nuiſances. It alſo takes for granted that there is viſiting the Fair a public, among whom two hundred tickets may be diſpoſed of at a guinea each. The great Cloiſter—now gone—in which this raffle was to take place, was the part of the Fair in which lotteries uſually were held, alſo the part in which lures were ſet for the licentious fops. The rent of ſtandings in the Cloiſter, formed a portion of the revenue of the Hoſpital.

The *Poſtman* for the 17th of Auguſt 1699, announces, that " at Mr. Barnes's and Mr. Appleby's Booth, between the Crown Tavern and the Hoſpital Gate, over againſt the Croſs Daggers, next to Miller's Droll Booth, in Weſt Smithfield, where the Engliſh and Dutch Flaggs, with Barnes's and the Two German Maidens' pictures will hang out, during the time of Bartholomew Fair, will be ſeen the moſt excellent and incomparable performances in Dancing on the Slack Rope, walking on the Slack Rope, Vaulting and Tumbling on the Stage, by theſe five, the moſt famous Companies in the Univerſe, viz., The Engliſh, Iriſh, High German, French, and Morocco, now united.

" The Two German Maidens, who exceeded all mankind in their performances, are within this twelve-month improved to a Miracle."

Two years afterwards, according to an advertiſement in the *Poſtboy*, it was " Her Majeſty's Company of Rope Dancers, at Mr. Barnes and Finley's Booth." The two young maiden rope dancers had " lately arrived from France," and there was ſpecification that " the Famous Mr. Barnes, of whoſe performances this king-

z 2

dom is fo fenfible, Dances with 2 Children at his Feet, and with Boots and Spurs.

" Mrs. Finley, diftinguifhed by the Name of Lady Mary for her incomparable Dancing, has much improv'd herfelf fince the laft Fair. You will likewife be entertained with fuch variety of Tumbling by Mr. Finley and his Company, as was never feen in the Fair before.

" Note, that for the conveniency of the Gentry, there is a back door in Smithfield Rounds."

The Lady Mary here mentioned, is fuppofed to be the perfon who efpecially fuggefted a remark made by Steele in the *Spectator*, that the humour of ftripping on the ftage introduced into playhoufes, came from Bartholomew Fair.

An announcement in the *London Poft* of Monday, Aug. 21 (1701), informs us that " The Lord Mayor and Court of Aldermen " (coming in aid of Government), " have thought fit to fupprefs the extravagant gaming ufual in St. Bartholomew's Cloifters during the Fair, to prevent quarrelling."

As we pafs into another century, again we take a ramble round the fcene.

In the year 1699, Edward Ward gave in his *London Spy* (Parts 9 and 10), a detailed fketch of Bartholomew Fair, from which I bring together all points that are noteworthy. The London Spy went to the playhoufe in Drury Lane, and there found that many of the players, " all the wifer part of the family of Tom Fools had tranflated themfelves to Bartholomew Fair," tempted by "the fifteen or twenty fhillings a day there to be earned."

The Spy then went alfo to the Fair, but in a coach to efcape the dirt and the crowd, and at the entrance was "faluted with Belphegor's concert, the rumbling of Drums, mix'd with the intolerable fqueaking of cat-calls and penny trumpets, made ftill more terrible with the fhrill belches of Lottery pickpockets, thro' Inftruments of the fame Metal with their Faces." The Spy having been fet down with his friend at the Hofpital Gate, went into a convenient houfe to fmoke a pipe and drink fmall beer bittered with colocynth. From one of its windows he looked down on a crowd rufhing, ancle-deep in filth, through an air tainted by fumes of tobacco and of fingeing overroafted pork, to fee the Merry Andrew. On their galleries ftrutted, in their buffoonery of ftatelinefs, the quality of the Fair, dreffed in tinfel robes and golden leather bufkins. "When they had taken a turn the length of their Gallery, to fhew the Gaping Crowd how Majeftically they could tread, each afcended to a feat agreeable to the Dignity of their Drefs, to fhew the Multitude how Imperioufly they could Sit." Then entered the Merry Andrew, whofe firft jeft was "a fingular Inftance of his Cleanlinefs, by blowing his Nofe upon the People, who were mightily pleaf'd, and Laugh'd heartily at the Jeft." Then having picked out a member of the Company to talk with, he began "a Tale of a Tub, illuftrated with abundance of ugly Faces and mimical Actions; for in that lay the chief of the Comedy, with which the Gazers feem'd moft to be affected." The Spy's friend fuggefted that "ever fince the Andrew was whipp'd for fingeing his Pig with Exchequer Notes, and roafting him with Tallies, it has made St. Bartholomew Jefters afraid of being witty, for fear of difobliging the Government." The Epilogue of Merry Andrew's Farce was, " Walk in, Gentlemen, and take your Places, whilft you may have 'em ; the Candles are all lighted, and we are juft agoing to begin ! " "Then fcrewing his Body into an ill-favoured Pofture, agreeable to his Intellects, he ftruts along before the glittering train of Imaginary Heroes, leading them to play the Fool infide."

Bartholomew Fair, as we have already obferved, ftill fat in judgment on the bufinefs of the nation. When, a year or two before the London Spy put his notes upon record, the Merry Andrew finged and roafted his pig with Exchequer Notes and Tallies, the country, helped by Paterfon, Locke, and Newton, was endeavouring to folve a hard financial problem. Loans were not eafily to be obtained by a Revolutionary Government, of which the ftability was not affured to foreigners, and the firft beginning of the Bank of England had juft been made (1694) by the incorporation of certain natural-born Englifh fubjects, among whom a loan had been raifed for the public fervice. The coinage had been clipped fo ferioufly, that a great recoinage, at a lofs of more than two millions, took place in 1696 ; during which, the twoyear old Bank was compelled for a time to fufpend the payment of its notes. While the Government was ftruggling with this great financial embarraffment, and Lord Halifax was endeavouring to direct it in the way of a found monetary fyftem, either in that year 1696, or

the year following, there was a Merry Andrew in the
Fair, whofe jefting, when it tended to create a popular
impreffion that might make the trouble greater, was
thought worthy of refentment.   For the credit of the
authorities we muft fuppofe that their wrath was fpent
not on an obfcure and ftarveling mummer, but that
Phillips, the great Merry Andrew of the day, of whom
all talked and to whom all crowded, was the man they
whipped.   Affuredly it is the fame man, one of whofe
jefts Prior, at the fame period, transformed into a poem,
and, we might almoft fay, paffed into a proverb.   The
jeft of which Ward fpeaks, and the iffue of it, feem
to have been the natural forerunners of that to which
Prior was a witnefs, in one of the years (poffibly
1697), when at Bartholomew Fair ftage plays had been
interdicted :

> " Sly Merry Andrew, the laft *Southwark* Fair
> (At *Barthol'mew* he did not much appear :
> So peevifh was the Edict of the May'r)
> At *Southwark*, therefore, as his Tricks he fhow'd,
> To pleafe our Mafters and his Friends, the Crowd ;
> A huge Neat's-Tongue He in his Right Hand held ;
> His Left was with a good Black-Pudding fill'd."

Thus furnifhed, he walked gravely up and down, and
was brought, in the ufual way, into converfation with
one of the Company, who declared that his joke feemed
a ftupid one.   In his reply, he faid—

> " That bufy fool I was, which Thou art now ;
> Defirous to Correct, not knowing how ;
> With very good Defign, but little wit,
> Blaming or Praifing Things, as I thought fit.
> I for this conduct had what I deferv'd ;
> And dealing honeftly was almoft ftarv'd."

But he has learnt the fecret to be great, and, on folicitation, tells it to his brother Droll :

> " Be of your Patron's Mind, whate'er He fays ;
> Sleep very much ; Think little ; and Talk lefs :
> Mind neither Good nor Bad, nor Right nor Wrong ;
> But Eat your Pudding, Slave ; and Hold your Tongue."

Thereupon, of courfe, holding the Tongue tight, he begins to eat the Pudding he has brought upon the ftage with him. William Phillips muft have been the planner of a jeft like that. The Poet, with full licence of his art, points it at one whom we fhould certainly not have expected to find in the crowd at Southwark Fair :

> " A Rev'rend Prelate ftopt his Coach and Six,
> To laugh a little at our Andrew's Tricks.
> But when He heard him give this Golden Rule ;
> ' Drive on, (he cried,) This Fellow is no Fool.'"

If Phillips was, indeed, the fubject of the whipping and the actor of the jeft cryftallized by Prior into couplets, it is not difficult to believe that this prince of the Merry Andrews may have been the man who, at the fame period, and under the fame name, by which no other man has been identified, is known as the writer of two tragedies, a comedy, and the Bartholomew Fair farce *Briton Strike Home.* If he be really their author, the plays probably were all written for a booth to which he was attached, fince it was in the dramatic companies that Merry Andrews ferved.

We return now to the fociety of the *Spy,* who, finding that the outfides of the Droll Booths were all garnifhed in this manner, and that there was no more

to be feen from his window, came with his friend out
of doors again. Buttoning their pockets they launched
themfelves, he fays, into the tempeft of the crowd, and
were foon off their feet, hurried along in the ftream
of the rabble. At the Rope-Dancers' Booth, they felt
the ground for the firft time, and there they remained to
watch the tumblers, among whom were women who
ftood on their heads. They paid their fixpences and
entered. Firft a little child crept about on the rope,
with a pole "not much bigger than a large tobacco
ftopper." Then came two ftout laffes, who began by
dancing on the rope in troufers, but "doffed their
petticoats after a gentle breathing," and began to caper
with more energy. Thefe were followed by a negro
woman and an Irifhwoman—this being the booth of
Barnes and Appleby. Then followed a man of authority, who with great airs required fundry adjuftments
of the rope; out of Fair time, this was an "Infallible
Phyfician." The perfon that danced againft him was
the German Maid, who as much out-danced the reft
as a Greyhound will out-run a hedgehog. After the
rope-dancing, followed tumbling, which the Spy pre-
ferred.

Out in the crowd again; befieged with the fhrill cry
of "Nuts and Damfons!" and again into a booth,
to fee a dwarf Comedy or Droll, called "the Devil of
a Wife." Here there were ten men to one woman in
the company, and they diverted themfelves by eating
pears and cracking filberts, while the mufic fcraped.
The curtain rofe on a fhort play, in which there was
every actor looking, notwithftanding his drefs, like

what he really was, and not like what he reprefented; "that I fancy'd," fays the Spy, "while they were playing, I heard fome of 'em crying *Flag-Brooms*, fome *Knives to Grind*, and others *Chimney-Sweep*; whilft their Ladies were making up the Concert with *Buy my Cucumbers to Pickle*; and *Here's your rare* Holland *Socks, four Pair for a Shilling*."

Needing refrefhment, the Spy and his friend having left this booth, refolved to eat a quarter of a Pig, on purpofe to be Fools in Fafhion; and with a great deal of elbow-labour, fcrambled through the throng that came pouring into the Fair from all adjacent ftreets. By inch and inch they gained " Pye-Corner, where *Cooks* ftood dripping at their doors, like their Roafted Swines' Flefh at their Fires; with painful Induftry, each fetting forth with an Audible Voice the Choice and Excellency of his Pig and Pork." Some pigs hung upon tenters in the fhop-windows, as big as large fpaniels, and half-baked by the funbeams. The vifitors entered a large fhop, where they had great expectancy of tolerable meat and cleanly ufage; " but had no fooner entered the fuffocating kitchen, but a fwingeing fat Fellow, who was appointed over-feer of the Roaft, to keep the Pigs from bliftering, was ftanding by the Spit in his Shirt, Rubbing of his Ears, Breaft, Neck, and Armpits with the fame Wet-cloth which he applied to his Pigs." That fight drove the vifitors quickly out again, "through an Army of Flies, encamped at the door, in order to attack the Pig-Sauce."

The Spy's next vifit was to a fhow in which was to be feen Doggett, the famous comedian, "who had manfully run the hazard of lofing that reputation in the *Fair* which he'd got in the *Playhoufe.*" The play was about Friar Bacon, and included in its attractions a Royal Court, Conjuration by Friar Bacon, the Devil, a cheating Miller, and his idiotic fon Ralph (that being the part there reprefented to perfection by the great comedian from Drury Lane), alfo a foolifh country juftice, a Flying Shoulder of Mutton, Dancing and Singing of Devils. It lafted three quarters of an hour, ending with a proceffion of the whole pomp of the perfons of the drama, and with the announcement that it would be repeated in half an hour. While waiting for it to begin, the audience cracked nuts, and there were handed round bafkets of plums, walnuts, pears, and peaches. Of the peaches of the Fair there is at this period of its life not unfrequent mention. They feem to have attempted a vain conteft for fame with its juicy pigs.

Oppofite the Hofpital Gate, this Fair time, was a comical figure between two life-like children in waxwork; the figure drummed, opened and fhut its mouth, and rolled its eyes. That was the invitation to a waxwork fhow, known as " the Temple of Diana." A young woman defcribed the figures, and the Spy beftows high praife on the illufion.

The next vifit was paid to a Mufic Booth. The Mufic Booths were chiefly to be found in a clufter on the North-weft fide of the Fair; two or three fcara-mouches, with forbidding faces and inviting voices being at the door of each. As they paffed the curtain into one of them and approached the Bar, a weather-beaten woman in white rang a bell, and the attendants, some in masks,—for here there was much masquerading,—came forward to welcome the newcomers and bad them to the further end of their Fools' Paradise, where they were placed upon "the Hoistings" exempt from the insult of low liquor and low charges. Kettle-drums, trumpets, and fiddles were there clanging and scraping. There followed upon the drums a ballad in two parts by seven voices, a "fine new Playhouse song, by the best composer." Then followed the Hautboys, "undoubtedly," observes the critic, "the best wind-pipes in the world, ill-played upon, to scare a man out of his wits; and I dare swear would raise the Father of all Discord, much sooner than ever Fryar Bacon or Cornelius Agrippa could." The public thus having had its ears boxed into deafness, there next followed "a Dance in imitation of a *Foot-Pad's Robbery;* and he that acted the Thief, I protest, did it so much like a Rogue, that had he not often committed the same thing in Earnest, I am very apt to believe he could never have made such a Jest on't; Firing the Pistol, Stripping his Victim, and Searching his Pockets, with so much Natural Humour, seeming Satisfaction and Dexterity, that he shew'd himself an absolute Master of what he pretended to." A fat woman then bounced about in a dance, with glasses full of liquor on the backs of her hands. Then a young damsel begged a number of swords from gentlemen in the room, and performed feats of apparent peril with them in a nimble sword-dance.

The rest of the entertainment was too obviously impudent and intolerably dull to be mentioned even by the Spy. The Company was of all ranks of men and many oftenfible varieties of women, but whatever their outward differences, few were fober, and all feemed at home in what Edward Ward, who was no "puritanical Alderman," denounced as "the Scandalous Nurferies of all Vice, Vanity, and Villany."

This feems to be the advertifement of the Mufic Booth above defcribed:

"THOMAS DALE, Drawer at the Crown Tavern at Allgate, keepeth the TURK's HEAD *Mufick Booth*, in Smithfield Rounds, over againft the *Greyhound* - Inn during the Time of *Bartholomew Fair*, Where is a Glafs of good Wine, Mum, Syder, Beer, Ale, and all other Sorts of Liquors, to be Sold; and where you will likewife be entertained with good Mufick, Singing, and Dancing. You will fee a Scaramouch Dance, the Italian Punch's Dance, the Quarter Staff, the Antick, the Countryman and Countrywoman's Dance, and the Merry Cuckolds of Hogfden.

"Alfo, a Young-Man that dances an Entry, Salabrand, and Jigg, and a Woman that dances with Six Naked Rapiers, that we Challenge the whole Fair to do the like. There is likewife a Young-Woman that Dances with Fourteen Glaffes on the Backs and Palms of her Hands, and turns round with them above an Hundred Times, as faft as a Windmill turns; and another Young Man that Dances a Jigg incomparably well, to the Admiration of all Spectators.

"*Vivat Rex.*"

In further illuftration of the entertainment at the

Mufic Booths, reference may be made alfo to the hand-bill of JAMES MILES from *Sadler's* Wells at *Iflington*; who kept the GUN MUSICK BOOTH in *Bartholomew* Fair, and fpecified nineteen of the dances performed at his eftablifhment. Among them were, a Dance between Three Bullies and Three Quakers; the Wonder of her Sex, a Young Woman who dances with the Swords and upon the Ladder with that Variety, that fhe challenges all her Sex to do the like; a Cripples' Dance by Six Perfons with Wooden Legs and Crutches in Imitation of a Jovial Crew; and a New Entertainment between a Scaramouch, a Harlequin, and a Punchinello, in imita-tion of Bilking a Reckoning.

By this time, the Spy having left the mufic booth, goes on to tell us that it was almoft dark, and he and his friend took a turn on the outfide of the Fair among the Whirligigs or Flying Coaches. They paffed two puppet-fhows, outfide which there were monkeys imi-tating men, and men mimicking monkeys. So they again came to the Hofpital Gate, and entering that came into the Cloifters, which they defcribed as a Bedlam for lovers. In the raffling fhops the fharpers who attended, led a fafhion of prefenting winnings to the next woman who might ftand near, although a perfect ftranger; and in this way the winners were enticed to return what they would otherwife have carried off, to the female accomplices of the proprietor. The laft event in this vifit to the Fair was a creep from the Cloifter "up a pair of Stairs as narrow and as fteep as the Stone Steps of a Belfry, over which was written in Golden Capitals, in two or three places, THE GROOM

PORTER'S; defign'd, as I fuppofe, for Fools to underftand it was the Honefter Place for his Name being
there, and that they might as fairly fling away their
Money here as in any place in Chriftendom." Thofe
ftairs led to a gambling den, containing a room in which
clerks and footmen could rifk fixpences, and a room in
which " money was toffed about as if a ufelefs com-
modity, and feveral parts of the Prodigal Son were being
acted to a miracle."

Surely there is in this picture of the Fair much
juftification of the efforts made for its reftriction. The
great Fair near Cambridge, Stourbridge Fair, was in
the days of which we are now fpeaking a place of large
commerce ; but at the Fair in the Metropolis, the
element of fober trade was choked by its exceffive
development as a great pleafure fair. The maffive
crowds of people that by the growth of London had
been placed ready to throng in upon Smithfield, by
their compact mafs almoft clofed the avenues of traffic
in its neighbourhood. The cloth trade in Bartholomew
Fair died naturally ; but the other trades that perifhed
from it, died by fuffocation.

In the year 1701, Bartholomew Fair was prefented as
a nuifance ("next only to that of the play-houfes ") by
the Grand Jury of London ; and of the nature of the
nuifance in the firft year of the new century of life
into which it had paffed, we have record, lefs elaborate,
indeed, than that for the laft year of the century
departed, but even more emphatic.

Four pages quarto printed for R. Hine near the
Royal Exchange, 1701, are entitled A WALK TO SMITH-

FIELD, or a TRUE DESCRIPTION OF THE HUMOURS
OF BARTHOLOMEW FAIR, with the very comical
Intrigues and Frolics that are acted in every particular
Booth in the Fair, by perfons of all ages and fexes, from
the Court Gallant to the Country Clown.

" With the Old Droll-players' Lamentation for the
lofs of their Yearly Revenues : being very Pleafing and
Diverting."   (Seven or eight lines of pointlefs verfe.)

The writer fays, in more words than we need repeat,
that he went on the firft day of the Fair, to vifit Saint
Bartholomew in Smithfield Rounds, to fupport there
the yearly cuftoms of debauchery; that he found a crowd
as thick as at a Covent Garden Conventicle or Quakers'
Meeting-houfe ; that the Bartholomew babes of Grace
were moft attentive to Jack-Pudding doctrine ; but that
he was himfelf fomewhat furfeited at the old threadbare
arguments of Merry Andrews and the other Fools
without the booths, and had an itching fancy to fee the
affes of both fexes within the wooden tents of Iniquity.
He found it difficult to ftir from booth to booth, three
yards in half-an-hour's time ; and for a man who would
have us think that he fcorns the booths as iniquitous,
the pamphleteer in the crowd proceeds to forget decency
to a remarkable extent.   Having at laft fqueezed his
way to Pye-Corner, he was informed that our Englifh
Sampfon was performing there, and having paid his
money at the door, was admitted to a feat three ftories
high, when prefently the Man of Kent appeared,
" equipped like one of the London Champions on the
Artillery Ground, at the mock-ftorming of a Caftle." We
have already, in company with King William the Third,

feen a performance by this Sampfon. The next booth was the puppet-fhow of *Jephthah's Rafh Vow :* or *the Virgin Sacrifice.* The explorer paid two pence and entered. While Jephthah made his vow, the author of the pamphlet boafts that he was indulging himfelf with more than a little naftinefs, and a gold watch and diamond ring were ftolen. If the behaviour of the audience at a puppet-fhow at all refembled the fketch here given, there was no company at the Virgin Sacrifice fit for an honeft woman to fit down among. Obliged to follow our foul guide, becaufe he gives us a few points of information, we next enter the booth that contained " Pinkeman's Medley." Having feen the Vaulting of the Horfe, and part of the Ladder Dance, our guide began to give his whole fympathy and attention to whatever was difgufting in the conduct of the audience. Then he fought " the Dutchwoman's booth," and " with fome difficulty made a hard fhift to get in where Danifh, Dutch, German, and Bohemian Frows made fuch a chattering in commendation of one another's dexterity, in derifion of Mr. Barnes and other Englifh heroes, that I fancied myfelf in the French camp in Flanders. However, confidering the Wheelbarrow dance by a little girl of ten years of age, and other ftrange performances, nothing but miracles could equal them." As he came out of that booth, a bill was thruft into his hand, with a picture of a man and woman fighting for the breeches, but the play was called *The Devil and Dr. Fauftus.* Content with the Dutch rope-dancers fent him to the Englifh performers taking the fame line, and in Barnes's booth he found " Lady Mary

A A

as far outdoing the Dutch Frows as a lady of honour
exceeds a milkmaid in dancing a borrie or minuet." I
leave out of account the filth with which every fact
given in this narrative is ftrongly feafoned. The author
looked to the Mufic booths, " but confidering that
Reformation of Manners had fuppreffed them all but
one (they were prohibited by an order of the Sixth of
Auguft, in the previous year), I declined going thither
left I fhould be thought a debauched perfon; therefore,
to compleat all but the Cloifter Walls, I defigned to
end my police in the booth called *The Creation of the
World."*

There is no more information to be gleaned from
the pamphlet, but feveral playbills of the puppet-fhow
of *The Creation of the World* are extant, curious reminders of the firft days of the Fair. It was in a
fubfequent year, at Heatley's Booth over againft the
Crofs Daggers, next to Mr. Miller's Booth, and was
there prefented during Bartholomew Fair as " a Little
Opera, called the Old Creation of the World, newly
reviv'd, with the addition of the glorious Battle obtain'd
over the French and Spaniards, by the Duke of Marl-
borough." At another Fair time, the fame puppets
were in Crawley's Booth, " newly reviv'd with the
addition of Noah's Flood; alfo feveral Fountains playing Water during the time of the Play."

" The laft fcene," fays the placard, " does prefent
Noah and his *Family* coming out of the Ark, with all
the Beafts, two by two, and all the Fowls of the Air
feen in a Profpect fitting upon the Trees. Likewife,
over the Ark is feen the Sun rifing in a moft glorious

manner; moreover, a multitude of Angels will be feen in a double rank, which prefents a double profpect, one for the Sun, the other for a Palace, where will be feen fix Angels ringing fix Bells. Likewife Machines defcends from above, double and trible, with *Dives* rifing out of Hell, and Lazarus feen in Abraham's Bofom, befides feveral *Figures* dancing *Jiggs*, *Sarabands* and *Country-Dances*, to the Admiration of all Spectators; with the merry conceits of Squire *Punch*, and Sir *John Spendall*.

"All this is completed with an Entertainment of Singing and Dancing with feveral Naked Swords, Perform'd by a Child of Eight Years of Age, to the general Satisfaction of all Perfons."

Jofeph Clark was a pofture mafter, famous at this period of Englifh hiftory. Clark lived in Pall Mall, and was rather ftout than thin, but he could imitate almoft every fort of deformity and diflocation. He had alfo a remarkable power of difguifing his identity by change of face. It was a trick of his to fend for a tailor and caufe himfelf to be meafured for new clothes as a man with a hump on the right fhoulder. When the clothes were brought home, the tailor reproached himfelf for negligence on finding that the hump was on the left fhoulder. He apologized for his miftake, made a new coat, and found his cuftomer's back, when he brought it, to be perfectly ftraight. Clark ufed alfo to pay fucceffive vifits with a fucceffion of new faces to Mr. Molins, an eminent furgeon of his day, and caufe himfelf to be examined for all kinds of horrible diflocations and contortions which were pro-

nounced to be of the moſt intereſting character, and
quite incurable. His ſucceſſor as a poſture maſter was
a man named Higgins, of whom leſs is known. To
Mr. Joſeph Clark's accompliſhments in his own art, his
portrait teſtifies. He died, it is ſuppoſed, towards the
cloſe of the ſeventeenth century.

CHAPTER XVIII.

The Playhouse at the Fair—Elkanah Settle.

ELKANAH SETTLE has been named already in these Memoirs as the manager in 1680, of the pageant of the Burning of the Pope. In that year, aged thirty-two, and already the author of five or six tragedies, he wrote "the Character of a Popish Succeffor, and what may be expected from such a one," opening a controversy which he pursued into a second pamphlet; and in 1681, author of two more tragedies, he had replied with " The Medal Reversed " to Dryden's poem of " The Medal." The reader knows how he appeared before the town as Dryden's rival, and advanced against " Abfalom and Ahithophel," his " Azaria and Hushai." When the Popish Succeffor was inevitable, Settle became a Tory, disgraced himself with " Animadversions on the Last Speech and Confession of William Lord Ruffell," and wrote in due time a poem on the Coronation of the Popish Succeffor, " the High and Mighty Monarch James II.," as he wrote also for the Corporation of London annual panegyrics on the Lord Mayor's Show, which he called " Triumphs for the Inauguration of the Lord Mayor."

There were men who had called Settle a better poet
than John Dryden; but none called him fo in the days
of his adverfity, after the expulfion of the Stuarts.
The Laureate of James the Second, became the laureate
of Mrs. Mynn in Bartholomew Fair, receiving from
that fhowwoman and her daughter, Mrs. Leigh, a falary
as their dramatic author. In the year 1707, Mrs. Mynn
produced in her booth, on a fcale of unprecedented
grandeur, Settle's *Siege of Troy*. It was not a political
play, but a Bartholomew fpectacle, upon one of the
themes known to the old Moralities.

To vifit Mrs. Mynn's booth is our main intention in
this chapter; but we muft walk to it at a leifurely pace,
along the high road of the annals of the Fair. The
handy Tiger who in the year 1701 fhowed how he had
been trained to pluck a fowl, is not to be denied his
fentence in the chronicle. And thofe fad-coloured threads
varying the pattern of our woof, the lines of melancholy admonition that were inceffantly being reeled
off by the Serjeant-Trumpet and the Mafter of the
Revels, muft not be fnapped fhort and thrown afide.
Impoverifhing was the obftinacy of the fhowmen; and
we manifeft only a decent refpect for infulted dignity,
in dwelling on the forrows of the Patentees. It will
be feen, that the Mafters of the Revels and the
Trumpeters have by this time difcovered a magnificent and charitable way of ftirring up on their behalf,
the dormant energies of magiftrates and conftables in
all the towns and villages of England. The following
appeared in the *Flying Poft* during Bartholomew Fair
time in the year 1700:

" Theſe are to give Notice, to all Trumpeters, Drums, Fifes, &c., who have, or ought to have Licences from the Serjeant-Trumpet, that Matthias Shore, Eſq., being lately deceaſed, the Licences by him granted are determined, and they are forthwith to apply themſelves for new ones to his ſon William Shore, at the *Adam* and *Eve*, near *Hungerford Market* in the *Strand*, who is ſworn into the Place of Serjeant-Trumpet. And all Civil Officers are deſired not to ſuffer any Perſon to Sound, Beat, or Play, without Licence from him, or paying the ſaid Serjeant-Trumpet's due of 12*d.* each day they ſo do, which he gives (as his Father formerly did) to the uſe of the Poor of the reſpective Places." In 1708, it was John Shore whom Her Majeſty had appointed to this office. Soon afterwards it was again during Bartholomew Fair time, that in the *Poſtman* for the 8th of September, 1702, Charles Killegrew, Eſq., as Maſter of the Revels, and Thomas Salby, Gent., Controller of the ſame, named ſeveral of the " Stage-players, Mountebanks, Rope-dancers, Prize-players, Puppet-ſhowers, and ſuch as make ſhew of motion and ſtrange ſights," who defied their licence ; and deſired all Conſtables, Borſholders, Churchwardens, and Overſeers of the Poor, to oppoſe and ſtay their actings, " unleſs they pay you 2*s.* per day for ſo long time as they ſtay among you, without the ſaid Maſter and Controller's Licence "— on which there are two ſixpenny ſtamps— " in part of what money is due from them to the ſaid Maſter and Controller, upon the account of their not having Licence." The money ſo paid is to be

diftributed to the poor of the diftrict, from which
it is raifed, but notice is to be given of the where-
abouts of the men, " fo as they may be profecuted."

The defiant fhowmen went on their accuftomed way.
They blew their horns in the face of the Trumpeter,
and fought the Mafter of the Revels with their puppets.
The Great Hog, the genius of the Fair, which had
been in the Fair fince Ben Jonfon's time, and was
there, perhaps, in Rayer's time, grunted againft the
claims of thefe private proprietors of taxes the contempt
begotten of his large experience.   It is an abfurd thing
to be reminded of the Wandering Jew by a ftationary
pig, but in that Great Hog there was fome likenefs
to Ahafuerus; and unpardonably defective would thefe
Annals be, if they did not contain one of his manifeftoes.   The fubjoined appeared in Queen Anne's day.
The reader will obferve that a myfterious filence is preferved as to the age of an animal which was a fhow in
almoft pre-hiftoric times, while we are told with alacrity
the age of the young colt that occupied the place of
companion in his eftablifhment :

" By Her Majefty's Permiffion.   This is to give
Notice, to all Gentlemen, Ladies, and others, that
at the Hofpital Gate in Smithfield, during the time of
Bartholomew Fair, is to be feen A LARGE BUCK-
INGHAMSHIRE HOG, about 10 feet long, 13
hands high, above feven foot and a-half round the
Body; alfo 5 feet round the neck, and 18 inches round
the fore Leg, above the Joynt."

" Likewife A COLT, about 5 months old, that was
foal'd without any fore Legs, and walks upright at the

word of Command on his two hind legs.—Thefe two
ftrange and Wonderful Creatures are to be feen at any
time of the day without lofs of time.

" *Vivat Regina.*"

Then, again, how can we venture to pafs by the
year 1702, and overlook the diftinction enjoyed by
the Fair that year in the prefence of a company " by
all owned to be the only amazing Wonders of the
World in Every thing they Do." The Documents
of thefe Minifters of Pleafure, are the true State papers
of our hiftory, and here is a State paper that I have
not difhonefty enough to fupprefs :

" At the Great Booth over againft the Hofpital
Gate in Bartholomew Fair, will be feen the Famous
Company of Rope-Dancers, they being the greateft
performers of Men, Women and Children that can
be found beyond the Seas, fo that the World cannot
parallel them for Dancing on the Low Rope, Vaulting
on the High Rope, and for Walking on the Slack, and
Sloaping Ropes, out-doing all others to that degree,
that it has highly recommended them, both in Bartholomew Fair and May Fair laft, to all the beft perfons
of Quality in England. And by all are owned to be
the only amazing Wonders of the World, in every
thing they do: It is there you will fee the Italian
Scaramouch dancing on the Rope, with a Wheelbarrow before him, with two Children and a Dog
in it, and with a Duck on his Head ; who fings
to the Company and caufes much Laughter. The
whole entertainment will be fo extremely fine and

diverting, as never was done by any but this Company alone."

Tempefts were frequent in the playhoufe of the Fair; chiefly, I am convinced, for the fine opportunity given by that particular theme to the big drums. The great emphafis laid in all acting booths upon the kettle-drum will hereafter become confpicuous, and Ben Jonfon, when he alluded years ago to plays on fuch a topic, in his Prologue to Every Man in His Humour, defined them by references to the "nimble fquib," and "the tempeftuous drum;" a few fquibs, and a little robuft exercife of the elbows, made, in fact, a cheap fenfation. Yet fhall we fay that expenfe was fpared in this perfectly new Tempeft?—

"Never acted before. At *Miller's Booth*, over againft *the Crofs-daggers*, near the *Crown* Tavern, during the time of *Bartholomew Fair*, will be prefented an Excellent New Droll, call'd THE TEMPEST; or *the Diftreffed Lovers*. With the *Englifh Hero* and the *Ifland Princefs*, with the Comical Humours of the Inchanted *Scotchman*; or *Jockey* and the *Three Witches*. Showing how a Nobleman of England was caft away upon the Indian Shore, and in his Travel found the Princefs of the Country, with whom he fell in Love, and after many Dangers and Perils, was married to her; and his faithful Scotchman, who was fav'd with him, travelling thorow Woods, fell in among Witches, when between 'em is abundance of comical Diverfions. There in the Tempeft is Neptune, with his Triton in his Chariot, drawn with Sea-Horfes and Mair Maids finging. With Variety of Entertainment, performed by the beft

Masters : the Particulers would be too tedious to be inserted here.   *Vivat Regina.*"

From among the actors at Drury Lane, there was always at this time a strong body detached for performance at the Fair, where there was more money to be earned than in the theatre. For this reason, and not because they began the world as strolling showmen, it has to be said of not a few good actors, that they performed in booths at Smithfield. William Penketh-man, or Pinke(th)man, a low comedian, of doubtful popularity, who had been, at the close of the seventeenth century, a member of the Drury Lane Company, an incorrigible talker to the galleries, in which he was dearly beloved by the name of Pinkey, did not overlook his own peculiar qualification for success at Bartholomew Fair. After the year 1700, if not earlier, he becomes an established feature of the festival whenever stage-plays are permitted by the City, keeping his booth in partnership with one or two brother actors. —Thus, in one year early in the century, it belongs to Pinkeman, Mills, and Bullock, and is " in the old place over against the Hospital Gate, where there is presented a New Droll called THE SIEGE OF BARCELONA, with the Taking of Fort Mount-jouy. Containing the pleasant and comical exploits of that Renown'd Hero, Captain Blunderbuss and his Man Squib : His adventures with the Conjurer, and a Surprising Scene of the Flying Machine, where he and his Man Squib are enchanted ; Also the Diverting Humour of Corporal Scare Devil." The actors are Mills, representative of ferious Gentlemen, as fecond to Wilks and Cibber; Bullock, another low comedian; Norris, who had performed in 1699, the part of Dicky in Farquhar's Conftant Couple, or a Trip to the Jubilee, and again in 1701, in its fequel, Sir Harry Wildair, and who appears in the Bartholomew Bill, as Mr. Norris *alias* Jubilee Dicky. Bullock muft have been tall and Norris fhort, for the *Spectator*, fpeaking of the fhifts of fmall dramatic wits to raife a laugh, fays, "Bullock in a long coat, and Norris in a fhort one, feldom fail of this effect." There were alfo three other performers.

A Dialogue printed in 1702, containing "a Comparifon between the Two Stages" (attributed to Gildon), thus defcribes two of the managers of this booth, Penkethman and Bullock:— "*Sullen*. But Pinkethman the flower of— *Critic*. Bartholomew Fair, and the idol of the rabble: a fellow that overdoes everything, and fpoils many a part with his own ftuff. *Sullen*. Oh, but Bullock— *Critic*. Is the beft comedian that has trod the ftage fince Nokes and Leigh, and a fellow that has a very humble opinion of himfelf."

After the play juft cited, in which Penkethman himfelf did not appear, that actor, who alfo performed harlequin parts at Drury Lane, added his own performance with Mr. Simpfon, a famous Vaulter, "who has had the honour to teach moft of the Nobility in England" (!), and who was with Mr. Pinkeman, "to let the world fee what Vaulting is. Being lately arrived from Italy." The laft claufe was added in deference to a tafte, then as ftrong in Bartholomew Fair as elfewhere, for minifters to entertainment who came from abroad. "About this time," fays Daniel O'Bryan in his Memoirs of the actor Wilks, "the Englifh Theatre was not only peftered with Tumblers, and Rope Dancers from France, but likewife Dancing Mafters and Dancing Dogs; fhoals of Italian Squallers were daily imported; and the Drury Lane Company almoft broke." Upon the production of Farquhar's Love in a Bottle (1698), "the facetious Jo. Haynes, compofed this Epilogue and fpoke it in mourning." As a fpeaker of Prologues and Epilogues written by himfelf, Haynes had a fpecial reputation. "This epilogue" we take for granted, but the tafte rebuked in it concerns us. Wright in his Hiftoria Hiftrionica, written in 1699, fays that plays could hardly draw an audience, unlefs fome foreign regale was exprefled in the bottom of the bill.

In 1702, Drury Lane Theatre clofed on the 22nd of Auguft until after Bartholomew Fair, and in that year the famous Thomas Doggett, praifed by Cibber as the moft natural actor of his time, who eight years before was acting leading comic parts in the fame caft with Leigh or Betterton and Mrs. Bracegirdle, was among the wooden horfes, Merry Andrews, and pickle herrings, ufing his famous fkill in the dreffing of parts, as actor for the Fair in an old woman's petticoats and a red waiftcoat. Though joint manager of Drury Lane, from which he retired with a competence when Booth, for his fuccefsful perfonation of Addifon's Cato, was by the interpofition of a noble lord thruft alfo into the direction, Doggett himfelf, during the Bartholomew holiday at Drury Lane, kept a booth in the Fair. Here is one of his bills :

"At *DOGGETT'S BOOTH*, at *Hofier - Lane End*, during the Time of *Bartholomew Fair*, will be Prefented a New DROLL call'd THE DISTRESSED VIRGIN or *the Unnatural Parents*. Being a True Hiftory of the *Fair Maid* of the WEST, or THE LOVING SISTERS. With the Comical Travels of *Poor Trufty*, in Search of his *Mafter's Daughter*, and his Encounter with *Three Witches*.

"*Alfo Variety of Comick Dances and Songs, with Scenes and Machines never feen before.* *Vivat Regina.*"

It was faid that Thomas Doggett could reprefent all degrees of age, and give character to the leaft detail of the drefs he wore. His name lives with the Coat and Badge, which, being a zealous Whig, he, after the acceffion of King George the Firft, gave to be rowed for by fix watermen on every 1ft of Auguft, that being the anniverfary of the event it was his loyal purpofe to commemorate. In 1704 Doggett's Booth at Bartholomew Fair was a partnerfhip venture, maintained by Parker and Doggett, the play being *Bateman*, or the Unhappy Marriage. Penkethman's Booth in that year was kept in partnerfhip with Bullock and Simpfon, and the play was *Jephthah's Rafh Vow ;* Penkethman and Bullock taking in it the Bartholomew farce characters of Toby and Ezekiel.

In 1705 Vanbrugh opened his new Theatre in the Haymarket ; and in the Haymarket alfo, under whatever management, the actors ufually or always clofed their Houfe during Bartholomew Fair. It was alfo ufual at Drury Lane and the Haymarket to perform, fhortly before or after the great feftival, Ben Jonfon's play of *Bartholomew Fair.* May Fair alfo feems at this time occafionally to have caufed the clofing of the theatres.

Thefe confiderations greatly leffen our fenfe of the fall experienced by Elkanah Settle, when he accepted a falary from Mrs. Mynn, and adapted to a Bartholomew audience in 1707, the operatic fpectacle of *the Siege of Troy,* which he had produced in 1701 at Drury Lane, Mills, one of Penkethman's partners, being then the Menelaus, Wilks and Mrs. Rogers Paris and Caffandra, and Mrs. Oldfield the Queen Helen.

The Drury Lane Play was a miferable piece of writing, full of directions for expenfive decoration of the Stage. The Prologue begins at once by calling it, in Mrs. Mynn's fafhion, " This coftly play." In adapting it for Mrs. Mynn, the poet left out four or five ferious characters, cut down all the ferious dialogue, and reduced his work from five acts to three, interpolating a fufficient quantity of right Bartholomew buffoonery. The new form of the play feems to have been tolerably popular ; for, in the following year, it was reprinted before a fixpenny Hiftory of Troy. Of the book iffued on behalf of Mrs. Mynn, and of the play as performed at the Fair, if the promife of the book may be trufted, this is an account :

The SIEGE OF TROY, A Dramatick Performance. Prefented in *Mrs. MYNN'S BOOTH,* Over againft the *Hofpital Gate,* in the *Rounds* in *Smithfield,* during the Time of the prefent *Bartholomew FAIR. Containing* A Defcription of all the *Scenes, Machines,* and *Movements,* with the whole decoration of the *Play,* and Particulars of the *Entertainment.*

LONDON, Printed and Sold by *Benj. Bragge* at the *Black Raven* in *Paternofter-Row*. And alfo at the *Booth* all the time of the Fair.

TO THE READER.

A Printed Publication of an Entertainment *performed on a* Smithfield-Stage, *which, how gay or richly foever fet off, will hardly reach to a higher Title, than the cuftomary name of a DROLL, may feem fomewhat new. But as the prefent undertaking, the work of ten Months' preparation, is fo extraordinary a Performance, that without Boaft or Vanity we may modeftly fay, In the whole feveral* Scenes, Movements, *and* Machines, *it is no ways Inferiour even to any one* Opera *yet feen in either of the* Royal Theaters; *we are therefore under fome fort of Neceffity to make this Publication, thereby to give ev'n the meaneft of our Audience a full Light into all the Objeƈt they will there meet in this* Expenfive Entertainment; *the* Proprietors *of which have adventur'd to make, under fome fmall Hopes, That as they yearly fee fome of their happier Brethren Undertakers in the* FAIR, *more cheaply obtain even the Engroft Smiles of the* Gentry *and* Quality *at fo much an eafier Price; fo on the other fide their own more coftly Projeƈtion (though lefs Favourites) might poffibly attain to that good Fortune, at leaft to attraƈt a little fhare of the good graces of the more Honourable part of the Audience; and perhaps be able to purchafe fome of thofe fmiles which elfewhere have been thus long the profufer Donation of particular Affeƈtion and Favour.*

Under the head of Aƈtors' Names, the Charaƈters of

Menelaus, Ulyffes, Helen, Caffandra, and the reft, are defcribed in a form fuitable to the tafte and underftanding of all patrons in the Fair.

The Siege of Troy. Act I. *The Curtain is drawn up, and difcovers King* Menelaus, Ulyffes, *Attendants, and Guards.*

The King and Ulyffes in a fhort difcourfe of four and thirty lines, reveal the whole fituation as it regards—

> " that tall Wooden Horfe
> We have prepar'd, in whofe dark Womb of Fate,
> Five hundred generous Volunteers all wait,
> All at one ftroke to give the fatal Blow:
> Fear not Succefs.
>   *King.*   No: wife *Ulyffes*, no.
> When thy great Hand's the Royal Engineer,
> 'Tis by fuch Pilots I to glory fteer.
>   *Ulys.* Confider, Sir, what managing Hand I've found
> To move this vaft Machine; the Honeft *Sinon*:
> A Man fo hearty in your Royal Caufe,
> That he has difmember'd even his very Face,
> Cut off his Lips and Nofe, and torn his Eyes out
> To make himfelf the Object of their Pity.
> That by his moving Looks and artful Tears
> He may fo lull the Credulous *Trojans'* Ears,
> To draw that fatal Horfe within their Walls.
>   *King.* Now Fate, curft Troy, for thy Deftruction calls.
> Revenge, Oh! dear Revenge,"

and fo on, but not for a long time fo on; becaufe the author of a booth-play muft remember, Time is Money. Next follows the comic fcene between Briftle a Cobler, and his Wife. The wife will go out of Troy " to fee the great Horfe the *Grecians* have left behind 'em," and the hufband will not let her go. Her talk is as the talk of Urfula the pigwoman; her hufband, to keep her at home, gives " a lick of Styrrup Leather."

"*Wife.* Help, help, Murder.

Within. Huzzah! huzzah!

Enter Mob.

1*ſt Mob.* ⎫ ſpeaking ⎧ The Horſe, the Horſe, the Horſe.
2*d Mob.* ⎬ all to- ⎨ The *Greeks*, the *Greeks*, the *Greeks*.
3*d Mob.* ⎭ gether ⎩ All run, run, run.

Briſtle. Hold, hold, hold, Neighbours. Let one Man ſpeak at once.

All. Ay, ay, let our Neighbour *Briſtle* ſpeak firſt.

Briſtle. Then mark me, good Folks; we are all going to ſee this great Horſe.

All. Ay, ay, the Horſe, the Horſe.

Briſtle. Look ye then, Neighbours; let us march Soberly and Decently, in roaring good Order, as thoſe Civil Gentlemen called the Mob, ſhould do; and I'll be Captain *Tom*, your Leader."

The Cobler therefore leads the mob to ſee the Horſe; leaving his wife behind with a member of the mob, whom ſhe, in Bartholomew phraſe, thanks kindly for kiſſing her.   [*Exeunt.*

The Scene opens and diſcovers Paris *and* Helen, *fronting the Audience, riding in a Triumphant Chariot, drawn by two White Elephants, mounted by two Pages in em-broyder'd livery. The ſide Wings are ten Elephants more, bearing on their Backs open Caſtles, umbraged with Canopies of Gold; the ten Caſtles fill'd with ten Perſons richly dreſt, the Retinue of Paris; and on the Elephants' Necks ride ten more Pages in the like rich Dreſs. Beyond and over the Chariot, is ſeen a Victor of the City of* Troy; *on the Walls of which, ſtand ſeveral Trumpeters, ſeen behind and over the Head of* Paris, *who ſound at the opening of the Scene.*

Poor indeed was the wit joined to theſe glories of ſtage upholſtery, in which Bartholomew Fair taught how a public might be ſatisfied with leaſt toil to the brain. Says Paris to Helen—

> " We 'll tune our trumps of War to Songs of Peace,"

and ſo forth; but Caſſandra comes. " Oh my dear Paris," exclaims Helen, " is that Screech owl here ! " Caſſandra calls her bad names, talks to Paris about angry gods " who with all the Bolts of Fate, Blood, Fire, and Sword, for his deſtruction wait." Paris, being annoyed, threatens the Screech owl, that if ſhe abuſes Helen any more—

> " by all the Pow'rs I ſwear
> Ile drive my Chariot o'er thy trampled Head,
> Beneath my rowling wheels Ile cruſh thee dead."

Caſſandra departs ſavagely ; then " Hark," ſays Paris, " what Celeſtial Muſick 's this I hear.

> [Venus *deſcends in a Chariot drawn by two Swans.*

She makes a ſoothing ſpeech in ſix lines ; upon which cries Paris—

> " Oh I am loſt in Raptures, this high Grace !
> But where 's my Vaſſals ? where 's my waiting Train ?
> Quick, quick, ye Slaves, for Goodneſs ſo Divine,
> Joyn all your Ayrs, your Songs of Triumph joyn."

The ten Rich Figures in the Caſtles of the Elephants, addreſs themſelves to the Goddeſs with this following piece of Muſick in Chorus:

SONG.

Hail Beauteous Goddefs all Divine,
Our upraif'd Eyes and Hearts all thine,
To Love we pray,
To Love we kneel:
Thy pow'r we own,
Thy Darts we feel.
To thy bright fway, thy Sovereign Throne
Not fuppliant mortals bend alone;
To the blind God, thy Boy, and Thee,
Even Jove, *Almighty* Jove, *here bows a knee.*

And upon that grand fpectacle of fong and fhow, the curtain falls, for fo the firft Act ends.

ACT II. *The Scene opens, and in a Wood without the Walls of* Troy, *appears the* Trojan Horfe, *being a Figure of that Magnitude, that 'tis* 17 *Foot high to the top of his Back. The whole Figure magnificently adorn'd with all the Trappings, Furniture of a War Horfe, fet off with rich Gildings, Plumes of Feathers, and all other fuitable Decorations. Under his Feet lies* Sinon, *with a mangled Face all bloody, his Nofe cut off, his Eyes out, &c., bound in Irons.*

The Mob enters, led by Briftle, to talk foolifhnefs. Briftle's wife enters, with her new friend, to talk foolifhnefs alfo. Ulyffes enters in difguife and beguiles them. Sinon is found and queftioned; Ulyffes perfuades the mob that, fince the gates are too low, they fhould make a breach in the wall, through which to drag into the city the horfe left, according to a warning of the gods, as a monument by the Greeks and pledge of peace ne'er to return in arms. The mob goes out huzzaing to pull down the walls. Ulyffes makes a fpeech by himfelf in fix lines, and exit. Enters Caffandra, makes another fpeech in feven lines, and exit.

The Scene opens and difcovers the Temple of Diana, *being a magnificent Structure richly adorn'd, the Capitals, Urns, Crefcents, Feftoons, and other carved Work, all gilt, confifting of ten pieces of Painting, in each of which, in a large Nych in each Front of thefe Paintings, are feen ten Statues of the Heathen gods, viz.,* Jupiter, Juno, Pallas, Apollo, Neptune, Thetis, Mars, Venus, Ceres, *and* Mercury, *each Figure near five Foot high, and all gilt. In the back of the Stage, in the Center of the Temple, is a rich Altar-piece, bearing* 3 *Nyches in the Walls, in the middle of which, on a Pedeftal* 18 *Inches high, ftands a young Woman dreft in Cloth of Gold, reprefenting the Statue of* Diana, *holding a Hunting Spear in her Hand; and on two other Pedeftals of the fame height on each hand of her, ftand two more young Women in the like Golden Habit, reprefenting two of her Nymphs, each with a Bow and a Quiver. Over this Altar-piece, and beyond the View of the Temple, are feen three Beautiful Circles of Clouds, and on the Back Scene beyond them in a ferene Heaven, is feen* Diana *driving in a Chariot drawn by two Hinds.*

Managers of London, with your Chriftmas and your Eafter glories, ye are but the great grandchildren of Mrs. Mynn; and it was in Bartholomew Fair that your great grandmother tickled the eyes of the mob, one hundred and fifty and more years ago! But Mrs. Mynn's pageant was a developing pageant, and fhe had alfo her transformation fcene; we are but at the firft burft of its glory.

Enter a Procession of Priests *and* Priestesses *in Vestments, adorned with Silver Crescents.*

VOCAL MUSICK.

Bright Cynthia, *Sovereign Queen of Light,*
With all thy Vassal Stars so bright,
Where thy Celestial Glories shine,
To Thee, to Thee,
We bend a Knee,
Our song of Triumph thine.

Cassandra comes, because the gods have given her power to work a miracle.

Seest thou those glittering Statues of the Deities,
　In all their shining Robes of Gold array'd ?
Paris. Yes, all too bright for thy weak blast to shade.
Cass. Those radiant Forms, if possible to sable,
　Dark as thy Crimes, I'll at one Breath transform,
　And hang yon smiling Skies, with all the Flames of Hell.

Here Cassandra *moves her Wand, and in the twinkling of an Eye the ten Golden Statues in the Painting, are all turned to black, and the three Figures on the Pedestals are likewise stript of their Cloth of Gold, and all drest in Black; and the whole Vista of the Heavens is changed to a flaming Hell.*

At Drury Lane there had been a more elaborate development, exactly according to the holiday taste of our own day; and upon that, when it was complete, a double transformation, first to Heaven, and then suddenly to Hell. This demoniacal change visible to the spectator, is seen by the Trojans only in Cassandra. The curtain falls upon them talking still about the shining of their golden gods. That is the one thing bordering on poetry in Settle's play. But upon new glories the curtain again rises.

ACT III. *The Scene opens, and difcovers the town of* Troy, *confifting of ten Pieces of Uniform Painting, repre-fenting a Street of Magnificent Buildings, terminating with a double Wall of the City, and over the Wall is feen an upper Town. In the Center of this City ftands the Horfe, out of whofe fides, in the fight of the Audience, two ladders flip, and immediately near forty Soldiers with their Officers, iffue out of the Body of the Horfe, all with their drawn Swords.*

Officers 1 and 2 agree, in eight lines, to lie clofe till Nightfall, and "the Scene fhuts."

Enter Mob, *drunk.*

Mob fober is not fo agreeable that we fhould care to enter into fellowfhip with Mob drunk. Cobler's wife enters to coax her hufband home, and home he goes, roaring a fnatch.

The Scene opens and difcovers the Town without the Horfe. Enter King, Ulyffes, Grecians, *Guards, and Attendants, all with drawn Swords in one Hand and lighted Flambeaux in the other.*

They talk together, and iffue orders in as much as eleven lines of fire and fword, and worfe.

During thefe Commands given by the King, the Soldiers run up and down the Streets, feemingly fetting the Town on Fire, whilft near forty Windows or Portholes in the feveral Paintings all appear on Fire, the Flames catching from Houfe to Houfe, and all perform'd by Illuminations and Tranfparent Paintings feen fcattered through the Scenes, both in the Upper and Lower Town. [Exeunt.

Here enter several Trojans *in various and distracted postures thro' the Flaming Streets, pursued by the* Grecians, *other* Grecians *running away with Young Women in their Arms, all with several Shrieks and Cries, &c.*

Paris comes in distracted ; is met by Caſſandra, who gives him not three minutes to repent.   The King enters ; there is a desperate broad-sword combat, and within the three minutes Paris is killed.   Then Helen, entering above, and seeing Paris dead, laments in two lines ;   is threatened horribly in three ;   and finally with an eight-line speech, "leaps down into the Fire." The King and Ulyſſes then exchange in five lines their obſervations on this incident, and the "scene shuts."   Briſtle and the mob enter and talk rubbiſh while the laſt scenic effect is being got ready.   When it is ready,

The Scene opens and diſcovers a Grove terminating with a Triumphal Arch, with two Figures of Fame *hanging beneath the Arch ; and beyond the Arch over a Terras Walk, is seen a Beautiful Garden of six Side Wings adorn'd with Statues, and ending in a Viſta of Garden-work.*

The King, Ulyſſes *and all his* Grecians *and Guards appearing by him.*

Twelve lines of unimportant talk then lead to *An Entertainment of several Dialogues and Dances. After which the King and the reſt come forward, and Ulyſſes ſpeaks*—four lines of an indifferent tag, which offer Helen as a warning to the Ladies !   Finally there is An EPILOGUE, ſpoken by the King.

" Now, if the Hundreds we have expended, more
Than e're adorned a Smithfield Stage before,
Can hope your Gen'rous Favours to obtain,
And all this coft is not laid out in vain ;
If you are pleaf'd our Moral Play fhall take,
Exprefs your Smiles, by the Applaufe you make."

Poor Settle was within a year of fixty when he thus
fpun Mrs. Mynn a play out of her own pocket, inftead
of his own brain.   And it was after this that he turned
actor in the Fair, and played the Dragon in a green
cafe of his own invention.

Though Settle was one of the worft poets, yet he
was the beft planner of fpectacles and pomps that his
day yielded.   His was a day alfo when Bartholomew
Fair was near the flood-tide of its fame as a Peru for
players, in which very foon we fhall find cleverer men
than himfelf looking for gold.   The pity in his cafe is,
not that he fhould have played the Dragon in the Fair,
but that he fhould have had to do fo when his hairs
were gray.

CHAPTER XIX.

𝕿𝖍𝖊 𝕮𝖎𝖙𝖞 𝖆𝖌𝖆𝖎𝖓𝖘𝖙 𝖙𝖍𝖊 𝕱𝖆𝖎𝖗.

THE ſtrong hold taken by the Fair on many claſſes
of the People, was not yet to be looſened, although
energetic efforts were made by thoſe citizens whoſe
ſlumbers were diſturbed at night by its kettle-drums,
whoſe traffic was ſtopped in the daytime by its crowds,
and who ſaw more than enough reaſon to be ſcandaliſed
at the profligacy of which it was the ſcene. There
was a ſtrong Puritanical feeling ſtill maintained by a
ſection of the people, and the proteſts againſt exceſſes
in the Fair, were, no doubt, very often tinged with it.
If the Mayors had dealt as ſeverely with the muſic
booths, as they did in their fitful courſe of reſtrictions
with the ſtage plays in the Fair, we might more readily
aſcribe their interference to a ſenſe of decency un-
tainted by prejudice. The evil chiefly to be dealt with,
was, of courſe, the long duration of the Fair, which
yet could not be forfeited by exceſs on the part of
its lords, for the Court of Piepowder ſat only for the
legal term of three days, and its Steward gave only
the lawful three days' licences for flying chairs and
flying horſes, puppet-ſhows, drolls, marble-boards,

counterboards, dice, hazard and roley-poley. The additional licence had been taken by the ſhowmen and the Fair-goers at the Reſtoration, when there were no perſons in authority at all diſpoſed to check it. Attempts to check it, made on the part of the Corporation, had been, ſince that time, cramped by the habit of farming the profits of the Fair to a City Officer, who would regard their curtailment as a fraud upon him. But in the Year 1708, the twenty-one years' leaſe of the Fair to the Sword Bearer was to expire, and in anticipation of that event, there were great efforts made to ſecure a new order of management. The argument for limitation of the Fair was formally ſtated in a Memorial, and in ſpite of a ſtrong oppoſition, the prayer of the petitioners was heard. When, afterwards, the efforts for a reſtoration of the fourteen days' Fair were continued, the original argument againſt it was reprinted (in 1711) for the fortification of the public mind as—

" REASONS Formerly publiſhed for the PUNCTUAL LIMITING of *Bartholomew Fair* to thoſe *Three Days* to which it is determined by the ROYAL GRANT of it to the City of LONDON. Now Reprinted with Additions, to prevent a *Deſign* ſet on Foot to procure an Eſtabliſhment of the ſaid *Fair* for Fourteen Days. Humbly Addreſſed to the preſent Right Honourable the Lord Mayor, to the Worſhipful Court of Aldermen, and to the Common Council of the ſaid City. London, Printed in the Year 1711."

This document purports to be an Addreſs, deſigned for the Happineſs and Proſperity of London, in ſubordination to the Glory of Almighty God, "by us who are a confiderable Number of the Citizens and Inhabitants of this City, and the Parts adjacent." It dilates on the affertion that "of Vice Extravagance is the Nature, Diforder the Product, Ruin the certain End. Men who have caft off the Fear of God, when they do not fee any fuch Execution of Penal Laws from the Magiftrate, as may be termed a Terror to Evildoers, become Thieves and Robbers, Coiners and Shoplifters, who annoy the Commerce of honeft Citizens in the Day, and difturb their Repofe in the Night. And when this lewd and ravenous Crew have greatly hardened themfelves, and multiplied their numbers, they ufually form themfelves into a fort of a Political Body, pitching on Places for their Rendezvous, and agreeing on Methods for the Management of their evil Purpofes. And thus they become an open and daring Enemy to good Government, are able to make a ftand againft Authority, and are evidently an Overmatch to inferior Officers."

It is declared to be an intolerable fhame "that the Thief, or his Compartner in Trade, dares to appear and treat with the injured Perfon on what Terms he fhall have his own Goods again; and this altogether as confidently as an honeft Tradefman fells his proper Wares in his fhop." It is recommended, by the way, to multiply workhoufes, and to enable vicious people to be fent to them for the inferior offences, for inftruction in "a fober, diligent, and frugal way of Life." It is fuggefted, that if fome perfons had not ftood up in the fpirit of Phineas "to oppofe, profecute, and puniſh great numbers of miſcreants," the impudence and blaſphemy of vice would have pulled down a Divine Vengeance upon London. It is thought wiſe not to uſe efforts only againſt open vice, "but alſo againſt all apparent *Inducements* to Lewdneſs and Debauchery, and againſt the viſible *Occaſion* of Diſorder and Miſdemeanour: for if we ſpare the *Roots*, we lop the *Branches* to no purpoſe." Reſtrict this Fair, then, to its ancient limits. All charters and writs, from the Reign of Edward the Firſt to this preſent time, ſpecify a three days' duration; "only in the Charter granted by King Charles the Firſt, the Time is not mentioned, but ſuppoſed to refer to the former grants; which do declare it to begin the day before the Feaſt of St. Bartholomew, and to continue one day after it, for the Sale of Live Cattle, Leather, and other Wares and Merchandiſe: And for this, Three Days are ſuffi-cient." But the prolonged Fair everybody knows "to be a mere Carnival, a ſeaſon of the utmoſt Diſorder and Debauchery, by reaſon of the Booths for Drink-ing, Muſic, Dancing, Stage-plays, Drolls, Lotteries, Gaming, Raffling, and what not."

The repreſentation cites as an inſtance of the cha-racter of the concourſe, the exhibition in a booth at the previous Fair, of a book filled with pictures of the utmoſt obſcenity, the exhibitors of which were then under proſecution by the Magiſtrates of the city. In that laſt Fair, eighty perſons had been apprehended by the Peace-officers in the act of Lewdneſs, Diſ-order, or Debauchery. But what were theſe diſorders to the multitudes that eſcaped the eyes of a few officers

in the crowd! The reprefentation dwells on the vice
of the fourteen days' Fair, in which even feveral
horrible murders had been perpetrated, and accounts
it "not only unreafonable, but unfufferable, that it
fhould continue longer than the lawful Bufinefs of it
requires, and than the Cryer publicly proclaims it, that
is, for Three Days : at which time alfo, the Court of
Pye-powders breaks up ; denoting that the juft term
of the Fair is then ended."

The Memorial goes on to urge that the time for a
redrefs of the grievance is at hand, fince the Leafe of the
Fair, which farmed its profits to the Sword Bearer for
twenty-one years, at a rent of a hundred a year, was
near its end, and there was a very prudent Order made
at a Court of Lord Mayor, Aldermen, and Common
Council, 26 October, 1705, in the Mayoralty of Sir
Owen Buckingham; "that no farther demife of Bartholomew Fair be entered upon, before publick Notice
be given to that Court, by Summons to that purpofe,
and the fpecial directions of that Court thereupon." A
Hundred Pounds was nothing to the city in comparifon
with the good to be derived from the fhutting of the
floodgates of Impiety and Diforder. The Hofpital of
St. Bartholomew might complain of its lofs, for it
profited by the better letting of its fhops in the
Cloifters. But the Fair-traffic in the Cloifters was
efpecially iniquitous, and begot more difeafe than the
money raifed by it for Hofpital ufes would fuffice to
cure. But why fpeak of worldly profit? What profit
is the gain of a World that involves lofs of one Soul?
Befides there is no profit in a hotbed for thieves, or for

riots that expoſe the city to a riſk of mulⅽt, and to a forfeit of the whole grant of the Fair by abuſe of privilege.

Again, the ſecond of September, anniverſary of the Fire of London, was kept as a day of Faſt and Humiliation, and although the booths were compelled to ſuppreſs open extravagance on that day, and had another day added to their time in lieu of it, yet they ſo trafficked as to ſet up the mockery of a town which lamented ſin in its churches, and indulged ſin in its ſtreets. "In the very laſt Fair much gaming and diſorder abounded therein, and we know one perſon that was on that very day ruined there by gaming." Now, at Southwark, a great Fire having broken out in the time of its Fair, A.D. 1689, "which conſumed many Houſes, and did much Damage; the Inhabitants prudently conſidering that this Deſolation came upon them by means of the Diſorderly Booths which were erected in this Fair, and by the juſt Vengeance of God for permitting ſuch pregnant cauſe of Licentiouſneſs, have ever ſince forbidden the ſetting up of Booths there, and have not ſuffered any to be erected.

"At Bartholomew Fair good orders of many Mayors had been fruitleſs by reaſon of the Twenty-one years' licence that maintained the Fair in its duration of a fortnight, ſo attracting from all parts throngs of booth-keepers, many of whom would not have encouragement to come, were the Fair to be concluded on the third day. That unhappy Leaſe expires Auguſt 10 next." The Memorial ends with a pious peroration, out of which I pick two facts, that the prolonged Fair had

been prefented for its immorality by feveral Grand
Juries, and that thirty of the more fubftantial inhabitants of Smithfield and its neighbourhood had figned
againft it a petition to the Lord Mayor and the Court
of Aldermen. The Memorial ends with crying to the
Citizens, " Difcern, O difcern ! in this your Day, the
things that belong to your Peace and Blifs, Temporal
and Eternal."

Not fo much the refult of this Memorial, as the iffue
of the prevalent opinion that fuggefted it, was the
following refolution paffed by a Court of Common
Council on the 2nd of June, 1708: " This Court
taking Notice, that the Fair of St. Bartholomew,
according to the Original Grant thereof, ought to be
holden Annually Three Days, and no longer. And
that by continuing the faid Fair for Fourteen Days, as
of late hath been practifed, and the Erecting and Setting
up Booths in Smithfield of extraordinary Largenefs, not
occupied by Dealers in Goods, Merchandifes, &c., proper
for a Fair; but ufed chiefly for Stage-plays, Mufick
and Tipling (being fo many Receptacles of vicious and
diforderly Perfons), Lewdnefs and Debauchery have
apparently encreafed, Tumults and Diforders frequently
arifen, and the Traffick of the faid Fair, by the Traders
and Fair-keepers reforting thereto, greatly interrupted
and diminifhed. After long Debate, and ferious Confideration had of the fame, and being defirous to put
a Stop (fo far as in them lies) to the further fpreading
of Wickednefs and Vice, to preferve the Peace of Her
Majefty's Subjects, and reftore the faid Fair to its
primitive Inftitution, and the Traders reforting thither,

to the full enjoyment of their Trades, without any hindrance or obſtruction. And this Court being of opinion, that no ways will be ſo effectual for the end aforeſaid, as reducing the ſaid Fair to its ancient Time of Continuance, doth *unanimouſly* reſolve, and ſo order, that for the future, the ſaid Fair ſhall be kept Three Days only, and no longer (that is to ſay) on the Eve of St. Bartholomew, that Day, and the Morrow after, being the 23rd, 24th, and 25th days of Auguſt, of which all Perſons concerned are to take Notice and govern them-ſelves accordingly." On the 3rd of July, the Common Council rejected certain ſtrong petitions for the revo-cation of this order; and that all perſons might the more readily take notice of it, this announcement in anticipation of the Fair, appeared in the *Gazette* for the 2nd of Auguſt (1708):

" The Committee for Letting the City's Lands in the account of the Chamberlain of the City of London, give Notice, That the Fair, commonly call'd Bartho-lomew Fair, annually held in Weſt Smithfield, London, is from henceforth to be held three Days, and no longer, viz. : On the Eve of St. Bartholomew, St. Bartho-lomew's Day, and the Morrow following, being the 23rd, 24th, and 25th days of Auguſt; and that the ſaid Committee will ſit every Wedneſday, at three of the Clock in the Afternoon, to Lett and Diſpoſe of the Ground in Weſt Smithfield, to perſons reſorting to the ſaid Fair ; of which more particular Information may be had at the Comptroler's Office in the Guildhall of the ſaid City."

In the ſame year, 1708, it is recorded by the

Poftman, of the 8th of June, that " a Perfon did Penance in the Chapter Houfe of St. Paul's, for publicly fhowing in Bartholomew Fair a book called a Blow-Book, in which were many filthy and obfcene pictures. The book was likewife burnt, and the Perfon paid cofts."

In the fame year, too, the temporary fuppreffion of May Fair was contrived in Weftminfter. The gentlemen of four fucceffive Grand Juries for the County of Middlefex and the City of Weftminfter, made prefentments of it in terms of abhorrence, as a vile and riotous affembly. Three of thefe juries took fpecial notice of the "commendable zeal and worthy to be imitated care " of the magiftrates of London, in the limitation of their Fair in Smithfield. The Bench of Juftices for Middlefex addreffed the Queen, and procured from her the Royal Proclamation by which May Fair was for a time fuppreffed. Bartholomew Fair, meanwhile, had only been confined within its old bounds, and was threatening to burft them. There was clamour for a reftoration of the fourteen days : care for the revenues of St. Bartholomew's Hofpital being the chief reafon affigned, as being the reafon moft likely to engage the public fympathy.

CHAPTER XX.

Under the First Georges.

COMMERCE in the Fair was ſtifled ; but its pleaſures were thoſe not only of the ignorant and vicious, whoſe ſtarved minds could take the coarſeſt aliment with pleaſure. Its vulgar appeals to an idle curioſity anſwered the taſte of London better than the higheſt efforts of the dramatiſt and the comedian. Shakeſpeare's pre-eminence in the firſt years of the eighteenth century was a fact yet to be diſcovered ; his works, though ſo much longer before the world, had not been diffuſed more widely than thoſe of Mrs. Aphra Behn. Theſe Memoirs have no right to diſcuſs ſocial truths of which the reaſons lie outſide the ſtory of the Fair ; it is their ſole purpoſe to ſhow how in the ſtory of the Fair they are developed and illuſtrated. The age of ſcoffers againſt virtue led by Charles the Second, turned nearly all that was great and ſound in our literature, into the way of a ſtern ſatire, and ſo, for example, forced into the only form that would compel reſpect, the poetry of Dryden ; which would have been mocked, had it been the gentle moraliſing by which it was ſucceeded. Againſt the energy of vice and folly repreſenting partly

the reaction from the preſſure of the Puritans, the true
Literature of England ſet an equal energy of ſatire.

But the laſſitude of vice and folly, and the indolent
frivolities that followed on a wild exceſs, ſat patiently
to hear the kindly voices of the moraliſts who next
addreſſed the town, year after year, in Tatlers, Spectators, Adventurers, Worlds, Ramblers, Moral Pieces,
both in verſe and proſe. Loud battle was not for thoſe
feeble ears. Society was then a ſort of invalid whom it
took long to bring to health by gentle applications, and
after any neceſſary bliſtering, by a light touch and
ſoft anointment of its bliſters. The whole tone of the
admonitions given in the Spectator ſuggeſts the exiſtence
of a public by which the ſights of Bartholomew Fair
were to be enjoyed,—heartily, I do not ſay, for it did
few things heartily,—but exquiſitely and coarſely.

We may ſtep here out of the ſtrict rule of chronological ſucceſſion to advance beyond the middle of the
eighteenth century, and ſhow how little change there is
in this reſpect as to the nature of the ground in which
the Fair laid its foundations. The *Adventurer* of the
3rd of February, 1753, commenting on the ſtate of the
Theatre, tells us, " It is to humour the TOWN that the
Necromancer Harlequin has aſſociated with Tumblers
and Savages, to profane the place which, under proper
regulations, would indeed be the ſchool of wiſdom and
virtue." Later ſtill, Goldſmith, writing his Citizen of
the World in the year 1760, makes his Chineſe philoſopher ſay that, " From the higheſt to the loweſt this
people ſeem fond of Sights and Monſters. . . A cat
with four legs is diſregarded, though never ſo uſeful;

but if it has but two, and is confequently incapable of catching mice, it is reckoned ineftimable, and every man of tafte is ready to raife the auction. A man, though in his perfon faultlefs as an aerial genius, might ftarve ; but if ftuck over with hideous warts like a porcupine, his fortune is made for ever, and he may propagate the breed with impunity and applaufe." One or two allufions in the effay here cited, will be illuftrated when its date has been reached. I cite it here, only to fhow why the efforts made by the Corporation of London to fubdue the Fair, continued to be almoft fruitlefs.

We pafs through the whole eighteenth century to one of the firft years following 1805, when the Towneley collection of Sculptures came into the poffeffion of the Britifh Mufeum, and read in a newfpaper of the day, this paragraph, which fuggefts a ftriking contraft between the temper of fociety upon which Bartholomew Fair lived, and the change of temper which in our own time has fecured its fall. I copy from an old newfpaper-cutting inferted in a MS. collection of Metropolitana in the Guildhall Library, which would have been more valuable than it is, had not the collector often omitted, as in this cafe, to label his extracts with an exact reference to their fource : " Though the admiffion to the Britifh Mufeum is open to the public three days in the week, only 2500 perfons availed themfelves, laft year, of that permiffion, and of thefe the greater part were foreigners. The fact is, John Bull, though a perfon of boundlefs curiofity, has no great tafte for the Fine Arts, and would rather fpend his time and money in feeing a Calf with two heads than the fineft piece of fculpture in the Towneley Collection for nothing."

Thefe notes may fufficiently account for the fact, that in fpite of all war made againſt it, we have now to purfue the Annals of Bartholomew Fair through yet another century.

John Edwards, Penkethman's Merry-Andrew, who was a quack horfe-doctor out of Fair time, died in the year 1706, in Caftle Street, St. Giles's; and in a neighbouring ftreet, there was at once printed a broadſheet of doggrel, called " *Pinkeman's Company in Mourning,* or an Elegy on the Much Unlamented Death of John Edwards, the Horfe Doctor, and Merry-Andrew," cruel in tone, and infamous in tafte. It gives the worſt character to the dead jefter, the worſt character to Bartholomew Fair, and ends with this character of his Employer :

> Dull, fneaking Pinkeman, this lofs bewail,
> And fing his Dirge o're half a Pint of Ale,
> For if thou more didſt fpend at once, your Note
> You'd change, and for your Charges cut your Throat.

Probably it was Settle who advifed Mrs. Mynn to dignify her eftablifhment with the name of BEN JONSON'S *Booth*. Certainly it was Settle who planned in that booth, at about this time, the Spectacle of Whittington, Lord Mayor of London, "concluding with a Lord Mayor's Triumph, in which are prefented nine feveral Pageants."

To Queen Anne's day, there belonged alfo "a Collection of Strange and Wonderful Creatures" dif-played in the Fair, without any proprietor's name, at

the Booth near the Hoſpital Gate, which included
"the Noble *Caſheware*, brought from the Iſland of
Java in the Eaſt Indies, one of the ſtrangeſt creatures
in the Univerſe, being half a Bird, and half a Beaſt,
reaches 16 Hands High from the Ground, his Head
is like a Bird, and ſo is his Feet, he hath no hinder
Claw, Wings, Tongue, nor Tail; his Body is like to
the Body of a Deer; inſtead of Feathers, his fore-part
is covered with Hair like an Ox, his hinder-part with
a double Feather in one Quill; he Eats Iron, Steel,
or Stones; he hath 2 Spears grows by his ſide."
Cuvier would have been edified by that deſcription of
a Caſſowary. There was alſo a Leopard from Lebanon;
an Eagle from Ruſſia; a Poſown (*i.e.* an opoſſum)
from Hiſpaniola; and "a little black hairy *Monſter*,
bred in the *Deſarts of Arabia*, a natural Ruff of Hair
about his Face, walks upright, takes a Glaſs of Ale
in his Hand, and drinks it off; and doth ſeveral other
things to admiration." After ſpecifying a few more
wonders, this State Paper of the Fair ends with the
Wonder of the World, the Great Mare of the Tar-
tarian Breed, which "had the Honour to be ſhow'd
before Queen Anne, Prince George, and moſt of the
Nobility." But let us not paſs by "the noble Caſheware" without remembering, that to the ſtudent, as well
as to the idler, he gave occupation. The exhibition of
rare animals was left entirely to the Showman. Sir
Hans Sloane ſtudied in Bartholomew Fair, and employed
alſo a draughtſman there.

An Elephant that fired a gun, was a ſight of the day.
He is alluded to in the *Medley* for Oct. 16, 1710, where

reference being made to harmlefs fquibs, thefe lines are quoted :

> " So have I feen at Smithfield's Wondrous Fair,
> When all his brother Monfters flourifh'd there,
> A lubber'd Elephant divert the town
> With making legs, and fhooting off a gun."

Dawk's Newfletter tells us, in the year 1715, that there is " one great playhoufe erected for the King's players, and the booth is the largeft that was ever built." They were the King's Players then, George the Firft having been proclaimed in the preceding year.

In the year 1719, there were twenty licenfed dice and hazard tables in Bartholomew Fair, and the reftriction to three days had long been over-ruled by public voice.

There was once fold in Bartholomew Fair a Fan on which the Fair was reprefented as it then appeared in the eyes of a Bartholomew artift, who having his own views of perfpective, carefully economifed the number of his figures, and left out at difcretion bodies or legs, in the treatment of which he was embarraffed. A coloured engraving of this picture was iffued by Mr. Setchel of Covent Garden, with a brief defcription commonly affigned to Caulfield, the bookfeller, author of four volumes of Remarkable Characters. The date of the Fan is here faid to be 1721 ; but this cannot be right, fince it dif- plays, among other things, a puppet fhow of the Siege of Gibraltar, which occurred in 1727. Almoft every great Siege in which England was concerned reappeared on the firft occafion in the fhows at the Fair. The date, therefore, of the Fan is evidently 1728. From this work Hone took for his *Table Book* fome (not abfolutely faithful) copies, that have fince been frequently re-copied.

The licence of the Fair is varioufly reprefented in it. One fource of ill manners muft have been the free ufe of untaxed gin at drinking-ftalls, difplayed in the annexed fketch. Here it will be feen that a leg of the table ☞ ferves alfo for leg to a man.

The introduction of a pick-

pocket—a juvenile offender—fhows that the artift did not mean wilfully to overlook any of the leading features of his fubject. The good children are but little to him.

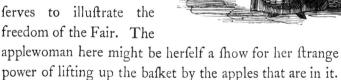

Alfo a falutation, at once diftant and familiar, ferves to illuftrate the freedom of the Fair. The applewoman here might be herfelf a fhow for her ftrange power of lifting up the bafket by the apples that are in it.

One of the plea-
fures reprefented is
the peepfhow of the
Siege of Gibraltar,
to which reference
has already been
made.

Another is Lee
and Harper's Booth,
prefently to be re-
ferred to.

Here, ſays the writer of the elucidation upon Setchel's print, the *Siege of Bethulia* is being acted. This was ſo far from being poſſible in 1721, that it was not poſſible in 1728. It was only in 1732 that there was firſt preſented at this booth " the Droll of the *Siege of Bethulia, containing the Ancient Hiſtory of Judith and Holofernes,* with the Comical Humours of Ruſtego and his Man Terrible." *Holofernes,* Mr. Mullart ; *Ruſtego,* Mr. Harper ; *Terrible,* Mr. Morgan ; *Judith,* Mr. Spiller ; *Dulcementa,* Mrs. Purden. The " Ancient Hiſtory " attached to the Siege of Bethulia was of old ſtanding in the Fair. Locke, early in his life, as we have found, ſaw *Judith and Holofernes* there, and there is not a word about Bethulia in the preceding picture.

Another glimpſe of pleaſure is a promiſe of Rope-dancing in " the Great Booth

over againſt the Hoſpital Gate." The proprietor invites attention with his trumpet, for blowing of which the Serjeant Trumpeter's man in the Fair has claimed his fee. There is a boy here in the corner wanting ſixpence.

This is the booth in which Fawkes the famous Conjuror difplays his dexterity of hand.

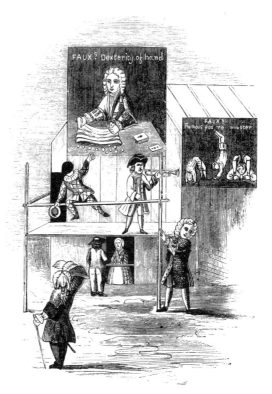

Here again the few lines of defcription attached to the print iffued by Setchel are in error. The fketch on the board is faid to be the only portrait of Fawkes extant. This ftatement leads me to believe that the defcription itfelf has been wrongly afcribed to Caulfield, who does indeed adopt from this fketch his picture of Fawkes in the " Remarkable Characters," but who there refers to a more elaborate portrait of him in another volume.

Below are Ups-and-Downs and ſauſages.   The artiſt, finding that the fourth ſtall in the machine would complicate his picture, has got it under altogether; and with a view alſo to artiſtic effect he has denied legs to the gentleman who is taſting his ale with ſo much reliſh, while the hot ſauſage grows cold upon his plate.   We are to ſuppoſe that he has been drinking till he loſt his legs.   Bad, however, as the art is, the repreſentation of details in theſe pictures is exceedingly inſtructive. Michael Angelo could not have diſplayed the anatomy of a Samſon with more care than the Fan painter has beſtowed on the anatomy of an Up-and-Down.

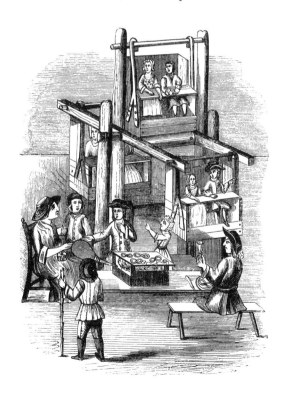

Finally there is Pye Corner with its " delicate Pig and Pork," upon which a high nobleman, who is confidently pronounced to be the premier, Sir Robert Walpole, has been feafting. It was always a tradition that Sir Robert Walpole frequently was to be feen among the vifitors to Bartholomew Fair.

The fketches here given, although detached, are exact facfimiles from portions of the coloured plate ; and, except fome unimportant figures with which fpaces are filled, they are all that it contains.

In Lee and Harper's booth, Harper was chief Comedian. He was a fat round-faced man, with a jolly laugh that qualified him, more than his wit, for the pofition he held as the Falftaff of his time. He is remembered alfo as one of the comedians who, in 1733, revolted from the patentees at Drury Lane, and eftablifhed themfelves at the Little Theatre in the Haymarket. George Lee was an adventurous printer, who did buſineſs in Blue-Maid Alley, Southwark. His name, except as manager, appears only as printer of the Drolls.

Fawkes, at his Booth at the lower end of Lee and Harper's, over againſt the The King's Head Inn in the Fair, exhibited entertainments in the manner following :

"His ſurpriſing and incomparable dexterity of hand, in which he will perform ſeveral entirely new Curioſities, that far ſurpaſſes any thing of that kind ever ſeen before. A curious muſical clock, that he lately purchaſed of Mr. Pinchbeck, Clockmaker in Fleet Street, that plays ſeveral fine Tunes on moſt Inſtruments of Muſick, and imitates the melodious Notes of various Kinds of Birds, as real Life : alſo Ships ſailing, with a number of curious and humorous Figures, repreſenting divers Motions as tho' alive." He had alſo a piece of clockwork called "Art's Maſter-piece, or the Venetian Lady's Invention," with a Dutch Tumbler and his little poſture-maſter, a child of about five years of age, ſome of whoſe feats are repreſented in the picture. Fawkes began his performances at two o'clock, and ended them at eight. His Chriſtian name is unknown ; we know only that he was married, and that he was the chief profeſſional Juggler of the days of George the Firſt. Hogarth has introduced his name in his print of Burlington Gate, as part of an inſcription on a board : "Fawkes's dexterity of hand." He died on the 25th of May, 1731, having acquired by his art a fortune of ten thouſand pounds.

CHAPTER XXI.

Fielding's Booth at the George Inn Yard.

THE authority of the Mafter of the Revels fuffered
a fevere blow in the year 1715, when Sir Richard Steele
was affociated with Wilks, Cibber, and Booth as a
playhoufe manager.   The office of the Mafter of the
Revels had been created in the year 1546, and Charles
Killegrew, in whofe perfon it practically became extinct,
reigned until January, 1724-5.   It was he who ex-
punged the whole firft act of Cibber's *Richard III.*,
becaufe he thought that the diftreffes of King Henry
the Sixth would remind people of King James.   Steele
and his friends refolved to try the right of this official
to be paid by them for meddling with their plays.   They
politely urged patent againft patent, and gained their
point.   In 1725, Charles Henry Lee fucceeded Killegrew in his office, and held it for nineteen years, unable
to affert his claims againft thofe who might fet them at
defiance.

In the year 1727-8, Gay's *Beggar's Opera* was produced and took the foremoft place among the pleafures
of the town.   It took a foremoft place, alfo, among the
pleafures of the next following Bartholomew Fair,

being acted during the time of the Fair, by the Company of Comedians from the New Theatre in the Haymarket, at the George Inn, in Smithfield. William Penkethman, one of the actors who had become famous as a booth manager, was then recently dead, and the Haymarket Comedians carried the *Beggar's Opera* out of Bartholomew into Southwark Fair, where " the late Mr. Penkethman's great Theatrical Booth" afforded them a ftage. One of the managers of this fpeculation was Henry Fielding, then only juft of age, a young man who with good birth, fine wit, and a liberal education both at Eton and at Leyden Univerfity, was left to find his own way in the world. His father agreed to allow him two hundred a-year in the clouds, and, as he afterwards faid, his choice lay between being a hackney writer and a hackney coachman. He lived to place himfelf, in refpect to literature, at the head of the profe writers of England,—I dare even venture to think, of the world. That his inclinations led him to begin his town life as dramatic author, and that he entered into clofe affociation with the players, everybody knows ; it is known alfo that he joined in the management of a booth at Bartholomew Fair in the year 1733 ; but the fimple act of turning over old newfpapers impofed as a duty on the writer of thefe Memoirs, firft brings to light the fact that Fielding, on beginning life in London, at once looked to the Fairs as a fource of income, and was a booth-keeper during not lefs than nine years of his life.

The management of the performance of the *Beggar's Opera* at Bartholomew Fair in 1728, was anonymous, but the removal of the fame company from the George Inn in Smithfield, to the late Mr. Penkethman's booth at Southwark Fair, is fpecified by a newfpaper of which I have feen only a cutting labelled fimply with the date, which, as complete files of old papers are not acceffible, I cannot directly verify. It is, however, indirectly and completely verified by the *Daily Poft* for the 12th of September, 1728, in which the company is advertifed as being at Southwark Fair, and Fielding's name ftands firft as manager.

At FIELDING and REYNOLDS'S

GREAT THEATRICAL BOOTH,

At the Lower End of Blue Maid Alley, on the Green in SOUTHWARK, during the time of the Fair, will be perform'd the BEGGAR'S OPERA, by the Company of Comedians from the Haymarket.

All the Songs and Dances fet to Mufic, as performed at the Theatre in Lincoln's Inn Fields.

N.B. There is a commodious Paffage for the Quality, and Coaches through the Half-Moon Inn, and care will be taken that there fhall be Lights, and People to conduct them to their Places.

It was at Lincoln's Inn Fields Theatre that the *Beggar's Opera* had been produced, on the 29th of the preceding January, and it was acted there for the fixty-third night of its memorable " run " on the day after the date of this advertifement. The Haymarket Company had, of courfe, never performed the piece in its own houfe.

Again in the year following, 1729, the *Beggar's Opera* was performed during the Fair, the place of performance being " the Black Boy on the Paved Stones near Hofier Lane, Smithfield," and the actors,

Rayner and Pullen's Company of Comedians.   That
is to fay, the company of Mrs. Rayner and of Mrs.
Pullen, who performed Polly and Lucy ; the Macheath
being that Mr. Powell whom the *Spectator*, not without
faving words of praife, accufed of a difpofition to
obtain "a loud clap" by the artifice of ufing violence
of manner where his author had been tranquil.   Mrs.
Rayner alfo fang and danced ; and the performances in
this booth were repeated fucceffively during twelve
hours, namely from eleven in the morning till eleven
at night.

Hall and Jo. Miller formed a theatrical firm at Bartholomew Fair in this year, and, in the *Daily Journal*
of Sept. 5th, on the twelfth day of the Fair—fo little
did the will of Mayors prevail—advertifed that they
would perform *Bateman* during its continuance : Bateman by Mr. Oates ; Sparrow by Mr. Miller ; Old
Sparrow, Mr. Hall.

Giffard, a comic actor, attached to the Haymarket
Company, fucceeded to the Management of Penkethman's Theatrical Booth, which he opened in the name
of Penkethman and Giffard, and in which he prefented
in the year 1730, "Wat Tyler and Jack Straw ; or the
Mob Reformers.   A Dramatic Entertainment."   From
Penkethman we may part alfo with a reference to the
good word written on his behalf by the *Spectator*.   After
faying that "the Craft of an Ufurer, the abfurdity
of a rich Fool, the awkward roughnefs of a fellow
of half-courage, the ungraceful mirth of a creature of
half-wit, might be for ever put out of countenance by
proper parts for Doggett," he goes on to obferve that

"the petulancy of a peevifh old fellow, who loves and
hates he knows not why, is very excellently performed
by the ingenious Mr. William Penkethman in *The
Fop's Fortune*, where he anfwers no queftions but to
thofe whom he likes, and wants no account of anything from thofe he appoves. Mr. Penkethman is
mafter alfo of as many faces in the dumb fcene, as
can be expected from a man in the circumftances of
being ready to perifh out of fear and hunger: he
wonders throughout the whole fcene very mafterly,
without neglecting his victuals." It is well to be
reminded of fuch praife in annals by which the actor
is prefented chiefly as a fhowman.

The fuccefs of the *Beggar's Opera* had excited inftant
imitation. The opera of the *Beggar's Wedding*, written
by Colley, was produced at Dublin, and then reproduced
at the Haymarket, to be performed again with its three
acts fufed into one long act at Drury Lane, when the
part of Juftice Quorum was fuftained upon the public
ftage by Henry Fielding.

One of the dated fcraps of newfpaper, pafted, without the name of the paper from which it came, into
the Guildhall collection, but corroborated perfectly as
we fhall fee, is, in anticipation of the Fair of 1729,
to this effect:—"We hear that Mr. Fielding, from
the Theatre Royal, Drury Lane, defigns to entertain
the town, at his Booth in the George Inn Yard," (the
phrafe may be thought to imply the fact that he
occupied it in the previous year,) "in Smithfield,"
during the Time of Bartholomew Fair, with the
BEGGAR'S WEDDING, having engaged Mr. Charke, Mr.

Hulett, Mrs. Egleton, Mrs. Roberts, Mifs Shireburn, and others, in order to give a general fatisfaction to all fpectators." I find, accordingly, in the *Daily Poft* for Saturday, the 23rd of Auguft, 1729, that

At Mr. FIELDING'S

GREAT THEATRICAL BOOTH,

In the George Inn Yard in Smithfield during the Time of Bartholomew Fair, will be Acted a diverting Dramatic Opera called

HUNTER, *or* THE BEGGAR'S WEDDING:

with Alterations. Confifting of Variety of Englifh, Scots, and Irifh Ballad Tunes, with additional Songs never perform'd therein before; particularly a Song of the Chimes of the Times, and the Conceited Farmer, fung by Mr. Mountfort.

The characters are as announced in the preceding extract; Mrs. Egleton plays *Tippit*. There is Dancing and Harlequinade, partly by Mr. St. Luce, lately arrived from Paris; the Songs and Mufic are to be

Perform'd by a good Band of Inftruments, accompany'd by a Chamber Organ provided on this occafion, and play'd upon by the beft Hand in England.

N.B. The Booth is very Commodious, and the Inn-yard has all the Conveniencies of Coach-room, Lights, &c., for Quality and others; and fhall perform this Evening at Four, and every day during the time of the Fair; beginning exactly at Two o'Clock, and continuing every Hour till Eleven at Night.

Of courfe every play or opera was much abridged in adaptation for the Fair.

In this year alfo there was a dramatic battle fought with Fielding by the members of the Haymarket Company. Fielding, attached to Drury Lane, was prefenting in the Fair the work that had been juft produced on their own ftage, giving it the new firft title of HUNTER, and, for an obvious reafon, advertifing Alterations.

The Haymarket actors, therefore, came into the Fair to act him down, and under the management of Reynolds, his former partner, opened " MR. REYNOLDS'S GREAT THEATRICAL BOOTH, Between the Hofpital Gate and the Crown Tavern, in Smithfield." Mrs. Nokes, though actreffes of note feldom repeated their parts in the Fair, retained her own Haymarket character of Tippit. Mr. Ray was brought over from Drury Lane to play the part of Hunter. They had alfo the Haymarket band and fcenery. But their original reprefentative of Chaunter, King of the Beggars, Fielding had lured away. His own men claimed him; Fielding claimed him; and throughout this Fair time, in every number of the *Daily Poft* from the 25th of Auguft to the 30th of Auguft, where there is a break in the file acceffible to me, Fielding and Reynolds advertife the fame play without a fyllable of allufion one to the other, and both claim to have Hulett acting in the part of Chaunter. How he managed to repeat the fame part every hour in two booths at once, I cannot fay. The defign of Reynolds probably was to eftablifh ground of action, if defirable. Hulett's name after this time difappears from the Haymarket play bills, and he is found to have been received among the actors at Lincoln's Inn Fields. On the firft day of the Fair, Auguft the 23rd, only Fielding's advertifement appears. Having acted the *Beggar's Wedding* until eight in the evening, Reynolds's Company went on until eleven at night with the Opera of *Damon and Phillida*, ending always with an entertainment of grotefque dancing, called the *Humours of Harlequin*.

Bullock had a booth to himſelf that year, in which was performed *Doraſtus and Faunia*, and the adaptation of Doggett's *Country Wake*, " after the manner of the *Beggar's Opera*," called *Flora*.

To Reynolds's advertiſement on the 2nd of September is the following : " Note. This being the Faſt for the Fire of London, we ſhall not play till to-morrow." The *Beggar's Opera* ſtill led the faſhion of the ſtage. There was produced at Lee and Harper's Great Theatrical Booth, in 1728, an adaptation of a piece that had been printed in 1725—" the Priſon Breaker, or the Adventures of John Shepherd, a Farce, as intended to be acted at the T. R. in Lincoln's Inn Fields ;" the adaptation of this other ſtory of a thief being ſtyled the *Quaker's Opera*. In 1730, Lee and Harper, ſtill dealing in ballad operas and outlaws, produced at Bartholomew Fair the Opera of *Robin Hood*.

To this year, 1730, belongs a characteriſtic ſtate paper, which will be found printed in the *Daily Poſt* for the laſt day of Auguſt :

" Theſe are to give notice to all Ladies, Gentlemen, and others,

" That at the end Hoſier Lane, in Smithfield, are to be ſeen, during the Time of the Fair, TWO RATTLE SNAKES, one a very large ſize, and rattles that you may hear him at a quarter of a mile almoſt, and ſomething of Muſick, that grows on the tails thereof; of divers colours, forms, and ſhapes, with darts, that they extend out of their Mouths, about two inches long. They were taken on the Mountains of Leamea. A Fine CREATURE, of a ſmall ſize, taken in Mocha, that burrows under ground. It is of divers colours, and very beautiful. The TEETH of a DEAD RATTLE SNAKE to be feen and handled, with the Rattles. A SEA SNAIL, taken on the Coaft of India. Alfo, the HORN of a FLYING BUCK. Together with a curious Collection of Animals and Infects from all Parts of the World. To be feen without Lofs of Time."

The dramatifts are not to have this part of the hiftory entirely to themfelves, and readers of thefe Memoirs muft be prepared for the occafionally fudden intrufion of a rattle-fnake or other monfter on their quiet meditations.

Another fhow in the year 1730, was Mr. Pinchbeck's (the watchmaker's) Grand Theatre of the Mufes. This probably was the machine containing a hundred moving figures which had been exhibited by Penkethman in the Little Piazzas, Covent Garden, as "the Pantheon, or the Temple of the Heathen Gods."

In 1730, Fielding was determined that nobody fhould accufe him of unfair play. He ftill occupied his booth at the George Inn, now, however, in partnerfhip with a Drury Lane Comedian, and acted himfelf in a new play, written by William Rufus Chetwood, tutor of Barry, and for many years Drury Lane Prompter. In the *Daily Poft* for Auguft 21ft, and following days, in 1730, it is announced that "At OATES and FIELDING's Great Theatrical Booth, at the *George Inn Yard, Smithfield*, during the time of *Bartholomew Fair*, will be prefented an entire new Opera, call'd THE GENEROUS FREE MASON, or the *Conftant Lady*. With the Comic Humours of Squire Noodle and his Man Doodle, by

perfons from both the Theatres. The parts of the
King of Tunis by Mr. Barcock; Mirza, Mr. Paget;
Sebaftian, Mr. Oates; CLERIMONT, MR. FIELDING,"
&c. (Here the Capitals are mine.) "Queen, Mrs.
Kilby; Maria, Mifs Oates," &c. All the characters
newly dreff'd with feveral entertainments of Dancing by
Mons. de Luce, Mademoifelle de Lorme, and others;
particularly the Wooden Shoe Dance; the Perrot and
Pierotte, and the Dance of the Black Joke, &c.
" Beginning every day at Two o'Clock."

Reynolds's Booth that year had alfo a new play. It
was called *Scipio's Triumph* or the *Siege of Carthage.*
With the Pantomime of *Harlequin's Contrivance,* or the
Plague of a Wanton Wife.

In the following year (1731), at MILLER's, MILLS's,
and OATES's Great Theatrical Booth over againſt the
Hofpital Gate, the play acted was the *Baniſhed General,*
or the *Diſtreſſed Lovers,* Mrs. Roberts being the chief
actrefs, and Mills, Oates, and Miller the chief actors.
At the end of the firſt act was "the Englifh Maggot"
dance. At the end of the fecond act, appeared two
Harlequins. "The whole concluding with a Grand
Dance and Chorus; accompany'd with Kettle Drums
and Trumpets. All the Scenes and Decorations
entirely new."

Oates had entered into a new partnerfhip, but Fielding
ftill held to his old ground in the George Inn Yard (in
1731), and was managing his booth at Bartholomew
Fair in company with Hippifley and Hall. It was
announced both in the *Daily Poſt* and in the *Daily
Advertiſer,* as FIELDING's, HIPPISLEY's, and HALL's

Great Theatrical Booth, in the George Inn Yard, Weft Smithfield, with a Company of Comedians from both the Theatres. They prefented a New Dramatic Opera, called *The Emperor of China, Grand Vulgi,* or *Love in Diftrefs and Virtue Rewarded :* written by the Author of the *Generous Free Mafon.* With the Comical Humours of Squire Shallow, in his Treatife of Marriage, and his Man Robin Booby, intermixt with Variety of Songs, Old Ballads, and Country Dances. The part of Shallow, the Welch Squire, by Mr. Hippifley, being the firft time of his appearing in the Fair. Emperor of China, by Mr. Roberts, &c. The other perfons of the play were Carlos ; Refident ; Eugenio ; Fidelia, Mrs. Templar ; Ifabella ; Robin Booby, Mr. Hall ; Sir Arthur Addleplot, Mr. Penkethman (Penkethman, the younger); Freelove, Mr. Berry ; " and the part of Loveit, the Chambermaid, by Mrs. Egleton." With Dancing, and " the whole to conclude with the favourite air in the Opera of *Porus ;* accompany'd with Fiddles, Hautbois, Trumpets, and Kettle Drums. Scenes and Cloaths entirely new. Beginning every day exactly at One o'Clock."

At that Fair time it is recorded that an alarm of fire in the booth next to Mrs. Fawkes, fcared Mrs. Fawkes into a premature confinement. This very flight record is the fole hint I have found of a cafualty by fire in the crowded, carelefs little town of boards and canvas.

In the next year, 1732, Fielding was ftill in the George Inn Yard, and held with Hippifley the Great Theatrical Booth there. Their advertifement is in fucceffive numbers of the *Daily Poft.* The play was,

The Envious Statesman, or the *Fall of Essex*; the Part of the Queen by Mrs. Mullart. With an adaptation, of course by Fielding, of Le Medecin Malgré Lui, called " the Humours of the *Forc'd Physician*, done from the French of Molière, and intermixed with Variety of Songs to old Ballad Tunes and Country Dances. The part of the Physician by Mr. Hippisley." John Hippisley was a wit and a low comedian, who had succeeded to the characters of Penkethman, and was a favourite at once with men of wit and with the mob. He was attached to the new Covent Garden Company, when, by the opening of Covent Garden, rivalry of other houses, and the competition of the foreign opera, the profits of the players were reduced so greatly in the year 1733, that an unusual effort was in that year made by the actors to draw treasure out of Bartholomew Fair. Cibber then first came into the Fair. There were four great Theatrical Booths. One of them, opened in the joint names of Cibber, Griffin, Bullock, and Hallam, performed the Drury Lane play of *Tamerlane the Great*, and Fielding's *Miser*, which he had at the close of the previous winter adapted from Molière, and in which Miss Raftor, better known to us as Mrs. Clive, had appeared at her last benefit. In *Tamerlane*, Cibber himself was the Bajazet, and Mrs. Charke, his youngest daughter—who descended in her latter days to the keeping of a puppet-show, and the selling of sausages—was Haly. In the *Miser*, Griffin played to the Fair people his own part of Lovegold, but Miss Raftor's part of Lappet was transferred to Mrs. Roberts, neither did any other of the ladies who firſt acted in it, travel with the play to Smithfield. There were alſo an Arlequin and Arlequinne dance, and there was an Epilogue by a little girl dreſſed in boy's clothes. Theſe entertainments were repeated ſeveral times a day. It is recorded that this booth had rich decorations, and was lighted by candles in glaſs luſtres.

A ſecond booth in 1733 was, of courſe, Lee and Harper's, in which *Jephthah's Raſh Vow*, was the entertainment, "with the comical humours of Captain Bluſter and his man Diddimo." Hulett, then attached to the Theatre in Goodman's Fields, was engaged to play the part of Diddimo, and ſtout Mr. Harper —who was ſtill a member of the company at Drury Lane—was Captain Bluſter. Mr. Harper, who has been already mentioned as the natural Falſtaff of his day, had to contradict, by public advertiſement, the rumour that he was engaged to perform Falſtaff in the Fair, at Cibber's Booth.

A third Great Theatrical Booth was maintained by three other members of the Drury Lane Company of Comedians, Miller, Mills, and Oates. They acted " the True and Tragical Story of *Jane Shore*, with the Comical and Diverting Humours of Sir Anthony Noodle and his Man Weazle." Noodle, Mr. Miller ; Mr. Shore, by Mr. Mills ; Timothy Stampwell, Mr. Oates ; Jane Shore, Miss Oates. They gave French Dancing at the end of one Act, and a hornpipe at the end of another. They concluded with a dancing entertainment called " the Gardens of Venus, or the Triumphs of Love," and they undertook to amuſe the company, while they were waiting for the play to begin, with rope-dancing and tumbling, by the celebrated Signor Morifini, Mons. Jano, and particularly the famous Italian Woman, Mademoifelle de Reverant, and (candour is great) her daughter.

Among the Drury Lane actors in that year, 1733, was the young Drury Lane author—then aged six-and-twenty—again at his old place in the George Inn Yard, and again opening his booth as partner with John Hippifley. The competition among the Theatrical Booths muft have been great. They were all doubly baited with French pofturing and rope-dancing. Fielding and Hippifley's play-bill for this year, is the following :

At *FIELDING's and HIPPISLEY's*

GREAT THEATRICAL BOOTH,

In the George Inn Yard in Smithfield, During the Time of Bartholomew Fair, will be prefented a Dramatick Entertainment (never perform'd there before), call'd

LOVE AND JEALOUSY,

OR

THE DOWNFALL OF ALEXANDER THE GREAT.

The Part of *Alexander* by Mr. Rofco; *Clytus*, Mr. Huddy; *Hepheftion*, Mr. Houghton; *Lyfimachus*, Mr. Mullart; *Rofana*, Mrs. Mullart; *Statira*, Mrs. Houghton.

To which will be added a Ballad Opera, call'd

A CURE FOR COVETOUSNESS,

OR

THE CHEATS OF SCAPIN.

Done from the French of MOLIERE.

The Part of *Scapin* by Mr. Hippifley, from the Theatre Royal in Covent Garden ; *Old Gripe*, Mr. Penkethman, Son to the late facetious Mr. Wm. Penkethman ; *Sly*, Mr. Salway ; *Octavian*, Mr. Jenkins ; *Shift*, Mr. Hewfon ; *Lucia*, Mifs Binks ; *Loveit*, Mrs. Pritchard ; *Medlar*, Mrs. Martin. With the diverting Humours of the Original Marquefs en Chian, from the Ridotto Al' Frefco. All the Characters, both Roman and Modern, entirely new drefs'd.

With feveral Entertainments of Dancing between the Acts, by Mons. Le Brun, Mrs. Ogden, Mr. Fifher Tench, and Mademoifelle D'Lorme.

And farther, to divert the Audience during the Filling of the Booth, the famous Mr. Phillips will perform his furprifing Poftures on the Stage.

N.B. An Extraordinary Band of Mufic is provided, confifting of Violins, Hautboys, Baffoons, Kettle Drums, Trumpets, and French Horns.

Note. The Paffage to the Booth will be commodioufly illuminated with feveral large Moons, for the Conveniency of the Company ; and Perfons of Quality's Coaches may drive up the Yard.

To begin every day at One o'Clock, and continue till Eleven at Night.

This was not Fielding's laft year in Bartholomew Fair, although the only one of which mention is made by his recent biographer.

Mrs. Pritchard, born Mifs Vaughan, had recently made her firft appearance before the public in one of Fielding's pieces at the Haymarket, and had performed alfo at Goodman's Fields ; but it was in this part at Bartholomew Fair, alfo one of Fielding's adaptation, that fhe firft won the popularity that fecured her an engagement at Drury Lane, and the opportunity of at once eftablifhing a high theatrical reputation in the character of Shakefpeare's *Rofalind.* A duet fung by her in the Fair with Mr. Salway, called " Sweet, if you love me, fmiling turn," created fo large a demand for copies, that Fielding and Hippifley caufed an unlimited number to be printed and given away gratis daily at their Booth while the Fair lafted. Mr. Hippifley added to the entertainments made unexpectedly fo popular, " his comic fcene call'd the Drunken Man."

Mrs. Pritchard came to the ftage a married woman ; her hufband Mr. Wm. Pritchard had fome office in Drury Lane Theatre ; fhe brought to her profeffion an unblemifhed character, and lived to the laft in private honour as a wife and mother, not lefs than in public honour as an actrefs. From the day of her firft fuccefs as Loveit, in Fielding's Booth at Bartholomew Fair, to the day thirty-four years afterwards when, a ftout woman advanced in life, fhe gave, in the year of her hufband's death, her farewell performance as Lady Macbeth to the Macbeth of Garrick, the refpect and admiration of the town abided firmly by her. In the midft of the feverities of his *Rofciad*, Churchill paufed to honour

> Pritchard by nature for the ftage defign'd
> In perfon graceful, and in fenfe refin'd ;
> Her art, as much as nature's friend became ;
> Her voice, as free from blemifh as her fame.
> Who knows fo well in majefty to pleafe,
> Attemper'd with the graceful charms of eafe ?

That praife was written fix-and-twenty years after the firft real difcovery of her genius made at Bartholomew Fair, when it was very creditable in P—— H——, to fend immediately to the *Daily Poft*, certain lines that atteft rather his faculty of criticifm than of fong :

To Mrs. Pritchard *on her playing the Part of* Loveit *at* Mr. Fielding's *Booth in Bartholomew Fair.*

> If to attract the *Eye*, to charm the *Ear*,
> And touch the *Heart*, an Actor's *Heights* appear ;
> Nature and Wit fo ftrong in thee combine,
> Excellent Fair !—thofe *Heights* will foon be thine.
> In thy *firft Effay* ev'ry *meaning* ftroke
> Awakes our Senfes, and fupports the Joke ;
> Surpriz'd we view thy dawning Excellence,
> Thy *Tones* and Geftures—all refult from *Senfe*.
> From hence tranfplanted to a brighter ftage,
> (And Prophet may I be !) thou'lt charm the Age

When *Art*, with delicate *Experience* join'd,
Shall form thy *Action* and improve thy *Mind*,
How wilt thou, perfect both in *Voice* and *Mien*,
Add pointed Beauties to the painted Scene ?

Thus far, then, it has appeared that in the first six
years of Fielding's literary life he looked to Bartholomew Fair as a fource of income. Frefh to his work,
dependent wholly on his ingenuity for bread, and only
twenty-one years old, he found London aftir with the
fame of Gay's operatic jeft, and fpeculated fafely in the
eftablifhment of a booth in the George Inn Yard,
wherein he alfo might profit by the crowding of the
public to the *Beggar's Opera*. The fpeculation was
inevitably profitable, and by the George Inn Yard,
Fielding abided. Next year he looked for profit to a
reproduction with fome colourable alterations, of the
Haymarket novelty, the *Beggar's Wedding*, and engaged
from the Haymarket its chief actor in the piece. The
Haymarket people, though the piece had not been
written for them, refented this poffeffion of their chofen
ground, ran their own play againft Fielding's in the
Fair, and battled with him for poffeffion of the truant
actor. The actor, doubtlefs, though announced to play
in both the booths, played only at the George, for
we find him from this date ftruck off the lift of the
Haymarket Company. There was perhaps temper
concerned in the fact that when, next year, Drury
Lane alfo feized upon the *Beggar's Wedding*, Fielding
appeared in it as actor. But at the Fair in that next year,
determined to avoid a repetition of unprofitable conteft,
he was cheering the heart of the Drury Lane Prompter

by producing a play of his compofition, an entirely new play, and himfelf acting before the Fair in one of its parts. The jefts that the Fair needed, he furnifhed then and afterwards, not by the ufual buffooneries, but by adapting for his booth the gayeft of the comedies of Molière. In this adventure he was profperous, for in the next year he produced another of the prompter's plays. In the fifth year of his booth management he entertained the Fair with a piece which feems to have been of his own devifing, called the *Earl of Effex*, and with another jeft from Molière adapted by himfelf. That his booth by this time had become famous for the good amufement he provided, is attefted by this paragraph from the *Daily Poft* of the 30th of Auguft, 1732 :—" Yefterday the Prince and Princeffes went to Bartholomew Fair, and faw Mr. Fielding's cele-brated Droll called the *Earl of Effex* and the *Forced Phyfician*, and were fo well pleafed as to ftay to fee it twice performed." A paragraph fuggeftive not only of the ftrength of Fielding, but of the ftrength alfo that yet abided by the Fair. Still renting the George Inn Yard at the next Bartholomew Fair, Fielding's booth became more than ever famous through the brilliant reputation fuddenly acquired in it by Mrs. Pritchard.

But that was not the clofing year of the career of Fielding as a booth-keeper. In 1734, he was again at Bartholomew Fair, for the feventh time manager of the booth in the Yard of the George Inn. Mrs. Pritchard, who in the interval had won her place at Drury Lane, did not withdraw herfelf from her firft hearty

and effectual public friends. It was then " Fielding
and Oates's Great Theatrical Booth in the George Inn
Yard, Weſt Smithfield, during the time of Bartholomew
Fair." The play was *Don Carlos, Prince of Spain,*
without interpolation of buffoonery. Then followed
a new ballad opera, the *Conſtant Lover,* in which
Oates was Ragout, Mr. Stoppelaer played the part of
Springgame, and Mrs. Pritchard was the Cloe. There
were dances, poſtures, kettle-drums. The performances
were continued every day from one o'clock until
eleven.

Even now we have not traced to the end this eſſential
feature in the life of the great Maſter of all Noveliſts.
The next year, 1735, is that in which the Court of
Aldermen came to a " final reſolve touching Bartholomew Fair, that the ſame ſhall not exceed
Bartholomew's Eve, Bartholomew's Day, and the Day
after ; and that during that time nothing but ſtalls
and booths ſhall be erected for the ſale of goods, wares,
and merchandiſe, and no acting be permitted." They
had come to many ſuch reſolves at divers times, but
the paſſive reſiſtance of the ſhowmen was too ſtrong
for them ; an energetic Mayor might compel obedience
in this year or that, but the fourteen day Fair had
recovered from all corporate attacks, chiefly becauſe
there was no law ſharp enough for uſe againſt rebellious
players. But in 1735 there was an energetic Mayor,
Sir John Barnard, who could defy a premier and compel
obedience from a ſhowman ; and ſhortly afterwards
the Licenſing Act became a law, which reduced all
unlicenſed players to the grade of vagrants, over whom

the Magiftrate had a defpotic power. That Act at laft gave to the City Magiftracy power enough to command obedience. For this reafon it happens that after the year 1735 Bartholomew Fair could be reftrained, actually and not nominally, to the original limit of three days. Neverthelefs, after a few years it again had broken bounds, and had to be confined again in the year 1750. A complete interdict upon ftage plays was in each year the perfonal act of the Mayor, and valid only in his mayoralty. In 1735 they were forbidden ; Fielding, therefore, was not at the George Inn Yard, nor were there any other players in the Fair. Had there not been an interdict, Fielding, no doubt, ftill would have been abfent, for that was the year of his marriage and retirement to the country.

But before the next Bartholomew Fair, when for the three days ftage plays were permitted, he was poor again, feeking a livelihood in London ; and again therefore, in the year 1736, he was to be found at his old quarters. It was then Fielding and Hippifley's booth in the George Inn Yard. *Don Carlos* was repeated, and Molière's *Fourberies de Scapin* was adapted for the Fairgoer in fearch of " Humours," as the *Cheats of Scapin.* Faithful Mrs. Pritchard came alfo to the Fair again to ferve her friend, taking a part in the Molière piece, with the old name of Loveit, which reminded people of her earlieft fuccefs. For the next year, record is wanting to me. In the acceffible files of newfpapers thofe are omitted which contain the booth advertifements, and I have only two or three dated flips

in the collections, among which there is no flip telling by
whom the booth at the George Inn Yard was occupied.
In the year following, Fielding having joined one of
the Inns of Court, his name does not appear as manager
of the booth in the George Yard. It was "Hallam's
Booth," and the play acted was the *Dragon of Wantley*,
to be played by the Company of Lilliputians from Drury
Lane. After that date, it is obvious that Fielding looked
no more to Bartholomew Fair for a portion of his income. If we may affume that Fielding occupied the
George Inn Yard in 1737, then it is over ten years of
his life that his connection with Bartholomew Fair muft
be faid to extend. If we reject what is a moft uncer-
tain furmife, the certain fact remains, that for nine
years of his life Fielding was connected with the Fair,
making his name familiar in men's mouths as a booth
proprietor; year after year renting the fame piece of
ground; holding it during Fair time, now with one
actor, now with another, as his partner, in uninterrupted
poffeffion during all that time; and never abfent
from the Fair, except in the one year when all ftage-
playing was excluded. This is fomething that entirely
differs from the accidental partnerfhip in a booth at
the Fair, during the year of diftrefs at Drury Lane,
which induced even Cibber to appear upon a ftage in
Smithfield.

In the Mufical Companion or Ladies Magazine for
1741 are fome verfes, entitled *A Trip to Bartholomew
Fair*. Though printed in 1741, they muft have been
written fome time before, or founded on old memoirs.
They begin by affuming that a wife fteals out to the

Fair during her hufband's abfence, in hope of finding a truftworthy fpark. With him fhe fays,

> ——I would ramble
> The Fair all around;
> I'd eat and I'd drink
> Of the beft could be found.
>
> There's *Fielding* and *Oates*,
> There's *Hippefley* and *Hall*,
> There's *Bullock* and *Lee*,
> And the Devil and all.

Here Fielding's connection with the Fair is, to a contemporary, fo obvious, that his name is the firft to come to mind in an enumeration.

CHAPTER XXII.

State Papers.

ALTHOUGH fuch monarchs of the ftage as Betterton, Quin, and Garrick, were not induced by large profits and quick returns to perform fix times a day before a Smithfield audience; and although no actrefs of high ftanding, except, for good reafon and in good company, Mrs. Pritchard, and in one year Mrs. Cibber, brought her genius to market in the Fair; yet had the Smith-field Drama certainly its golden age in the days of which we have been fpeaking and now fpeak. The three or four "Great Theatrical Booths" were, in fact, three or four playhoufes, fuftained by nearly all the favourite comedians of the day. The names of actors who had made themfelves moft clearly the favourites of the town by their drollery, ferved as attractive labels to the booths they managed. If, for the fake of illuftration, I may take a moment's liberty with the names of actors living in our time, I fhould fay that had they lived in the middle of the laft century they would have eftablifhed, without lofs of profeffional or focial credit, fuch Thea-trical Booths in Bartholomew Fair as " Robfon's and Keeley's," or "Buckftone's, Compton's, and Wright's;"

and that they would have acted pieces altered or written
to fuit the occafions of the Fair in affociation rather
with their brother actors of the playhoufe, than with the
ftrolling players who were left a few years later in the fole
poffeffion of the booths. We have feen that a Smithfield Theatre was in thofe days able to attract to itfelf
Royal vifitors. Two playhoufes, at leaft, were clofed
during the Fair, and their audiences flocked into Smithfield for amufement. That a large part of the audience
in one of the principal Theatrical Booths was compofed
of the regular play-goers is fuggefted by the fact that
when, in 1733, Cibber the younger announced from the
ftage in the Fair, that on the 20th of September next
following, the Haymarket Theatre would be opened with
Congreve's *Love for Love*, fuch an announcement made
in that place was received with ftrong applaufe.

Of courfe there was alfo in the Fair the party of the
Pig-Woman to be confidered, and the rough Englifh
mob, raw material of the more polifhed Englifh people,
which has a predominant delight in jefters. I believe
that the quiet love of what is beft called " fun," in which
the Englifhman ftands high above all rivalry, and his
quick inftinct for the ridiculous, which is a part of it,
have been even more ferviceable than his patriotifm in
checking dangerous extravagance and keeping fafe fenfe
uppermoft in public writing and in public action. If
there had been no fpirit of fun in us, we might have
gone to ruin in one Revolution ; and then, good patriots
as we all are, have clafhed about the fragments of our
conftitution in the chaos of a dozen revolutions more.
Therefore I look with no contempt at all the fooleries of

Bartholomew Fair. The jack-puddings are gone, but we have ftill good ftore of clowns every Chriftmas, and the nation is the ftronger for its power of enjoying them. The "Humours interfperfed" at the Fair with tales of Rome and Babylon, ftill live in the farces and burlefques which keep us merry at the theatres. We practife ourfelves well in laughter over feigned abfurdities, and we in the meantime learn to fubdue with laughter alfo real abfurdities of life, which, in a nation holding itfelf to be wifer for its want of foolifhnefs, would prompt only to follies that occafion tears and groans. Then let us not ftand aloof magnificently from the nonfenfe of the Fair. The ludicrous things to be read in the Manifeftoes of its Minifters of Pleafure, are in the worthieft fenfe State Papers to us, if we underftand them thoroughly. Such State Papers have done more good to England than will ever be done to her neighbour country by the programmes, with no fun in them, proceeding from the manager, who, regardlefs of expenfe, has produced the Tragi-Comedy of "the Empire" at his Great Theatrical Booth fomewhere in Paris. It is wifer as well as merrier to have at Bartholomew Fair than at Weftminfter a Dragon of Wantley reprefented by a Company of Lilliputians.

Having thus claimed due refpect for them, I fhall produce fome more Bartholomew State Papers. A juft intereft in Henry Fielding makes it right that we fhould clearly know what the Fair was when he was part of it, and how, therefore, his booth-keeping touches our impreffion of his character.

The George Inn Yard and the ground facing the

Hofpital gate were the two principal fites for a Smithfield playhoufe. In (1736) the firft year of plays after
the reduction of the Fair to its original three·days, the
only Great Booth, except Fielding and Hippifley's, was
Hallam and Chapman's, where, as the managers mourn-
fully announced, " during the Short Time of Bartholomew Fair," the performances confifted of *Fair Rofamond*
and a Ballad Opera.

In 1737, at Hallam's Great Booth, over againft the
Hofpital Gate, the play was *All Alive and Merry*, with
the furprifing performances of various Tumblers and
Pofture mafters, having French and Dutch names, alfo
the Italian Shadows by " the beft Mafters from Italy,
and which have not been feen here thefe Twenty years."
The whole to conclude with a grand Ballet Dance call'd
Le Badinage Champêtre. " With a Complete Band of
Mufick of Hautboys, Violins, Trumpets, and Kettle
Drums. All the Decorations entirely new. To begin
every Day at One o'Clock, and continue till eleven at
Night. The Fair begins to-morrow at One o'Clock."

In the fame year at Yeates' Senior and Junior's Great
booth facing the Hofpital Gate, the Artificial Moving
Wax Work, five feet high, prefented the *Lover his
own Rival.* There was alfo a machine coach and horfes
made by Mr. Cornues of France. Yeates' junior's
dexterity of hand. Alfo the famous tumbler. All new.
" Note. The Tap is to be lett."

In 1738, at Penkethman's Great Theatrical Booth,
againft the Hofpital Gate, there was, " during the Short
Time of Bartholomew Fair," a New entertainment called
The Man's Bewitched, or the *Devil to Do About Her.*

Diego, Furiofo's Man, Mr. Penkethman (the Younger). Added to this was the *Country Wedding* or the *Roving Shepherd*, and an Extraordinary Band of Mufic, not forgetting kettle-drums. Time 1 a.m.—11 p.m. At Hallam's Great Theatrical Booth in the George Inn Yard, a celebrated burlefque opera, *The Dragon of Wantley*, was performed by the Lilliputian Company from the Theatre Royal, Drury Lane. And during the time of filling the Booth, the famous Mons. Rapinefe was to perform his furprifing poftures on the Stage. "Note the extraordinary band of mufic, Violins, Hautboys, Baffoons, Kettle-Drums, Trumpets, and French Horns. The Paffage to the Booth will be commodioufly illuminated with feveral large Moons and Lanthorns, for the Conveniency of the Company, and that Perfons of Quality's coaches may drive up the yard.

"The Fair begins to-morrow and will end on Saturday Night. Time, 1—11."

In 1739, at Lee and Phillips' Great Theatrical Booth, corner of Hofier Lane, there were ferious and comic entertainments. 1. A Grand Scene of Cupid and Pfyche. 2. A Scaramouch Dance by Mr. Phillips and others, which he perform'd at the Opera Houfe in Paris, upwards of forty fucceffive nights, with univerfal applaufe. 3. A Dialogue between Punch and Columbine. 4. The Drunken Peafant, by Mr. Phillips. To which was added, a Dramatic Pantomime Entertainment, call'd *Columbine Courtefan.* Harlequin, Mr. Phillips from the Theatre Royal Drury Lane. Columbine, Mrs. Phillips. Spaniard and Clown.

The Booth at the George Inn was occupied that year

by Hippifley, Chapman, and Legar, who played *The Top of the Tree*, with a (then famous) dog fcene, and a Harlequinade of *Perfeus and Andromeda*. A new tafte for harlequinade was then predominant in the playgoer, and the Booths of the Fair made hafte to take advantage of it. Hallam, oppofite the Hofpital Gate, played in this year *Harlequin turned Philofopher* and the *Sailor's Wedding*.

In 1740, at the Booth in the George Yard, Hippifley and Chapman played the *Cheats of Scapin*, which Fielding had prefented as a ballad opera, at a time when the *Beggar's Opera* had brought all kinds of Ballad opera into requeft, but which was prefented now in accordance with the change of tafte that Rich eftablifhed, as *Harlequin Scapin*. In this Booth, Hippifley, Oates, and Yates all acted. This was the bill:—" At HIPPISLEY's and CHAPMAN's G. T. B., in the George Inn, Smithfield. HARLEQUIN SCAPIN, or the OLD ONE CAUGHT IN A SACK, with the Comical Tricks, Cheats, and Shifts of *Scapin's* Two Companions, *Tim the Barber* and *Bounce-about the Bully*. The part of Scapin by Mr. Hippifley; Tim, Mr. Chapman ; Bounce-about, Mr. Arthur ; . . . Slyboots, Mr. Yates. With entertainments of Singing and Dancing by Mr. Oates, . . . Mr. Yates, Mrs. Phillips and others, particularly a new Whimfical and Diverting Dance called the *Spanifh Beauties*. The whole to conclude with a new Mufical Entertainment called *The Parting Lovers*, or the *Prefs-gang*. The part of Tom Trueblue, by Mr. Bencroft ; Old Briton, Mr. Arthur ; Lieut. Dreadnought, Mr. Arthur ; Nancy, Mrs. Villeneuve. With a grand chorus accompanied by

Violins, Baſſoons, Hautboys, French Horns, Trumpets, and Kettle-Drums. Note. The Fair ends this Day."

In the ſame year, Yeates and Hallam maintained ſeparate booths oppoſite the Hoſpital Gate, one playing *Orpheus and the Death of Eurydice*, with the Metamorphoſes of Harlequin, the other playing *The Rambling Lover*, with Comical Humours of Squire Softhead, his Man Bullcalf, Mother Catterwawl, and ſo forth. There was alſo a Great Theatrical Booth maintained in that year, by Fawkes, Pinchbeck, and Terwin.

In the following year there was ſo large a muſter of the players in the Fair, that we might ſuppoſe they had already conquered the three days' reſtriction, if they were not all advertiſing their performances for "the ſhort time of Bartholomew Fair." Hippiſley and Chapman were at the George Inn acting a Droll called *The Devil of a Duke*, with the Comical Humours of Capt. Tipple. Hallam from Covent Garden had *Fair Roſamond ;* another Hallam produced Rope Dancers and Tumblers. Fawkes and Pinchbeck had a working model of the ingenious clockmaker's manufacture, advertiſed as "the true and exact Siege of Cartagena," with an announcement that "Before the Siege begins, will be ſpoken and given gratis the authenticated Speech of the Admiral;" —a reflection again of the great world in the Fair, thrown back, not from the paſſions of the people, but from the mechanical ſkill in which they had begun to excel and delight, and of which the Fair, therefore, now diſplayed abundant evidence. Fawkes and Pinchbeck promiſed a Comedy after the mechaniſm, and invited cuſtom with a burleſque flouriſh meant for fun.

The Comedian Yates, in this year, 1741, appears for the firſt time as a manager at Bartholomew Fair, where he was deſtined to be very popular :

> In charaĉters of low and vulgar mould,
> Where nature's coarſeſt features we behold,
> Where deſtitute of every decent grace,
> Unmanner'd jeſts are blurted in your face,
> There Yates with juſtice ſtriĉt attention draws,
> Aĉts truly from himſelf and gains applauſe.

In the Fair, if anywhere, he could earn that opinion from Churchill. We have ſeen that he made his firſt appearance there in the preceding year. This year he ruled the booth of Turbutt and Yates, oppoſite the King's Head and Greyhound, where, after the dramatic pantomime of *Thamas Kouli Kan, the Perſian Hero*—founded on news of the day from the Eaſt—he aĉted "a Drunken Epilogue, in the charaĉter of an Engliſh Sailor." Engliſh ſailors now, in war time, begin to form an important and liberal part of the public at the Fair, and performances not ſeldom conclude with a tribute to them in a grand ſcene of the Temple of Neptune.

Finally, there was in this year, the theatrical booth of Lee and Woodward, oppoſite the Hoſpital Gate, in which was to be ſeen *Darius, King of Perſia,* or the *Noble Engliſhman,* with the Comical Humours of Sir Andrew Aguecheek, at the Siege of Babylon (!)

Fielding, it will be ſeen, had parted altogether from the Fair. It was in the next year, 1742, that his firſt novel was iſſued. We paſs on—croſſing the blank year 1744, in which the Mayor and Aldermen of London again interdiĉted ſtage-plays at the Fair—to the year

1748, in which we find a hint of Smollett's popularity. The George Inn Yard was then occupied by Bridges, Crofs, Barton, and Vaughan, with a Company from the Theatres Royal, and they acted An Hiſtorical Drama (on events comparatively recent), never acted before, called, the *Northern Heroes*, or the *Bloody Conteſt between Charles the Twelfth and Peter the Great, Czar of Muſcovy, &c.*, Interſperſed with a Comic Interlude, never acted before, called *the Volunteers*, or the *Adventures of Roderick Random and his Friend Strap*, with entertainments of dancing, &c. Boxes, 2*s.* 6*d.* Pit, 1*s.* 6*d.* Firſt Gallery, 1*s.* Upper Gallery, 6*d.* New Dreſſes. Begin at 12. In the ſame year, Couſins and Reynolds, at the G. T. B. over againſt Cow Lane, played the *True and Ancient Hiſtory of King Henry IV.*, or the *Blind Beggar of Bethnal Green*, &c., with several diverting Scenes between Squire Punch and his Man Gudgeon. Likewiſe there was a beautiful repreſentation of the Court of the Queen of Hungary in Waxwork, being the moſt beautiful figures in England, and as big as life. With Variety of dancing between the Acts. To conclude with the Italian Sword dancers, who had the honour to perform before His Royal Highneſs the Prince of Wales, with great applauſe. Pit, 1*s.* Firſt Gallery, 6*d.* Upper Gallery, 3*d.*

In the ſame year we find reference to Foote, for by a Company of Comedians from the Theatres, after there had been performed for the delight of the ſailors, at Huſſey's G. T. B., facing the Hoſpital Gate, a new Droll, called *the Conſtant Quaker*, or the *Humours of Wapping ;* there was ſinging and dancing, including " a new dance, called *Punch's Maggot,* or *Foote's Vagaries,* by Mafter Harrifon and Mafter Dominique. Then a Pantomime, *Harlequin's Frolics,* or the *Rambles of Covent Garden.* "The whole to conclude with a magnificent Piece of Fireworks, never exhibited before, in Honour of the approaching Peace ; in which will be reprefented a fuperb Temple of Apollo, adorn'd with a grand Triumphal Arch, decorated and embellifhed with various Trophies of War ; to be accompanied with a chorus of vocal and inftrumental mufic. Boxes, 2s. Pit, 1s. Gallery, 6d. To begin each day at Twelve o'clock."

In that year alfo there was a fhow at the firft houfe on the pavement from the end of Hofier Lane, which contained a Camel, a Hyæna, a Panther, a "young Oronutu Savage," and "the wonderful and furprifing fatyr, call'd by Latin authors, Pan."

The genius of the Fair has not departed from it : ftill there is—

The greateft Prodigy in Nature. To be feen, during the Fair, on the Pavement, near the End of Cow-Lane, Smithfield, A moft extraordinary Large Hog, near Twelve Feet long, and weighs 120 Stone. Being the moft remarkable Sight ever offered to the Public. His Keeper is the amazing little Dwarf, Being the fmalleft Man in the World.

Admittance only 3d. each.

The Hog is of all time. The next advertifement is probably of older date than the year under which it is inferted.

THE GERMAINE MASTERPIECE,

BEING

That Famous Kniffe, which hath been for fome time in England, and highly applauded by yᵉ moft Exquifite Artifts, containing in the Haft fixty odd feveral Figures, fome Engraved, others Carved, and all to the admiration of thofe that behold them ; it hath two Keys, which open feaven Locks, including thofe various Rarities contrived therein : it was feaven years a Making, and Valued by the Authour, that famous Artift of Germany, at Fifteene Hundred Pounds, and is now expofed to publique View, for Englands fatisfaction. To be feen At Bartholomew Faire, againft the King's Head, with other Rarities.

By me, JOHN GIFFORD.

To the Nobility and Gentry, and to all who are Admirers of the Extraordinary Productions of Nature.

There is to be feen in a commodious Apartment, at the Corner of Cow-Lane, facing the Sheep-Pens, Weft Smithfield, During the fhort time of Bartholomew Fair,

MARIA TERESIA,

the Amazing CORSICAN FAIRY, who has had the Honour of being fhown three Times before their Majefties.

☞ She was exhibited in Cockfpur-Street, Hay-market, at two fhillings and fixpence each Perfon ; but that Perfons of every Degree may have a Sight of fo extraordinary a Curiofity, fhe will be fhown to the Gentry at fixpence each, and to Working People, Servants, and Children, at Three-pence, during this Fair.

This moft aftonifhing Part of the Human Species was born in the Ifland of Corfica, on the Mountain of Stata Ota, in the year 1743. She is only thirty-four Inches high, weighs but twenty-fix Pounds, and a Child of two Years of Age has larger Hands and Feet. Her furprifing Littlenefs makes a ftrong Impreffion at firft Sight on the Spectator's Mind. Nothing difagreeable, either in Perfon or Converfation, is to be found in her; although moft of Nature's Productions, in Miniature, are generally fo in both. Her Form affords a pleafing Surprife, her Limbs are exceedingly well proportioned, her admirable Symmetry engages the attention ; and, upon the whole, is acknowledged a perfect Beauty. She is poffeffed of a great deal of Vivacity of Spirit ; can fpeak Italian and French, and gives the inquifitive Mind an agreeable Entertainment. In fhort, fhe is the moft extraordinary Curiofity ever known, or ever heard of in Hiftory ; and the Curious, in all countries where fhe has been fhown, pronounce her to be the fineft Difplay of Human Nature, in Miniature, they ever faw.

⁎ She is to be feen, by any Number of Perfons, from Ten in the Morning till Nine at Night.

In 1749, Crofs and Bridges, oppofite the Hofpital Gate, announced in the *General Advertizer*, that they would prefent a New Dramatic Droll, called the *Fair Lunatick*, or the *Generous Sailor*. Being founded on a Story in Real Life, as related in the Memoirs of Mrs. Conſtantia Phillips. In which will be introduc'd a new Scene of Bedlam, call'd *Modern Madneſs*, or, *A Touch at the Times*. Interſperſ'd with a merry interlude, call'd the *Jovial Jack Tars*, with the Comical Humours of Nurſe Prate and Will Bowling, the Jovial Tars; as alſo of Jack Handſpike, Nick Hatchway, and Simon Buckely, Sailors; with Mary the Chambermaid, Suſan of the Dairy; Kate of the Kitchen, and Nan the Spinner. The whole to conclude with the *Jubilee Ball*, dances, trumpets, and kettledrums.

In the ſame year, Yeates was alone, oppoſite the George Inn, with the *Blind Beggar of Bethnal Green*, and the *Bottle Conjuror out-done*. He was alſo oppoſite the Hoſpital Gate (during the Short Time of Bartholomew Fair), with Lee and Warner, acting the *Hiſtory of Whittington* "perform'd in the ſame manner as it was by Mrs. Lee, fifteen years ago."

Alſo in this year, " YATES *from the* Theatre Royal *in* Drury Lane," had the Great Theatrical Booth in the George Inn, and performed according to announcement in the *General Advertizer*,

A New, Pleaſant, and Diverting Droll, call'd the DESCENT of the HEATHEN GODS, with the LOVES of JUPITER and ALCMENA; or Cuckoldom no Scandal. Interſperſed with ſeveral Diverting Scenes, both Satyrical and Comical, particularly the Surpriſing Metamorphoſis of *Jupiter* and *Mercury*; the very remarkable Tryal before *Judge Puzzlecauſe*, with many Learned Arguments on both Sides, to prove that One can't be Two. Likewiſe the Adventures and whimſical Perplexities of *Gormandize Simple* the Hungarian Footman; with the wonderful Converſation he had with, and the dreadful Drubbing he received from, *His Own Apparition*; together with the Intrigues of *Dorothy Squeezepurſe* the Wanton Chambermaid,

And so forth, very much reminding us of Hero a

Wench o' the Bankfide, who was fpied by Leander landing at Trig-ftairs. The part of Jupiter was by Mr. Oates. Mr. Yates mixed with the Heathen Gods as the Hungarian Footman, and Mifs Hippifley was Dorothy the Chambermaid.

The laft booth-bill belonging to this fchool of Bartholomew Fair drama that I care to quote, is that iffued ·in the fame year of the Fair by "CUSHING, *from the* Theatre Royal *in* Covent Garden." His booth was oppofite the King's Head, Smithfield, and he alfo announced in the *General Advertizer*, with fpecial emphafis, that it was during the Short Time of Bartholomew Fair, he meant to prefent " The Tragical Hiftory of the LIFE and DEATH of KING JOHN. Interfperfed with a Comic Piece, call'd the Adventures of Sir LUBBERLY LACKBRAINS, and His Man BLUN-DERBUSS. The Tragedy contains the barbarous contrivances of King John, againft his Nephew, Prince Arthur; his method of perfuading Hubert to undertake the cruel Murder of that Youth; the Sufferings of Arthur in his confinement, where Hubert attempts to put out his eyes, with Red-hot Iron " &c. " The comic contains the exquifite Drolleries of Sir Lubberly," and includes a Tom Rafh, a Jeffery Holdfaft, and a Moll Tatler. Sir Lubberly, Mr. Cufhing; Lady Conftance, Mrs. Cufhing; Prince Arthur, by Mifs Yates, from Drury Lane. " Violins, Hautboys, Baffoons, Trumpets, Kettledrums."

There is a man here named Ford, who was famous in Bartholomew Fair and in London by the name that his cry gave him, of Tiddy Doll the Gingerbread Baker.

His difappearance from his ufual ftation in the Haymarket in 1752 (when he was gone among the country

fairs) gave rife to a Grub-ftreet halfpenny account of his
murder, which produced a week's wealth to its publifher.
The annexed fketch of him is by Hogarth, who intro-
duces him into the picture of the Idle Apprentice executed at Tyburn.

After a few years, one more of the beft comedians
of this generation, became famous alfo as a booth-
manager in Smithfield. Yates in the Fair was foon
followed by Edward Shuter:

> Shuter who never cared a fingle pin
> Whether he left out nonfenfe or put in.

F F 2

It is a hard fate for the actors of a hundred years ago, that their features come most readily to mind in the sharp lines with which Churchill drew them in *The Rosciad.* Shuter, it is to be remembered, was the man who took the thrust into his ribs with the best humour. In him the line of true comedians acting at the Fair became extinct, but while he played he ruled there, for he was the darling of the crowd:

> From galleries loud peals of laughter roll,
> And thunder Shuter's praises—he's so droll.

In 1760, when *The Rosciad* was written, he was monarch of the Smithfield stage, on which the Satirist bade Murphy seek his proper throne:

> A vacant throne, high placed in Smithfield, view,
> To sacred Dulness and her first-born due.
> Thither with haste in happy hour repair;
> Thy birthright claim, nor fear a rival there.
> Shuter himself shall own thy juster claim,
> And venal *Ledgers* puff their Murphy's name;
> While Vaughan, or Dapper, call him which you will,
> Shall blow the trumpet and give out the bill.

A writer in the *St. James's Chronicle* (March 24, 1791) wished to place upon record the fact, that it was Shuter who, in the year 1759, when Master of a Droll in Smithfield, invented a way, since become general at Fairs, of informing players in the booth when they may drop the curtain and dismiss the company, because there are enough people waiting outside to form another audience. The man at the door pops in his head and makes a loud inquiry for " John Audley ? "

There lived about this time a popular Merry-Andrew,

who fold Gingerbread nuts in the neighbourhood of Covent Garden, and becaufe he received a guinea a-day for his fun during the Fair, he was at pains never to cheapen himfelf by laughing, or by noticing a joke, during the other three hundred and fixty-two days of the year.

In 1760, there was ftill enough life in the Smithfield drama to give expectation of a Smithfield Rofciad from Churchill. But very foon afterwards, the Hiftory of the Englifh Stage parted entirely from the Story of the Fair. No actor of note appeared in a booth after Shuter's time. Garrick's name is connected with the Fair only by ftories that regard him as a vifitor out of another world. He offers his money at the entrance to a Theatrical booth, and it is thought a jeft worth tranfmitting to pofterity, that he is told by the check-taker, " We never takes money of one another." He fees one of his own fturdy Drury Lane porters inftalled at a booth door, when he is preffed forely in the crowd and calls for help. " It's no ufe," he is told, " I can't help you. There's very few people in Smithfield as knows Mr. Garrick off the ftage." The great actor was in the Fair fimply a little man, born to be always worfted in the crufh. Bartholomew Fair did indeed witnefs fome of the firft flafhes of the genius of Edmund Kean, as Mafter Carey, and may alfo have feen him, as tradition fays it did, with no known father, and a doubtful mother, falling as a boy-rider, in the circus, and receiving the hurt to his leg of which the mark remained in later years; but I have fought in vain among its ftate papers for any mention of the name of " Mafter Carey." The playhoufe of the Fair left to itfelf by the playhoufe of the Town, had no more royalty of rank or wit before the curtain. Every year it fank, till it had fairly fuited itfelf to the tafte of its new public. Abfurd and wretched as were the pieces played in Yates's and Shuter's time, yet it was certainly a notable fall when the Bartholomew Addifon tumbled into a pit full of fkeletons, and murderers, and fpeɛtre brides, out of the company of Cephalus and Procris, or Orpheus and Eurydice, even though Squire Gawky intruded there, and Mafter Ferg performed a folo on the kettle-drums.

Smithfield, no longer in the fuburbs, had not only been hemmed in by the growth of London until it had become a central point in the Metropolis, but it chanced alfo that it was immediately hemmed in by regions, black with negleɛted ignorance, in which were fome of the moft famous haunts of London thieves. By every thief living in London, Bartholomew Fair was regarded as an annual performance for his benefit; and all the ignorance and vice of the town, poured therefore, as it had always done, into the Fair: but the town was become larger, the tide of evil in it fuller and ftronger, and the old breakwaters were gone. Decency did indeed go to the Fair to buy toys, and enjoy the outfide gaiety of all its buftle; but its receffes were left ufually unexplored by creditable vifitors, and fhowmen were left to difcover, that an ignorant and vicious rabble was the public by whofe pleafure they muft live. One evidence of this we fhall find in the faɛt that, during the laft years of Bartholomew Fair, nearly all the fhows charged but a fingle penny for admiffion.

But in the year 1760, there was outfide Smithfield
ftill a tafte that made fome corners of it, in due feafon,
an Elyfium to the fafhionable. "Thefe people," faid
Goldfmith's Citizen Philofopher, writing in that year,
"are not more fond of wonders than liberal in rewarding
thofe who fhow them .... A fellow fhall make a
fortune by toffing a ftraw
from his toe to his nofe;
one in particular has found
that eating fire was the moft
ready way to live;"

This is the man ☞
His name was Powell.

"and another, who gingles
feveral bells fixed to his cap,
is the only man that I know
of, who has received emolument from the labours of his
head."

This is the man ☞
His name was Roger
Smith.

I have no wifh to
be the fhowman's Plu-
tarch. Details of the
laft and leaft interefting
part of the Fair's hiftory
are thofe which moft

abound, but the main facts illuftrated by them are few
in number.   The accidental excefs of material muft not
divert our attention from the plan and purpofe of the
hiftory we build.   The roof is not to be as large as the
houfe, becaufe we chance to have more tiles than bricks
at our difpofal.   One ufe, however, it will be worth while
to make of the increafed mafs of documents connected
with the laft days of the Fair.   In thefe laft days, as
ordinary arts of life advanced in England, picture makers
multiplied, and fhowmen indulged freely in cheap illuftrations to their handbills.   Comic engravings alfo found
both publifhers and purchafers in plenty.   Therefore it is
now eafy to tell much to the eye that formerly was to be
told only through the ears, and from this new advantage
we muft get what benefit we can.   A Fair is full of
fights, and we muft ufe our eyes as much as poffible
before we leave it.

CHAPTER XXIII.

Laſt Years of the Condemned.

OLD cuſtom had eſtabliſhed that as the civic proceffion paſſed, on its way to Cloth Fair, under Newgate,
it pauſed while the Keeper of that priſon drank to the
Mayor in what is uſually deſcribed as "a cool tankard,"
but is more particularly defined in the *Weekly Journal* or
Britiſh Gazetteer for the Fair time in 1728, as "a
lemonade." It is defined, however, as a "cup of fack,
&c.," in a newſpaper for September, 1779. Doubtleſs,
it was a very comfortable lemonade. Sir John Shorter,
Mayor in 1688, and maternal grandfather to Horace
Walpole, let the lid of the tankard fall with a click that
ſtartled the horſe, and cauſed the rider a fall of which he
died. Succeeding Mayors changed, therefore, the new
faddle for the State Coach, and lumbered in it to the
Fair, where they were received, again according to old
cuſtom, by three ſtrokes from the bells of St. Bartholomew. The State Coach at firſt traverſed Cloth Fair,
but after the time of Alderman Bull's Mayoralty, it was
left in the ſtreet, and the Mayor walked through the
adjoining houſe of a Smithfield tradeſman into the gateway between Smithfield and Cloth Fair, which was the

place of proclamation. The proclamation was read in the Mayor's prefence by a clerk, who then announced whether his Lordfhip would allow ftage plays and interludes. If he forbade them, yells and riots followed. If he allowed them, all the drums, kettle-drums, and trumpets, wild men and wild beafts in the Fair, clafhed and roared to their fatisfaction.

There remained a memorial of the ancient privileges of the Priory, in a toll payable to the reprefentatives of the Rich Family, from thofe who brought goods to the Fair in Weft Smithfield. The Earldoms of Warwick and Holland, together with the Barony of Kenfington, became extinct in the year 1759, in the perfon of Edward Rich, coufin and heir male of the Earl, whofe mother had married Jofeph Addifon. But Francis Edwardes married a daughter of the houfe of Rich, and their fon William Edwardes became in default of the direct line, heir to its eftates. This William was created, in 1776, Baron Kenfington of the Peerage of Ireland, and the inheritors of his barony inherited alfo his rights over Bartholomew Fair.

Even as late as the year 1826, when the collectors of Lord Kenfington were refifted in an attempt to levy toll for ftandings even outfide Smithfield, in Giltfpur Street, the claim fo made was regarded not as an unjuft but as a doubtful one. But on behalf of the citizens of London, in the year 1752, a leather-feller in Newgate Street, Mr. Richard Holland, refolved to claim immunity from toll. On the firft day of the Fair in that year, Mr. Holland entered it carrying under his arm a fmall bundle of leather, and when this was feized for

the fee by a Toll collector, Mr. Holland fetched a
conſtable to take him into cuſtody for an unlawful
invaſion of the rights of citizens. On the 30th of
June in the next year, there was a large crowd aſſembled
at Guildhall, to hear the trial of the caſe between Mr.
Richard Holland, plaintiff, and the Proprietors of the
Bartholomew Fair Toll, defendants. Objection was made
on the part of the defence to a jury of citizens, and
the cauſe was poſtponed, but it was determined at
Guildhall, on the 17th of July, 1754, in favour of the
right claimed for the citizens. At the Fair time in
1753, while the queſtion in diſpute ſtill remained open,
on Monday the 3rd of September—Mr. Richard Holland's cart, loaded with hay, paſſed unmoleſted by the
Toll collectors at Smithfield Bars and Pye Corner into
Bartholomew Fair. On one of the Horſes' foreheads
was fixed a writing, and round his neck a halter dreſſed
with flowers. On the front of the Hay another writing
was fixed, with a halter hanging by the ſide of it. As
the Crowd might prevent many perſons from reading
the two papers, Mr. Holland made his appearance in
good time before the Cart, and read his poems to the
populace.

On the Horſe's forehead he had inſcribed :

> My maſter keeps me well, 'tis true,
> And juſtly pays whatever is due.
> Now plainly, not to mince the matter,
> No Toll he pays, but with a Halter.

On the Hay was written :

> The Time is approaching, if not already come,
> That all Britiſh Subjects may freely paſs on ;

And not on pretence becaufe it's Bartholomew Fair,
Make you pay for your paffage with all you bring near.
When once it is try'd, ever after depend on,
Will incur the fame fate as on Finchley Common.
Give Cæfar his due, when by law 'tis demanded,
And thofe that deferve, with this Halter be hanged.

To complete the ftory of this civic patriot and poet, I have only to add that on the 9th of Auguft, 1758, at the Election of Sheriffs, Richard Holland, Efq., Leather Seller in Newgate Street, was propofed, but pleaded incapacity on account of his advanced age. He was then 69 years old, and in his addrefs to the livery fet forth that " he had been always a zealous afferter of the rights and privileges of the Corporation, and had not been fparing of either time or money on that account." He died in 1760, worth a quarter of a million, and left 5000*l.* to the perfon by whom he was firft placed out in the world.

It was a part of the Mayor's duty when he proclaimed the Fair, to open formally the Court of Piepowder, which was a part of the Fair to the end. Its efficiency was increafed by the Act, 19 Geo. III., cap. 70, which fecured that againft the decifions of the Piepowder Courts a writ of error might lie in the nature of an appeal to the Courts of Weftminfter, and that fuch Courts fhould have the right to iffue writs of execution, in aid of their procefs after judgment, where the perfon or effects of the defendant were not in the Fair, and therefore beyond the ancient limits of their jurifdiction. The officers of the Piepowder Court were—until fome years before the clofe of the feventeenth century, but never later—an Affociate, who was the Common Serjeant

or one of the Attorneys of the Mayor's or Sheriff's
Court; ſix Serjeants at Mace (two for the Mayor,
two for the Poultry, and two for the Giltſpur Street
Compters); and in later days, a Conſtable appointed by
the ſteward of Lord Kenſington to attend on his behalf.
Its jury was termed "the Homage."

In the year 1804, a newſpaper reports an action
brought in the Fair, before the Court of Piepowder on
the 5th of September, by a fire-eater againſt one of the
ſpectators of his tricks, who had half ſuffocated him by
ſuddenly clapping a bundle of lighted matches under his
noſe. The defendant was fined a guinea by the Homage,
and the Steward gave charge to the conſtables to turn the
man out of the Fair if he appeared in it again. The appearance of the Court of Piepowder is repreſented in the
ſubjoined picture. The caſe before the Court is a diſpute
between ſeveral members of a Grand Theatrical Booth.

The degeneration of thefe booths is forcibly fhown in another fketch which difplays Proteus and his Brother Actors taking refrefhment during the fhort interval between the performances at Bartholomew Fair.

After the Mayor had made proclamation of the Fair and opened the Piepowder Court, it was ufual for him to ftation at the Ram Inn one of the City Marfhals and a ftrong body of Conftables to keep the peace. The City Marfhal, when the Fair was over, gathered from the fhowmen fees for his fervices in this refpect, varying from one guinea to three from each proprietor.

His fervices, however, were not in the higheft degree valuable. The conftables of old had never dared to cope with Lady Holland's Mob. And yet upon the eftablifhment of a good fyftem of City Police, it was fuppreffed at will, and fo came to its end before the Fair of which it had fo long remained a formidable feature. This Mob made, with an orderly and folemn form of words, its premature and illegal proclamation. This was the form of it :

" The Form of the Proclamation for Proclaiming *The Fair of Saint Bartholomew :* at 12 o'clock of the Night Previous to the Day on which it is Proclaimed By the Lord Mayor of London.

O yez ! O yez ! O yez ! All manner of perſons may take notice, that in the Cloſe of Saint Bartholomew the Great and Weſt Smithfield, London, and the ſtreets, lanes, and places adjoining, is now to be held a Fair for this day and the two days following, to which all people may freely reſort and buy and ſell according to the Liberties and Privileges of the ſaid Fair, and may depart without diſturbance, paying their duties. And all perſons are ſtrictly charged and commanded in His Majeſty's name, to keep the peace, and to do nothing in the diſturbance of the ſaid Fair, as they will anſwer the contrary at their peril, and that there be no manner of arreſt or arreſts, but by ſuch officers as are appointed : And if any perſon be aggrieved, let them repair to the Court of Pie-Powder, where they will have ſpeedy relief, according to Juſtice and Equity.

GOD SAVE THE KING."

The Mob proceeded then to break the peace. In the year 1735, three armed horſemen met the proclaimers at night, in Long Lane. "Smugglers ! Smugglers ! " was the cry. The Horſemen turned and fled ; the Mob following in a wild hunt through the ſtreets, and therein accounting itſelf faithful ſervant of the law. But its ordinary character is not ill repreſented by the record of its behaviour in 1802, when its members abuſed, knocked down, or robbed, almoſt every perſon they met ; knocked down a carpenter who came to his door with a light ; ſnatched a watch from a tradeſman who was at his own door, and beat him ſeriouſly with bludgeons upon his endeavouring to ſeize the thief. Thoſe who came with lights to their windows were aſſailed with volleys of ftones, and " it was impoffible for the watchmen " to fecure even one offender.

The courfe of this narrative again follows the order of the years.

In 1750, Alderman Blackford, being Mayor, proclaimed in the middle of July his determination to reduce the Fair to its original three days, and to ufe the powers of the Licenfing Act (10 Geo. II.) for the more effectual punifhment of rogues and vagabonds. He acted upon the reprefentation of more than a hundred of the chief graziers, falefmen, and inhabitants of Smithfield, who complained that the "infolent violation of the law " by the fair people, not only encouraged profligacy, but alfo obftructed bufinefs for fix weeks ; the time occupied in putting up and taking down the booths being a time alfo of great hindrance to the ufual Smithfield marketing and trading. The Mayor and Aldermen refolved that this fhould be fuppreffed ; and from this year the real fuppreffion of the Fair as a fourteen day riot, may be dated.

In the fame year, there was at No. 20, Hofier Lane, during the time of the Fair, " the Wonderful and Aftonifhing Arabian Poney," who could count the fpots on cards, and tell the time to a minute by the watch of any vifitor. He could find out particular perfons, and do other clever things before an audience that had paid for admiffion fixpences and threepences.

In 1752, Mr. Birch, Deputy Marfhal, died of a beating received in the Fair, and a detected pickpocket was very roughly treated. Evans, a rope-dancer, fell from a wire in the George Yard, and broke his thigh.

In that year there was " At the Greyhound in Weſt Smithfield, the famous ITALIAN FEMALE SAMSON, who has been applauded in Courts of Europe and in England at laſt Briſtol Fair. Walks barefoot on a bar of red-hot Iron. A block of marble, 2 or 3 thouſand weight, on her perſon, ſhe will throw to a diſtance of 6 feet, without uſing her hands. She puts her head on one chair, and feet on another, and bears ſix large men from her ſtomach to her inſtep. Performs from 9 a.m. to 10 p.m. Pit, 1s. Gallery, 6d."

In 1752, occurred an event that worked ſtrongly in aid of the Licenſing Act to ſecure permanence to the reſtriction of time for the Fair. The alteration of the Calendar transformed in that year the third of September into the fourteenth, to the conſternation of the million who thought themſelves defrauded of ſo many days' work and income, and ſhouted " Give us back our Eleven Days!" Old Bartholomew's Day thus ſtood at a new date in the Calendar; and in the following year, 1753, the Fair that was aſſociated with it, alſo paſſing out of the Month of Auguſt, was proclaimed—then and from that time forward—on the third of September. From the third of September onward a fourteen day Fair would have carried Smithfield Revels to an unaccuſtomed date. Its firſt days had been effectually ſevered from it, but uſe and habit were againſt addition to its laſt days of a period with which it ſeemed at no time to have been aſſociated. A rough inſtinct againſt innovation came, therefore, in aid of the endeavours of the London Corporation.

The " Ups and Downs " in the Fair broke down in

1754, but none of the perfons who fell with them were ferioufly hurt. The Mob feized and burnt them, and to make the better bonfire, burnt alfo the chairs, tables, and other properties of the black-pudding fellers.

In the year following, four or five boys from Bridewell efcaped into the Fair. In a fubfequent year, for fuch a caufe, a crowd of people out of Smithfield, mobbed the gates of Bridewell, and knocked down officers of the place who came out to fpeak to them.

In 1758, we find a writer in the *Chronicle*, complaining of the conduct of the rabble at Bartholomew Fair, which bawled " King George for Ever ! " while knocking down every perfon who came in their way, and behaving otherwife in an outrageous manner. A fad little fragment from the life of the Fair in the following year, further illuftrates the dark fide of its character. A woman with a child in her arms went into a public-houfe there, and called for a pint of beer. About the payment for this there enfued a quarrel, and the drawer, ftriking at the woman, ftruck the child and killed it on the fpot.

On the third of December, in the year 1760, the London Court of Common Council referred it to its City Land's Committee to confider the Tenures of the City Fairs, with a view to their abolition. The fubject was then carefully difcuffed, and a final report fent in, with the opinions of counfel, upon which the Court came to a Refolution, that our Lady Fair at Southwark, over which they had the fole control, fhould be thenceforward abolifhed; but that, becaufe of the intereft of Lord Kenfington in Bartholomew Fair, that was a nuiſance which they could endeavour only by a firm practice of reſtriction to abate.

In 1760, George the Third came to the throne, and in the year following, Shuter preſented at his booth in the Fair, the *Triumph of Hymen*, a Maſque, with the landing of the Queen. (It was printed in Wignell's Poems, 1762.)

The Court of Common Council recommended, in the Mayoralty of Sir Samuel Fludyer (1762), that plays ſhould be interdicted at the Fair; and at the legal cloſe of the Fair time, the Mayor ſent conſtables to prevent its unlawful continuance. There can be no doubt whatever, that in all this conteſt with the people of the Fair, the London Corporation fought the battle of good order, and deſerved well of the citizens; but, as regards the players, certainly the battle was at times fought with ungenerous ſeverity. Sometimes, as in this year, the announcement that there were to be no plays, was not made until after poor men, who were ſtruggling for a livelihood, had incurred expenſe in the erection of ſtages which they ſuddenly were ordered not to uſe. A comedian in 1762, had paid to an innkeeper, forty pounds for the right to erect a booth upon his ground, and had begun to build. But when the interdict appeared, the publican retained the money and diſpute aroſe. It was decided that the money paid by him to the innkeeper, ſhould be returned to the comedian, and that the comedian was to pay for the booth he had begun. Theſe meaſures alſo preſſed ſeverely againſt innkeepers, in whoſe rents Bartholomew Fair perquiſites had been conſidered by the landlord.

The following was, in the year 1762,

A Description of Bartholomew Fair in London. By George Alexander Stevens:

While gentlefolks ſtrut in their ſilver and ſatins,
We poor folks are tramping in ſtraw hat and pattens;
Yet as merrily old Engliſh ballads can ſing-o,
As they at their opperores outlandiſh ling-o;
Calling out bravo, ankcoro, and caro,
Tho'f I will ſing nothing but Bartlemew fair-o.

Here was, firſt of all, crowds againſt other crowds driving,
Like wind and tide meeting, each contrary ſtriving;
Shrill fiddling, ſharp fighting, and ſhouting and ſhrieking,
Fifes, trumpets, drums, bagpipes, and barrow girls ſqueaking,
Come my rare round and ſound, here's choice of fine ware-o;
Though all was not ſound ſold at Bartlemew fair-o.

There was drolls, hornpipe dancing, and ſhowing of poſtures,
With frying blackpuddings; and op'ning of oyſters;
With ſalt-boxes ſolos, and gallery folks ſquawling;
The taphouſe gueſts roaring, and mouthpieces bawling,
Pimps, pawnbrokers, ſtrollers, fat landladies, ſailors,
Bawds, bailiffs, jilts, jockies, thieves, tumblers, and taylors.

Here's Punch's whole play of the gun-powder plot, Sir,
With beaſts all alive, and peaſe-porridge all hot, Sir;
Fine ſauſages fry'd, and the black on the wire,
The whole court of France, and nice pig at the fire.
Here's the up and downs; who'll take a ſeat in the chair-o?
Tho' there's more up and downs than at Bartlemew fair-o.

Here's Whittington's cat, and the tall dromedary,
The chaiſe without horſes, and queen of Hungary:
Here's the merry-go-rounds, come who rides, come who rides, Sir?
Wine, beer, ale and cakes, fire-eating beſides, Sir;
The fam'd learn'd dog that can tell all his letters,
And ſome men, as ſcholars, are not much his betters.

The world's a wide fair, where we ramble 'mong gay things:
Our parſons, like children, are tempted by play-things;

By found and by ſhow, by traſh and by trumpery,
The fal-lals of faſhion and Frenchify'd frumpery.
What is life but a droll, rather wretched than rare-o ?
And thus ends the ballad of Bartlemew fair-o.

In 1769, not only were plays and puppet-ſhows prohibited, but feventy-two officers were appointed to prevent all gambling within the Fair, and to fee all places of refort in it clear by eleven o'clock at night.

At this period of the Fair's hiſtory, the great Wild Beaſt Show in the Fair was Pidcock's, confiſting of animals brought from the Menagerie in Exeter Change. Pidcock, whofe charge for admiſſion was a ſhilling, afterwards gave up attending, and to his place of honour there fucceeded a Wild Beaſt Showman named Polito. Miles was another chief of a menagerie. There was a fine collection of ſtuffed birds and beaſts exhibited between the years 1779 and 1782, by " the ingenious Mr. Hall of the City Road, Iſlington."

In 1775, an account of profits of the Mayoralty, delivered to Alderman Wither on his taking office, ſhows that the profits of the Fair no longer formed an element in the Chief Magiſtrate's official income. In lieu of it there are fet down, " two Freedoms yearly," value twenty-five pounds each. In that year a Turkiſh artiſt danced on a rope thirty-eight feet high above the ground.

Alderman Bull, Mayor in 1776, who was re-elected two years afterwards, was a tea-dealer in Leadenhall Street, and a leading man among City Diſſenters, attached warmly to Wilkes and Liberty. As he refufed to permit the erection of booths for ſhows during his Mayoralty, the mob broke the windows of almoſt every inhabitant of Smithfield.   Alderman Sawbridge alfo, when Mayor, fuppreffed the fhows, and riot was the confequence.

In 1778, a foreigner exhibited at Bartholomew Fair, curious ferpents from the Eaft, who danced on filk ropes to the found of mufic.

Flockton, who was nearly throughout the laft half of the eighteenth century one of the great fhowmen of Bartholomew Fair, was at this time in his meridian fplendour.   He was the Prince of Puppet-fhowmen, and his puppets were called the Italian Fantoccini.   He had alfo at one time a fine Newfoundland, whom he taught to fight with and overcome the Devil.   This is the form of one of his ftate-papers, iffued in 1789.

" MR. FLOCKTON's Moft Grand and Unparallelled Exhibition.   Confifting firft, in the difplay of the Original and Univerfally admired ITALIAN FANTOC-CINI, exhibited in the fame Skilful and Wonderful Manner, as well as Striking Imitations of Living Performers, as reprefented and exhibited before the Royal Family, and the moft illuftrious Characters in this Kingdom.   MR. FLOCKTON will difplay his inimi-table DEXTERITY OF HAND, Different from all pre-tenders to the faid Art.   To which will be perform'd an ingenious and Spirited Opera called The PADLOCK " . . . . principal vocal performers, Signor Giovanni Orfi and Signora Vidina.   " The whole to conclude with his grand and inimitable MUSICAL CLOCK, at firft view, a curious organ, exhibited three times before their Majefties."   In this clock there were nine hundred figures at work upon a variety of trades.   His prices were for the pit 1*s.*, and for the gallery 6*d.*

" The celebrated Mr. Flockton, of facetious memory," died at Camberwell upon the 12th of April in the year 1794. He had made a little fortune of five thouſand pounds. His Company was his family ; and for diviſion among the members of it, he was generous enough to bequeath the chief part of the money they had helped him to acquire. It is well to think of the relations of good fellowſhip that muſt have been maintained among theſe booth companions.

The fame of Flockton's Puppet-ſhow ſuggeſted, in 1790, the publication of a ſixpenny mechanical ſheet of pictures opening and ſhutting to diſplay a whole performance. This is the outſide ſketch of Punch's Puppet-ſhow.

The next is a ſcene inſide—on the old ſtory of " Pull devil, pull baker," which ſhows that not only did Flockton retain the traditions of the puppet-ſhow, but

that he retained alfo fome of the earlieft traditions of
the Englifh ftage.   The picture carries our thoughts
back to one of the firft chapters of thefe Memoirs.

In 1792, a Puppet Showman, venturing to revive
in another form an ancient humour of the Fair, turned
fatirift upon the Camp at Bagfhot, with wooden puppets
which he gave out as "equal if not fuperior" to the
originals.   He carved one of his puppets into a likenefs
of the Chancellor of the Exchequer, attacked Henry
Dundas, and introduced a figure drefled in black,
labelled in brafs upon the forehead, "Dirty work done
at a moment's warning by the Rofe of the Treafury."

Treaſury Servants-of-all-Work followed, with a Toad upon their banner.

In 1797, Jobſon and other puppet-ſhowmen were proſecuted for having made their puppets talk, and do the buſineſs of players in ſpite of the Licenſing Act.

The enormous ſale of pig in Bartholomew Fair came to an end in the middle of the laſt century, and its place was taken by beef ſauſage. There was a ſtrong gale from the S.S.W. when the Fair opened in 1778, and a contemporary newſpaper reporter found it adviſable to "ſteer half a point to windward of the ſauſage ſtalls." In that year the Duke and Ducheſs of Glouceſter rode through the Fair, by Flockton's, Jobſon's Grand Medley, Ives's, Baſil's, Clarkſon's, and the other booths, entering at Giltſpur Street, and paſſing out through Cow Lane into Holborn. They paſſed the eſtabliſhment of Mr. Lane, his Majeſty's Conjuror,

who repreſented himſelf thus upon his handbills, and by that of Mr. Robinſon, Conjurer to the Queen.

Some of Mr. Lane's manifeftoes headed by the preceding picture were in verfe. The painter and the poet joined to do him honour; the painter as above, the poet in this happy vein.

> It will make you to laugh, it will drive away gloom,
> To fee how the egg it will dance round the room;
> And from another egg a bird there will fly,
> Which makes the company all for to cry,
> O rare Lane, Cockalorum for Lane, well done Lane,
>   You are the Man.

He ended his entertainment with "the two Mifs Lane's Surprifing Pofturing, and a Hornpipe by Mifs Ann Lane."

Many perfons, that year, were impreffed in the Fair, and among the reft a Merry Andrew, of whom a newfpaper wit afked how it could be conceived that he had no vifible way of living, when he was afking all the Fair to look at him.

In 1779, the Britifh Prefs paid homage to the Genius of Smithfield, ftill in the midft of the Fair, and faid, "Of all the curiofities that are now to be feen at Bartholomew Fair, it is a furprifing large Hog, who receives the greateft applaufe. This amazing animal is near fourteen feet long, and when he rifes from the ground for the fpectators to fee him, he roars in fuch a manner that his voice feems to mix, as it were, with the earth." He is an Earth fpirit of courfe. Still, a profound filence about his age.

The American War came to an end in the year 1783, and the Peace of Paris was figned at Bartholomew Fair time. In the Fair, that year, this little tract was diſtributed among the great number of ſailors who attended it.

LARGE SIEVES AND PLAIN TRUTHS.

Attend you Seamen all unto the Lines I have here penn'd ; the Truth doth ſpeak. You are all my Countrymen; and if you are not, I am yours. My Tongue and my Heart, and my Pen goes now to ſpeak my Mind ; for we poor Sailors are compelled to ſpeak the Truth, for now the War is over, we poor Sailors, who it pleaſed God to let live, where many of us was born and brought up ; who was taken away from our Wives and Children, from our Fathers and Mothers, Siſters and Brothers, Trades and Callings, full ſore againſt our Will, to ſerve our King and Country, to face our Enemies where Balls do wilfully fly, to ſpill our Blood, to receive our Wounds, and leave our Limbs. I'll tell you how we are rewarded for all our pains, to go in the ſtreets and beg, thieve, or ſtarve and be Hanged for what they care what become of us. We once fought like Men, the ſame as we go unregarded, and die like Dogs ; we who was prized once, are now deſpiſed, and become the Objeċts of hatred. I will only aſk you my countrymen, what muſt we do, to ſee my poor children cry for bread, I turn into the ſtreets publickly to declare it.

Dare I to ſpeak my mind,—I ſay we have been uſed cruel after all our ſervice ; can any one of you ſay we are well uſed after all our ſervice ; I muſt ſay, we leave it to any man to judge how hard we have fought for our Country and the Gold, and cannot get it now, for the War is over. For to ſee the Numbers of poor Seamen ſwarm about the Navy Office to demand their Wages and Prize Money ; it would grieve you to ſee the French Horn, Lamb, the Globe, the Ship, the White Horſe, the Cheſhire Cheeſe, crowded with Wives and Widows, Fathers and Mothers, Siſters and Brothers, how they come for it, and return as they come.

Suppoſe a War breaks out with England again, what will we do to get Men ; for my part I do not know. I do pray to God to bleſs our good and gracious King, to preſerve him and his Crown and his Land, all gallant officers, ſuch as Hood and Elliot. Now I conclude in hopes that ſome of you will take compaſſion on us poor Sailors, who fought for the honour of the Nation, its Rights to maintain. My prayers to God that we may be paid with all ſpeed, ſo farewell my countrymen.

The above is printed for the benefit of Anthony Jackſon, late Mariner of the Warwick of 50 guns, commanded by Robert Clayton, Eſq. ; the above Seaman is ſtab'd in his left Breaſt with a Bayonet, ſhot in his right arm, and wounded in his head, having a wife and one child, humbly hopes for generoſity.

Here is a copy of a pen-and-ink fketch of a flower of the Fair, taken in the year 1787. It is Kelham

Whitelamb, born at Wifbeach, age twenty-two, height (?) inches.

This is the famous Unicorn Ram, fhown at Bartholomew Fair, in the year 1790.

Of the laft of the true Comedians in Smithfield, the memory furvived in 1790, when the Fair alfo paid its refpects to the French Revolution. There was

entertainment "during the Short Time of St. Bartholomew Fair, Smithfield. At the Original Theatre (Late the celebrated YATES and SHUTER, of facetious Memory), Up the *Greyhound* Inn Yard, the only real and commodious place for Theatrical Performances. The Performers ſelected from the moſt diſtinguiſhed Theatres in England, Scotland, &c. The Repreſentation conſiſts of an entirely New Piece, called, The Spaniard Well Drub'd, or the Britiſh Tar Victorious . . . . The Piece concludes with a GRAND PROCESSION of the King, French Heroes, Guards, Municipal Troops, &c., to the Champ de Mars, to ſwear to the Revolution Laws, as eſtabliſhed by the *Magnificent National Aſſembly*, on the 14th of July, 1790. Hornpipe dancing by the renound JACK BOWLING," and, among other things, "Mr. Swords will deliver his Olio of wit, whim, and fancy, in Song, Speech, and Grimace." Box and Pit, 1*s.* Gallery, 6*d.*

This is the famous Ram with Six Legs, ſhown at Bartholomew Fair, in the year 1790.

The Fair had given birth to ſo many public-houſes in the pariſhes of St. Bartholomew the Great, that on the 30th of March, 1791, the Court of Aldermen agreed to fuggeft to the General and Quarter Seffions, to receive no recommendation for licences in that parifh which was not figned by the Alderman either of Alderfgate, or Farringdon Without.

In 1792, with the preamble that the Author of Nature is wonderful even in the LEAST of His Works, it was announced that a Caravan in Bartholomew Fair contained MR. THOMAS ALLEN, the moft furprifing SMALL MAN ever before the Public. He had at the Lyceum in the Strand excited in the breafts of the Dukes of York and Clarence, fenfations of wonder and delight.

Alfo MISS MORGAN, the Celebrated WINDSOR FAIRY, known in *London* and *Windfor* by the Addition of LADY MORGAN, *a Title which His Majefty was pleafed to confer on her.*

This unparallelled Woman is in the 35th year of her age, and only 18 pounds weight. Her form affords a pleafing furprife, and her admirable fymmetry engages attention. She was introduced to Their MAJESTIES at the *Queen's Lodge, Windfor,* on Saturday the 4th of Auguft, 1781, by the recommendation of the late Dr. *Hunter ;* when they were pleafed to pronounce her the fineft Difplay of Human Nature in *miniature* they ever faw.—But we fhall fay no more of thefe great Wonders of Nature : let thofe who honour them with their vifits, judge for themfelves.

> Let others boaft of ftature, or of birth,
> This Glorious Truth fhall fill our fouls with mirth :
> " That we now are, and hope, for years, to fing
> The SMALLEST fubjects of the GREATEST King !"

☞ Admittance to Ladies and Gentlemen, 1*s.*—Children, Half Price.

§ In this and many other parts of the Kingdom, it is too common to fhow deformed perfons, with various arts and deceptions, under denominations of perfons in miniature, to impofe on the public.

This Little Couple are, beyond contradiction, the moft wonderful difplay of nature ever held out to the admiration of mankind.

N.B. The above Lady's mother is with her, and will attend at any Lady or Gentleman's houfe, if required.

As another illuftration of the literary powers of the

ſhowmen's author at the cloſe of the eighteenth century, I quote the deſcription of a Lion, from a handbill iſſued in the Fair in 1794.

The Noble Lion and Lioneſs (from the Tower of London),

Whoſe like Earth bears not on her ſpacious Face
Alone of Nature ſtands the wond'rous Race.

Theſe moſt magnanimous Animals need no other Recommendation than to behold them. The Lion is univerſally allowed to be the King of all the Brute Creation, whoſe majeſtic Looks, and Voice like Thunder, ſtrikes Terror to the whole kingdom of Quadrupeds; yet theſe tremendous Beaſts are ſo Tame, by being brought up from a few days old by ſuckling of Goats inſtead of their Dam, that the moſt Timorous may approach them with the greateſt ſafety.

Flockton's ſucceſſors, when he had retired on his ſmall fortune, were "the Widow Flint and Gyngell, at Flockton's original Theatre up the Greyhound Yard, Smithfield." They preſented in one year Mr. Gyngell's ſleight of hand and muſical glaſſes, Mrs. Gyngell's ſinging with Fantoccini, from Sadler's Wells, and (late Flockton's) the Grand Muſical Clock, with five hundred (Flockton had advertiſed nine hundred) "figures at work in different trades and callings."

In 1798, a pickpocket, caught in the Fair, proteſted to the City Marſhal that he got a very honeſt living by buying and ſelling bad ſhillings. There were in the Fair that year according to a newſpaper wit, "Some of the firſt actors, the firſt ſingers, the firſt dancers, and the firſt horſemen in the whole world; ghoſts, ſpectres, bluebeards, and bleeding nuns, deſcending amidſt flaſhes of roſin, and aſcending amidſt clouds of tobacco."

In a coloured picture of Bartholomew Fair, by

Rowlandſon, publiſhed in 1799, we ſee ſome things
that hitherto we have but talked about. Here is part
of the line of ſhows drawn up againſt the pavement,

with their backs to the backs of the gingerbread ſtalls
that faced the houſes, and their fronts to the free area
of Smithfield. The chaiſe without horſes introduced
into the picture, is, outſide, a place of frolic and a poſt
of obſervation ; inſide, a reception room.

And here is a corner of a booth, ſhowing how folks before the ſcenes enjoy their entrances and exits.

The author of theſe ſketches is Thomas Rowlandſon, a famous political and ſocial caricaturiſt, beſt known as the illuſtrator of Dr. Syntax's Tour in Search of the Picturefque. He died in the year 1827, at the age of ſeventy-one. Among his works are two pictures of Bartholomew Fair, which, as the reader will perceive, admit of being ſeparated into groups; for while, in each cafe, the whole picture is effective, every group in it is a perfect little ſtudy of ſome inci-

dent or feature of the ſcene. One of the two pictures is founded on a drawing by another hand.

H H

The kind of audience obtained by the actors, is expressed in other ways than by the bill at the booth

door, announcing the " Demand of Fashion " for " Red Devils." The Theatrical Booth may possibly be the next pleasure sought by the folks whom we here see luxuriating in the pleasures of the swing, and to whom there is a hot pie readily accessible when they touch earth again.

Mr. Bull's servant and his lantern, when he chooses to retire betimes through the dim throng, with the young family that he has been amusing, seem to be hardly brilliant enough to make him independent of the link-boys, who are anxious that his lady ſhall not ſtep into a puddle.

But there is firelight enough to ſhow him as he paſſes out the gamblers and the gluttons in the ſauſage market—

and he needs muſt meet the revellers who, when the quiet people go, begin the loudeſt frolic of the Fair.

The picture on page 465, contains a libel on Mifs
Biffin, who was a perfon really capable of fhowing talent
as a miniature painter, without hands or arms.   She was
found in the Fair, and affifted by the Earl of Morton,
who fat for his likenefs to her, always taking the un-
finifhed picture away with him when he left, that he
might prove it to be all the work of her own fhoulder.
When it was done he laid it before George the Third,
in the year 1808 ; obtained the King's favour for Mifs
Biffin ; and caufed her to receive, at his own expenfe,

further inftruction in her art from Mr. Craig.   For
the laft twenty years of his life he maintained a corre-
fpondence with her ; and after having enjoyed favour
from two King Georges, fhe received from William
the Fourth a fmall penfion, with which, at the Earl's
requeft, fhe retired from a life among caravans.   But

fourteen years later, having been married in the interval, ſhe found it neceſſary to reſume, as Mrs. Wright late Miſs Biffin, her buſineſs as a ſkilful miniature painter, in one or two of our chief provincial Towns. Her picture is here given from a lithograph, publiſhed in 1817, before her complete retirement from the Fairs.

A Biffin of the Nurſery was Maſter Vine, who, by the annexed picture, is ſhown to have been not an armleſs miniature painter, but a producer of ineſtimable pieces of another ſort. It was his peculiar merit to draw landſcapes in pencil with the ſhrunken, misformed ſtump that repreſented hand and arm.

In 1803, there was to be ſeen at Bartholomew Fair, in a commodious caravan, " A Surpriſing large Fiſh, THE NONDESCRIPT. This ſurpriſing Inhabitant of the Watery Kingdom, was drawn on the ſhore by 7 horſes, and about 100 men. She meaſured 25 Feet in length, and about 18 in circumference, and had in her belly, when found, one thouſand ſeven hundred mackerel." With her were ſhown two amazing calves, one with a compound of heads, the other with a compound of bodies.

At the beginning of the nineteenth century, all that was vile in London held its revel at the expenſe of

much that was refpectable.   In 1801, a mob of thieves
and pickpockets furrounded helplefs women in exulting
crowds, tearing their clothes from their backs.   In
1802, Lady Holland's Mob, as has been faid before,
committed robberies, beat paffengers with bludgeons,
and fired volleys of ftones at thofe perfons who, difturbed in their fleep, came with lights to the windows.

A fhow of the Fairs at this time, was " the Beautiful
Albinefs," whofe portrait was carefully engraved ; but

with whofe beauty a Mob at Glafgow Fair had been
fo little affected, that they turned her out of her booth,
as they turned out alfo a fhow full of wild beafts.

In 1807, the King's Deputy Trumpeter having
found great difficulty in collecting his fees, obtained
on his own behalf a proclamation from the Lord Cham-

berlain's office; but a lady, who was acting Belvidera, in *Venice Preſerved*, and occaſionally came out to blow a trumpet, being applied to by the King's Deputy Trumpeter's collector, knocked him down with her trumpet, and was compelled by the officers who came up, to make him compenſation.

Again comes a reminder of the vice that the Fair foſtered. Among offenders in this year, was a gang of children, under a boy, aged fifteen, called Captain Stirrick, who diſpoſed of the plunder of the band through a ſauſage man, named William Perfect. The gang was brought to juſtice at Guildhall, by help of a king's evidence, aged 10; and theſe were found to be its members: 1. Ned Stirrick, Captain, about 15 years of age, dreſſed in a thickſet jacket and coarſe canvas trouſers. 2. Caroline Cottenham, a girl of about 13 years of age; wore a grey cloth ſpencer, and coarſe old cotton gown, and barefooted. 3. Billy Long, about 12 years old; ragged and bare legged. 4. Maria Taylor, a beggar-girl, 11 years old. 5. Peg Green, a match-girl, 11 years old. 6. Joe Coverley, a boy about 10 years old. 7. Charles Clark, ditto, ditto. 8. Thomas Grey, aged 12. 9. Jack Wilkes, aged 11. 10. A girl about 10 years old; a ballad-ſinger. 11. A boy, Jones. 12. Scott, a beggar-boy. 13. Jem Barnes, a plaiſterer's boy, about 13 years old. 14. Donougho, aged about 12; a naked, ſickly-looking boy. Truly a melancholy group of children at the Fair; and they ſtole toys, ſays the record, but to barter, not to play with !

The Playbills of Richardſon's Theatre, the Chief

Dramatic Booth in the laſt days of which we are now ſpeaking, ſhow how completely the amuſements of the Fair were planned to the taſte of the moſt uncultivated playgoers. This is one of them :

A CHANGE *of Performances each Day,*
RICHARDSON'S THEATRE.

MR. RICHARDSON has the honour to inform the Public, that for the extraordinary Patronage he has experienced, it has been his great objeƈt to contribute to the convenience and gratification of his audience. Mr. R. has a ſplendid colleƈtion of Scenery, unrivalled in any Theatre ; and, as they are painted and deſigned by the firſt Artiſts in England, he hopes with ſuch Decorations, and a Change of Performances each day, the Public will continue him that Patronage it has been his greateſt pride to deſerve.

The Entertainments to commence with a New Melo-Dramatic Romance, with New Scenery, Dreſſes, Decorations, &c., by the moſt eminent Artiſts, called, The

MONK AND MURDERER !
Or, The Skeleton Speƈtre.

Baron Montaldi . . . . . Mr. H. CAREY.
Deſperado (his Confidant) . Mr. REED
Nicolina (Steward of the Caſtle) . . Mr. WILMOT.
Edmund (Page to Edgar) . Mr. ODEY.
St. Julian of France . . . .⎫⎧Mr. DENNEY.
Harold, the Dane . . .⎬Knights⎨Mr. WATERS.
Mohammed, the Perſian . . .⎭⎩Mr. HUNTER.
Edgar (an Engliſh Knight) . Mr. SEYMOUR.
Romaldo (the Myſterious Monk) . . Mr. BROWN.
Emilina (Daughter to the Baron) Mrs. H. CAREY.
Lauretta (her Confidante) Mrs. WILMOT.

A ſhort Sketch of the Scenery : 1. A Gothic Hall in Montaldi's Caſtle.—2. View of the Rocks of Calabria, with the appearance of the Myſterious Monk.— 3. Myſterious Foreſt.—4. A ruſtic Bridge, with diſtant View of the Caſtle : a Grand Proceſſion of Knights, &c.—5. Gothic Chamber.—6. Interior of the Caſtle, decorated with Banners, Trophies, &c., and a Grand Combat with Shield and Battle-Axe.

The Piece terminated with the fall of the Murderers, the aſcenſion of the Spectre Monk, and the predicted union of the Engliſh Knight and Emilina.

The whole to conclude with an entire New Pantomime, called

MIRTH AND MAGIC!

Or, a Trip to Gibraltar.

Harlequin, Mr. RILEY.—Panteloon, Mr. GREEN.
Lover, Mr. SMITH.
Sailor, with the Song of " The Britiſh Flag," Mr. RAYMOND.
Market Woman, Mr. WILMOT. — Countryman, Mr. WATERS.
Landlord, Mr. SEWELL.
Clown, Mr. BERGEMAN.—Columbine, Mrs. WILMOT.

The whole to conclude with the Grand Panorama View of

THE ROCK OF GIBRALTAR,

PAINTED BY THE FIRST ARTIST.

Boxes 2s., Pit 1s., Gallery 6d.

Mrs. Carey's name will be obſerved in this bill. I ſhall form no theory upon a very doubtful queſtion, but record ſimply that if Ann Carey, ſaid to have been one of Richardſon's actreſſes and an itinerant flower-woman, who figures as the aſſumed mother in the early hiſtory of Edmund Kean, be the ſame Mrs. H. Carey here mentioned, and the only Mrs. Carey I have found in a conſiderable file of Richardſon's announcements, then it is worth obſerving that there was a Mr. H. Carey, who for ſome time played firſt male parts in the ſame caſt with her, and that ſhe appears to have been one of the chief ladies, if not the chief, who was permanently attached to Richardſon's Company. Her portrait, as here copied, was engraved in a fmall medallion with fome care. The fingular head-drefs reprefented in it is

not ftage coftume, but a form of lady's bonnet fafhionable when the fketch was made.

Richardfon fometimes had the only Theatrical Booth in the Fair, but his rival ufually was Scowton. Sometimes Richardfon and Scowton worked as partners. Mr. Scowton in the opening to his Farewell Bill

pleafantly combines his gratitude to his patrons with a defire to recommend " the whole of his extenfive concern " to anybody who defires to fpend his latter days in Comfortable Retirement.

SCOWTON'S THEATRE.

Mr. Scowton, deeply imprefled with heart-felt Gratitude for the liberal Patronage and Support which he has for a feries of Years experienced from his Friends and a generous Public, and which will enable him to fpend his future Days in comfortable Retirement: begs leave to announce that the whole of his Extenfive Concern, is to be difpofed of by Private Contract; and therefore, at the fame time, as he takes leave, requefts them to believe that the Memory of their favours and indulgence will never be eradicated from his Memory. For this Day only. Will be performed a new grand Dramatic Romance, called THE TREACHEROUS FRIEND, or *Innocence Protected.*

Alphonfus, Mr. Scowton, &c. With a Pantomime.

Boxes 2*s.*, Pit 1*s.*, Gallery 6*d.*

A famous perfon in the Fair, before and after the year 1814, was the Fireproof Lady, Madam Giradelli. This lady put melted lead into her mouth, and fpat it out marked with her teeth, paffed red-hot iron over her body and limbs, her tongue and her hair, thruft her arm into fire, and waſhed her hands, not only in boiling lead, but alſo in boiling oil and aquafortis.

Mr. Simon Paap, the celebrated Dutch Dwarf, 26 years of age, weighs 27 Pounds, and only 28 Inches high, had the honour of being Preſented to the Prince Regent and the whole of the Royal Family, at Carlton Houſe, May 5th, 1815. He was introduced by Mr. Daniel Gyngell to the Lord Mayor on the 1ſt of September 1815, and was exhibited in the courfe of four days in Smithfield to upwards of 20,000 Perfons.

A colleƈtor of the autographs of little men procured the following :

The fourteen day Carnival had now been effeƈtually fuppreffed, and the utmoft licence obtained by the fhowmen was the holding of Bartholomew Fair for three days, in which the day of proclamation (made at noon by the

Mayor, Sheriffs, and City Marſhals) was not counted. The Mayor, having made his proclamation, uſually returned as he came ; but John Wilkes, Eſquire, diſtinguiſhed himſelf by making the entire circuit of the booths in his State Coach.

The ground of Smithfield was entirely parcelled out in booths and ſtandings.   In the centre among the ſheep-pens, were thoſe who ſold in booths or at ſtalls oyſters and ſauſages.   Tables were ſet for company in a moſt faſcinating ſtyle, and in 1808 women invited paſſers by into the ſauſage rooms with an appeal to their patriotiſm—for the popular political feeling ſtill had its repreſentation in the Fair. " Walk into Wilkes's parlour," was their cry ; the ſauſage-rooms being in thoſe days called Wilkes's parlours.   Outſide the pens, the exhibitions were ſet in a row cloſely ſide by ſide, with their backs to the pavement and their fronts to the central ſpace of Smithfield.   There alſo was the immenſe multitude of up-and-downs and round-abouts, many of them elevated to a dangerous and painful height.   On the pavement before the houſes, fronting their cloſed doors and ſhutters, were the lines of gilt gingerbread and toy ſtalls.   The ſhow booths had, in 1808, lately become gay with unwonted decoration, and with many-coloured lamps.   Horſe-riders were favourite performers.   Aſtley, in his day, uſed to attend with his " learned horſe."   In 1808, Saunders kept the beſt of three or four horſe-riding exhibitions.   Itinerant muſicians congregated in the Fair.   There was a famous London ſtreet-band conſiſting of a double drum, a Dutch organ, a tambourine, violin, pipes, and " the new Turkiſh jingle,

ufed in the army," which ufed to play military pieces
for a long time on winter evenings before the Spring-
Gardens coffee-houfe, and oppofite Wigley's great room,
to entertain the diners. This well known ftreet orcheftra
was generally engaged by one of the chief booths in
Bartholomew Fair; but there was always too much jangle
of more difcordant inftruments, and too much bawling of
" Show them in ! Juft going to begin ! " to make their
harmonies of any confequence to the fair-goers. There
was a large caravan of well known tumblers and pofture-
men. Bear dancing, a ftreet fight, was an incident of
buftle in the outer crowd. The bear now and then
turned a good fummerfault and generally danced to the
bagpipes. His companions were fome little dogs
dreffed in red jackets, and a monkey who ufually rode
on the bear's back.

Pupils of the celebrated Fair conjuror, Mr. Lane,
practifed the fublime art of legerdemain. There were
tricks with cards, and tricks with balls, and there was
fortune-telling. Knives were run through the hand
without producing blood ; knives and forks were taken
as pills ; flames and fparks, as from a forge, were blown
out of men's mouths. The more ambitious Puppet-
fhows were in their decline, and Punch in the full tide
of his popularity rioted over their decay.

At this date there was a noted perfon in the Fair,
who walked about hatlefs, to fell flices of hot plum-
pudding, with his hair powdered and tied *en queue,* his
drefs neat and his apron fpotlefs, jefting wherever he
went, with a mighty voice in recommendation of the
pudding, which for the fake of greater oddity he fome-

times carried on a wooden platter. This was James Sharp England, the flying pie-man.

Rowlandſon, in one of the extracts I have taken from his pictures, repre-ſents a negro pieman of the ſame deſcrip-tion, who ſeems to have been England's pre-deceſſor. Other ſuch characters

of the Fair are theſe two which ſpeak for themſelves:

The blind pig-dealer's wares are made of piecruſt, and have currant eyes.

Certainly not a piecruſt pig, hardly indeed to be thought of as pork, was the learned Toby, to whom we are now brought a little prematurely by aſſociation of ideas. The genuine Toby firſt appeared in the Fair in the year 1817, and is ſaid to have been the pupil of one Maſter Nicholas Hoare. He muſt have arrived therefore at a pig's years of diſcretion, when he appeared in the year 1833, as the "Unrivalled Chineſe Swiniſh Philoſopher, TOBY THE REAL LEARNED PIG. He will ſpell, read, and caſt accounts, tell the points of the ſun's riſing and ſetting, diſcover the four grand diviſions of the Earth, kneel at command, perform blindfold with 20 handkerchiefs over his eyes, tell the hour to a minute by a watch, tell a card, and the age of any party. He is in colour the moſt beautiful of his race, in ſymmetry the moſt perfect, in temper the moſt docile. And when aſked a queſtion, he will give an Immediate Anſwer." On the faith of the handbill, here is the portrait of the moſt beautiful of pigs.

Inſolent, indeed, was the pretenſion that oppoſed againſt Toby, this counterfeit beaſt, under the name of the Amazing Pig of Knowledge. A peculiarity, however, about the Amazing Pig of Knowledge (who was to be ſeen in a commodious room at the George), which may account for his ſomewhat ſhabby appearance, is, that he knew the value of money.

He alſo could tell black from white, diſtinguiſh colours; with a ſhrewd eye count his audience; and even tell people their thoughts.   J. Fawkes, the proprietor of "this moſt amazing pig," which was to be ſeen for three-pence, ſummed up his handbill with theſe very ſuitable and lucid obſervations:

> A learned Pig in George's reign
>   To Æſop's Brutes an equal Boaſt;
> Then let Mankind again combine,
>   To render Friendſhip ſtill a Toaſt.
>
> Let Albion's Fair ſuperior ſoar,
>   To Gallic Fraud, or Gallic Art;
> Britons will e'er bow down before
>   The Virtues ſeated in the Heart.

But while the Great Hog of the Fair was thus ſubliming himſelf into pure intellect againſt the day when he was to vaniſh altogether, human life in the Fair was dropping faſt into the hog's old poſition. In September, 1815, there were heard in one morning at Guildhall, forty-five cafes of felony, mifdemeanour, and affault, committed in Bartholomew Fair. To this fact let me add the titles of a few of the plays performed at Richardfon's Great Booth. I felect fome of thofe in which Mrs. Carey was an actrefs. *The Caftles of Athlin and Dunbaine,* or *the Spectre of the North.* Glenroy, Mr. H. Carey. Julia (of the Houfe of Rofs), Mrs. H. Carey. (After this play, Mr. Carey played the Pantaloon, in a Fair verfion of Mother Goofe.) *Donald and Rofaline,* or *the Spectre of the Rocks.* Donald (rightful heir of Athlin), Mr. H. Carey. Spectre of Marian, Mrs. Carey. *Agnes of Bavaria,* or *the Spectre of the Danube* (no Mr. Carey); Agnes, Mrs. H. Carey. *The Haunted Cavern,* or *Myfterious Cheft* (no Mr. Carey); Emeline, Mrs. H. Carey. *The Hall of Death,* or *Who's the Murderer?* Cardinal Gonzaria, Mr. H. Carey. Ducheza Rofanna Vinfenza, Mrs. H. Carey.

One does not wonder that the men zealous for fouls began to flock into the Fair with pious tracts; that exhortations to difcountenance the Fair were diftributed among houfeholders in its neighbourhood; that, in one year, "Boatfwain Smith" fet up a pulpit at the end of Long Lane, over which floated a flag, with the infcription, "Bethel Union," and opened his bufinefs with a hymn, beginning—

> Hinder me not; for I 'll proceed,
> Though Earth and Hell oppofe!

Wifer men than that rude enthufiaft, longed for the releafe of London from a yearly riot of iniquity. In one year a ftrong mob of pickpockets formed wild rings about decent women who approached the Fair, and tore their garments from their backs.

There was a disfigurement upon the Fair greater than that here repreſented in the picture of " the Beautiful Spotted Negro Boy," who was to be ſeen in his travelling pavilion, and who was afterwards engaged by Mr. Richardſon to appear at his theatre, where he ſtood on the bills between the *Monk and Murderer*, or the *Skeleton Spectre*, and *Love and Liberty*, or *Harlequin in his Glory*.

The writer, in 1837, of a ſmall pamphlet called *A Poetical Deſcription of Bartholomew Fair*, by One under a Hood, a lamentable imitation of the puns of Thomas Hood without his wit, tells pleaſantly enough what, no doubt, was a real incident, and a ſtrange one :—

> At Richardſon's ſo tedious 'twas
> Before they would begin ;
> A wag propoſed the gap to ſtop,
> By giving out an *imn* !
>
> This ſtriking *im*-propriety
> Made one and all to crave it :
> It was ſo obviouſly wrong,
> They cried that's right, let's have it !

In 1825, Mr. Hone, in his Table Book, expecting the end of the Fair, carefully deſcribed it as it then was for the information of poſterity. At the ſame time

he publifhed a few interefting notes by way of con-
tribution to its early hiftory. In that year, the Fair
began on Saturday, and trading was forbidden on the
Sunday, although thoufands then vifited in its quietude
the fcene of noife and buftle. He tells us that the
largeft of the toy-ftalls had eighteen or five-and-twenty
feet of frontage ; that the fhutters of the houfes were
all up, and the doors clofed ; that faufages and oyfters,
yielding three-penny or four-penny dinners, were fold
at tables with cloths on them, in the fheep-pens ; but
that the ftalls were no longer called by fuch names as
Brighton Pavilions, or Fair Rofamond's Bowers. Among
the fhows were thefe : A peep-fhow of the Murder
of Mr. Weare, of King Solomon and the Queen of
Sheba, &c., to be feen for one penny. A penny giant.
Penny tumbling at Ball's Theatre. A Sixpenny wild
beaft fhow—Atkins's—with " that Coloffal Animal,
the wonderful performing ELEPHANT, upwards of ten
feet high ! ! Five tons weight ! ! His confumption of
Hay, Corn, Straw, Carrots, Water, &c., exceeds 800lbs.
daily." Eight muficians were outfide this booth, in
fcarlet beefeater's coats and with fkin caps, and a ften-
torian fhowman drowned the mufic with his fhouts of
" Don't be deceived. The only Lion and Tigrefs in one
den that are to be feen in the Fair, or the proprietor will
forfeit One Thoufand Guineas. Walk in ! walk in ! "

Richardfon's platform was lined with green baize,
feftooned with crimfon curtains, and lighted with fifteen
hundred variegated lamps. His moneytakers fat in
Gothic feats. He had a band of ten beefeaters, and
a parade of his dramatic force.

Samwell, a very fat man in tight ſatin jacket, led a troop of tight-rope-dancing children, and the Dancing Horſe.

Clarke, from Aſtley's, had a ſpacious platform, ten feet high, and a large booth of which the interior was lighted by gas in a ſingle hoop.

Wombwell is ſharply cenſured by Hone for having expoſed his fine Lion Nero, to be baited by dogs, at Warwick. He diſplayed a diſguſting picture of the fight outſide his ſhow. He is deſcribed in the Table Book as " underſized in mind, as well as in form, a weazen, ſharped-faced man, with a ſkin reddened by more than natural ſpirits, and he ſpeaks in a voice and language that accords with his 'feelings and pro-penſities." Of this man, who began life as a cobbler  in Monmouth Street, I find only unfavourable record. He had a yellow card, with a Tiger above his addreſs, of " Wombwell, Wild Beaſt Merchant, Commercial Road, London. All ſorts of Foreign Animals, Birds, &c., bought, ſold, or ex-changed, at the Repoſitory, or the Travelling Ména-gerie." He muſt, however, have had unuſual ability and energy in his pecu-liar way. His collection  was good. Its boaſt, in 1830, was the Elephant of Siam, a theatrical performer in the ſpectacle of the *Fire-*

fiend, wherein it uncorked bottles and decided for the Rightful Prince. On each fide of it he had in his fhow two miniature elephants the " fmalleft ever feen in Europe."

Mr. Hone faw the Mermaid, and fketches the beautiful firen, painted on the outfide canvas of the booth. But if things of the earth fallen in water fuffer "a fea-change into fomething rich and ftrange," things of the water being hauled on earth may have a land change to go through. In the cafe of a Sea Nymph this is proved to be the cafe by the annexed ftudy publifhed at the time by Mr. George Cruikfhank, of the Mermaid as exhibited infide the booth.

The kind of public to which the fights of the Fair were left, is indicated by the fact that in 1830, except that Wombwell, Atkins, and Richardfon charged 6*d*., and Morgan, a part of Wombwell's, 3*d*., all the fhows were penny fhows. Ball's Theatre; Ballard's Beafts (including a Seal in a tub); Key's Conjuror; Frafier, Conjuror; Pike; the Learned Pony; the Pig-faced Lady; the Shaved Bear, fhown in oppofition to her, and pronounced by Smithfield wit a bear-faced impofition; the Living Skeleton; the Red Barn Tragedy; the Court of Pekin; the Fat Boy and Girl; the Fire Eater; the Diorama of Navarino; the Scotch Giant; and, George the Fourth being lately dead, two or three fhows of His Late Majefty Lying in State.

In 1832, Clarke from Aſtleys, who had a good exhibition, inſcribed on his booth, " We have Met the Times—Lowered the Price—only Threepence."

Signor Capelli was at one Fair time during this period, exhibiting his own ſleight of hand and the powers of the LEARNED CATS. They beat a drum, turned a ſpit, ground knives, played muſic, ſtruck an anvil, roaſted coffee, rang bells ; and one of them obeyed orders in French or Italian. Alſo, the Signor announced that " the Wonderful Dog will play any gentleman at Dominoes that will play with him." This exhibition was at a houſe in Giltſpur Street.   The admiſſion charge was for gentlemen, 4*d.* ; work-people, 2*d.*

This, printed in 1842, is ſuppoſed to be the laſt of the handbills iſſued in Bartholomew Fair :

EXTRAORDINARY PHENOMENON !!!

THE GREATEST WONDER IN THE WORLD

Now Exhibiting Alive,

AT THE GLOBE COFFEE HOUSE, No. 30, *KING STREET,*

𝔖𝔪𝔦𝔱𝔥𝔣𝔦𝔢𝔩𝔡,

A FEMALE CHILD WITH TWO PERFECT HEADS,

Named Elizabeth Bedbury, Daughter of Daniel and Jane Bedbury, Born at Wandſworth, Surrey, April 17th, 1842. The public is reſpectfully informed that the Child is now LIVING ; and hundreds of perſons has been to ſee it, and declares that it is the moſt Wonderful Phenomenon of Nature that they 'd ever ſeen.

ADMISSION 1*d.* Each.

No Deception ; if diſſatisfied the Money Returned.

In 1849, from the 3rd to the 6th of September, the
Fair contained only a dozen gingerbread ftalls; fhows
having been removed to the New North Road,
Iflington; where a large fpace was taken for their
occupation. They were obliged to clofe at ten at night,
and were not fuffered to be ftirring before fix.

Earth to earth. Bartholomew Fair, after long ficknefs,
was dead, and bred corruption. That which it now
remains for me to tell is, not the manner of its death,
but of its burial.

CHAPTER XXIV.

Earth to Earth.

In what manner the body of the Fair was removed,
few words will tell. For a dead man there needs but a
coffin and a coach, for a dead inftitution there need
certain acts and ordinances. In the year 1798, when
the queftion of abolifhing the Fair was difcuffed very
ferioufly by the Corporation, a propofal to reftrict it
to one day was made and fet afide, becaufe that meafure might produce in London a concentrated tumult,
dangerous to life. In the courfe of a trial at Guildhall
in the year 1827, involving the rights of Lord Kenfington, it was ftated on Lord Kenfington's behalf,
that confidering the corrupt ftate of the Fair, and the
nuifance caufed by it in the neighbourhood of Smithfield,
he fhould throw no obftacle in the way of its removal,
and was ready to give up his own rights over it, on
being paid their value. His receipts from toll were
ftated to be thirty or forty pounds a-year, and their
eftimated value five or fix hundred pounds. In the
year 1830, the Corporation of London did accordingly
buy from Lord Kenfington the old Priory rights, vefted
in the heirs of Chancellor Rich, and all the rights and

interefts in Bartholomew Fair then became vefted in the City. Having thus fecured full power over the remains in queftion, the Corporation could take into its own hands the whole bufinefs of their removal.

That the Fair was dead there could be no doubt. In 1831, Richardfon paid, not only for his own booth, but alfo for the ground, fhutters, and making up of Ewing's Wax Work, on condition that he received half of what was taken in the fhow. But he loft fifty pounds that year; and Wombwell, who had a fecond booth called Morgan's, at the corner of the Greyhound Yard, made only his expenfes.

After Bartholomew Fair in the year 1839, a Memorial having been prefented to the Corporation by the London City Miffion, pointing out the pollution fpread by the retention of the Fair in Smithfield, it was referred to the City Lands' Committee, to confider the power of the Corporation to remove the fame. The City Solicitor, Mr. Charles Pearfon, gave in an able Report the opinion for which he was afked. He refpected the queftion of privilege which had induced a former City Solicitor, advifed by counfel, to recommend that an Act of Parliament be fought; and did not therefore recommend the immediate and entire abolition of the Fair. He advifed the abridgment of it to two, inftead of three clear days, and the refufal to let ftandings for fhow-booths in a Fair that was created in the firft inftance for purpofes of trade.

This advice was followed by a refolution of the Market Committee, Mr. Deputy Hicks, Chairman, which abolifhed the irregular midnight proclamation

until then accepted as a legal act on behalf of Lord
Kenfington, advifing a proclamation by the Mayor (if
neceffary), but without the ufual ftate, on the afternoon
of the Eve of St. Bartholomew, and that the Fair be
permitted to continue only for the remainder of that day
and the two following days. It advifed alfo that all
theatrical reprefentations fhould be thenceforth entirely
excluded, and that the Mayor and Corporation, as well
as the Commiffioner of Police be requefted to enforce
thefe regulations. Further, it was refolved that no
difturbance of the pavement be permitted, and that there
fhould be no roundabouts or flying wheels in any part of
Smithfield Market; that no perfon fhould be admitted
who was in debt to the City for his ftandings in a former
year; and that the ground about all ftandings fhould be
cleaned morning and night by thofe who held them.
Thefe regulations were confirmed by the Corporation;
and the ufual renters of ground were informed of their
effential claufes in a lithographed circular, dated the 23rd
of July, 1840, which ftated alfo that no ftalls whatever
might be erected until the morning of the day on which
the Fair would open, and that they muft be all removed
on the day of its clofing.

This very effective meafure followed on a courfe of
beneficent and difinterefted extortion practifed upon the
fhowmen by the Market Committee, with a view to
their exclufion from the Fair. Though their number
decreafed every year, yet in the income of Smithfield
Bartholomew Fair (in the account of receipts from
Smithfield Market) was an item of 162*l.* in 1836, of
206*l.* in the year following, of 284*l.* in 1838, and of

305*l.* in 1839. Thus, in 1837, Mr. Clark the eque-
trian was charged 25*l.* for his ground, but next year, he
had 50*l.* to pay. Wombwell's rent was raifed from
35*l.* to 70*l.*, and Johnfon's rent was in like manner
doubled. In 1839, the rents, though not doubled,
were again raifed. Wombwell paid more than 80*l.* for
his ground, which was let at 15*s.* 6*d.* a foot on the
Grand Line; and at prices varying from 10*s.* to 16*s.* a
foot—the higher charge for double frontages—in other
places.

The next year, 1840, ftruck away the exhibitions;
and from the meagre lift of applicants even the dwarfs
and giants were excluded, but wild beaft fhows were
allowed. I copy the Chairman's notes of the—

MEETING OF THE SPECIAL COMMITTEE FOR LETTING THE CITY
    GROUND IN SMITHFIELD PREVIOUS TO ST. BARTHOLOMEW
    FAIR, *Auguft* 29*th*, 1840.

20*s.* per Pen for Toy Stalls, &c., &c.
        Mr. Clark, Equeftrian, excluded.
        Mr. Frafer, Gymnaftics,   do.
Let, 31*l.* — Mr. Hylton, Wild Beaft, Ground the fame Terms as laft Year.
        Mr. Lafkey, Living Giant and Giantefs, excluded.
        Mr. Crockett, Living Curiofities, Giantefs, Dwarf, Serpents,
            Crocodile, &c., excluded.
        Mr. Reader,   do.
27*l.* 18*s.*— Mr. Wright, Wild Beaft, 36 feet at 15*s.* 6*d.*, North end.
        Meffrs. Lee and Johnfon, do., 30 feet at 15*s.* 6*d.*, South or
            Centre.
        Mr. Groves, Works of Art, Machinery, &c.

The neceffary refult of thefe meafures was that in a
very few years, Bartholomew Fair was attended only by
the proprietors of a few handfuls of ginger-bread, who
had no proteft to make againft the laft aét requifite to
complete the ceremony of interment, the fuppreffion of

the ufual proclamation. Proclamation of Bartholomew Fair had been made fince the year 1840 without any of the luftre fhed of old by a gilt coach over the ceremony. The Mayors had withdrawn the formality as much as poffible from public obfervation, until in the year 1850, and in the Mayoralty of Alderman Mufgrove, his worfhip having walked quietly to the appointed gateway, with the neceffary attendants, found that there was not any Fair left worth a Mayor's proclaiming. After that year, therefore, no Mayor accompanied the gentleman whofe duty it was to read a certain form of words out of a certain parchment fcroll, under a quiet gateway. After five years this form alfo was difpenfed with, and Bartholomew Fair was proclaimed for the laft time in the year 1855. The fole exifting veftige of it is the old fee of three and fixpence ftill paid by the City, to the Rector of St. Bartholomew the Great, for a proclamation in his parifh. The Monday Cattle Market when the Fair happened on Monday, neverthelefs was held and clafhed with it in a wild uproar ; but even that alfo has quitted Smithfield. There is entire filence now on the hiftoric ground over which, century after century, the hearts of our forefathers have throbbed with the outfpoken joys of life, and with the fuppreffed agonies of death ; in which the concourfe of a heroic people has in its youth enjoyed the life and the wit of a grofs Fair : even as Prince Hal, till he came to his Royalty, enjoyed his fellowfhip with Falftaff.

I have told from firft to laft the ftory of a Feftival which was maintained for feven centuries in England. Of the few popular Feftivals that occafion yearly gatherings of ftrangers in the open ftreets of one of our great cities, this was the chief. In its humours, we have feen the humour of the nation blended with the riot of its mob. Yet when the nation had out-grown it, a Municipal Court with the help of but a few policemen put it quietly away.

INDEX.

THE END.

BRADBURY AND EVANS, PRINTERS, WHITEFRIARS.